INDIAN ARRIVALS 18

Indian Arrivals 1870–1915: Networks of British Empire explores the rich and complicated landscape of intercultural contact between Indians and Britons on British soil at the height of empire, as reflected in a range of literary writing, including poetry and life-writing. The book's four decade-based case studies, leading from 1870 and the opening of the Suez Canal, to the first years of the Great War, investigate from several different textual and cultural angles the central place of India in the British metropolitan imagination at this relatively early stage for Indian migration. Focussing on a range of remarkable Indian 'arrivants'—scholars, poets, religious seekers, and political activists including Toru Dutt and Sarojini Naidu, Mohandas Gandhi and Rabindranath Tagore—*Indian Arrivals* examines the take-up in the metropolis of the influences and ideas that accompanied their transcontinental movement, including concepts of the west and of cultural decadence, of urban modernity and of cosmopolitan exchange. If, as is now widely accepted, vocabularies of inhabitation, education, citizenship, and the law were in many cases developed in colonial spaces like India, and imported into Britain, then, the book suggests, the presence of Indian travellers and migrants needs to be seen as much more central to Britain's understanding of itself, both in historical terms and in relation to the present-day. The book demonstrates how the colonial encounter in all its ambivalence and complexity inflected social relations throughout the empire, including at its heart, in Britain itself: Indian as well as other colonial travellers enacted the diversity of the empire on London's streets.

Elleke Boehmer FRSL FRHistS is Professor of World Literature in English at the University of Oxford, and Professorial Governing Body Fellow at Wolfson College. She is Director of the Oxford Centre for Life Writing at Wolfson. She has published *Colonial and Postcolonial Literature* (1995, 2005), *Empire, the National and the Postcolonial, 1890–1920* (2002), *Stories of Women* (2005), the biography *Nelson Mandela* (2008), *Indian Arrivals* (2015), and *Postcolonial Poetics* (2018). She is the author of five acclaimed novels, and the short-story collections *Sharmilla and Other Portraits* (2010) and *To the Volcano* (2019). Her 2015 novel *The Shouting in the Dark* won the EASA Olive Schreiner Prize for Prose. She edited Robert Baden-Powell's *Scouting for Boys* (2004), and the anthology *Empire Writing* (1998), and has co-edited over five other books including *The Indian Postcolonial* (2010) and *The Postcolonial Low Countries* (2012). She is the General Editor of the Oxford Studies in Postcolonial Literatures Series. In 2019 she became Fellow of the Royal Society of Literature and Fellow of the Royal Historical Society.

Praise for *Indian Arrivals 1870–1915*

'a luminous literary history.'

Times Higher Education

'[a] carefully researched and beautifully written book [. . .] which sensitively and empathetically explores the multi-layered meanings of 'arrival'.'

Amelia Bona, ***H-Net Reviews***

'A comprehensive and rewarding exploration of a fascinating period in British and Indian literary history'

Máire ní Fhlathuin, ***Review of English Studies***

'*Indian Arrivals* [. . .] makes for very engaging reading. It twins impressive archival research with an imaginative handling of the material.'

Victorian Studies

'Elleke Boehmer is one of the very few genuine literary all-rounders'

Anshuman A. Mondal, ***Interventions***

Indian Arrivals 1870–1915

Networks of British Empire

ELLEKE BOEHMER

UNIVERSITY PRESS

OXFORD
UNIVERSITY PRESS

Great Clarendon Street, Oxford, OX2 6DP,
United Kingdom

Oxford University Press is a department of the University of Oxford.
It furthers the University's objective of excellence in research, scholarship,
and education by publishing worldwide. Oxford is a registered trade mark of
Oxford University Press in the UK and in certain other countries

First published 2015
First published in paperback 2021

Published in the United States of America by Oxford University Press
198 Madison Avenue, New York, NY 10016, United States of America

British Library Cataloguing in Publication Data
Data available

Library of Congress Cataloging in Publication Data
Data available

ISBN 978–0–19–874418–4 (Hbk.)
ISBN 978–0–19–285567–1 (Pbk.)

In memory
Jon Stallworthy
(1935–2014)

Acknowledgements

A work of literary and cultural history like *Indian Arrivals 1870–1915: Networks of British Empire*, which seeks to make a particular contribution to a specialized yet increasingly populated field, would be inconceivable without extensive collaboration, and hence owes many debts of gratitude. First and foremost, I would like to acknowledge the support of the 'Making Britain: South Asian Visions of Home and Abroad' research project, funded by an Arts and Humanities Research Council Major Research Award, 2007–2010 (AH/E009859/1), with funding also from the University of Oxford English Faculty and the Open University. A substantial portion of the research for *Indian Arrivals* was carried out while I worked as a co-investigator on this flagship project. Piloted by Susheila Nasta of the Open University, 'Making Britain' explored migrant South Asian contributions to British culture and society between 1870 and 1950 and succeeded, via a range of outputs, persuasively to challenge representations of a racially homogeneous Britain in that period. My heartfelt thanks go to Susheila for her generosity, collegiality, and commitment to the subject of pre-1950 Indian immigration, as well as her discerning eye for what this history reveals about the long-term heterogeneous make-up of the 'small island' of the UK. It was also Susheila who made the link between the project and the pioneering historical and archival work of Rozina Visram. Throughout the project, Rozina was so courageous as to take a gamble on working with a group of literary critics, and so open-hearted as to share her copious research notes compiled across an entire career of scholarship, on which her own keynote study *Asians in Britain: 400 Years of History* (2002) was built. All of those who were involved in 'Making Britain' are indebted to her work.

We are also extremely grateful to Lyn Innes, another senior consultant on the project, who offered invaluable advice on all aspects of our work. The leading historian of modern British imperialism, Antoinette Burton, unfailingly gave of her time, advice, and door-opening insights to the project, becoming in the process a much-valued colleague and friend. I will always be grateful to Mohanlal Keshav, my friend Satish's late father, for giving me Rozina Visram's *Ayahs, Lascars and Princes: Indians in Britain, 1700–1947* (1986) to read when I was a guest in his home in 1990, and for sowing the seed that would eventually grow into this book.

As co-investigator, I served as the lead researcher on the 1870–1920 strand of 'Making Britain', a period marked (in my view) by some of high imperialism's most subtle and fascinating contradictions. Though my 2002 *Empire, the National, and the Postcolonial: Resistance in Interaction* had investigated these fault-lines in so far as they manifested as cross-empire connections, closer attention to the literary 'diaspora space' of Britain in the long close-of-century period opened up an even wider range of interesting and unexpected interrelationships. In this work I was ably assisted by the AHRC 'Making Britain' Postdoctoral Research Fellow Sumita Mukherjee. My indebtedness to her work is acknowledged in the notes and bibliography, but should also be taken as a golden thread running through the book. I am extremely grateful to Sumita's parents, Arabinda and Nita Mukherjee, for the energetic and patient support they gave to Sumita's work on the project, and also for Arabinda's hospitality in Santiniketan, a place where Rabindranath Tagore's far-sighted universalist vision continues to make a palpable impression on daily life. I will always remember mid-March 2009 as a very special time. Sanjukta Dasgupta at the University of Calcutta and Rosinka Chaudhuri at CSSS both gave me a warm welcome in that city in the same month. I am grateful to Amit Chaudhuri for the booking at the Bengal Club and for his encouragement throughout.

Other researchers on the project, Rehana Ahmed, now at Queen Mary, University of London, Ruvani Ranasinha at King's College London, and Florian Stadtler, now at Exeter University, carried out excellent research on the 1920–50 strand of 'Making Britain'. I am particularly indebted to Florian's investigations into the Sarojini Naidu and Rabindranath Tagore papers in the National Archives in Delhi and the Houghton Library in Harvard, respectively. Other members of the Advisory Committee, in particular Penny Brook, Lead Curator of the India Office Records at the British Library, and the art historian Partha Mitter, gave invaluable advice as to key figures and sources. I am grateful to the John Fell Fund (083/049), the English Faculty, Wolfson College, and the Bodleian Library, in particular Chris Fletcher, Wilma Minty, and Dana Josephson, for support in mounting the 'Indian Traces in Oxford' exhibition in March 2010, which was opened by Amitav Ghosh. It was a pleasure to collaborate with Talking Pictures manager Neena Sohal on her OxAsians exhibition, which ran at the Pitt Rivers Museum in Oxford concurrently with 'Indian Traces in Oxford'.

As happens when research is at once exploratory and topical, 'Making Britain' generated many other collaborative links and collegial ties. Here I should especially acknowledge the advice and input of the following scholars: Richard Rupert Arrowsmith with his important work on South Asian influences in the visual and plastic arts 1900–20; Siobhan Lambert-Hurley, a specialist on Muslims in early twentieth-century Britain, Atia

Fyzee in particular; Alexander Riddiford and his fascinating research on the Bengali classicist poet M. M. Dutt; and the art historian of the networked Edwardian empire, Sarah V. Turner. I should also like warmly to thank Anna Snaith at King's College London for our always fruitful, ongoing conversation about women's writing in the time of high empire, and for showing me the KCL documentation relating to Sarojini Naidu's years as a student in London. Alex Tickell at the Open University, a leading literary historian of India in the long nineteenth century, has also been a highly valued interlocutor for more years than we may both care to remember. I am grateful to Chandani Lokugé for sharing insights into the work of Cornelia Sorabji and Toru Dutt. From long before 'Making Britain' began, Cornelia's nephew Richard Sorabji and his wife Kate showed me great generosity in my research on the lives of his remarkable aunts, the doctor Alice as well as the lawyer Cornelia. It was my great good fortune that Richard Sorabji's compendious biography of Cornelia, *Opening Doors*, with its in-depth account of her British life, appeared a few years before *Indian Arrivals*.

Though the 'Making Britain' project allowed substantial research on pre-1945 India-in-Britain to take place, my writing up of these findings would not have been possible without the support provided in 2010–2011 by the AHRC Fellowships Scheme Award (AH/I001123/1), 'India Arrived: Seeing and Being in Britain 1870–1914', matched by Oxford University Humanities Division and Faculty Research leave in the same academic year. The 'India Arrived' Research Fellowship gave me the time and opportunity to develop a more independent literary trajectory of investigation on cultural networking and intercultural poetic collaborations between 1870 and 1915, and to explore in more textual detail the core concepts of the extended west, Greater Britain, and decadent orientalism. Across the entire period of the work on early South Asian Britain, my English Faculty colleague and friend Ankhi Mukherjee was generous with her trademark razor-sharp insights into theories of hospitality and migration, always backed by a sympathetic understanding of how these concepts play out between individuals as well as cultures. President of Wolfson College, Hermione Lee, showed infinite patience and kindness across 2012–2013 in tolerating my sometimes all-consuming focus on completing *Indian Arrivals*. I am also extremely grateful to many other English Faculty colleagues for the interest they showed in the project over the years, and the encouragement they gave in many different forms, including: Rebecca Beasley, Faith Binckes, David Bradshaw, Stefano Evangelista, Patrick Hayes, Michelle Kelly, Peter D. McDonald, Laura Marcus, Michèle Mendelssohn, Lloyd Pratt, Kirsten Shepherd-Barr, Helen Small, and Michael Whitworth.

I should like to acknowledge two other major research projects with which I had the privilege to become involved during the five years of working on South Asian migration to Britain: the 'Literature as an Object of Knowledge' project funded by the Balzan Foundation, investigating literature and cognition, led by Terence Cave (2010–2013), based at St John's College, Oxford, and the Marie Curie-funded International Training Network CoHaB (2012–2015), on which the University of Oxford (the English Faculty together with COMPAS, the Centre on Migration, Policy and Society) was a partner. The workshops of the Balzan group gave invaluable conceptual support to my efforts to bring literature to centre-stage in understanding migration. Balzan meetings always created safe, stimulating spaces for (re)thinking literary expression as one of the most important ways through which human beings conceive, shape, move through, and reflect on their experiences (be it of displacement or of connection), and made it possible also to consider how mental processes manifest in interpersonal and cross-cultural ways. I am extremely grateful to all the participants at these seminars, in particular to my inspired and inspiring long-time friend Terence Cave. The conferences and workshops on diaspora organized under the auspices of the ITN project, expertly led by Klaus Stierstorfer at the University of Muenster, afforded valuable links with contemporary debates on diaspora, migration, and concepts of home and belonging.

I am very grateful to the multitalented doctoral students I supervised across the period of writing about India-in-Britain, for their understanding, generosity with references, and plain ongoing interest in the progress of this work (in chronological order of first meeting): Dobrota Pucherova, Mithu Banerji, Konstantin Sofianos, Scott Teal, Vincent van Bever Donker, Ed Flett, Alexander Bubb, Charne Lavery, Nisha Manocha, Ruth Bush, Karim Mattar, Tamara Moellenberg, Hazra Medica, Dominic Davies, Erica Lombard, and Priyasha Mukhopadhyay. Two of this group I should single out in particular, as without their specific contributions to the research and writing-up process *Indian Arrivals* could not have come to fruition as it has (any flaws are, of course, entirely my own). Alex Bubb gave outstanding support to the 'Making Britain' project from the start, not least in the form of the 'Indians in Oxford' and 'Asian Bloomsbury' tours he devised and led. Charne Lavery provided indispensable assistance at the crucial stage of pre-submission, not only with the editorial apparatus but also with her insightful and sensitive read-through of the entire manuscript. I should also gratefully acknowledge Nilanjana Banerji's research on Edward Thompson and Rabindranath Tagore, and Michael Collins's research on Tagore, Yeats, and Gandhi: it was a pleasure to examine these theses. Warm thanks to Dom Davies and Erica Lombard for amazing help with the index and final corrections.

I am grateful to the organizers of and audiences at the following lectures, conferences, and seminars for their kind and constructive receptiveness to earlier versions of Chapters 1–3 in particular: the 'Britishness, Identity and Citizenship' conference, St Catherine's College, Oxford, June 2008 (a paper co-written with Sumita Mukherjee); the University of Calcutta conference on Britain and Bengal, March 2009 (in particular Sanjukta Dasgupta, and also Tapati Gupta and Jharna Sanyal); the Mellon Distinguished Visiting Professor lecture, University of the Witwatersrand, September 2009 (in particular Leon de Kock); the Postcolonial Forum at Queen's University, Belfast, March 2010, in collaboration with Susheila Nasta (in particular Anthony Soares, Eamonn Hughes, and Daniel Sanjiv Roberts); the University of Stellenbosch research seminar, May 2010 (in particular Dirk Klopper and Meg Samuelson); the 'Bharat Britain: South Asians Making Britain' conference, the British Library, September 2010; the 'Concurrences' workshop, Linnaeus University, May 2012; the 16th Biennial Conference for the International Society for Religion, Literature and Culture, on 'Cultures of Transition', University of Copenhagen, Denmark, October 2012 (in particular Inge-Birgitte Siegumfeldt); and the Annual keynote lecture at the Centre for British Studies, Humboldt University, Berlin, October 2012 (in particular Gesa Stedman). I spent a stimulating time in January 2011 as Edward Mellon visiting fellow at UCLA, hosted by the Professor of Comparative Literature, Françoise Lionnet. I am grateful to Françoise for her hospitality, as well as to David Theo Goldberg at Irvine and David Palumbo-Liu at Stanford for their invitations to present from my research. It was a privilege also to engage with Nile Green, Professor of History at UCLA, on his investigations into early Muslim travellers in Britain.

To those friends and interlocutors in more informal contexts across these past several years, who have provided a listening ear and given advice on the topic of discovering the (Indian) familiar in the (British) foreign, I am also very grateful. They include: Derek Attridge, Barnita Bagchi, Annemie Boehmer, Shirley Chew, John Coetzee, Julie Curtis, Santanu Das, Elizabeth De Loughrey, Sarah de Mul, Alison Donnell, Ketaki Dyson, Gunlög Fur, Leela Gandhi, Barbara Harriss-White, Isabel Hofmeyr, Victor Lal, David Lambert, Josephine McDonagh, Linda McDowell, Pablo Mukherjee, Geoff Mulligan, Zoe Norridge, Maria Olaussen, Makarand Paranjape, Tamson Pietsch, Rajeswari Sunder Rajan, Jahan Ramazani, the late Jon Stallworthy, Robert J. C. Young, and Jarad Zimbler; also members of The Oxford Research Centre in the Humanities (TORCH) 'Race and Resistance across Borders in the Long Twentieth Century' network, especially Stephen Tuck, and all participants in the English Faculty's remarkable Postcolonial Writing and Theory seminar from 2007 to the present day. During her time as Head of the Humanities Division at

Oxford, Sally Shuttleworth was always encouraging of 'Making Britain' research, and invited presentations from work-in-progress at the Oxford Alumni weekend, September 2008, and at the Oxford India day, June 2011. I dedicate this book to the memory of my former supervisor, dear friend, and first reader, Jon Stallworthy.

I owe a big debt of thanks to the librarians and archivists of the libraries in which I have worked towards *Indian Arrivals 1870–1915*: to staff at Oxford's English Faculty Library, Rhodes House Library (especially Lucy McCann) and the Bodleian Library; the British Library; Special Collections at the University of Reading, in particular the Hogarth Press and Swan Sonnenschein archives, with thanks also to Jean Rose, the Library Manager of the Random House Group Archive and Library; the Modern Records Centre at the University of Warwick Library; the National Library Kolkata, including the Ashutosh collection; the International House Library, Ramakrishna Centre, Kolkata; and the library of the Bengal Club, and the Rabindra-Bhavana Library, Visva Bharati, Santiniketan (especially the Director Swapan Majumdar). Paragraphs from the Introduction and Chapters 2 and 3 appear as part of the essay 'The Zigzag Lines of Tentative Connection: Indian–British Contacts in the Late Nineteenth Century', published in *India in Britain 1858–1950*, edited by Susheila Nasta (2013); and in an article co-written with Sumita Mukherjee, 'Re-making Britishness: Indians at Oxford at the Turn of the Century', published in *Britishness, Identity and Citizenship: The View From Abroad*, edited by Catherine McGlynn and Andrew Mycock (2011).

None of these research findings, however, would have moved out of the snug compartments of my filing cabinets without the amazing support and love of my family across the often daunting process of turning my findings into serviceable literary historical narrative (while at the same time writing a novel). I owe Steven Matthews inexpressible gratitude for all he has offered and suffered across the five long years when it seemed many times that 'India won't ever arrive', to quote our son Sam. During a period in which Steven himself produced books and poems, he put nutritious meals on the table, was Assistant Dean, expressed a healthy scepticism that any project could be worth so many eye-blurring sessions peering at screens, and offered both jokes and sympathy at almost any time of day and night.

To our sons, Thomas and Sam, how can I begin to thank you for everything we have shared across the past five busy years, which have also been momentous and transitional in your lives? Thomas's incredible archaeological imagination, historical acumen, deep memory, and almost preternatural understanding of the ways in which myth and story can work as a culture's archive, on many occasions shed light for me on how the layers of time can manifest in the texture of narrative and other writings, as well as in marks left on stone, wood, and paper. Helping Sumita and me to photocopy the 'Making Britain' archive in 2009, Thomas 'got' the ethics of the project early on, as captured in his marvellous understatement that same day, 'It looks like there's quite a lot in this'. He was also my companion on a 2009 visit to Ypres and Brussels to look for traces of Indian sepoys: I could not have wished for a better, more informed guide.

But if Thomas's will to historicize helped to drive the writing forwards, it could not have arrived in the world without irrepressible Sam's will to complete anything he undertakes with grace and precision, including pressing his mother both towards and away from the laptop at the appropriate times. It was Sam who encouraged me to play, updated us on football scores and celebrity gossip, and insisted on peanut butter sandwiches. Thank you Thomas and Sam—you may find bits of this book to like, especially what it says about brotherliness and friendship.

Contents

List of Figures

The author and publisher gratefully acknowledge the permission granted to reproduce the copyright material in this book. Every effort has been made to trace copyright holders and to obtain their permission for the use of copyright material. The publisher apologizes for any errors or omissions and would be grateful if notified of any corrections that should be incorporated in future reprints or editions of this book.

Introduction

Indian Arrival—Encounters Between Indians and Britons, 1870–1915

Near Hastings, on the shingle beach,
We loitered at the time
When ripens on the wall the peach,
The autumn's lovely prime.
Far off,—the sea and sky seemed blent,
The day was wholly done,
The distant town its murmurs sent
Strangers,—we were alone.

We wandered slow; sick, weary, faint,
Then one of us sat down,
No nature hers, to make complaint;—
The shadows deepened brown.
A lady past,[1]—she was not young,
But oh! Her gentle face
No painter-poet ever sung,
Or saw such saintlike grace.

She past us,—then she came again,
Observing at a glance
That we were strangers; one, in pain,—
Then asked,—Were we from France?
We talked awhile,—some roses red
That seemed as wet with tears,
She gave my sister, and she said,
'God bless you both, my dears!'
Sweet were the roses,—sweet and full,
And large as lotus flowers
That in our own wide tank we cull
To deck our Indian bowers.
But sweeter was the love that gave
Those flowers to one unknown,

I think that He who came to save
The gift a debt will own.

The lady's name I do not know,
Her face no more may see,
But yet, oh yet, I love her so!
Blest, happy, may she be!
Her memory will not depart,
Though grief my years should shade.
Still bloom her roses in my heart!
And they shall never fade!

Toru Dutt, 'Near Hastings', from *Ancient Ballads and Legends of Hindustan* (1876/1882)

I ENCOUNTER

The Victorian Indian poet Toru Dutt's lyric 'Near Hastings' is notable for being probably the first poem in the English language to represent a British–Indian encounter on British soil.[2] Set at an iconic place of arrival in British history, the site of the 1066 Battle of Hastings, not far from where William the Conqueror landed, the two 'strange' women walking on the shingle beach seem themselves to have arrived on British shores after a long journey: 'weary, faint', they are mistaken for Frenchwomen by the passing British 'lady'. A conversation then begins, a gift exchanges hands, and spontaneous mutual affection is expressed. Throughout, the poem interweaves British and Indian glances, greetings, and blessings, if also a pervasive taint of uncertainty, so offering an apt object lesson with which to begin a study entitled *Indian Arrivals 1870–1915*: *Networks of British Empire*. By the poem's close, Indian arrival has been staged, in more ways than one.

With 'Near Hastings', Dutt precociously explored something of the cultural strangeness, anxiety, and hesitation mixed with curiosity and recognition that is involved in arriving in a new culture. Writing from her own pioneering experience of travel and education in Europe as a young Bengali woman, she evokes in surprisingly assured Romantic terms the process of finding the linguistic and aesthetic means through which to articulate the discovery of sameness within difference.[3] For Kwame Appiah, in his work on cosmopolitanism, an ethical position informed by cosmopolitan values is based on a respect for the other's difference in its absolute specificity, balanced by a willingness to find areas of agreement and concord.[4] Although the Indians and the Britons who are discussed in this book, most of them distinctively Victorian liberals and reformers, may not consciously or consistently have espoused cosmopolitan values, yet they displayed a commitment to such openness to another culture, even while often grappling with the feelings of racial distrust and antagonism that imperial structures inevitably fomented. These contrary impulses, for and against harmonious interaction, run through and across the broad spectrum of the memoirs, poetry, letters, essays, and other writing produced out of their encounters with one another. Many of these texts also outline, as I will show, that this cosmopolitan respect for difference is something negotiated through the give-and-take of conversation in its broadest sense, a trading of recognitions, 'the respect and candid exchange of views among individuals and cultures' in Appiah's terms, in spite of moments of doubt and disjuncture. The picture that emerges is of a more dialectical late Victorian or imperial cosmopolitanism than may hitherto have been conceived—one in which turn-of-the-century Indian travellers not only participated, but to which they also contributed in important ways.

Set on a significant piece of English ground, Dutt's 'Near Hastings' captures the dynamic moment of such exchange in its pivotal third stanza in particular, when a conversational overture is made and then accepted. As such, the poem gives an anticipatory snapshot of an encounter scene that acknowledges sameness as well as difference—one that would be repeated across the decades from 1870, as travellers from the subcontinent began to travel to Britain in ever greater numbers, as did Dutt, in quest of education, or political representation, or social reform, until at last, in 1914–15, over a million Indian sepoys arrived in Europe, to safeguard the Western Front.[5] While Dutt's much-anthologized ode 'Our Casuarina Tree' represents perhaps her most poignant expression of intercultural translation, 'Near Hastings' addresses itself more precisely to the purposes of this book and to a specific scene of Indian arrival, and therefore furnishes the more fitting exemplary text with which to open.[6]

Made up of five stanzas, like 'Our Casuarina Tree', the progressive rhyme scheme *abab cdcd* of 'Near Hastings', different from the other poem's Keatsian frame, immediately evokes a sense of forward movement and underlying harmony. Though for the imperial historian Antoinette Burton 'Near Hastings' suggests how conspicuous Toru and her sister felt as Indians whenever they travelled outside London, and though the overall mood of the poem is unmistakeably plangent, in fact the poem also highlights the tenderness of the contact with the English lady, and, despite her out-of-the-ordinary saintliness, the relative terms of equality on which the women meet.[7] Throughout, 'Near Hastings' also interestingly recalls Matthew Arnold's 'Dover Beach' (1867), famously set on the English shoreline facing France, with which an avid reader of poetry like Dutt would surely have been familiar. Yet the 'naked shingles' of Arnold's well-known poem of foreboding are in Dutt touched by the soft light of an autumn evening, and the poem's focus rapidly shifts from the potentially desolate beach scene to the floral gift that connects three people and three geographies—not only France and England, but also India.

The first two stanzas of 'Near Hastings' lay down the conditions under which the encounter takes place, building to the initial crossing of paths at the end of stanza two, with the opening of the conversation—'we talked'—and the giving of the symbolic gift of roses that then follows in the central stanza. Wandering on a 'shingle beach' near Hastings at the end of an autumn evening, the speaker's companion, presumably her ailing sister Aru, feels faint, and the two sit down, whereupon they are spotted by the passing woman. She observes that they are 'strangers' (the word is repeated in stanzas one and three), yet at the same time casts them as proximate rather than distant others, by asking whether they are Frenchwomen.[8] Then, spontaneously bestowing her floral gift, which somewhat miraculously lies to hand, the lady asks for God's blessing upon them. In the final two stanzas, the speaker shifts to an overtly Christian register and boldly compares the lady's selfless unqualified love to Christ's. This rather predictable move (for the Christianized Dutt) is shadowed by a more interesting symbolic transfer in which the gift of the roses is said to be transposed into the speaker's memory and heart—in which form, she avers, their image will never fade.

The sense of inextricable fusion rising out of the brief yet telling encounter between strangers sheds a retrospective light on other suggestions of merging and mingling in the rest of the poem: the 'blending' of 'sea and sky' in the evening light; the 'browning' of the deepening shadows, which in context is a significant chromatic choice; and then, suggestively, the red roses—English blooms—that are, however, described as 'large as [the] lotus flowers' that float on the tank at home in India and are used to 'deck our Indian bowers'. There is some passing hint that the English lady may herself have been bound for a shrine or grave on which she was to lay the flowers (or why did she have them so conveniently to hand?). However, in an act of profound hospitality to the two strangers, women like herself, she gives the lotus-sized red English roses to them, so drawing from the speaker a reciprocal, if perhaps overcompensatory assertion of emotion: 'I love her so!' A recognition of foreignness shifts into a profound (and for Appiah cosmopolitan) exchange of love, trust, and understanding which, in its final wishful expression 'Blest, happy, may she be', returns the blessing the Englishwoman gave the Indian sisters and turns the poem itself into a further confirmation, however evanescent, of the friendship between the two of them and England, as embodied in the rose-bearing lady.

Despite the pervasive Arnoldian mournfulness, the poem is imbued with the sense that England's welcome to India, as perceived by at least some Indians, is warm and genuine, and as such the poem embraces those English people who have extended a hand of friendship to travellers from the subcontinent.[9] India, the assurance is made, will repay the benefits of this hospitality in manifold ways. Its Christian sentimentality aside, 'Near Hastings' makes clear that the reciprocation of affection described is contingent upon the Englishwoman's initial overture, upon the giving and receiving. Viewed in this light, 'Near Hastings' looks ahead to the complicated dialogic lineaments of the many encounters that were to take place between 'arriving' Indians and their British hosts in the decades featured in this book—from 1870 and the opening of the Suez Canal to the outbreak of the First World War.

II INTERCONNECTED CULTURAL TERRAINS

Indian Arrivals 1870–1915: Networks of British Empire sets out to paint a more textured picture than previously available, not only of cross-cultural contact between Indians and Britons in Britain, but also of the place of India in the British metropolitan imagination at this relatively early stage for Indian migration.[10] The book explores, through a series of four roughly decade-based case studies and a coda on the First World War period, the late nineteenth-century arrival in Britain of a number of remarkable Indian individuals, including scholars, poets, and political activists. To do so it examines, where appropriate, the take-up in the metropolis of the literary, social, and cultural influences and ideas that accompanied their transcontinental movement. Each chapter reflects critically on various literary and historical accounts of significant Indian arrivals and 'arrivants', in two cases including actual portraits (a pen sketch and two photographs: Figures 1 and 2 in Chapter 3, and Figure 3 in Chapter 4). For if, as is now widely accepted, vocabularies of inhabitation, education, citizenship, and the law were in many cases developed in colonial spaces like India, and imported into Britain, then, the book suggests, the presence of Indian travellers and migrants needs to be seen as much more central to Britain's understanding of itself, both in historical terms and in relation to the present day.[11] Plainly expressed, the colonial encounter in all its ambivalence and complexity inflected social relations throughout the empire, *including* in Britain. Indian as well as other colonial travellers enacted the diversity of the empire on London's streets.

Indian Arrivals 1870–1915 builds on the pioneering work of historians of Indian migration such as Rozina Visram, Antoinette Burton, and

Kusoom Vadgama in investigating the ways in which individual Indians 'at the heart of empire', like B. M. Malabari or Cornelia Sorabji, negotiated the colonial and racialized meanings that were often attached to their encounters with Britons.[12] Its perspective is shaped also by the valuable work of Catherine Hall on how empire (concepts of 'new colonial selves', for example) lay at the heart of nineteenth-century understanding of Britishness.[13] However, *Indian Arrivals* goes further than Burton or Visram in one particular sense, in that it looks closely and critically at how cross-cultural and interpersonal negotiations between Indian and British individuals on British soil figured and reconfigured Britain in literary and textual terms. It is specifically interested therefore in negotiations that were conducted in writing, with a special emphasis on poetry—at a time before modernist iconoclasm created opportunities for an Indian author like Mulk Raj Anand to join in with 'conversations in Bloomsbury'.[14] Each chapter reads the ramifications of Indian presences in Britain, as expressed within literary and related texts, in order to track, as Edward Said writes, the 'interdependence of [Indian and British] cultural terrains' in the making of British as well as Indian identities and cultural perceptions at the turn of the nineteenth century.[15] So, whereas Visram's approach rests on an accretion of hitherto buried evidence relating to Indian migration, and Burton's interest is in the specific biographical trajectories of Pandita Ramabai, Behramji Malabari, and Cornelia Sorabji, the focus of the chapters that follow is on those arrivals and encounters that can be seen to have made a certain distinct impression on British cultural and literary life before the First World War, yet that to date have tended to be marginalized or overlooked by the colonial archive.

In dialogue with the findings of the major research project 'Making Britain: South Asian Visions of Home and Abroad, 1870–1950' (2007–2010), the different case studies in *Indian Arrivals 1870–1915* examine a range of British–Indian interrelations, especially one-to-one collaborations, partnerships, and friendships.[16] The more finely meshed, networked picture of early Indian immigration to Britain that emerges from this investigation goes some way towards responding, at least for this period, to Edward Said's compelling invitation in *Culture and Imperialism* (1993) to interrogate the binaries of colonial self and colonized other, European metropolis and non-western periphery, that have conventionally underpinned the rhetoric of empire. To the same end of 'unthinking Eurocentrism' in Said's terms, *Indian Arrivals* also draws in insights from Rasheed Araeen's work on the deconstructed and expanded metropolis, and Partha Mitter's account of global cosmopolitanism, in order to develop an understanding of the imperial world as at once more complicated and as integrated.[17] As Mitter suggests, non-metropolitan movements in the arts, including early twentieth-century modernism, exhibited remarkable 'plurality, heterogeneity and difference' even when compared to their western, apparently pre-eminent counterparts. *Indian Arrivals* seeks to evoke something akin to the asymmetrical, uneven yet interconnected world pictures modelled by these peripheral modernisms, and uses critical terms drawn from its own readings of the individual writers' texts (with their accent on interchange and reciprocity, as will be seen) in order to do so. Yet, as this book several times has occasion to observe, metropolitan writers, too, such as Sir Arthur Conan Doyle, used rhetorical strategies drawn from colonial texts in order to '[imagine] the imperial centre' as fluidity, darkness, and cesspool, and in this way also disturbed conventional centre–periphery divides.[18]

Indian Arrivals 1870–1915 is premised on an understanding of empire as multilayered and interconnected, as well as divided and dichotomous. As the work of historians and historiographers such as Frederick Cooper, Nicholas Thomas, and Daniel E. White shows, empire made up an intercalated field of meanings not confined to the oppositions of colonizer and colonized which have dominated both materialist and nationalist postcolonial historiography.[19] The structures and devices put in place by colonialism were never merely accepted by its subjects, but were always contested, revised, interrupted, and creatively reinterpreted, such as when Indians and Britons collaborated in the production of Decadent poetry, or when the Parsi Dadabhai Naoroji served in 1892–1895 as the first South Asian Westminster MP, representing the constituency of Finsbury Central. Joining with the new scholarship on imperial circulation that has developed in the past two decades or so, this book considers how networked relations operated as modes of identity and knowledge production in the diasporic space of 'India-in-Britain'.[20] Or, as Antoinette Burton reminds us, 'colonialism . . . was made, contested, and remade in the . . . local spaces of the everyday'—spaces such as might be found in London or in Liverpool—or in Calcutta. Concurring, P. D. Morgan observes that empire operated as 'an entire interactive system, one vast interconnected world'.[21] As in Burton, many of the case studies brought together here focus on London; however, an expanded narrative of Indian arrival could equally include Bristol, Brighton, or Edinburgh in legitimate and lively ways.

The emphasis throughout *Indian Arrivals* on circulation and exchange should not, however, be read as claiming that such interactions were not often impeded as well as facilitated by empire. Under colonialism, Appiah's definitive encounter between two individuals sharing cosmopolitan values would in many cases be distorted by experiences of racism and cultural misrecognition. Given that otherness must be ceaselessly recreated in order for colonialism to sustain itself, imperial cosmopolitanism rarely involved entirely emollient relations. Indeed, the postcolonial identification of the cosmopolitan as transnational notwithstanding, the genealogy of cosmopolitan values is ineluctably bound up with the west's history of imperial domination.[22] Relating cosmopolitan approaches, historically developed within the west, to individuals coming from outside the west, therefore demands from us a constant critical vigilance as to geopolitical location. Cosmopolitanism espoused in any unequal situation, even if in the metropolis, would always have been different from the open exchange that Appiah and others describe.

Leela Gandhi's *Affective Communities* (2006) makes an important contribution to our view of empire as cross-connected, as well as to postcolonial theories of transnational migration and exchange, with its readings of Indian–British friendship in roughly the same turn-of-the-century period as that explored in this book. However, the predominant focus of *Affective Communities* is not on the intercultural dynamics of Indian–British transactions *per se*.[23] Drawing on Marx, Derrida, and Nancy, Gandhi's concern is rather to take the interrelationships of, say, M. K. Gandhi and C. F. Andrews, or Manmohan Ghose and Laurence Binyon, as paradigmatic instances of the radical aesthetic 'autonomies' that the disparate, often risky affiliations of the European *fin de siècle* made possible. Her predominantly philosophical study asks how hospitable collaborations between members of the oppressed and oppressor echelons at the turn of the century anticipated 'new and better forms of community and relationality', and how, in effect, such anti-colonial practices helped to generate an anti- or postcolonial ethics.

Indian Arrivals responds to Leela Gandhi's work through its reflection on some of the specific channels through which Indian ideas, mentalities, and encounters contributed to shaping metropolitan cultural life. It takes an approach at once literary and historicist, by considering how interrelations between Indians and Britons served as catalysts in the moulding of metropolitan cultural and social perceptions in the 1870–1915 period, and how this was refracted, calibrated, and in some cases made possible through literary writing—in the travelogues, memoirs, letters, poems, and other records of contact produced by Indians and their British hosts across these turn-of-the-century years. The book's methodology, therefore, combines both sifting through archives and close reading; both the decoding of textual traces and the literary-critical recuperation of forgotten, buried, or partially erased contacts and connections. Inspired by Paul Gilroy's notion of British migrant history as produced through 'a fusion of [cultural] horizons', the different chapters consider how the presence of Indians and Indian texts in late nineteenth- and early twentieth-century metropolitan society intervened in literary movements and other cultural developments until now seen as almost exclusively British. The picture of 'knotted . . . histories' that emerges, certainly disturbs any understanding of the cosmopolitan as frictionless.[24] Diverse 'voyages in', including salon conversations, street-side interactions, and drawing-room friendships, suggest in each case how Indian identities abroad came into articulation in contrapuntal ways, through representations of the familiarity and unfamiliarity of England as well as of India. The book's readings will therefore be interested in the unsaid as well as the said of these encounters, in particular in those textual traces of early Indian presences in Britain (bodies, knowledge, forms of awareness) that suggest even in their inadvertency and contingency how the metropolis that ruled over a quarter of the planet was striated at its core by its contact with India.[25]

At this point, it may well be objected that in *per capita* terms the number of Indians in British cities in the period was relatively small—at the turn of the century, about 10,000 in 8 million (as against 100,000 African-origin people).[26] Moreover, as well as being relatively few and far between, Indians in Britain at this time—mostly men, but also a small number of women—were rarely at large in public spaces, and did not freely mingle with Britons. They tended to inhabit the relatively closed environments of college quads and designated hostels and dormitories, and congregated for mutual support. In the course of this study therefore, it may seem from time to time that a great deal of theorizing and speculation will be made to bear down on relatively thin evidence.

Yet, as Antoinette Burton also recognizes, for those who had the eyes to see it (the novelists Wilkie Collins and Charles Dickens were among them), Indians were everywhere present in Britain's larger cities, 'on street corners, in West End theatres, in travelling shows', and of course on the quaysides and in the sailors' hostels that lascars frequented as they waited for a berth on an India-bound ship.[27] As commentators observed at the time, 'Asia Minor' might be found in the neighbourhood of the London docks.[28] The less-than-privileged Indian lascars or seamen who were mostly designated in these descriptions were in fact those who most actively plied the networks of travel that connected Britain and the subcontinent in the nineteenth century: they were perhaps the first Indians to develop a global awareness, an experience of the world that was mobile, multilingual, creolized, and networked through the planet's constellation of port cities.[29] Though their presence and that of other Indians may not at first have made a strong demographic impression, nonetheless these travellers were able to have an impact precisely because their numbers were perceived as relatively small and therefore unthreatening, an effect which their occasional displays of exceptionalism only reinforced (as in the case of Sarojini Naidu, in Chapter 3). Their ways of seeing and being in the metropolis laid down a store of experience and memory that would not only serve as a guide and an inspiration for later generations of migrant Indians, but at certain points also sparked change, initially often slight, yet incrementally influential, in Britain's cultural and social make-up. Significantly, the lascars' metropolitan presence in this early period also reflected in microcosm the flow of Indian labour through the world system of imperial capitalism, as expressed in indenture. Developed to fill the labour vacuum that the abolition of slavery had created, the structures of indenture interconnected the far-flung plantations of Fiji, Mauritius, Trinidad, and Natal in a new, highly uneven, and fateful global network.[30]

The mention of lascars draws attention to a further important fact concerning Indian demographics abroad, which is that the Indian travellers who plied between Europe and the subcontinent in this period fell into two main groups—the privileged and educated, and the unprivileged; elite travellers as against lascars, ayahs, soldiers, and other working people. Considering that the preoccupations of this study are literary and textual, the focus here falls primarily on the first group, Indians who travelled to Europe as paying passengers, who tended to be educated members of elites. As Thomas Babington Macaulay's Minute on Indian Education of 1835 had recommended, these elite Indians were products of an education in British history and the English literary classics explicitly designed to anglicize their cultural values and beliefs.[31] Nehru, for instance, had read Dickens, Thackeray, Kipling, Wells, and Conan Doyle before he ever arrived in England. He and his migrant compatriots therefore interpreted the metropolitan world using the cultural and linguistic codes that had been made available to them back in India, not excluding, of course, the English language. In fact, as Dipesh Chakrabarty observes, almost everything that nineteenth-century elite Indians were taught was refracted through the concepts and books of Europe, through a bifocal lens that affirmed European cultural superiority, yet at the same time cast liberalizing ideas and practices as applicable to the wider world.[32] In short, the class and, to an extent, race coordinates of this group of travellers were a world away from those of the larger population of working-class Indians also present in Britain at that time.

However, whether they were privileged scholars or stranded lascars, the contribution of early Indian migrants to the life of the metropolis has not until recently been formally acknowledged to any significant degree, including not in literary historical studies, despite the far-reaching historical investigations of Visram, Burton, and others. So Ann Thwaite's 1985 biography of Edmund Gosse pays no attention to this Victorian scholar's mutually formative friendships with the innovative Indian poets Toru

Dutt or Sarojini Naidu, or how these reflected his lifelong interest in the aesthetic perspectives offered by other cultures and literary traditions.[33] And the several Indians that W. B. Yeats befriended across his long career as a poet and spiritual seeker until recently merited little more than a passing mention in studies of his life and work.[34] This lack of recognition for pre-1914 Indian migration can in part be attributed to the question of numbers already raised; in part to the fact that its traces lie in documents, texts, and other sources often deemed evanescent and peripheral; and in part to how the dominant narrative of British national history operates (like most national stories) in unifying and homogenizing ways. 'Events', as the historiographer Hayden White writes, 'are made into a story by the suppression or subordination of certain of them and the highlighting of others.'[35] In many cases, as women's histories also show, historical details, voices, strands, and traces relating to minorities are not registered within the authoritative or 'highlighted' narrative frameworks through which national histories are read. Or, as the anthropologist Michel-Rolphe Trouillot observes: 'Historical narratives necessarily produce silences that are themselves meaningful.' The meaningfulness of such silences is asserted in particular when minority voices resist how canonical history has interpreted them.[36] To address these gaps in the historical record, *Indian Arrivals* is particularly interested in combining views from a range of different sources, relating to both incomers and their hosts, and so creating a deeper, even stereoscopic, understanding of the obscure and overlooked stories that nonetheless also helped shape turn-of-the-century British cultural life.

III CROSS-BORDER POETICS

Indian Arrivals 1870–1915 is informed throughout by an interest in textuality as it is manifested in literary, as well as some non-literary, writing; that is, in how textual forms mould and model intercultural contacts and relationships. It takes this writing—its tropes and formal structures—as both reflective and diagnostic of the Indian–British encounter, and therefore as bearing a critical impression of the salient features of the Indian interaction with Britain. As Nile Green's research also recognizes, Britain, and in particular England, had been 'textualized' by Asian travellers from as far back as the early nineteenth century. Their travel writing not only testified to the reciprocity of the religious and social exchanges they conducted with Britons, but also laid down an archive of written observations with which later travellers and arrivants might interact—one, moreover, that cuts across colonial dichotomies and fills historical silences with presence.[37] It is this archive to which the Indian scholars, students, teachers, poets, and activists covered in these pages contributed in their turn as they wrote up their experiences of travel to, and within, the west.

As with Green's travellers, textual sources such as journals and memoirs, based on evocative narrative genres such as the picaresque, provide rich contemporary impressions of the complex of perceptions and emotions associated with the Indian–British encounter. In the worked, encoded forms of such writing, the subtleties of interaction are traced, and the associated anxieties and aspirations of travel captured. Here it is important not to forget that English-born writers, too, such as Wilkie Collins or Frances Hodgson Burnett, played a key role in exploring and articulating some of the complicated dimensions of intercultural encounter between Britain and the subcontinent on British soil. So Collins in *The Moonstone* (1868/1871) intriguingly represents Indians as not merely forming a part of the hustle and bustle of London's streets, as is discussed in Chapter 2, but also as maintaining their self-mastery even under pressure, unlike many of his British characters.

As this implies, *Indian Arrivals* approaches in particular literary texts in two interrelated ways: first, as actual records of travel and cultural transaction, but also in their particularity, as imaginative structures or 'technologies', in Cara Murray's definition, or as cognitive models or 'affordances', in the definition of Terence Cave.[38] We will be interested in how literary texts, not least lyric poetry, shaped and were in turn shaped by the encounters in question. For example, how did a British–Indian poetic collaboration, such as that of Manmohan Ghose and Lawrence Binyon, imprint on a cultural movement like 1890s decadence (as in Chapter 3)? Or how might the concept of a spiritualized modernity explored by Rabindranath Tagore and his promoter friend William Rothenstein have shaped the emergence of the 1910s modernist poem, not least in terms of providing it with a necessary foil against which to react (as in Chapter 4)? In each case, the literary text will be taken as an instrument through which to understand and reflect critically on the world, as it indeed was by the writers and artists in their time. Or, as Cara Murray recognizes, in the late nineteenth century certain generic forms (such as the colonial romance) made possible new modes of global imagining, new symbolic investments in space that was until then uncharted.

As part of its critical methodology, the book also gives attention to and reads in-depth contemporary postcolonial or transnational writing that attempts to retrieve and flesh out encounters that the historical record to date has not captured, or that have slipped from historical memory, such as we find in Michael Ondaatje's *The Cat's Table* (2011) or Julian Barnes's *Arthur & George* (2006). As this implies, postcolonial novels and poems, themselves moulded by experiences of migration and displacement, help to set up diagnostic frameworks for reading earlier colonial-era texts. Critical perceptions adapted from these works draw out in particular the complexities and tensions of cosmopolitan relations inflected by orientalism, and its simultaneous assertions of intimacy and distance. Both in this introduction and elsewhere in the book, V. S. Naipaul's moving evocation in *The Enigma of Arrival* (1987) of his long-anticipated encounter with England as an Indian-origin immigrant from the New World, deepens the thematic resonances of arrival.

Several chapters consider poetry, especially the lyric poem, as a particularly suggestive and mobile medium for forging connection across cultures, and for giving expression to understandings that might as yet appear inchoate or even inconceivable in other forms. Whereas large-scale, formal contacts between Britons and Indians, whether they were durbars, exhibitions, or dance performances, were documented in a variety of public media, including newspapers, court circulars, and periodicals, private one-to-one interactions tended to go unrecorded, or, at least, were not recorded in direct or easily accessible form. On this more muted, intimate level of Indian–British connection, poetry, with its intensities of expression and concentrations of meaning, afforded rich possibilities for cross-cultural exchange to be both pursued and consolidated, as is especially evident in the friendship by poetic collaboration of Lawrence Binyon and Manmohan Ghose (chapter 3). Poetry's symbolic resonances and openness to mystery also captured the combined wonder and apprehension involved when individuals sometimes more familiar with the English language and its literary traditions than with one another's cultures, forged interactions. To borrow from Jahan Ramazani's persuasive exegesis in *The Hybrid Muse* and *A Transnational Poetics*, the 'exceptional figural and formal density' of poetry afforded the poets concerned delicate and sensitive ways of exploring intercultural and other cross-border links, as well as excavating layered histories.[39]

The Irish poet W. B. Yeats, for example, who, as we already saw, cultivated several important Indian interlocutors, takes on an Indian persona to expound his thoughts on embodied godhead in his early poems. And Sarojini Naidu in the 1890s laid claim to an at once English yet Oriental poetic voice through the insistent beat of her sultry, decadent refrains. Expanding Ramazani's term 'transnational poetics', the readings of these and other poets that follow will begin to develop the idea of a *cross-border poetics*—that is, a poetics that explores the tentative, complicated textures of (here) Indian–British encounters and that itself plays out something of the troubling of the boundaries between the cultures involved.[40] It is not coincidental that the cross-border poetics associated with many of the poets featured in the following chapters arose from or formed a response to their collaboration and friendship with poets from 'the other side' of the India–Britain divide.

Yet writing in all forms, not forgetting journalism, allowed travelling Indians not merely to articulate their experience of migration but also to give it conceptual shape. While there are no major novels of the period by Indians that evoke passages to England, journals and letters home, and the more retrospective forms of the travelogue and the memoir, provided effective means through which these travellers could reflect on the modern imperial world that they themselves were making and remaking in the process of moving through it. Chapter 1 in particular focuses on the ways in which travel writing allowed Indian travellers to respond to and critically evaluate the new and changing human situations which they encountered both en route to Britain and in the metropolis. As for the European colonial traveller in South America, Australia, or the Cape, as Mary Louise Pratt and Paul Carter amongst others have described, the linear and denotative forms of the travelogue allowed Indian migrants to plot familiar day-to-day patterns within unfamiliar spaces.[41]

The newspaper and the periodical, too, provided the migrant imagination with the diagnostic tools through which to make sense of the pell-mell contingencies of their experience, especially given the stark juxtapositions of geographies and social worlds their layout made possible wherever in the world they were published.[42] If, as Benedict Anderson contends, the world was conceptualized, reconceptualized, and consumed on a daily basis by way of the nineteenth-century newspaper's format and its mass propagation, this was something that happened not only in London or New York, but in Bombay and Calcutta too.[43] The serial generation of modern meanings in the newspaper, therefore, far from moving outwards from the single source of the metropolis, is more accurately described as a two-way or even multidirectional process.[44] As Indian migrants moved across the world and mingled with strangers—as did other modern travellers, most notably Africans on the middle passage—their relatively stable local and regional identities and belief systems brought over from home were thrown into new, unpredictable, and quintessentially modern mixes, as Chapter 2 in particular describes. In interpreting these experiences, it could not but be helpful that processes of confronting and then convening a heterogeneous world were encapsulated in the very pages of the newspapers and periodicals they bought and read, and to which some contributed.[45] Within the metropolis, Indian newspaper readers therefore became involved participants in, as well as observers of, Britain's public culture. The situation represents an interesting expansion and complication of Benedict Anderson's largely monadic model of newspaper reading as nation making, where the primary reference is to the metropolitan reading population.

IV ARRIVALS AND ARRIVANTS

Indian Arrivals 1870–1915 offers a sustained reflection on what it is to arrive in another culture, in all senses of the word. To the Indians who formed part of the early phase of migration to Britain the idea of arrival certainly bore a special suggestiveness. The term 'India Arrived'—from which the book's title is adapted—makes play with the Indian-English term of disapprobation 'England Returned', used in elite Indian circles from the late nineteenth century to refer to Indians who, having studied abroad, returned to the subcontinent affecting English manners and attitudes. There is a rough synonym in the creolized Bengali term *ingabanga*, which appears in Rabindranath Tagore's letters home to describe the behaviour of deferential anglicized Bengalis in Britain.[46] As the shadowy mirror-image to 'England Returned', the coinage 'India Arrived' shares a sense of identities constructed and reconstructed as part of the process of moving through the transport and communications networks of empire. At the same time, it represents that process at its promising first stage, the moment when arrival signifies excited anticipation and openness to new experiences, as it does to some extent for a V. S. Naipaul newly arrived in England in *The Enigma of Arrival* (1987). The phrase holds out the prospect that, despite prevailing prejudices, cross-cultural understanding and exchange may yet take place. At the same time, the term carries the connotations of social climbing also borne by the English verb 'to arrive', pointing to the acquisition of snobbish airs and graces that accompanied a long-term visit to the heart of the empire (as *ingabanga* also suggests). Many of the Indians who will be observed arriving in this book did indeed secure social and professional advancement by way of the educational and cultural rewards that their travelling brought.

Arrival, arriving: reaching a destination; landing in a new place; establishing a position but then discovering that the completion of one journey in fact leads to a new departure. The *Oxford English Dictionary* defines 'arrival' both as the achievement of one's destination and as the founding of a reputation. From the point of view of the colonial traveller, however, these meanings may lay too strong an accent on finality and resolution. For the migrant whose cultural home would always in some sense be located elsewhere, *arrival* carried the countervailing connotations both of movement and coming to rest, of welcome and incursion, of encountering an ostensibly strange new world that was, however, in many ways foreseen and charted in advance. Certainly, from the point of view of the Indians profiled in this book, it is the *process* of arrival that is particularly significant—a process that is often understood as falling into two phases: both the journey for which arrival is the end-point (which is central to Chapter 1 and some of Chapter 2), and the aftermath of arrival, of what happens next (the focus of the book's second half). To cite from the Eliotesque title of the fifth volume of Leonard Woolf's autobiography: for this study *both* the journey *and* the arrival matters—and the arrival is not end-stopped.[47]

As the Indians who journeyed to Britain in the final decades of the nineteenth century did so largely to study and obtain professional qualifications (Mohandas Gandhi, Manmohan Ghose, Jawaharlal Nehru), to expand business and commercial links (Dadabhai Naoroji, Mancherjee Bhownagree), or to petition for economic reform and political representation in India (Naoroji, R. C. Dutt), their time in Britain usually represented a means to an end. They aimed not to settle but to return: their arrival was open-ended. Crucially, Indians in this period travelled through the empire and lived in Britain as recognized imperial citizens. Under Queen Victoria's proclamation of 1858, they were held to be subjects of the British Crown and so could travel freely without papers throughout the empire's transport networks.[48] Indians stood to gain no particular advantage or status therefore from living on in Britain. Though there are exceptions to the rule, the knowledge and expertise they acquired in Britain was ultimately always geared to fostering and mobilizing nationalist, legal, or social projects back in India.[49]

In *Nationalist Thought and the Colonial World* (1986)—his influential interrogation of the transmission of European nationalist thought to India—Partha Chatterjee deploys the term 'arrival' in a specifically historical and political sense informed by Gramsci's theory of revolution, yet expands the concept to embrace how arrivants' interests remain to some extent connected to the place left behind.[50] The transition from colonial to postcolonial nation-states in the Third World, in Chatterjee's view, can be divided into three phases: the moment of departure, where nationalist consciousness is synonymous with the adoption of European modernity and capitalist production (yet the preservation of an 'eastern' spirituality), as in the Bengal Renaissance; the moment of manoeuvre, associated with M. K. Gandhi, where the historical consolidation of the nation decries the modern; and the moment of arrival, embodied in Jawaharlal Nehru, in which integrated nationalist thought combining modern and traditional elements seeks expression in 'the unified life of the [modern] state'. For Chatterjee, as this suggests, concepts of departure, transition, and arrival are specifically bound up with the differential transfer of ideological inputs from west to east. However, the connotations of arrival in his work cross-refer to the cultural history of east–west migration that is developed here, in the sense that arrival to a greater or lesser extent always involves the incorporation of the difference of the new place into the social and imaginative structures the arriving party carries with it. For example, the idealistic nationalist Nehru on his return to India after an education in the west, at Harrow and Cambridge, endeavoured to pass off his strong interest in western science as something that in fact bore close ties to eastern forms of rationality.[51] For colonial travellers under empire, as we will shortly see again, arrival was on some level always already scripted in advance.

From an overview of book titles published in Britain across the first post-millennium decade, *arrival* tends once again to carry connotations of transport and migration, pertaining to people as well as to birds, and often has to do with cross-border movement.[52] A small subset of titles associate the word with the coming of a god or a presence through some form of incursion or annunciation—a meaning which can be related to the appearance of the mysterious stranger figure in Toru Dutt's poem, who offers blessings rather than the curses a more forbidding godhead might bestow. A related sense of arrival is captured in the Alexandrine poet Constantine Cavafy's atmospheric 1904 'Waiting for the Barbarians', which gave J. M. Coetzee's 1980 novel its title: 'What are we waiting for, gathered in the market place?/ The Barbarians are to arrive today'.[53]

To the Jamaican poet E. K. Brathwaite in *Arrivants* (1973), a trilogy charting Afro-Caribbean trajectories of Black Atlantic travel, arrival ambivalently signifies both conventional arrival in a new place (for post-war Caribbean immigrants, England), yet also a return to somewhere familiar from ancestral memory, such as Africa for the descendants of slaves. The poem 'Arrival' in *Masks*, the second volume in the *Arrivants* trilogy, for instance, is built on a rhythmic structure of images of leave-taking and arrival back in Africa, that poignant return journey to the place where the cultural or racial navel string is buried. Brathwaite's coinage 'arrivants', which I adopt in this section's title and throughout this study, therefore helps to highlight the condition of those displaced and culturally untethered persons whom empire has committed to ceaseless processes of arrival and departure (where 'arrivers' might suggest those whose task is completed with one process of arrival).[54] In partial contrast with Brathwaite, the New York-based Indian writer Meena Alexander, in her collection *The Shock of Arrival* (1996), gestures repeatedly at the 'multifold' shock of the new that arrival brings, which is contingent upon the old life left behind '[being] shattered open', and the dispersal and loss of cultural knowledge that follows. For Alexander, unlike for Brathwaite, therefore, arrival is a one-way process, involving a complete reinvention of the self.[55] For pre-1914 Indians in Britain, different from Alexander and more like Brathwaite, arrival could often mean recursion, where recognitions of similarity existed in dynamic relationship with perceptions of difference. To arrive in a new place was at once to recognize it, yet to know it 'for the first time', as the émigré T. S. Eliot perceives in *Four Quartets*.[56] Discovery was always in some sense a rediscovery, a seeing anew moulded by some form of prior knowledge. Such prescripted cultural awareness of a context that in sensory and geographical terms is unfamiliar is fundamental to the idea of Indian arrival explored in this study.

It was due in great part to the book-knowledge they had acquired as part of their colonial education that the Indian migrants discussed in *Indian Arrivals* lived out in visceral ways some of these interlocking paradoxes of arrival. For them, arrival pointed not only to eventual return to the homeland, but also committed them to a perpetual cycle of attempted arrival and rearrival in a Britain or a Europe that was always strongly anticipated in the imagination before it was ever reached. This also meant that true arrival (or staying on) was almost inevitably doomed not to succeed and therefore had to be reattempted each time. Importantly, these places of mostly temporary arrival were not always confined to Western Europe. Travelling Indian scholars, artists, and religious seekers were, at different points in time, intellectually or spiritually oriented also, among other destinations, to the United States, the venue of the 1893 World Parliament of Religions, as well as places east of India, in particular Japan, already perceived by the 1890s as a triumph of modern development on non-western lines.

The period of Indian arrival in question begins with the four-month opening from November 1869 of the Suez Canal, that 'passage' which would rapidly become the arterial route of travel between India and Britain. The starting date of 1870, however, is significant for other reasons also, which began to converge in the first two decades of the nineteenth century's second half. Due to a combination of Hindu caste restrictions upon ocean-going travel across the *kala pani* or black water, and the difficulty and expense of shipboard journeys, up to this point in history elite Indians had not yet travelled in significant numbers to the west. Religious restrictions applied also to Parsis, though for a different reason, as steamships were powered by fire, sacred to the Zoroastrian faith of India's Parsi community. The aversion to sea travel changed in part because the building of the Canal shortened the time of travel between India and Britain, but also in part because, from 1869, the Indian Civil Service examinations were opened to Indians for the first time. Even though discriminatory regulations continued to pertain, in that non-British candidates were required to sit and therefore also study for the examinations in London, Indians, aware of the new channel for career and social promotion that had been opened in the capital, began to seek permission from their caste elders to travel. In due course, more flexible caste regulations (involving procedures for caste reinstatement) were put in place. From the mid-century, too, Oxbridge colleges, the primary destination of the Indian student, began gradually to relax their religious restrictions on Indian enrolment.

On the British side, the 1870 Education Act made provision for primary school education for all, which meant that Britons across the social classes tended from this point on to be better informed in their encounter with Indians.[57] From the point of view of the imperial economy, the American Civil War of 1861–65 shifted the flow of the global cotton trade to Britain, as the booming Bombay cotton industry extended its trade networks to Britain and the Lancashire textile industry became dependent on Indian cotton. Several Parsi cotton companies based in Bombay set up offices in Liverpool and London, and from the early 1870s there were Parsis working in the Lancashire cotton industry.[58] In global terms, the final decades of the nineteenth century, from around 1870, represent the period of high British imperialism, characterized by a massive expansion of the empire's trade, travel, and communications networks. And in 1876, with the passing of the Royal Titles Act proclaiming Victoria Empress of India, the paramountcy of British rule in India was made more secure than ever.

The period closes with two key movements of arrival—one an arrival in terms of prestige, the other a decisive mass arrival in military terms. First there was, in 1913, the award of the Nobel Prize for Literature to the feted Bengali poet Rabindranath Tagore, the first non-European dark-skinned person to receive the prize. Then, in 1914–15, there was the arrival on the Western Front, around the Ypres Salient, of over one million Indian sepoys, without whose participation, it is now widely believed, the Allies could not have held out. It was a brief moment in which the presence of India-in-Britain (or India-in-Europe) was held to be indispensable and life-sustaining. Beyond this period, the landscape of Indian–British interaction became cross-cut with political tensions connected to the anti-colonial struggle in India and the disappointment of nationalist hopes at Versailles.

V THE ENIGMA OF ARRIVAL

Tacking between 'discourses of displacement and dwelling', Trinidad-born V. S. Naipaul's *The Enigma of Arrival* charts the complicated, often intertwined ambiguities that for the migrant are associated with living in a new, yet also in some sense familiar (culturally well-known), country.[59] As such, the novel with its resonant title provides a symbolic index to many of this book's meditations on Indian arrivals in England, both early and late. With *The Enigma of Arrival*, Naipaul measures out in cadenced, reiterative prose what seems on one level to be an incremental, step-by-step process of approaching the long-imagined English landscape, aided and encouraged by the terms of description his colonial education in Trinidad has bestowed. Yet the linearity of this process is all too soon revealed to be an illusion, in as much as the landscape is shown to be fantastical and remote, despite its apparent pastoral stasis. The measured steps of Naipaul's actual daily walk, during which he meditates on arrival, similar to the measured steps of his prose, are punctuated by innumerable pauses, repetitions, retakes, and backward glances to something said before. The interruptions powerfully suggest that Naipaul's arrival within a seemingly real-life England at the same time involves a retreat from his dream image of England. Yet, as he recognizes, the real England is ultimately only accessible through the dream image.

Naipaul begins *The Enigma of Arrival* by observing that the English landscape only began to gather meaning for him as he learned little by little to 'absorb' it into his frameworks of reference. At first he lacked the historical and aesthetic means through which to 'fit' it in (pp. 11–12). He felt a stranger in 'the other man's country', an unanchored 'oddity', whose sense of displacement was increased by his awareness that his very presence represented a significant change, even an upheaval, within the apparently changeless English landscape (not unlike Dutt on the beach near Hastings) (p. 13). Yet, almost in the same breath, he concedes that even as a stranger he brought to this setting, like Nehru, certain kinds of linguistic and literary–cultural knowledge that allowed him imaginatively to inhabit it, to 'reconceptualize migration into a mode of dwelling'.[60] Beside the Wiltshire water meadows he finds 'a physical beauty perfectly suited to my temperament and answering, besides, every good idea I could have had, as a child in Trinidad, of the physical aspect of England' (p. 52). Even as he speaks of his presence in Wiltshire, on the downs overlooking Stonehenge, as an 'accident', he again and again sees with his trained 'literary eye, or with the aid of literature', certain patterns that are not accidents, that are in fact fully explicable as products of his education (pp. 22, 23).

Wordsworthian figures in the landscape, images from *Sir Gawain and the Green Knight*, lines from King Lear (p. 23)—these transform his adopted new country into something seen before: 'I felt I had always known them' (pp. 20, 23, 24, 26, 31, 38). He comes in this way to calibrate his own sense of contingency in the landscape with the subtle changes he discerns around him, to the extent that his own surprising arrival in this rural setting ('at the time of empire, there would have been no room for me') can itself be seen as part of a process of slow accretion and gradual change: 'the world—in places like this—is never absolutely new, there is always something that has gone before' (pp. 51, 52). His years in Wiltshire become a 'second life': a 'second arrival (but with an adult's perception) at a knowledge of natural things'; almost, one might say, a rearrival (pp. 83, 91).

Following Naipaul's carefully orchestrated evocation of second arrivals at the end of 'Jack's Garden', the first section of the novel, he offers at the start of 'The Journey', the second section, a description of De Chirico's surrealist painting, entitled by Apollinaire, which gives his own book its title (pp. 91–4). This core scene within the novel—of a classical harbour, a set of cloaked figures, and an arriving or departing ship—is presented both as an escape fantasy, 'a free ride of the imagination' from the book he is working on, and as an atmospheric encapsulation of his own story of arrival and rearrival. Repeating as an insistent chord across the novel, the De Chiroco scene not only shapes Naipaul's personal experience of alienation and fracture, but also captures for him the mystery of all arrival, its feelings of loss and desolation, yet also the sense that every arrival is, through the force of imaginative expectation, a second arrival (pp. 91–3, 102, 113). Every arrival, too, is haunted by the fear of no return—that fear which would have powerfully gripped Indians crossing the black water for the first time.

The keynotes of the experience of arrival which Naipaul finds in the 'Enigma of Arrival' painting, which are also the keynotes of his own migrant experience, are picked up in many of the travellers' tales, memoirs, notes, and jottings that are observed in this book. In these travellers' accounts, too, there are journeys by ship powered by fantasies and dreams; ambitions to arrive and stay constantly undercut by the longing to retreat and return home; the clash between abstract ideas derived from education and reading, and actual experience; and then always the discovery on return that home has irrevocably changed, due not only to the passing of time but the experience of the journeying itself. Indeed, though Naipaul sees himself in many ways as a precursor figure, he is also rightly aware of forming part of a great intercontinental movement of peoples that has defined the twentieth century: that 'a great shaking up of the world' for which the migrant Indians discussed here were themselves precursors. These travelling Indians, too, like Naipaul, took their 'proofs from books' (pp. 120, 122, 145).

As for Naipaul in *The Enigma of Arrival*, the experience of arriving somewhere new and yet knowing the place (remembering from cultural memory rather than experience), is central to the writing and observation of nearly all the Indian arrivants who are discussed in the following chapters.[61] Far from being parochial in their outlook and habits, as their caste-driven reluctance to travel might suggest, these Indians imaginatively inhabited a cultural—and to some extent cosmopolitan—world that extended far beyond the bounds of India. Abroad, on the streets of London, Edinburgh, Brighton, or Bristol they would find their urban experiences of Calcutta or Bombay echoed back to them. 'I felt Indian by birth,' a later traveller, J. P. Reddy, wrote, 'but decidedly European in interest.'[62] Or, as the England-educated lawyer Nagarajan typically wrote in the early twentieth century: 'I enjoyed every minute of my stay in Britain. To me Britain was English history and literature come to life.'[63]

VI CHAPTERS

Each chapter in *Indian Arrivals* dwells on a key historical moment, phase, or development in the process of Indian arrival in Britain, 1870–1915, many of these fitting around or into a decade-long time span. Chapter 1, 'Passages to England: Suez, the Indian Pathway', collates Indian accounts of 'voyages in' from various Indian ports through the Suez Canal to London in order to explore the symbolism of Indian crossings over. A book on arrivals therefore opens, appropriately, with that primary phase of passing into the west. Travelogues, memoirs, diaries, and related documents from S. A. Ali, Lala Baijnath, R. C. Dutt, Toru Dutt, and the Raja of Kolhapur, among others, set against those from western travellers like Edwin Arnold, cast the metropolis as both distant and near, and the homeland as defined from a vantage point abroad. From the moment of their departure from India, we will observe, Indian travellers often saw themselves as moving *through* as well as *towards* a 'Greater Britain' located beyond the seas, yet at the same time not significantly distant from India. On board ship, many of the experiences that would later become definitive of arrival in the metropolis were anticipated, the apprehension at being a stranger amongst strangers balanced by the familiarity of certain urban scenes and cultural artifacts. The initial process of travelling to Britain therefore represented the opening chapter in an ongoing reiterative experience of arrival that pre-empted or forecast the phases to come. On this journey, as Michael Ondaatje recognizes in *The Cat's Table* (2011), the experience of travelling through the Suez Canal was perceived as a watershed passage, a cross-section of the layered, complicated voyage that brought Indians from the subcontinent to Europe.

Moving from the *process* of arriving to the phase of 'touch down', Chapter 2, 'The Spasm of the Familiar: Indians in Late Nineteenth-century London', considers the Indian encounter with the imperial metropolis, the primary destination of their travels. The high imperial decade of the 1880s, the heyday of Liberal Britain, forms a dominant point of focus, though examples are chosen from across the final thirty years of the century. How did the teeming city strike Indians in this period, yet, equally, how did their presence on its streets strike the city? The chapter contends that although Indian travellers, students, business-men, and so on, were perceived—and indeed perceived themselves—as foreigners in London, many at the same time were longstanding city-dwellers and bore with them a keen awareness of what it was to inhabit an industrialized, modern world. A significant number of Indian writers and commentators in this period—including B. M. Malabari, T. N. Mukharji, M. K. Gandhi, and Dadabhai Naoroji—pictured Indians as forming an intrinsic and definitive part of the energy and modernity of London's crowded streets, and found some of their views corroborated in the work of their British counterparts—Wilkie Collins, George Meredith, and F. Max Müller, amongst others.

Chapter 3, 'Lotus Artists: Self-orientalism and Decadence', explores the complicated ways in which the end-of-century Indian-English poets Manmohan Ghose and the slightly later Sarojini Naidu, as well as Ghose's Oxford contemporary the law student Cornelia Sorabji, both anglicized and yet orientalized their writing, and the personas they presented to British society. They contributed to creating, yet were at the same time shaped by, the orientalist effects of 1890s decadence. As in the previous chapters, the accent lies on how Indians in Britain fell in line with, yet also actively participated in, the cultural inscription of India and Indians. An important feature of this self-orientalization is how these Indian artists and writers, not omitting Tagore in the 1910s, were inducted into their aesthetic preoccupations through the medium of close friendships with leading British men of letters and cultural critics, especially Laurence Binyon, Edmund Gosse, and Arthur Symons, as well as through their affiliation with the avant-garde circles, clubs, and groups that defined the era, such as the Rhymers Club. Feted by Yeats's friends, mentored by Symons and Gosse, published in the *Savoy Magazine,* Naidu, for example, was inspired to orientalize both her writing and appearance to the extent that she was widely seen as an embodiment of the modern age in eastern dress.

Chapter 4 'Edwardian Extremes and Extremists, 1901–13' traces the marked bifurcation in the representation of India-in-Britain that accompanied the radicalization of Indian politics in the first decade of the twentieth century. As Indian nationalists in India began to protest ever more concertedly against the intransigent British presence on the subcontinent, a growing number of Indian students in British universities, especially those clustered around India House, set about defining themselves in opposition rather than in relation to the imperial 'homeland'. Though the law continued to regard Indians as being more a part of Britain than Jews and other East European immigrants, in literary writing and journalism Indians were generally viewed as foreign and exotic, perhaps to a more marked degree than before, as Julian Barnes reflects in his searing 2000s novel *Arthur & George*. In a related development, despite the fact that Britain now played host to increasingly more Indian students and other visitors, some Indians in Britain, resistant to incorporation into the British social landscape, began to single themselves out as different and exotic, rather than as integrated and urbane citizens of the empire. Indian art criticism, produced by both Britons and South Asians, provided an especially sensitive barometer to these developments, with its ethnographic and primitivist readings of Indian art and architecture. These polarizing tendencies came to a head with the assassination in 1901, by an Indian extremist, of a high-ranking colonial civil servant on the steps of the Indian Institute in South Kensington. In its second half, Chapter 4 looks at the *annus mirabilis* of the Bengali poet Rabindranath Tagore's reception in London during 1912–13. The dichotomous representation of India-in-Britain manifested strongly in how Tagore was represented, as will be shown—that is, as both the embodiment of an ancient spiritual tradition, against which a fierce secular modernity might pit itself, and as a cosmopolitan interlocutor from a not unrelated cultural context, in dialogue with whom modernity might be defined. The central portrait of the remarkable friendship between Tagore and the art critic William Rothenstein, supported by connections both enjoyed with Yeats and others, captures in microcosm the dynamic relationship that formed between Anglo-Irish, British, and Indian artists and avant-gardes in London in the years before the outbreak of the First World War.

The coda 'Indian Salients' touches briefly on three paradigmatic Indian–British 1910s 'scenes'—one mathematical, one military, and one poetic. It observes how, at around the same time as the Indian mathematician Ramanujan began collaborating in Cambridge with his British counterpart G. H. Hardy, Indian troops at Ypres and Neuve-Chapelle on the Western Front helped to hold this crucial salient for the Allies.

Beside these two scenes is finally placed an end-of-war image. When Wilfred Owen was killed in the closing days of the First World War, a poem from Tagore's 1912 *Gitanjali* was found in the breast pocket of the uniform he had been wearing. Taken together, the vignettes powerfully signify how intimately Indian knowledge and awareness (one might say 'soul-force') had been incorporated into the heart of the empire and how closely Britain was networked with India even in this relatively early period for cross-cultural contact.

As the full title *Indian Arrivals 1870–1915: Networks of British Empire* suggests, this study is preoccupied in a sustained way with how travel, communications, organizational, and other networks underpinned Indian–British cultural interactions in the period between 1870 and 1915, not excluding the ways in which the formal networks supplied by groups and organizations such as the National Indian Association (1870), India House (1904), and the India Society (1910) forged partnerships and collaborations. Across its length, the book turns through a set of interlocking paradoxes involving Indian arrivants—of perceptions of the familiar locked inside the strange, of the intercalation of home and abroad, of the contradictory experience of being both a cultural insider to Britain and a foreigner, a self-styled oriental and yet an anglicized Indian.

NOTES

1. The spelling convention of 'past' followed here, taken from the Oxford India edition of Dutt's work, may reflect the poet's delight in archaism.
2. Toru Dutt, 'Near Hastings', *Ancient Ballads and Legends of Hindustan*, intr. Amaranatha Jha (Allahabad: Kitabistan, 1941), pp. 163–4; also Chandani Lokugé, ed., *Toru Dutt: Collected Poetry and Prose* (New Delhi: Oxford University Press, 2006), pp. 206–7. First published in 1882, the poem was probably written in 1876.
3. Edmund Gosse, 'Toru Dutt: Introductory Memoir', in Toru Dutt, *Ancient Ballads and Legends of Hindustan* (London: Kegan, Paul, Trench and Co., 1882), pp. vii–xxvii, speaks of Toru's interest in travel and the 'great zeal and application' with which she applied herself to the 'Higher Lectures for Women' at Cambridge.
4. Kwame Anthony Appiah, *Cosmopolitanism: Ethics in a World of Strangers* (London: Allen Lane, 2006). See also <http://www.motherjones.com/interview/2006/02/anthony_appiah.html> (accessed 7 January 2015). On the recognition of the singularity of the other that defines in particular a situation of friendship, see also Maurice Blanchot, *Friendship*, trans. Elizabeth Rottenberg (Stanford, CA: Stanford University Press, 1997).

5. As the Coda to this volume will show, the Indian troops were to be sent back east as soon as they had fulfilled their purpose, and, until recently, their contribution was largely forgotten.
6. See Tricia Lootens, 'Bengal, Britain, France: The Locations and Translations of Toru Dutt', *Victorian Literature and Culture* 34.2 (2006): 573–90; and her 'Alien Homelands: Rudyard Kipling, Toru Dutt and the Poetry of Empire', *The Fin-de-siècle Poem: English Literary Culture and the 1890s*, ed. Joseph Bristow (Athens, OH: Ohio University Press, 2007), pp. 284–310. See Edmund Gosse, 'Toru Dutt: Introductory Memoir', in Toru Dutt, *Ancient Ballads and Legends of Hindustan* (London: Kegan, Paul, Trench and Co., 1882), pp. vii–xxvii.
7. Antoinette Burton, *At the Heart of the Empire: Indians and the Colonial Encounter in Late Victorian Britain* (Berkeley, CA: University of California Press, 1998), p. 53.
8. In France, Toru Dutt had found an intimate friend in a Frenchwoman of her age, Clarice Bader: the misidentification in the poem is a possible sign of fellow feeling with the French.
9. This would include Toru Dutt's mentor, the English man of letters Edmund Gosse. See Edmund Gosse, *Father and Son*, ed. and intr. Michael Newton (Oxford: Oxford University Press, 2004), in particular p. 41.
10. Throughout, the term 'India' designates the entire Indian subcontinent, as it did across the colonial period up to independence and the partition of India and Pakistan in 1947.
11. Pablo Mukherjee, *Crime and Empire: The Colony in Nineteenth-century Fictions of Crime* (Oxford: Oxford University Press, 2003), p. 2.
12. Amongst other readings: Antoinette Burton, *At the Heart of the Empire* (1998); Kusoom Vadgama, *India in Britain: The Indian Contribution to the British Way of Life* (London: Royce, 1984); Rozina Visram, *Ayahs, Lascars and Princes: Indians in Britain, 1700–1947* (London: Pluto Press, 1986), and *Asians in Britain: 400 Years of History* (London: Pluto Press, 2002); James Walvin, *Passage to Britain: Immigration in British History and Politics* (London: Penguin, 1984). Also salient throughout this study is Antoinette Burton, *Empire in Question: Reading, Writing and Teaching British Imperialism* (Durham, NC, and London: Duke University Press, 2011), which offers a rigorous rethinking of some of the core interpretations underpinning imperial history and colonial discourse theory.
13. Catherine Hall, *Civilising Subjects: Metropole and Colony in the English Imagination 1830–1867* (Cambridge: Polity Press, 2002).
14. See Mulk Raj Anand, *Conversations in Bloomsbury* (London: Wildwood House, 1981). See also Jessica Berman's discussion of Anand's often disillusioned cosmopolitanism in *Modernist Commitments: Ethics, Politics, and Transnational Modernism* (New York: Columbia University Press, 2011).
15. See Edward Said, 'Introduction', in *Culture and Imperialism* (London: Cape, 1993), in particular pp. xviii, and xxii–xxiii, in which he begins to lay out his case for empire as a 'central area of concern' in the making of metropolitan

culture and literature. See also Burton's related discussion of this passage in *At the Heart of the Empire*, pp. 70–1.

16. The AHRC-funded interdisciplinary research project, completed in 2010, entitled 'Making Britain: South Asian Visions of Home and Abroad, 1870–1950', focused on the early presence of South Asians in Britain and sought to highlight South Asian contributions to British culture. It produced, among other outputs, an online interactive database that provides information and bibliographical references on 450 South Asians in Britain during the period, available at <http://www.open.ac.uk/researchprojects/makingbritain/> (last accessed 7 January 2015). For more detail on the project, see the Acknowledgements to this volume.
17. See Rasheed Araeen, 'A Very Special British Issue: Modernity, Art History and the Crisis of Art Today', *Third Text* 22.2 (March 2008): 125–44; Partha Mitter, *The Triumph of Modernism* (London: Reaktion, 2009), in particular pp. 8–10. It is salient at this point to reference also the 'large-scale' conceptualization of the global spread of modernity that is developed in the world-systems theory of Immanuel Wallerstein. Throughout *Indian Arrivals*, however, the focus is consistently on countervailing literary and cultural flows from the (Indian) periphery to the centre. See Immanuel Wallerstein, *Historical Capitalism with Capitalist Civilization* (London: Verso, 1996), and also David Palumbo-Liu, Bruce Robbins, and Nirvana Tanoukhi, eds., *Immanuel Wallerstein* (Durham, NC: Duke University Press, 2011).
18. See Joseph McLaughlin, *Writing the Urban Jungle: Reading Empire in London From Doyle to Eliot* (Charlottesville, VA, and London: University Press of Virginia, 2000), pp. 1–3 in particular. Deirdre David, *Rule Britannia: Women, Empire and Victorian Writing* (Ithaca, NY, and London: Cornell University Press, 1995), early on traced the 'links between metropolitan culture and the material practices of empire' and discerned the many presences of empire that lay at its heart.
19. Frederick Cooper, *Colonialism in Question: Theory, Knowledge History* (Berkeley, CA: University of California Press, 2005); Nicholas Thomas, *Colonialism's Culture: Anthropology, Travel and Government* (Cambridge: Polity Press, 1994); Daniel E. White, *From Little London to Little Bengal: Religion, Print, and Modernity in Early British India, 1793–1835* (Baltimore, MD: Johns Hopkins University Press, 2013). See also Elleke Boehmer, *Empire, the National, and the Postcolonial: Resistance in Interaction* (Oxford: Oxford University Press, 2002).
20. See, for example, Frederick Cooper and A. Laura Stoler, eds., *Tensions of Empire: Colonial Cultures in a Bourgeois World* (Berkeley, CA: University of California Press, 1997); David Lambert and Alan Lester, eds., *Colonial Lives Across the British Empire: Imperial Careering in the Long Nineteenth Century* (Cambridge: Cambridge University Press, 2006); Tamson Pietsch, *Empire of Scholars: Universities, Networks and the British Academic World* (Manchester: Manchester University Press, 2013).
21. Burton, *At the Heart of the Empire*, p. 189; P. D. Morgan, 'Encounters Between British and "Indigenous" Peoples, *c.* 1500–*c.* 1800', in M. J. Daunton and

R. Halpern, eds., *Empire and Others: British Encounters with Indigenous Peoples, 1600–1800* (London: UCL Press, 1999), p. 68.

22. See, respectively, Pheng Cheah and Bruce Robbins, eds., *Cosmopolitics: Thinking and Feeling Beyond the Nation* (Minneapolis, MN: University of Minnesota Press, 1998); Daniel Carey and Lynn Festa, eds., *Postcolonial Enlightenment* (Oxford: Oxford University Press, 2009); and Timothy Brennan, *At Home in the World: Cosmopolitanism Now* (Cambridge, MA: Harvard University Press, 1997).
23. Leela Gandhi, *Affective Communities: Anti-colonial Thought and the Politics of Friendship* (Durham, NC: Duke University Press, 2006), in particular pp. 1–33.
24. Paul Gilroy, *Between Camps: Race, Identity and Nationalism at the End of the Colour Line* (London: Allen Lane, 2000), p. 78.
25. Amitav Ghosh, *In an Antique Land* (Delhi: Seagull, 1992), especially pp. 16–17, is astute on locating and reading traces buried in the seemingly silent archive. See also Elleke Boehmer and Anshuman Mondal, 'Networks and Traces: Interview with Amitav Ghosh', *Wasafiri* 27.2 (June 2012): 31.
26. Jose Harris, *Private Lives, Public Spirit: A Social History of Britain 1870–1914* (Oxford: Oxford University Press, 1993), especially p. 44.
27. Burton, *At the Heart of the Empire*, pp. 16, 26, 28, 30.
28. See 'Opium Smoking in Bluegate Fields', *Chemist and Druggist* 11 (1870): 259–60: quoted in McLaughlin, *Writing the Urban Jungle*, p. 196 n. 9.
29. Amitav Ghosh's *Ibis Trilogy* represents probably the first fictional recuperation of the buried history of Indian lascars. See *Sea of Poppies* (London: John Murray, 2008) and *River of Smoke* (London: John Murray, 2011).
30. The exilic *imaginaire* associated with indentured Indians' transoceanic southern journeys have in recent decades taken the defiant critical term 'coolitude'. Though Indian arrivals in England took no part in the painful, obscure pathways being traced by their fellow countrymen, what they did share with these other travellers was a perception of India 'from a mosaic stance', a sense of the subcontinent as both distant and plural. See Marina Carter and Khal Torabully, *Coolitude: An Anthology of Indian Labour Diaspora* (London: Anthem, 2002), in particular pp. 145–6 and 212; Khal Torabully, *Cale d'étoiles-Coolitude* (Réunion: Editions Azalées, 1992).
31. See Elleke Boehmer, *Colonial and Postcolonial Literature: Migrant Metaphors* (Oxford: Oxford University Press, 2005), especially ch. 3; Gauri Viswanathan, *Masks of Conquest: Literary Study and British Rule in India* (New York, NY: Columbia University Press, 1989). The Minute made notorious claims about Indian in comparison with British cultures, including that 'a single shelf of a good European library' was worth 'the whole native literature of India and Arabia'. See Thomas Babington Macaulay, *Prose and Poetry*, ed., G. M. Young (Cambridge, MA: Massachusetts, 1952), p. 722; E. L. Woodward, *Age of Reform 1815–1879* (Oxford: Clarendon Press, 1938), p. 148.
32. Dipesh Chakrabarty, *Provincializing Europe: Postcolonial Thought and Historical Difference* (Princeton, NJ: Princeton University Press, 2000).

33. Ann Thwaite, *Edmund Gosse: A Literary Landscape, 1849–1928* (Oxford: Oxford University Press, 1985).
34. See, for example, Richard Ellman, *Yeats: The Man and the Masks* (London: Macmillan, 1949). R. F. Foster, *W. B. Yeats: A Life*, 2 vols. (Oxford: Oxford University Press, 1997–2003) was the first biographical study to give proper attention to Yeats's interactions with Indian theosophists and poets, though the implications of these for his work are not treated in very great depth.
35. Hayden White, 'The Historical Text as Artefact', in *Tropics of Discourse: Essays in Cultural Criticism* (London: Johns Hopkins University Press, 1978), pp. 84–5.
36. Michel-Rolphe Trouillot, *Global Transformations: Anthropology and the Modern World* (Basingstoke: Palgrave Macmillan, 2003), pp. 1, 10. Thomas, in *Colonialism's Culture* and elsewhere, also points out that minority histories and peripheral subjectivities are often written out of the picture by monolithic definitions, for him of colonialism as a 'unitary totality', whereas, as he writes, 'colonialism can only be traced through its plural and particularized expressions' (p. x).
37. See Nile Green, 'Among the Dissenters: Reciprocal Ethnography in Nineteenth-century Inglistan', *Journal of Global History* 4 (2009): 293–315.
38. Cara Murray, *Victorian Narrative Technologies in the Middle East* (London and New York: Routledge, 2008), especially pp. 14–19, 159; Terence Cave, 'Cognitive Affinities', *Times Literary Supplement* 5739 (29 March 2013): 22–3. My thinking is also informed at this point by Terence Cave's to-date-unpublished essays, collectively entitled 'Thinking with Literature', in particular 'Literary Affordances'. Cara Murray's study is aptly in part about the Suez Canal.
39. See Jahan Ramazani, *The Hybrid Muse: Postcolonial Poetry in English* (Chicago, IL: University of Chicago Press, 2001), and the later and even more pertinent cross-border study *A Transnational Poetics* (Chicago, IL: University of Chicago Press, 2009). The quotation is from Ramazani, *The Hybrid Muse*, p. 4.
40. Gandhi, *Affective Communities*, p. 121, quoting Logie Barrow, reminds us that Indian–British connections in this period were often 'zigzag' in character, marked by a heterodoxy and political dissent that drew individuals into unlikely and secret alliances.
41. Paul Carter, *The Road to Botany Bay* (London: Faber, 1987); Mary Louise Pratt, *Imperial Eyes: Travel Writing and Transculturation* (London and New York: Routledge, 1992). See also J. M. Coetzee, *White Writing* (Boston, MA: Harvard University Press, 1988).
42. See Paul Gilroy, *The Black Atlantic* (London: Verso, 1993), ch. 1, in particular in this context his discussion of Martin Delany's identity as formed through a 'process of movement and mediation'.
43. See Benedict Anderson, *Imagined Communities*, rev. edn (London: Verso, 1991); and his *The Spectre of Comparisons: Nationalism, South-East Asia and the World* (London: Verso, 1998).

44. Visram, *Asians in Britain* (2002), lays particular accent on the relative multiplicity and diversity of early Indian presences in Britain, and Burton, *At the Heart of the Empire* (1998), on the many contingencies through which their cultural identities were shaped.
45. See Antoinette Burton and Isabel Hofmeyr, eds., *Ten Books that Shaped the British Empire: Creating an Imperial Commons* (Durham, NC: Duke University Press, 2014).
46. Rabindranath Tagore, *Selected Letters*, ed. Krishna Datta and Andrew Robinson (Cambridge: Cambridge University Press, 1997), pp. 8–10.
47. Leonard Woolf, *The Journey not the Arrival Matters: An Autobiography of the Years 1939–1969* (London: Hogarth Press, 1969).
48. See Sukanya Banerjee, *Becoming Imperial Citizens: Indians in the Late-Victorian Empire* (Durham, NC: Duke University Press, 2010), a thoroughgoing investigation of how ideas of imperial citizenship provided late nineteenth-century Indians with the conceptual and legal grounds for articulating civil rights within India, and for developing the idea of a common and equal status for all across the empire.
49. Partha Chatterjee, 'Nationalism, Colonialism and Colonized Women', *The American Ethnologist* 16.4 (1989): 622–33. As is often the case in diasporic communities, as Roy Foster has observed of the Irish, the distance from home clarifies ideas of the homeland. Their transcontinental journeys therefore afforded Indian travellers a sharper sense of themselves as Indians *and at the same time* as citizens of the modern world. See Roy Foster, *Modern Ireland, 1600–1972* (London: Allen Lane, 1988).
50. Partha Chatterjee, *Nationalist Thought and the Colonial World: A Derivative Discourse?* (London: Zed Press, 1986), especially pp. 49–53.
51. On one level, however, Nehru was not deluded in finding the forms of western science at work in India, and not in a merely imitative, colonial way. From the 1880s, India was treated as a vast laboratory in which to develop not only new educational policies, but also new scientific methods of statistical and population analysis, amongst other innovations. See Nigel Leask, *British Romantic Writers and the East: Anxieties of Empire* (Cambridge: Cambridge University Press, 1992); Jawaharlal Nehru, *The Discovery of India* (London: Meridian Books, 1946), and his *An Autobiography: With Musings on Recent Events in India* (London: Bodley Head, 1936).
52. The word search of titles containing the word 'arrival' and its cognate forms was conducted via SOLO in the Bodleian library on 18 October 2010.
53. C. P. Cavafy, *Collected Poems*, trans. Edmund Keeley and Philip Sherrard (Princeton, NJ: Princeton University Press, 1992).
54. E. K. Brathwaite, *Arrivants: A New World Trilogy* (Oxford: Oxford University Press, 1973). *Arrivants* comprises *Rights of Passage* (1967), *Masks* (1968), and *Islands* (1969).
55. Meena Alexander, *The Shock of Arrival* (Boston, MA: South End Press, 1996), pp. 1–2.

56. T. S. Eliot, '"Little Gidding" V', in *Four Quartets* (1944; London: Faber and Faber, 1963), p. 222.
57. See Roger Oldfield, *Outrage: The Edalji Five and the Shadow of Sherlock Holmes* (Cambridge: Vanguard Press, 2010), p. 158.
58. Oldfield, *Outrage*, p. 178.
59. V. S. Naipaul, *The Enigma of Arrival: A Novel* (London: Penguin, 1987). Page references will appear in gathered form in the text. See also Weihsin Gui, 'Post-heritage Narratives: Migrancy and Travelling Theory in V. S. Naipaul's *The Enigma of Arrival* and Andrea Levy's *Fruit of the Lemon*', *Journal of Commonwealth Literature* 47.1 (2012): 73–90.
60. Gui, 'Post-heritage Narratives': 74.
61. Naipaul's *Half a Life* (London: Picador, 2001) also considers how twentieth-century Indian arrival in Britain is informed by ideals derived from education and cultural myth.
62. J. P. Reddy, *Down Memory Lane: The Revolutions I have Lived Through* (Hyderabad: Booklinks, 2000), p. 165.
63. K. Nagarajan, 'Lawyer at Large', unpublished autobiography, Centre for South Asian Studies, Cambridge, n.d., loose leaves, of which the quotation is from p. 240.

1

Passages to England

Suez, the Indian Pathway

1 Singing my days,
Singing the great achievements of the present,
Singing the strong light works of engineers,
Our modern wonders, (the antique ponderous Seven outvied,)
In the Old World the east the Suez canal,
The New by its mighty railroad spann'd
The seas inlaid with eloquent gentle wires...

2 Passage O soul to India!
Eclaircise the myths Asiatic, the primitive fables.

Not you alone proud truths of the world,
Nor you alone ye facts of modern science,
But myths and fables of eld, Asia's, Africa's fables,
The far darting beams of the spirit, the unloos'd dreams,
The deep diving bibles and legends,
The daring plots of the poets, the elder religions...

Walt Whitman, 'Passage to India', from
Leaves of Grass (1871)[1]

Bound in the wheel of Empire, one by one,
The chain-gangs of the East from sire to son,
The Exiles' Line takes out the exiles' line
And ships them homeward when their work is done.

Rudyard Kipling, 'The Exiles' Line' (1890)[2]

It was the night we never slept.

In less than half an hour we were sidling alongside a concrete dock with crates stacked into giant pyramids and men running with electrical cables and baggage carts alongside the slow-moving *Oronsay*. Everywhere there was fast, intense work under the pockets of sulphurous light...This night turned out to be our most vivid memory of the journey, the time I stumble upon now and then in a dream. We were not active, but a constantly changing world slid past our ship, the darkness various and full of suggestion . . . We had crossed open seas at twenty-two knots, and now we moved as if hobbled, at the speed of a slow bicycle, as if within the gradual unrolling of a scroll.

Who knows what was exchanged that night, and what cross-fertilization occurred as the legal papers of entrance and exit were signed and passed back down to land, while we entered and left the brief and temporary world of El Suweis.

Michael Ondaatje, *The Cat's Table* (2011)

I ONDAATJE'S 'FRAGMENTARY TABLEAUX'

Michael Ondaatje's perplexed and wistful reminiscence, *The Cat's Table*, traces a mid-1950s westward journey of the cruise ship the *SS Oronsay* of the Orient Line.[3] The journey begins in the east, in Colombo, Ceylon (as it then was); its destination point is Tilbury docks in London. Told from the perspective of the narrator Mynah's eleven-year-old self, sent to school in England, this coming-of-age story is transmitted via a series of oblique slivers and compressed character vignettes. In these, many of the *Oronsay*'s passengers are represented as, in effect, walking adventure tales, always hiding more than they make known at first sight. On one level (deck-level, as it were), as the narrator explains late on in the novel, his trip aboard the *Oronsay* appears to his memory as no more than 'an innocent story within the small parameter of my youth': 'just three or four children at its centre, on a voyage whose clear map and sure destination would suggest nothing to fear or unravel' (p. 264). Yet at another level (deep down in the hold), the familiar crossing of 'the Indian Ocean and the Arabian Sea and the Red Sea . . . through the Suez Canal into the Mediterranean . . . [to] a small pier in England', comes back to him as a dynamic though at times threatening spectacle in which most of the central characters are concerned with finding ways of escaping their land-locked pasts and reinventing themselves (pp. 7, 14). The journey that at first seemed to Mynah and his friends a chance to run wild for three weeks, their high jinks always eventually circumscribed by the boundaries of the ship's island world, becomes 'something significant in a life', a freighted passage from childhood into adulthood (p. 58). As many of the other wayfarers from South Asian homelands into the wide world of the west who appear below also discover, in the course of this passage everything becomes altered, shifting from innocence to experience, opening from a youthful, unchecked involvement in life's adventures, to a wary detachment from its potential to deal out pain (pp. 214, 264). Indeed, as Mynah–Michael sees, his experience with the outcasts at the Cat's Table, the least desirable dinner placement on board ship, in many ways prefigures the rest of his personal formation, and the *Oronsay*, this floating city of migrants, will understandably be remembered as the 'first and only ship of his life' (p. 4). His three weeks on board come to stand in his memory as do the vivid pictures of the Suez night-passage itself, as in the epigraph from the novel above: a 'series of time-lapse criss-crossings', captured in a photograph of a city at night (p. 84).

As if mimicking the unreliable processes of memory, the narrative perspective in *The Cat's Table* shuttles between the adult narrator's present day, and his memories of his unsupervised younger self prowling the decks of the *Oronsay* as one of an unruly trio of friends. In the course of this shuttling it is gradually revealed that many of the relationships on board ship, seemingly so temporary and adventitious, in fact date from many years before, and bear dark secrets and destructive intent.[4] All the mysterious characters involved sit with the boys at the Cat's Table, which becomes a privileged venue for eavesdropping on their many intrigues, and, for Mynah in particular, the precursor of the many other Cat's Table situations that will change his life (pp. 189, 211).

Fittingly, the moment when the surface simplicity of things begins to peel back to reveal these many underlying complexities comes at the approach to the 190 kilometres of El Suweis, which, again fittingly, occurs around the middle point of the novel. A harbour pilot boards the ship to 'take us into even shallower waters and adjust [its] angle . . . so we could slip into the narrower canal' (pp. 137–40). The now awe-struck, now curious South Asian travellers who feature in this chapter will observe very similar procedures being undertaken, and will witness startlingly similar proximities being exposed. On the night that follows, as Mynah watches the 'constantly changing world' of Suez slide past the decks, he comes 'to understand that small and important thing, that our lives could be large with interesting strangers who would pass us without any personal involvement': 'Who knows what was exchanged that night, and what cross-fertilization occurred . . . while we entered and left the brief and temporary world of El Suweis' (pp. 139–40).[5] After the revelatory moment of crossing over, the picaresque form of Mynah's tale begins to unravel even as its sense of allegory intensifies. Suez becomes in compressed form the testing passage from one state of being to another: 'the cleavage between east and west floods their consciousness'.[6] After the Canal, the ship is duly given a makeover: blasted en route by the deserts sands of Arabia and Africa, it needs repainting (p. 171).

Years later, Mynah's extrovert friend Cassius, who becomes a painter, will distil scenes from the voyage, and this phase of it in particular, into his work, as the adult Michael, too, will do in his writing (pp. 140–3). The 'traced map of the world' without 'names on it' the eleven-year-old carries in his pocket, will become in his memory something even more ambiguous and open-ended, a voyage into the dark, 'west and north, away from Colombo', away from 'exuberance' (pp. 7, 39, 58, 200). Both will show in their art how the journey on board the vast layered domain of the *Oronsay* allowed them sudden, unpredictable shifts of perspective that exposed the bigotry, inequities, and weird juxtapositions of empire: the separate 'contrapuntal' film-screenings of A. E. W. Mason's colonialist *The Four Feathers* for the ship's different classes; the knighted Ceylonese entrepreneur travelling to Harley Street for treatment as Harley Street will not come to him; the cyclone off Aden that bumps the 'cream of the East' up against pickpockets and thieves (pp. 94–5, 68, 107). As in Ondaatje's *The English Patient* (1992), the *Oronsay*'s world is populated with the 'international bastards' empire spawns, 'born in one place and choosing to live everywhere'—those who are, amongst others, also Naipaul's subjects.[7] In that earlier novel, the desert created 'nationless' people; here, it is the sea and the ship. The overriding effect ultimately produced by the novel is of the strange alchemy of journeying, of the enigma of the voyage as well as the arrival, something that all the Indian travellers in this study experience, a mix that is titrated by the experience of passing through the Suez Canal.[8] The makeshift community of the Cat's Table 'cannot be attached either to the East or to the West', as Pico Iyer writes. This is 'the English story of passage' remade by those travelling to rather than from England, in which it is the west and not the east that is revealed after a tussle with the sea (to adapt from Conrad's *Youth*, a passage Ondaatje cites as his epigraph). Yet, as Ondaatje overtly recognizes in a vignette of the teacher Mr Fonseka, this ambiguous journey is also a time-tried path, which earlier South Asian travellers traced in 'a more dangerous time', suffering the insults and embarrassments of the brown stranger marooned in the 'centre of culture', whose voyage out is always at the same time potentially a longed-for voyage back, the India Arrived soon turning into the '*London Returned*'—a term the novel italicizes (pp. 64–5).

Though it refers to a time many decades on from that covered in this book, Ondaatje's *The Cat's Table* provides an apt curtain-raiser to an account of early Indian passages to England via Suez. As will be seen, many of the travelogues examined here are marked by a similar sense of significance and amazement at the passage through the famous Canal (hailed also in Whitman's 'Passage to India', quoted above). The Canal is not only the vital new artery of the British Empire's transport networks, but also, to them in particular, their gateway to the west. They, too, like Mynah, have a strong awareness of new beginnings, of the journey as a passage not merely into a new world but into a new experience of the self, a more 'worlded' identity.[9] Whereas before these travelling Indians may have seen themselves as members of a family, a caste, a community, now they acquired through their travel a host of new personae, becoming at once cross-cultural migrants, citizens of the world, and self-conscious Indians. In their writings, first the journey and then the retrospective narrative about it work as 'technologies' that at once shape, and critically reflect upon, this process of self-production, just as Mynah's growing up on the twenty-one-day journey from Colombo to Tilbury moulds the transcultural imagination he will carry into adulthood.[10] Like Ondaatje's *The Cat's Table*, these writings carry out one of the primary tasks of the postcolonial novel since V. S. Naipaul's *In a Free State*, according to Philip Hensher, which is to map migratory identities onto migrant lives (pp. 77–8).[11]

Linking to the sense of suppressed danger that Mynah experiences at the Cat's Table, the *Oronsay*'s divided world also presents a dynamic illustration of the contradictoriness even of seemingly amicable cosmopolitan gatherings under empire. In a situation where most such relations were on an uneven race or class footing, as here, interactions were always fractious as well as friendly, and concord was laced with anxiety. At the same time, though the international bastards thrown together on the decks of the *Oronsay* make up a random assemblage, they are nonetheless bonded together by a surprising range of shared enterprises, intrigues, and commitments. As this suggests, imperial cosmopolitanism entailed at once the assertion of common bonds and identities, *and* a simultaneous heightening of the strangeness associated with any such encounter, as we will see many times in this study. Cosmopolitanism in such contexts always exceeded and complicated Appiah's paradigmatic encounter between two well-meaning individuals.

II ACROSS THE BLACK WATERS

As did Ondaatje's Mynah, the late nineteenth-century South Asian travellers who stand at the heart of this book experienced their journey from the subcontinent to Britain as a stage-by-stage passage into an expansive and speeded-up modern world, as well as, simultaneously, a process of finding or laying claim to a new self. The travellers' movement through and beyond Suez involved a series of shifts along a sliding scale of difference and wonderment, where each new phase seemed freighted with both individual and mythical significance. The linear trajectory of their ocean crossing decanted each one of these travelling provincials from the layered, multiple temporalities of India into the channel of progressive, modern time—an induction which would eventually lead them, it was believed, towards the rights and privileges of imperial citizenship and 'universal humanity'.[12] Elite as they were, it was in an immediate sense through their travel that they laid claim to these rights. The very act of journeying entailed putting their proclaimed citizenship of the wider empire into play.[13] If their status and education gave them a certain cultural know-how and ability to 'read' Europe in advance, their travel to and sojourn in the metropolis then embedded, confirmed, and embellished their cosmopolitan credentials. As Priya Joshi observes in *In Another Country*, her study of nineteenth-century Indian book cultures, 'literate Indians [in this period] addressed, absorbed, consumed and otherwise responded to the world of textuality and print that originated in and arrived from Britain'.[14] In short, the travellers' view of the wider world and their place in it was moulded by English books. Yet, though travel to Britain was bound in many ways to consolidate the expectations raised by this reading, it also allowed them to take possession of new worlds in the imagination, not only the western world beyond Suez, but also the concept of an idealized England, 'the home of [their] rulers'—and, in due course, of an Indian homeland.[15]

From the inaugural point of 1869, when the Suez Canal formally opened, Indian journeys manifested across at least two levels of spatio-temporal symbolization, as will be seen: both across a chronologically unfolding series of well-known transit points—the Indian Ocean, Aden, the Red Sea, the Suez Canal, Port Said, the Mediterranean—and as a formative phase in space–time plotted in linear terms, as secular pilgrimage, voyage of (re)discovery, or rite of passage. The beginning of this long process of arrival was the moment of boarding in Calcutta or Bombay, Colombo or Madras, where the deck of the British steamer was often seen as a surrogate for British soil—and the terminus of the journey as the achievement of something as idealized and nebulous as the west. Though the movement of these 'citizens' via Suez to Britain was on one level therefore a significant voyage, taking them 6,000 miles across the Black Waters away from home, it was at the same time a journey within 'an elite imperial geography'.[16] Though they might in actuality be travelling over the Indian Ocean and through the Middle East, they were, as Amitav Ghosh discerningly writes in *In An Antique Land*, travelling *in* the west.[17] Or as Satadru Sen observes of Shri Kumar Ranjitsinhji, who in 1900 was the first Indian to play cricket for England, they had gone abroad even before they embarked for England.[18]

Growing like desert sand crystals on a porthole window—almost as many hopes and expectations would accumulate in the minds of travelling Indians around the trajectory of the east–Suez–west journey as around the touch-down in Britain itself. Shifting from one legendary port of call to another was perceived not only as an arc of movement through the vast empire, as it was by many travellers moving in the opposite direction also, but as a gradual movement into the heart of Greater Britain itself. The Indian journey via Suez therefore captures very precisely how arrival could be an extended and incremental process, at once a *longue durée* and an unfolding series of paradigmatic moments—a series that culminated at last with disembarkation at Portsmouth, Southampton, or Tilbury. As with Ondaatje's 'time-lapse criss-crossings' that trace the *Oronsay* passengers' daily journeys around the ship, many of the Indian travellers' representation of the significant stages in their journey read as cross-sections, or scenes in miniature, of the broader trajectory that took them from towns and cities within the Indian Empire to the metropolitan centre of the wider British Empire. So Aden was widely seen as a window onto the Middle East, while 'squalid' Port Said with its saloons and souks at the other end of the Canal was perceived by many as the last of Asia, offering a final glance back to a steadily retreating eastern homeland.[19] At the same time, the tiered society on board ship, with its different decks and classes, its Captain's Table versus its Cat's Table, was often experienced—as in shipboard literature from Sebastian Brant to Joseph Conrad—as a cross-section of the wider world, mirroring its social divisions.

For nostalgic travellers like Ondaatje's Mynah, or the young Rabindranath Tagore, each stage of the journey out was shadowed by its opposite, a stage in the imagined journey back, a perception thrown into relief whenever homebound ships were encountered en route. In 1889, the young student Cornelia Sorabji, on her way to Oxford, yearned so for her 'Dear Home Circle' that she daydreamed in a letter to them about transferring straight to the 'P & O homeward mails' which her *SS Asia* passed on its way to collect her latest letter from Aden, and so personally taking it home.[20] In a letter to his wife on board the westbound *SS Siam* in 1890, Tagore, feeling seasick in the vicinity of Aden, was overcome by an experience in which his spirit seemed to fly back to 136 Jorasanko, Calcutta, his home address.[21] For Tagore, there was both freedom and constraint in travel: in quest always of the specific and the individual, travel to him generalized and blurred sensory impressions which could only, therefore, be appreciated in their singularity once back at home. Just two years earlier, the colonial head-teacher and poet Edwin Arnold in the prologue 'Adieu' to his memoir *India Revisited* (1886) pictured his steamship, seemingly the same *SS Siam*, steaming over the 'Arab main' with its flag and his thoughts at the same time streaming back to India.[22] Ondaatje captures these different though related yearnings in a single shipboard image: 'An eastbound steamer passed us at dusk one evening, all of its lights on, and it was a fantasy among the three of us to row over to it and return with them to Colombo' (*The Cat's Table*, p. 104). So the journey out became in memory one half of an oscillating pattern in which the outward-bound phases of arrival were counterpointed by corresponding phases of return.

There was no phase along the east–west trajectory, however, that appeared more significant than the passage through the Suez Canal. Across the varied accounts that the early travellers kept, whether in the form of journals, letters, or memoirs, the experience of Suez is nearly always highlighted. Only M. K. Gandhi in 1888, anxious to reach London as soon as possible and begin his long-planned legal studies, became so shy about speaking English to fellow passengers while en route to England that he spent most of his passage in his cabin, as his *Autobiography* records.[23] But for most on the pilgrimage to, and within, the west, El Suweis stood as 'a sign of the promise of a new world order'—as it also did, of course, to the colonial travellers moving in reverse, towards the radiant east that Conrad evokes in *Youth*.[24] The Canal was universally regarded as a watershed arrival moment, a 'rite of passage' in microcosm, a point of crisis, the east-to-west divide encapsulated, as if writ small but in bold.[25] Even the phases in the Indians' approach to the Canal assumed an at once generic and symbolic significance: the invariably smooth journey across the Arabian Sea to Aden; the Red Sea passage north-west, where Africa and Asia appeared to come face to face across the water; and then the geometric narrowness of the Canal itself, the gateway to the Mediterranean. For some, the Red Sea approach to the Canal, with its dangerous coral reefs, heat, and threats of fever, carried sinister associations, as if it were a hazardous birth canal or passage into the after-life. In a letter, Lockwood Kipling described the disturbing (but by no means untypical) end of a lascar who, maddened by heat exhaustion when his ship reached the mouth of the Canal, jumped overboard—the sense of crisis and panic which the Canal could occasion tragically brought to a head in the suicide of this nameless man.[26] The poet Tennyson's son Lionel also found in the same area of the Red Sea before the Gulf of Suez his 'vast and wandering grave'.[27] 'Your India', Tennyson wrote in his poem 'To the Marquis of Dufferin and Ava', addressed to the then Viceroy of India, 'was his Fate.' And Gandhi's reclusive act of shutting himself away, too, betrays considerable social panic about taking the narrow passage into the west.

To gain insight into how early migrants from the subcontinent came to understand themselves as at once citizens of the modern world and cosmopolitan Indians, the crossing via Suez therefore is symptomatic and crucial. The passage west shaped their perceptions of their place in the world, poised between the empire towards whose heartland they were moving, and the emergent nation they were leaving behind, yet to which they would ceaselessly hark back. As in Ondaatje, Suez also represented a confrontation with an elaborated modernity, embodied in the technological paraphernalia of entering and then moving through the channel's 'hobbled' aperture after the days on the open sea (*The Cat's Table*, pp. 137–8). Above all perhaps, the 'magnificent ditch', in the phrase of Edwin Arnold, represented for the traveller suspension between two states of being—on the one hand the legendary and timeless east caught at the point of its encounter with Africa, and on the other all the noisy, fraught, electric-lit, time-bound modernity of a mode of transport made possible by imperial capitalism.[28] If, for E. M. Forster's Fielding in *A Passage to India*, Suez is a portal to the Mediterranean, the cradle of the west, for Indian travellers it is that and something more, a phase in which their eastern identity crystallizes, yet is in part left behind. Indian travellers therefore gave a contrapuntal resonance to Rudyard Kipling's 'The Exiles' Line', an anthem-like poem of Anglo-Indian exile from two homelands, from which the second epigraph to this chapter is taken. They had the sense that they, too, were exiles from their mother country; they, too, were bound in 'the wheel of Empire' through their quest for education, qualifications, and profit, first transported into the wider world by powerful steamship lines, then shipped back home when their work was done.

Indians' significantly intensified travel in the period after 1870 was, as the Introduction began to suggest, motivated by several factors. These included the loosening of traditional caste restrictions on travel across the black waters; the gradual opening of Indian Civil Service examinations to Indians, as these had to be sat in London; and the widespread perception that education at a British university, at this time usually Oxford, Cambridge, Edinburgh, or London, was academically at a higher standard than what might be obtained in India. For would-be lawyers in fact there was no choice in the matter: Indian-trained *vakils* could only be called to the bar in London. Restrictions such as these provided a powerful means of ensuring that for colonial Indians the pinnacle of their educational pilgrimages would for the foreseeable future continue to be situated in the metropolitan heartland; in other words, the socio-economic gains that were to be had from making the journey could safely be deemed to outweigh the caste costs. When Gandhi set out for England in 1888 to pursue his legal studies—which he was told would be 'easier' there—he was excluded from his caste, and, on his return, his new status as a trained lawyer notwithstanding, he had to appeal formally to be readmitted.[29] Members of India's princely classes, who had the means to travel, were unsurprisingly well represented on the east–west route—and their travelogues predictably supply the bulk of illustrative quotations in this chapter. Indeed, whenever disputes arose in the princely states in matters of inheritance and succession, study in England provided an effective means of removing potential troublemakers from the scene.[30]

The rest of this chapter explores in more detail the experience of the Suez passage from both eastern and western perspectives, the connecting thread throughout being the simultaneous opening and shifting of social and cultural horizons brought about by Indian travel west from 1869. Journeying, these well-educated, English-speaking travellers, who were already possessed of a rough-and-ready awareness of English manners and society, imaginatively took possession of the wider world beyond India and achieved an important modern worldliness in so doing. What they saw and recorded of their journeys demonstrates emphatically the degree to which empire constituted a field of meanings at once contested and shared to which both colonizing and colonized parties contributed.

III THE 'MAGNIFICENT DITCH' IN ITS IMPERIAL CONTEXT

Opened with pomp and ceremony across five days in November 1869, the Suez Canal, the brainchild of the French diplomat and later engineer supremo Vicomte Ferdinand de Lesseps, was hailed worldwide as a marvel of European engineering and a piece of inspired, initially French, investment. With his ditch, De Lesseps had conclusively overstepped the apparently insurmountable physical, technological, and financial challenges of building a 168-kilometre canal through the waterless desert between the Red Sea and a Mediterranean that lay nine metres lower at high tide. A glorious pathway to 'the ends of all the Earth' was certainly how de Lesseps conceived of his Canal, as if proleptically singing to Kipling's 'A Song of the English' sheet. As the 30 November 1854 charter exclusively granted him by the Viceroy of Egypt Mohammad Said-Pacha declared, the Universal Company now established would '[cut] the Isthmus of Suez, [and open] a passage suitable for large vessels' between the Mediterranean and the Red Sea.[31] With this cut, the engineer enthused to one of his British benefactors, Viscount Stratford de Redcliffe, something that was once confined to 'the views of Providence', would now 'be in the power of man'. It would allow the traveller, like some anti-Moses, not so much to part the waters of the Red Sea as move along a sea 'bridge' through dry land.[32] Yet de Lesseps did not conceive the benefit of his Canal to be one-way only. Regulating communications through an 'uncertain' Egypt, in his view, could potentially transform and modernize the whole of the chaotic, disputatious, and backward east.

It remains an irony of British imperial history that de Lesseps' technologically ambitious project initially met with resistance on Britain's part, with the notion of the speeded-up journey to India brushed aside at the time as impossible to achieve. Despite the strong nineteenth-century association between imperial capital and the global expansion of trade and transport networks, British disaffection in respect of technological development in the Middle East marked the first half of Queen Victoria's reign. Even Thomas Waghorn's early—1830s—attempts to persuade Indian Steam Committees to invest in an overland route had encountered only a lukewarm official response.[33] Yet from the moment ocean-going ships began to move smoothly through the completed length of the Canal, with its eight stations for passing ships and absence of locks, the world's supreme maritime power belatedly awoke to a sense of the opportunity, and the potential threat, that a canal through the Isthmus of Suez represented to its global hegemony.[34]

Almost from the moment of the Canal's opening, the British began to work determinedly and deftly to establish financial and then political control over Suez, and, by extension, Egypt. In 1875, the British Prime Minister Benjamin Disraeli outmanoeuvred the French to purchase the bankrupt Egyptian Khedive Ismail's 44-per-cent shares in the Suez Canal Company, so turning Britain overnight into the Canal's largest single shareholder. Disraeli's telegram to Queen Victoria informing her of this news was pregnant with a brash new imperial insouciance: 'you have it, Madam', he wrote. The following year, Britain and France established dual control over Egypt's finances, putting the government in the hands of bankers, and in 1879 Tawfiq ousted his modernizing but spendthrift father, the sultan Ismail. Within another two years, British forces, unassisted by France, sent troops to put down a nationalist rebellion against Tawfiq, led by the charismatic Ahmad Arabi, and then moved quickly to establish a protectorate over Egypt by seizing the Canal. From henceforth the magnificent water gateway could legitimately be seen as a manifestation not of French but of British imperial power. Suez for the British now came to work as a 180-degree hinge, opening both India and Africa to its widening skirts of influence. It was not before time. Bismarck's Berlin Convention that launched the so-called Scramble for Africa lay but seven or so years in the future. From now on, control over the 'lifeline' would become the driver of political and economic decisions in territories as far apart as Afghanistan and Kenya.[35] Far into the twentieth century, post the Second World War, Britain would continue to go to extraordinary lengths to safeguard this premier route to what had been its most valuable imperial possession, India.[36]

In British colonial literature of the period, whether the work of Kipling, Edwin Arnold, or Forster, the Suez Canal, as we will see, is universally viewed as a vital channel for imperial transport, communications, and expansion. It is invariably, and unsurprisingly, cast as a passage to the opulent east and back home again, weighed down with riches.[37] In a context where, as the imperial bard Rudyard Kipling wrote, 'the Lord our God' had made 'the deep as dry', and 'smote for [the English] a pathway to the ends of all the Earth', the Suez Canal represented one of the major technological advances that had made and continued to make this world-wide grid of pathways possible.[38] In the imperial imagination, therefore, the Canal rapidly transmogrified into a grandiose yet eminently useful manifestation of European engineering might and venture capital; an ur-symbol of the ever-widening, world-enveloping empire. Yet there was also a perceived dark underside to the Canal's magnificent modernity—one that arose from the political instability of Egypt, and found expression in a new genre of paranoid popular fiction, of which a leading example was Richard Marsh's orientalist sensation novel *The Beetle* (1897).[39] The remarkable time–space compression that the Suez Canal afforded, was by definition also seen to increase the speed at which threatening elements in the colonies might be able to reach Britain's doorstep.

On a day-to-day level, the immediately perceptible advantage of the Suez Canal's opening was the dramatic shortening of the travel distance between Europe and 'East of Suez', the Occident and the Orient, so in effect drawing these imaginative oppositions, as theorized by Edward Said, into closer conjunction. The journey from London to Bombay by the Suez Canal measured about 6,300 miles, whereas via the Cape of Good Hope the route was about 11,000 miles. Bombay to Aden therefore usually represented two weeks of sailing time, followed by seven days from Port Said to Marseilles, one of the points of disembarkation for those taking the boat train on to London. Leonard Woolf records that his journey from Tilbury to Ceylon as a rookie colonial officer in 1904 took three weeks; for Ondaatje some fifty years later it was still a twenty-one-day journey.[40] Speed through the Canal itself, however, was always felt to be relatively slow and restricted—about 5 or 6 knots through a surprisingly narrow channel. The 'short-cut' passage in fact took two days to complete. The impression was exacerbated for those journeying out from Europe, or back to India, as northbound ships had right of way. The southbound pulled over and waited in berths positioned along the length of the Canal for the purpose. Such was the frequency of crossing that already in the 1880s, Edwin Arnold observed, the Canal was being eroded by the bow wave and wash from the passing ships.[41] Edward Carpenter in his Indian travelogue *From Adam's Peak to Elephanta*

(1892) speaks also of the enormous traffic and the heat (and notices the ancient crossing-point at Kantarak).[42]

Yet, as much as the British tended to picture the Canal as following always a west–east vector, Suez was to the same degree but from a different subcontinental perspective, increasingly viewed as the pathway through which the Indian elite might reach England, travelling east–west. For these travellers, too, Suez would become a crucial link in the imperial network that extended from India, across the Arabian and Mediterranean seas, to London. For them, too, it was perceived as an almost wholly 'British waterway', both a convenient passage west and a gateway to the wonders of the metropolitan world.[43] Rajah Jagatjit Singh of Kapurthala in *My Travels in Europe and America 1893*, for example, picked out the unadorned engineering brilliance and commercial utility of the 'famous' Canal as particularly noteworthy features. In stilted, formal tones, as if of a respectable colonial tour guide, he wrote:

> At three this morning we entered the famous Suez Canal. It is much narrower than I expected to find it: indeed there is not room for two ships to pass except at fixed stations, and the traffic seems to be very heavy. As a piece of engineering it is marvellous, and its immense utility in saving distance and consequent expense between Europe and the East is of course of the highest commercial and political importance.[44]

Rajah Singh's predecessor, T. N. (Trilokya Nath) Mukharji, the Indian ethnographer, setting out for Europe in the mid-1880s to help showcase the subcontinent at the Indian and Colonial Exhibition, had been even more explicit about the shipboard journey to Europe as providing an entry point to cosmopolitan enlightenment. In his *A Visit to Europe* (1889), he describes how proud he is to be on board his ship, the *SS Nepaul*. England's imperial destiny, he writes, has provided a levelling moral influence which now has enabled 'many of [India's] sons to break though the trammels of caste . . . and to seek education and enlightenment at the very fountain-head of modern civilization'.[45] As this imperial destiny rests on ships, so it follows, in Mukharji's precise syllogism, that the east–west journey—facilitated by the technological innovations of the compression engine, fast new propellers, and the Canal itself—was a pathway direct to that fountainhead. His compatriot the Nawab Mahdi Hasan Khan in his 1888 European travel diary was likewise concerned from the moment of embarkation to index all the up-to-date technologies of the ship taking him into the heartland of the modern world.[46] For two or three of these travellers, Port Said, at the far end of the Canal, in spite of its seediness, was perceived as a gateway point marking their entry to this world. B. M. Malabari was particularly impressed at the town's modern connectivity, his sharp disapproval of its immorality and dirt notwithstanding. The local telegraph operator, he found to his surprise, was acquainted with his own journal, the *Indian Spectator*, which he edited out of Bombay.[47]

Another important Indian presence on the new marine pathway to England should, of course, be noted at this point, though their imprint in official historical records is faint and has often been overlooked. Lascars in great numbers formed a close acquaintance with the Canal from its beginning, plying this route just as they had done the ramifying shipping routes of the world for hundreds of years before. While the lascar labour force had already proved itself to be essential to the operation of the British merchant fleet in the Indian Ocean, as Rozina Visram observes, the opening of the Suez Canal, and the introduction of steam navigation, had created a new category of engine-room labour on board ship, which in tropical climates lascars were deemed best suited to fill.[48] The heat suffered by firemen and trimmers in the engine room (which *The Cat's Table* also evokes), is a likely explanation for the desperation of the lascar observed by Lockwood Kipling above. British colonial officers bound for India who, from the Gulf of Suez onwards often chose to sleep on deck, saw lascars in a different but related role, again demonstrating their ubiquity and indispensability: upon entering the Red Sea, it was the lascars' task to sluice down the decks in the early morning, to lower temperatures on board.[49] In his sea-chantry poem, 'For to Admire', Rudyard Kipling presciently—and fittingly—pictures a lascar in another key position on this same stretch of treacherous water, this time calling look-out, 'Hum deckty hai', from a high forward mast.[50] In his travelogue *The Indian Eye on English Life*, B. M. Malabari contributed to the general picture of the lascar's omnipresence by marvelling, perhaps a little facetiously, at how the Indian lascars on board his Austro-Hungarian steamship *Imperator* made 'capital sailors'. However, he harmonized with colonial stereotype in opining also that Indians did not yet seem cut out to be ship's officers.[51]

IV BRITISH PERSPECTIVES

The Anglo-Indian civil servants and their families crossing from Britain to India and back again, though in many ways so remote from lascars' lives, shared one important aspect of their exiles' existence with them—the condition that Kipling describes as the colonials' permanent impermanence. These travellers, too, if from a different social vantage point, experienced the restless 'shuttling' of P & O liners on the loom of imperial service, between their mutually remote and often phantom-seeming homes.[52] For these British travellers, both first-time ICS officers, 'dutiful Englishmen bound on the service of the Queen', and colonials returning from leave, the Suez Canal did not simply signify the east; sometimes in fact it signified home. However, what it did always point to was the seemingly endless movement back and forth to which their lives were now committed, which Kipling resonantly evokes in 'The Exiles' Line'.[53] By its very existence, the Canal had made the India–Britain trip more feasible for Anglo-Indian families, and therefore it contributed to the vast increase in colonial traffic that the Red Sea and Mediterranean now began to witness—something that Walt Whitman, too, celebrates in the 1871 'A Passage to India' section of *Leaves of Grass* (in the epigraph above).

As Elizabeth Buettner writes in *Empire Families,* which also takes Kipling's poem as its epigraph, ceaselessly journeying Anglo-Indians made up a loose 'imperial social formation' whose contours bridged continents, cultures, and already interconnected seas—a formation 'reducible neither to metropolitan nor indigenous colonized society but rather [characterized by] the transnational intermediate zone bridging them'.[54] To late nineteenth-century middle-class colonial families strung out between England and India, therefore, Suez represented not only a connection with the home country, from which they felt they were in permanent exile, as Kipling recognized; it was also the vital roadway through which to maintain filial links. It made the separation of these families slightly more bearable than if the connection home had had to go around the Cape, as before. The journey, and the ability of families to make it, to bring out British wives and relatives, and send children home to be educated, safeguarded lineages and preserved emotional ties, as well as guaranteeing social and racial purities.

Inevitably, given the make-up of the Indian Civil Service, and related British institutions and services such as the Indian army, many more single British men than other members of families travelled out to India via Suez. It is their voice that probably rings loudest in the published record, and lays down a number of its core tropes. So Edwin Arnold, the one-time principal of the Government College at Poona (Pune), and author of the best-selling *The Light of Asia*, described his return journey to India in his travelogue *India Revisited* in fairly typical terms, pointing to scenes and recreating emotions which would be meaningful also to other travellers, European and Indian, and would be corroborated in later travel writing (see also Chapter 2). His fairly humdrum physical passage, he writes, was throughout thickened and complicated by multiple associations and reminiscences. Outward bound, on the *SS Parramatta*, he notes idiosyncratic details of the passing scene that catch his attention, as they might any traveller's.[55] The sea at Port Said, he observes, is tinged green by the amount of equatorial silt brought down the Nile from central Africa. And the native café has its predictable Ghawazi dancing girl, performing in the traditional way, 'as old as the Pharoahs' (p. 30). In the Port Said harbour lie Egyptian corvettes (with the sailors on board reciting afternoon prayers), a French troop-vessel under quarantine, and Her Majesty's troopship the *Crocodile* full of tanned soldiers (pp. 25–7). In Arnold's view, however, this crossroads of nations and continents at Port Said is noteworthy in particular for the predominance of British warships and steamers in the harbour. The perception is not unique to his account, nor, interestingly, to British travelogues. As in the Suez Canal scenes recounted in other India–Britain and Britain–India travelogues, an acknowledgement of what postcolonial theory would much later call cultural hybridity is made safe, or at least permissible, by the presence of British power.

Moving on towards the Canal, Arnold describes the 'fowl-haunted swamps and dreary barren flats' on either bank preceding it, the crossing points in the 'ditch' itself, and then the widening into the Gulf of Suez and the blistering heat of the Red Sea beyond. The *SS Parramatta* then follows the treacherous 'coral-line belt' right out to the Indian Ocean, whose stillness, Arnold takes pains to observe, 'stretches without a break in its vast expanse from the Arabian mountains to the Antarctic Circle'. This phase of the journey from the Canal out to the Indian Ocean in *India Revisited* is worth highlighting, as the criss-crossed cultural history of the region that Arnold describes is reminiscent of the archaeology of intercultural migration between India, Arabia, and Africa excavated in Amitav Ghosh's *In an Antique Land*, set in this same part of the world. Arnold remarks, for instance, on the legendary site of Eve's tomb on the Arabian shore and on age-old Arab fears of the Red Sea coral reefs. Ghosh, too, is aware of the deeply embedded myths and memories of trade and exchange that interconnect the region. Arnold is also preoccupied with the *Arabian Nights* associations of the Indian Ocean's 'calm blue' 'lake' with its flying fish. His terms of description highlight those ways in which the travel literature of the England–India journey built many of the sites en route into clusters of cultural and literary association, or points of attachment where memories might be recalled and refreshed.

A number of Indian travellers sailing in the opposite direction from Aden into the Red Sea and on to the Canal were similarly struck by the region as representing a complicated meeting point of cultures and geographies. R. C. Dutt observed, as his ship passed along, the rising sun tingeing the 'yellow rocks and hills of Africa' and on the other side throwing into relief the rocks of Arabia.[56] For the Christianized N. L. Doss, the Sinai Peninsula was redolent of biblical references, just as it was for Muslim travellers of Islamic history and traditions. The

Nawab Mahdi Hasan Khan, for example, was pleased to identify the hot, bare rocks around Aden as the land of the Prophet.[57] As these accretions of meaning suggest, the different travel texts, all published within about two decades of one another, feed into what might be termed a Suez discourse, at this time still embryonic and far from univocal, yet clearly discernible. Emerging out of the loose colonial formation that knitted together the passenger contributors, this Suez discourse as it gathered symbolic significance itself worked to bind that formation more tightly together. Moreover, as the examples illustrate throughout, it was a discourse in which *both* west–east *and* east–west travel writings participated, even while they at times cut across or overrode one another.[58]

The later socialist thinker and critic of empire Leonard Woolf, too, saw his passage to the east to begin a career as a Cadet in the Ceylon Civil Service as the beginning of a new life, indeed, as a 'second birth'. In that section of his autobiography entitled *Growing*, Woolf borrows the suggestive title of his wife Virginia's first novel, *The Voyage Out*, to mark the chapter dealing with his experience of sailing from Tilbury docks in the P & O liner *Syria*.[59] 'Filthy' Port Said he predictably describes in letters home as his first brush with the east—an experience that then opens out to something far more other.[60] *East of Suez*, in Kipling's phrase, strange new experiences and awakenings awaited an expectant Briton like Woolf, as they do the Anglo-Indians featured in Alice Perrin's collection of gothic short stories bearing that same title.[61] In his 1921 short story 'Pearls and Swine', Woolf gives his description of this same place and phase in his journey more memorable fluency and colour: 'the brothel and *café chantant* at Port Said suddenly open out into that pink and blue desert that leads you through Africa and Asia into the heart of the East'.[62] According to the account in his letters, Woolf finds the Red Sea beyond the dusty straits of the Canal hot, 'no doubt about [it]'—again a standard response for west–east travellers. The Indian Ocean (with its flying fish) is, once again, almost preternaturally calm.[63] Like Mynah and many other colonial officers on their first voyage, Woolf takes to sleeping on deck: 'it's very charming with the stars & the noise of the sea & the waking up at sunrise'.[64]

Though Leonard Woolf does not explicitly speak of it as such, his vocabulary across the 'Voyage Out' chapter anticipates something of the break with Europe, or at least with empire, that Ceylon will initiate in him. As in Ondaatje, the Suez Canal is positioned as a kind of birth passage on that journey, one that leads Woolf on into his 'second birth' and new life.[65] Thinking of his correspondent Lytton Strachey's family ties to India, he observes: 'You have seen it all of course, & the canal with its weird colours under searchlight by night, & its melancholy sand & its melancholy camels by day.'[66] Similar to Edwin Arnold's account, the ship is described as a microcosm of a stratified colonial society, though Woolf, writing some two decades later, and as yet without Arnold's colonial experience, takes a less idealizing view of these hierarchies and divisions. In this respect, his depiction is closer to that of the Indian travel writers, who put on record their awareness of the exclusivity of the Anglo-Indian community on board ship—clearly a carry-over from colonial arrangements on the subcontinent.

If Woolf's transformational journey east contributes to that unfolding index of symbolic reference points that could be called a Suez discourse, then E. M. Forster in his elegiac Indian novel *A Passage to India* visibly synthesizes and heightens many of these associations. Published in 1924, its title referencing Walt Whitman's hymning of the Canal, the novel draws on Forster's experiences of voyages to and back from India in 1913 and again in the early 1920s, and so builds the discourse of the Suez crossing into a point of particular intensity. Suez is first approached in the novel, but fittingly only approached and not reached, by Mrs Moore on her attempted return journey to England. In *A Passage to India*, as the reader already knows, bridges between the east and the west are scarce. Adela Quested sees Suez as a tipping-point between her 'turning' to the east, and then her 'return' from it. The self-conscious westerner Fielding finally also passes through it on his own return to Europe. 'Somewhere about Suez there is always a social change', the novel's narrator almost hyperbolically observes.[67]

World-weary and spiritually jaded after the events of the Caves, Mrs Moore, who has understood some of the 'attitude towards life' that characterizes the Islamic east through her contact with Dr Aziz, leaves for England before Aziz's trial, but dies '[journeying] across the Indian Ocean', having fallen ill 'on leaving Bombay', before reaching Aden. By the time the news of her death arrives back in Chandrapore, her memory has famously been transmuted into an 'Indianized' chant in court, invoked by the Indian crowd as a mantra, as if she were a goddess. She is, in effect, claimed for the Indian side of Suez, her body committed to the Indian Ocean, 'lowered into yet another India', evading thereby 'the great net [of empire] Great Britain had thrown over [the subcontinent]' (p. 18). Reflecting on her death, Forster's narrator gives an interestingly orientalized map of the passage back to England that is Mrs Moore's last journey:

> Dead she was—committed to the deep while still on the southward track, for the boats from Bombay cannot point towards Europe until Arabia has been rounded; she was further in the tropics than ever achieved while on shore, when the sun touched her for the last time... A ghost followed the ship up

> the Red Sea, but failed to enter the Mediterranean. Somewhere about Suez there is always a social change: the arrangements of Asia weaken and those of Europe begin to be felt, and during the transition Mrs Moore was shaken off. At Port Said the grey blustery north began. (p. 249)

By contrast, Fielding experiences no such orientalizing transition. Resisting Aziz's call to 'give in to the East', he returns to England 'for a little time', reversing the 'romantic' journey out across the Mediterranean and 'through the sands of Egypt to the harbour of Bombay', which both Mrs Moore and Adela remember fondly before they meet 'the gridiron of bungalows at the end of it' (pp. 254, 269, 26). In the impressionistic chapter that closes the 'Caves' section of the novel, Fielding is pictured glorying in the structural harmonies of Venice, having detoured via 'charming' Egypt, where the intricacies of Bombay are already stripped away (pp. 26, 275–6). In the Mediterranean, he feels himself in his western element, within 'the human norm'. At this point, the novel's symbolic east–west geography appears to be briefly balanced or straddled, at least in the narrator's representation. However, the short evocation continues, 'when men leave that exquisite lake, whether through the Bosphorus or the Pillars of Hercules, they approach the monstrous and extraordinary; and the Southern exit leads to the strangest experience of all' (p. 275). Fielding's feelings of exultation in Venice confirm that he sees India from the point of view of the passage east, as a westerner, unlike his educated Indian friends.

Appropriately enough, Adela Quested, as the novel's vacillator, is the only character pictured at a fixed point on the passage through the Suez Canal itself, in the snapshot scene in which she stands at the foot of the giant statue of de Lesseps in Port Said.[68] At this celebrated site of passage, a fellow traveller, a missionary, pontificates about the experience of return in terms I anticipated earlier, suggesting that the western traveller's turn to the east is always shadowed by his *re*turn from it. Like Fielding, Adela becomes aware of an altered atmosphere, a cleaner light: 'even Port Said looked pure and charming in the light of a rose-grey morning'. She feels she is able to see more clearly than she has at any point before on her eastern journey (p. 258).

As Forster's imagery of well-worn west–east routes suggests, *A Passage to India*, for all its interest in indirect southern passages, follows a long established tradition of India-bound travel writing, in which the assumption is that Europeans are the chief—not to say sole—travellers, and the easterly direction of their travel is the predominant direction. The keen-eyed postcolonial traveller Naipaul in *The Enigma of Arrival* also commits this oversight when he observes of England-to-India travel writing: 'India was special to England; for two hundred years there had been any number of English travellers' accounts and, latterly, novels.' And therefore: 'There was no model for me here, in this exploration; neither Forster nor Ackerley nor Kipling could help. To get anywhere in the writing, I had first of all to define myself very clearly to myself.'[69] His implication is that he has no precursor—and in so far as he is an Asian-Trinidadian in quest of 'peasant India', he is, of course, right. Yet he chooses to overlook the nonetheless significant fact that the ocean pathway he took 'from England' to India had been traced by any number of Indians first moving in the reverse direction. Moreover, it was also their route home.

V INDIAN PASSAGES TO ENGLAND: TRAVELLING IN THE WEST

Just as Anglo-Indians created colonial formations facilitated by the Suez Canal, so, too, did Europe-bound travelling Indians. Like the Anglo-Indians, their loose transconfigurations also bridged subcontinent and metropole, and crisscrossed geographical and some social boundaries, connecting elites at home with elites abroad. They, too, as we have already seen, felt the countervailing pulls of Suez, both back, to communities left behind, and on, to the promises and prizes of the west. Within these loose social formations, travelling Indians—students and activists in particular, but also seers, lawyers, proselytizers, and business people—began the process of forging Indian identities from the vantage point of a position abroad, in that well-described proto-nationalist and cross-border way.[70]

While the act of travel is typically enunciative, establishing a here, India, against a there, Britain—that is, positing both a background and a destination—at the same time, it puts these apparent dualities into play along a continuum, a shifting spectrum of familiarity and unfamiliarity, or home and away.[71] The experience of what we might call the expanded Suez Canal—from Aden through the Red Sea to Port Said and the Mediterranean—both away from South Asia but not yet within Britain—was for these early travelling Indians a formal inauguration of the experience of travel and also an opening to the complexities, dynamism, ambiguities, and uncertainties of the wider world. Moving towards, through, beyond, and eventually back through the Suez Canal, Indian travellers contributed to a growing tradition, as the previous sections began to show. At the same time, they also laid down a circuitry of travel and communication that would become form-giving for diasporic South Asians to come. Elite Indians who had been homebound due to caste, now began to experience in significant numbers the 'untidy workings' of migrant identity formation—well described by Paul Gilroy as 'creolized, syncretized, hybridized and chronically impure'.[72]

In Indian travelogues, just as in many British accounts, therefore, the Suez passage is developed into a complex trope of horizontal as well as vertical transition, between geographies and up or down social hierarchies, in which physical movement through space often also encoded social elevation. The symbolic importance of this journey operated at several temporal levels, signifying now transition point and now watershed; now passageway (or diachronic process) and now gateway (or synchronic cross-section). For these travellers, therefore, the movement from India through Suez to England in many ways worked as a geophysical embodiment of the pathways they traced between regions within the empire, and sites within imperial hierarchies. This was especially in so far as many of these elite travellers moved between echelons of comparable social status in India and Britain, and sought acceptance within social structures in Britain at matching levels of privilege and prestige, as the work of David Cannadine and Martin Wainwright recognizes (see also Chapter 2).[73]

Far from being undiscovered country, the north-west passage to England was one that Indians had anticipated in some detail not only through their reading, as we saw, but also through other forms of psychosocial preparation. They approached the Canal as one point along a cross-cultural vector of which they already had clear-cut expectations. Due to their education in English, in British-run schools, following a syllabus that embodied English cultural values, even if developed largely in India, they had an expanded sense of Fielding's 'human norm' as encompassing both England and India. They also possessed that intimate knowledge of their colonizers which is transferred by subtle processes of cultural osmosis in any experience of colonization.[74] Naipaul puts it thus: 'The migration, within the British Empire, from India to Trinidad had given me the English language as my own, and a particular kind of education.'[75] The prescient 1890s traveller Malabari laid a similar emphasis on the acquisition of the English language as entailing the adoption of a particular cultural point of view. In the Preface to his verse collection *The Indian Muse in English Garb*, he makes a point of outlining his concerted attempts as a Bombay businessman and journalist to learn English, this soon-to-be 'world language', in ways that bear comparison with Naipaul's painstaking efforts some six decades later.[76] Interestingly, he is concerned to underline that this effort of learning is widely shared across the subcontinent. He sees Indians as coming together to form an anglophone literary culture, which is founded on and stimulated by literary materials from England:

> We have schools and colleges enough to rear the rising generations of all Asia; and week by week the English have been sending us the freshest 'thought-crystals' of the West, in the form of books and reviews and pamphlets.[77]

Priya Joshi's reading of India's influential English-language book culture in the nineteenth century corroborates Malabari's view—especially her sense that 'Indians actually "saw" the imperial centre through their literary and not physiological eyes, layering their actual experiences with rich, concomitant images drawn from an already familiar literary imaginary.'[78]

Along with Dadabhai Naoroji, the economic historian Romesh Chunder Dutt (cousin of Toru) was one of the more prominent and peripatetic Indians to ply the Suez route between India and Britain in the later decades of the nineteenth century. As one of the few Indians to be elevated to the Indian Civil Service (ICS) in this period, Dutt was granted regular periods of furlough in England across his career and, after retirement, from 1897, became a lecturer in Indian history at University College, London. Yet the journey that stands out, at least in his own account of the period, *Three Years in Europe 1868–71* (1872), was, unsurprisingly, the first. In 1868, the year before the Canal was opened, Dutt set out with two friends, Bihari Lal Gupta and Surendranath Banerjee, on the *SS Mooltan* from Calcutta in order to study for and sit the ICS examination in London.[79] Though the ICS was in principle, by the Queen's Proclamation of 1853, open to 'all natural born subjects of the Crown', at this point in time only one Indian had as yet passed the entrance examination and qualified: Satyendranath Tagore, in 1863. Vexing barriers existed in the form of the age restrictions that favoured English candidates, reinforced by the regulation stipulating that the examination venue had to be in England. Dutt's biographer Meenakshi Mukherjee expands on the disadvantages facing the would-be candidates:

> The odds, indeed, were heavily against the Indian students, not only because they had to make an expensive trip to a distant country at the risk of losing caste and also to adjust to inclement weather, but also because the examination was based on a curriculum alien to them.[80]

Dutt himself wrote to his brother about the 'madness' of '[venturing] on this impossible undertaking' and his fear of being 'cut off from our countrymen'. Yet there was little choice in the matter: for those Indians who wished to try for the tests, transoceanic travel could not be avoided.

Dutt and his companions duly departed from Calcutta, if in 'a clandestine manner', the local paper *Amrita Bazar Patrika* reported. Yet, in spite of their apprehensions, the friends' youthful excitement at the adventure they were undertaking lent a certain radiance and definition to all they now experienced. Dutt noticed, for example, the great blueness of sea and sky surrounding the Mooltan on leaving Diamond Harbour—a fateful blueness for a Hindu setting out across uncharted waters, yet nonetheless a 'novel' and 'mighty' one.[81] His entire account of the journey makes a self-conscious contribution to the standard descriptive grammar of Indian travel to the west, something that comes through most prominently at those points where he connects the sites en route to well-known myths and legends. Ceylon, he observes, is the 'golden region' of Valmiki's *Ramayana*; 'Gibraltar', in Arabic, designates the 'rock of Tariq', the Muslim Conqueror of Spain.[82] Repeatedly associating geography and cultural history, *Three Years* thus participates in laying down a set of procedures that would rapidly become customary in the articulation and negotiation of Indian crossings into the west—procedures in which the demonstration of prior knowledge worked to legitimate the passage of the traveller. The travelogue works in effect as a repeat performance of this demonstration and so underwrites the author's achievement of his new cosmopolitan or outer-national self, in Gilroy's definition. Or, as the ICS trainee and later lawyer Lala Baijnath wrote when setting out for England in the early 1890s, it was his intention, on board the P & O steamship *Rohilla*, to '[adapt] one's self to a new way of life as soon as possible'.[83]

A clear illustration of the Indian travellers' collective contribution to a grammar of east–west crossing is found in their often repetitive descriptions of Aden—especially of the first residents of Aden travellers tended to encounter, the local diving boys. So Dutt records the Red Sea port as being a dry and barren place, adding as a touch of local colour the fact that the diving children are adept at remaining afloat 'like sea-animals'. Lala Baijnath in his travel 'impressions' *England and India* sees the dark 'Somali' divers with their 'shining, black, negro-like faces' as signs of the proximity of the African coast. They are all that distinguishes unprepossessing Aden.[84] Coming after the generally smooth crossing from Bombay, the dullness of Aden was as it were offset by the boys' amphibious displays, as Rajah Jagatjit Singh of Kapurthala, too, noted.[85] For N. L. Doss in *Reminiscences,* the underwhelming effect of 'the bold and barren coast approaching Aden' was also counterpointed by a detailed description of these same Arab boys' incredible diving techniques.[86] And Malabari's account of his two journeys to England drew special (if characteristically censorious) attention to Aden's precocious diving boys: 'sprightly little imps of Satan' who resembled both dolphins and squirrels in their quick movements, and were, he claimed, cleverer at extricating money from travellers than 'sharpers' on the London stock exchange.[87]

By way of drawing these examples together, Aden's young black divers epitomized for the Indian traveller some of the more unfamiliar and exotic aspects of the new world that their steamship journeys were beginning to approach. Written into the opening pages of virtually all the Indian travelogues, the stock image of the boys provided a curtain-raiser for their subsequent evocations of the marvellous Canal and so vouched for the Indians' status as travellers, much as a photograph of a famous tourist site might do in the present day. Equally as important, because the boys were usually the first foreigners the travellers from India would have encountered on their journey, they also functioned in predictable ways as oriental figures—reference points for the elite Indian's feelings of cultural and in some cases religious superiority in confronting a world deemed not as civilized as British India. As with the Arabs, Somalis, and other foreigners they met en route, descriptions that objectified 'wicked' and seemingly backward eastern elements like the boys afforded the Indian travellers an effective means of distancing themselves. Though they might be easterners themselves, they chose not to identify with, even as they identified, the divers' oriental characteristics. The boys belonged to a space tantalizingly poised between a mysterious African coast and an Arabia associated with myth and legend, yet in which these self-conscious imperial citizens, to their evident relief, had no part to play.

Lala Baijnath the ICS trainee, for instance, was particularly concerned to mark himself out as distinct from the strange places and peoples encountered en route—as more cultural and civilized, less eastern.[88] Aden, he wrote, would 'not do credit to even a third rate Indian town'. N. L. Doss, too, felt little to no kinship or sympathy either with a 'Negro' trickster who came on board in Aden, or with the 'poor . . . moral atmosphere' of Port Said, with its European cafés. He noted also the 'funny' aspect of veiled Egyptian women in Port Said, while at the same time conceding that Muslim women in Calcutta were as swathed.[89] In the opinion of Nawab Mahdi Hasan Khan, even had there been more Muslims on board his steamship to England, their internal social differences would have prevented them from creating the pleasant community that, by contrast, drew the English together. For him, too, the degenerate state of Port Said was reflected in the corrupted Arabic of the touts and porters. On arrival at the same port, the reformer T. B. Pandian in his late-century *England to an Indian Eye* (1897) expressed related feelings of superiority to the Turks, whom he viewed as subjects of a very different, autocratic eastern empire than that to which he felt he belonged.

The port city of Aden, the home of the diving boys and usually the first landfall on the journey west, invariably struck both British and Indian travellers as dry, dusty, hot, and 'uninviting'.[90] But the port was also for many, especially those who hailed from India's western seaboard, something of a fragment of India, even an outpost of Bombay.[91] This stood to reason: Aden's commercial prosperity was to a large extent 'the creation of

Bombay Indians, craftsmen, builders, blacksmiths and coolies'—in particular, as Malabari is pleased to note, the Parsi community, just as in Bombay. Occupied in 1837 by the British for its strategic position, and developed as a secure coaling station on the route to India, Aden at a practical level offered through-Suez traffic a convenient harbour with an easily navigable channel.[92] As we find in both Ondaatje and Malabari, it was recommended to go on shore here to avoid the dust produced by bunkering and coaling. Yet this 'gate of India' (in Baijnath's words) also first made visible to the Indian travellers that going abroad would involve an ever-greater proximity to imperial modernity.[93] Looking back from the torrid wastes of the Red Sea or relative desolation of the Canal region, many recalled aspects of Aden's 'development'—its parade ground, Crescent Hotel, cable station—which the port city in great part, of course, owed to the building of the Canal. On going ashore to visit his Parsi friend Mr Cowasji Dinshaw, Malabari observed that though the Indian networks that had extended to Aden might be distinguished by their Bombay personnel, they were also founded on sound British infrastructure, 'some trophy of the Englishman's practical genius—roads, drives, tunnels, tanks . . . admirable works of engineering'.[94] Aden therefore began to point to the infrastructural complexity that the travelling Indian might expect to find in the west, and specifically in England: 'roads, drives, tunnels, tanks', and even tree-lined roads. In Aden, Ondaatje's Mynah experiences for the first time how individuals can melt away into the heterogeneous crush of a city's streets, as they will again in London. 'In the streets [of Aden]', writes Malabari, as if concurring, 'we meet a variety of faces representing almost all known types'—a cosmopolitan variety which he, and others, will again observe, though to a far greater degree, in London.[95]

Appearing only a decade-and-a-half after Dutt's travelogue, the Indian ethnographer T. N. Mukharji's *A Visit to Europe* benefits from and itself builds on the grammar Dutt and others have already laid down, as its confident approach and digressive, annotative style straightaway announce to readers. Its references to European technological sophistication as against Indian backwardness also engage in fairly explicit ways in an ongoing discussion pursued by Indian reformers in these years concerning the merits of empire—and as such his account draws comparison with Malabari's. *A Visit to Europe* ticks off in business-like fashion the expected markers of the journey: the Indian Ocean's flying fish, the 'bleak hills of Aden', the diving boys 'of African descent', the Jewish and Arab tradesmen, the bazaar, which is filthy, yet which the coming of English 'commerce, peace and prosperity' is gradually changing, the 'sunken coral reefs' of the Red Sea (also noted by Edwin Arnold and Kipling's lascar), the feat of Suez, and immoral Port Said.[96] In the same way as Arnold and also Dutt 'read' legendary and historical events off the ancient landmarks of the east, so, too, is Mukharji intensely aware of the layers of ancient history as it were laid bare by his journeying, digressing repeatedly to give potted narratives of interesting incidents. Aden, for example, sparks a digression on the Hindu myth of Ravan the ten-headed giant (for whom Aden was a place of banishment). He is reminded, as are so many others, of the cosmopolitan exchanges that have moved across these waters for centuries, writing that Indians and Arabs have had close commercial intercourse in the region from 'ancient times'.

Yet it is not a knowledge and understanding of the past alone that Mukharji is interested in showcasing. As if to be true in all possible respects to the professional role of ethnographic curator that he in fact occupied, he talks his reader through the modern colonial world with its lighthouses, mail boats, and great Canal (against which he weighs the 'corruptions' of present-day Hinduism), even more faithfully perhaps than other of his countrymen. Addressing himself to an implied Indian reader, he looks forward to the day when all the peoples of the world will be able to utilize such technological bounties, as America and Australia already do, assisted by the more horizontal and democratic structure of their societies.[97] Like Woolf or Arnold, he is interested, too, in the different social groupings and worlds-within-worlds that can be found on board ship, yet it is the integration across social divides that draws him in particular, not the reconfirmed hierarchies that Leonard Woolf's mordant eye discerns. Despite the heterogeneity of the Indians on board ship, by forging one-to-one bonds they manage nonetheless in Mukharji's view to form that modern entity, a more horizontally appointed Indian community, drawn together in its Indianness once it is away from India. He interestingly links concepts of England, modernity, and social levelling within the same passage.[98]

Finally, at the culmination point of the Indian travellers' first phase of their journey, there was that 'splendid piece of work', the Suez Canal itself.[99] To several writers, the passage through the Canal represented, at least on first encounter, something of an experiential paradox, at once fascinating to observe, yet monotonous to endure. In general, however, the Canal's modernity proved startling and unforgettable, as was often captured in the electric effulgence in which it was bathed at night. Given that transshipment was usually arranged to begin at midnight, to limit the time the passengers would spend baking in the desert sun, electric lighting had been installed throughout the length of the Canal to help with navigation. This was a well-known fact, yet any number of Indian travelogues, including those of Pandian and Baijnath, express amazement at this to them unprecedented spectacle, this brilliantly illuminated entrance to Fielding's 'human norm'. From this magnificent point onwards, the Indians' travelogues anticipate, the different cultural ecumene of the west would begin to open up, one to which the writers, as self-consciously civilized imperial citizens, assumed access.[100] Beyond Suez and Port Said, the Indian travelogues devote noticeably less attention to the scenes and sites of the second phase of the journey, in the main singling out those details that might accord with accepted views of the west's rationality and order: in Dutt, the 'neat and stone-paved streets' of Malta and garden-like Isle of Wight. This change of focus no doubt had something to do with the fact that, practically speaking, Indians' travel routes tended to ramify after Port Said, some reaching England via the overland routes from Brindisi or Marseilles, some going on by boat round the Iberian Peninsula.

As travel via Suez became established, and Indian travellers grew more seasoned, with individuals like Dutt and Dadabhai Naoroji making the journey several times in their career, the passage to England via the Canal in some travel accounts came to be taken for granted, as the fact of elite Indian travel itself increasingly also was. By and by, the crossing of the Isthmus, hot and dusty at the best of times, became merely another humdrum phase in the twenty-one-day journey, to be endured along with the rest. As elite Indians began successfully to establish themselves as part of the western cultural landscape, there was less of a need to lay down in writing, through their deployment of the standard, ritualized tropes of travel enumerated above, their cosmopolitan credentials. Especially in the case of those who frequently shuttled east–west, their intercultural and transoceanic movements could be inferred from where they carried out their work or published their writing; that is, in both India and Britain.

Of these shuttling cosmopolitans, there were few more tireless and well travelled than the Parsi businessman and then politician Dadabhai Naoroji, who spent much of his long and active career seesawing between Bombay, Liverpool, and London. Naoroji's shuttling began when he first travelled to London in 1855 as a partner in the firm Cama and Company, though at this point, of course, he took the overland route at Suez. Thereafter, the existence of the Canal route facilitated his trading interests as well as his political activities, and also allowed his business in Egyptian cotton to flourish during the period of the American Civil War (though it was to fold in the early 1880s). Through occupying influential political positions in the Bombay municipal corporation and then the Legislative Council, Naoroji came strongly to believe that reform in India depended upon a direct approach to the imperial Parliament in London. British politicians had to be addressed and petitioned on the Indian question *in situ*, and he was the man for the job: he believed he had the language of civil intercourse required, as well as the financial backing and the contacts, including with Irish activists and politicians. From its inception, his second, political career, like his first in business, developed through transnational networking and cross-border campaigning. Looking only at the period from 1859 to 1869, the year of the Suez Canal opening, Naoroji plied back and forth between India and Britain six times. Even so, he is not a significant contributor to Suez discourse. His cosmopolitan sense of India and of modern Indianness as something that might be shaped, defended, and consolidated abroad is crystallized instead in the number of different Indian societies he managed to found in London, including the East India Association, the London India Society, and the British Committee of the Indian National Congress (see also Chapter 2).

Cornelia Sorabji, in her 1934 memoir *India Calling*, refers to the repeated 'to-and-fro-ings' that punctuated her varied career as a lawyer divided between India and England.[101] These many back-and-forth journeys would all have been via the Bombay–Aden–Suez Canal route, but, apart from her letters home on her first journey, in September 1839, she, too, is largely silent on the subject of the Canal, whether the Canal as the passageway that facilitated her double life, as she often described it, or as a symbol of her intra-imperial journeying, her varifocal east–west identity.[102] For the goal-driven Sorabji, the enforced idleness, discomfort, and waiting imposed by shipboard travel—its unfavourable winds, quarantines, and missed mail boats—probably brought frustrations that even the novelty of travel could not allay. Even so, it is worth noting that where she does mention the passage in the early letters home, she relies on the Indian grammar of Suez travel that was by now standard. Aden is predictably 'dreary'; the Arab traders she meets 'rough' and 'horrid-looking'.[103] However, the 'Dear Delightful Canal' meets with her full approval, not so much because of its modernity, but for touristic and anthropological reasons: her eyes are 'gladdened' by the greenery of the settlements that border the Canal, and she enjoys the glimpses of 'picturesque' 'scenes from Arab life' that the passage through exposes. As for Baijnath and others, her narrative position in the letters is self-consciously that of a westernized observer, surveying the 'unwashed' Arab children and dirty 'wicked' Port Said from an elevated distance.

In 'Love and Death', a short story Sorabji published a decade or so later, in *Love and Life Behind the Purdah* (1901), the presence of the Canal as a border zone between a primitive east and a rational west is interestingly inferred from the vantage point of Brindisi on the Italian coast, a well-known point of Indian embarcation for the journey home.[104] 'Love and Death' opens on the deck of the *SS Khartoum* bound for India, where the narrator, a 'foreigner', is in conversation with an interlocutor, presumably an Englishman, during which he tells him of his feelings of apprehension at the prospect of a return to India after many years of education abroad. Beyond 'squalid' Brindisi, he says, lies the east, which he casts as a place of superstition and primitive ritual. The second half of the story then proceeds to confirm his worst apprehensions, culminating in his fiancée's gruesome death in a fire ceremony in which she herself has chosen to participate. Modern 'to-and-fro-ings', in Sorabji's view, did not easily succeed in bridging the age-old cultural and religious differences dividing the west from the east.[105]

VI FORGED THROUGH THE MEDIUM OF TRAVEL: TORU DUTT AND SAROJINI NAIDU

Toru Dutt and Sarojini Naidu, both Indian-English poets whose careers Edmund Gosse helped to foster, also created work that was shaped by their experience of east–west crossing: Dutt's in the early 1870s, Naidu's in the 1890s. Though Dutt's oeuvre is less obviously a product of the passage to England than is Naidu's, it begins to model how an intercultural perspective and a modern sense of Indian selfhood might be composed through the very process of moving between cultures and countries, through what Chapter 2 will call 'Greater Britain'. In several ways, certainly, Dutt's poetic career anticipated and laid the ground for that of Sarojini Naidu. As is clear from 'Near Hastings', which the reader will remember from the introduction, Dutt's cross-border poetics is never unaware of the actual east–west interfaces it inhabits: her imagination, as Tricia Lootens writes, is 'sheltered, constricted, yet in many ways deeply cosmopolitan'.[106] This is clearly reflected in her *Ancient Ballads and Legends of Hindustan* (1882), adaptations into English stanzaic forms of 'lessons' from the Sanskrit Puranas, and *Mahabharata*, in which portraits of Indian mythic heroines are cast into English rhymes and cadences. Similar crossings are scored through the history of her publication and reception in Europe, as Gosse traces in his famous 'Introductory Memoir' to her posthumously published work.[107]

Toru Dutt was probably one of the first Indian women to travel to Europe via the Isthmus of Suez. Setting out with her family for England in November 1869, she must have seen the Canal in its final stages of construction; and then sailed along it for the first time, in the opposite direction, when travelling back to Calcutta in 1873. In a letter of 19 December 1873 to her friend Mary Martin in England, her first on return to Calcutta, her description of the journey home is largely devoted to describing the fellow passengers she met on board, and to recording a stop-over in Ceylon.[108] She mentions as something of an afterthought her steamship becoming temporarily 'stuck' while passing through the 'narrow' Canal. She also notices the aridity of the surrounding land, apart from the area around Ismailia.

Yet, though the east–west crossing at Suez did not much grab Dutt's attention, her threshold position as an Indian-English poet straddling different cultural worlds imprints everywhere in her work: in its 'Anglicized' yet 'pure Hindu' perceptions, in Gosse's terms; in how she transports themes, motifs, and structures in both directions, between Europe and the subcontinent, as is particularly evident in her best-known poem, 'Our Casuarina Tree'; in how she translates constantly between different languages and cultural forms, most ostentatiously perhaps in her translations into English of contemporary French poetry.[109] Fittingly, Gosse's posthumous interaction with her legacy, in the introduction in which he strove to bring her work to western literary awareness, is similarly marked by east–west crossings both actual and metaphorical.[110]

Gosse begins the 'Introductory Memoir' by describing the 'melancholy satisfaction' he experienced on finding himself in the position of being one among only two of Toru Dutt's European reviewers, when *A Sheaf Gleaned in French Fields* was published. In the review he then produced, he further writes, he sounded a 'note of welcome' that, he hoped, reached 'the dying poetess from England'—that crossed, therefore, from England to India.[111] This was the first and only live contact between them. He records his initial lack of excitement at encountering 'a thin and sallow packet with a wonderful Indian postmark on it, and containing a most unattractive orange pamphlet of verse, printed at Bhowanipur' (a response that was rapidly overturned, however), and anticipates her possibly gratified response at hearing rare appreciation, in print, from England. 'This shabby little book' 'with its queer type', he thought at the time, might 'hastily' be consigned to the 'waste-paper basket'—they are words he would later echo in his editorial advice to Sarojini Naidu. In the event, however, his underwhelmed response did not survive the reading. Acknowledging this, Gosse's Introductory Memoir makes a rapid change of direction or crossing, both in respect of the terms of his description, and of what is being described. The apparently odd, 'hopeless', saffron-coloured book, once read, elicited from him, he writes, 'surprise and almost rapture'. Out of an experience of profound strangeness and indifference came a sudden recognition of sameness that appeared also to bridge the barrier between the living and the dying: he experienced an intense impulse of identification with that final 'feverish dream of intellectual effort and imaginative production' that went into her last poems, including 'Our Casuarina Tree' and 'Near Hastings'.

Other than Cornelia Sorabji, the poet and later nationalist activist Sarojini Naidu was one of the few Indian women regularly plying the route from Bombay to England in the period from 1890 onwards. As Chapter 3 explores in detail, Naidu, as a student in 1890s London, associated herself with the wrought late Romantic aesthetic of W. B. Yeats, Lionel Johnson, and others, and responded to their work by cultivating a heated orientalist style in her poetry, as in her social manner. Yet, authentically oriental though her appearance and verse may have seemed, she presents an even more symptomatic case than does Toru Dutt of a poetic persona forged through the medium of shipboard travel, in response to that same experience of steaming west. Drafts of Naidu's poems written on shipboard letterhead paper suggest that the eastern self she fostered, one projected through her English poetry and addressed to her English mentors, was generated almost literally while at sea.[112] Shipboard travel was instrumental to her formation as an eastern poet.

Naidu (then Chattopadhyay) travelled to England for the first of many visits in 1895, accompanied by the reformer and theosophist Annie Besant, as she was still a minor. She was inducted into the interstitial zone of east–west travel by an already seasoned Suez voyager, therefore, whose own intercultural identity had by this stage been profoundly shaped by similar cross-border movements. It was in the 1900s, however, when Naidu first submitted her work for publication in Britain, that she began seriously to compose, rewrite, and edit her poems in transit, and on materials marked by transit. So it was that the very features of her work that her British reviewers acclaimed—its 'fresh' 'Eastern colour', 'sumptuously coloured words', and assurance of a common humanity—were crafted in the crucible of her intercultural travelling experience.[113] Her poems were in effect transoceanic compositions. A draft of *The Bird of Time* poem, 'In praise of Gulmohur Blossoms', for example, is written on notepaper bearing the address, 'H. H. Nizam's Camp, Delhi Durbar', a glittering 1903 event to mark Edward VII's accession to the throne. Naidu attended this elaborate performance of imperial might and fiefdom as part of the Nizam of Hyderabad's party, and presumably contributed with her poetry to the 'gothic efflorescence' of the occasion (as she is known to have done on other occasions).[114]

An even clearer sign of the making-in-transit of Naidu's cross-border poetics is found in the corrected fair copies of *The Bird of Time* poems. 'A Persian Lute Song', 'Renunciation', and 'The Gift' are written on the red letterhead paper of the *SS Olympic*, 'The Island Sanctuary' on the notepaper of the Taj Mahal hotel, on 'Apollo Bunder, Bombay', which was from 1911 the well-known place of embarcation for Europe. Regardless of whether or not Naidu was a compulsive copier of her poems and often ran out of paper (she makes few significant changes from version to version, often tinkering only with alliterative synonyms), her notepaper provides unabashed evidence of composition en route, suggesting that her breathless, sexually charged aesthetic was made possible by her growing distance from home, suspended on a floating island in the middle of the sea. Certainly, the cosmopolitan social formation first of the colonial hotel, and then of the steamship, would appear to have at once inspired and sanctioned the risqué expressions of feminine sexual submission liberally distributed across her poems (the perfume-covered limbs of 'At Dusk'; the 'garden of the mouth' of 'At Dawn').[115]

*

As Indian travellers from R. C. Dutt through to Sarojini Naidu would do within months, if not weeks of their time in Britain, on the expanded stage of London's cosmopolitan world, they began on their shipboard journeys to take possession, as Indians, of the mobile, cross-border experience of travel—in a word, to play the part of peripatetic cosmopolitans and modern imperial citizens. As the Indian seer Vivekananda wrote in a letter to one of his English friends, remarking on the experience of going through Suez after extensive travel in the west: 'Once more Asia. Am I Asiatic, European, American? . . . I feel a curious medley of personalities within me.'[116] Especially with the formation of the Indian National Congress in 1885, it became politically as well as culturally important to project new modern selves in this fashion—selves that were conversant with the accelerated and interconnected modern world, yet at the same time retained cultural, religious, or linguistic bonds with India.

As this chapter's many examples have demonstrated, travel writing, whether in the form of letters or memoirs or even, as with Naidu, poems, much of it in English, formed a powerful way of dramatizing and consolidating these mobile new Indian identities. This writing was distinguished in particular by its deployment of certain interrelated motifs, repeated and sometimes elaborated from one text to another to form what has been termed a Suez discourse. Of these discursive devices, there were few more elaborate and emphatic than the extended trope of the passage from India through the Suez Canal itself, usually positioned at the very opening or 'gateway' of the text. The trope unequivocally established the writer within the mobile, intercultural, quintessentially modern domain of the steamship, not only as a modern traveller, with an equivalent status to other travellers on board ship, the British included, but also, more subtly, as a citizen of the vast, interconnected British Empire. Though the Suez Canal was at the time very much regarded as a British waterway, Indians in their journeying and their writing began to contribute to how the empire could at the same time be viewed in a more expansive, transnational light. As is implied throughout, Indian travellers in this period were not so much concerned with a cultural transition from east to west, such as Fielding effects in Forster's *A Passage to India*, but were rather shifting their position within a more or less integrated cultural geography, that of Greater Britain, within which their cosmopolitan selves would be defined contingently, unpredictably, and sometimes awkwardly, as Gilroy writes, always more in terms of movement than fixity.[117]

NOTES

1. Walt Whitman, 'Passage to India', in *Leaves of Grass*, ed. Michael Moon (New York and London: W. W. Norton Company, 2002), pp. 345–53; this quotation is on pp. 345–6. 'Passage to India' appeared as a supplement to Whitman's long accumulative poem *Leaves of Grass*, in its 1871 edition.
2. Rudyard Kipling, 'The Exiles' Line', in *Complete Verse: Definitive Edition* (London: Hodder and Stoughton, 1989), pp. 162–4.
3. Michael Ondaatje, *The Cat's Table* (London: Jonathan Cape, 2011), pp. 137–8, 140. Page references henceforth will be included in the text.
4. The silent tailor Gunesekera turns out to be an undercover police officer; the deaf Asuntha is the daughter of the ship's mysterious prisoner Niemeyer, whom a small party on board has an audacious plot to set free, with dire consequences; the pale linguist and pigeon-fancier Miss Lasqueti is revealed to be a CID markswoman with a key role to play in the final escape of the prisoner. And so on.
5. Nearly all the South Asian Suez narratives brought together in this chapter trace the same route, in the same direction: the 'turmoil of the ocean' gives way to the stillness of the Arabian Sea that leads to Aden, 'keyhole into Arabia', which then narrows to the 'confines of the Red Sea' and the Canal, and finally opens again on to the brightness of the Mediterranean, entered at daylight. See Ondaatje, *The Cat's Table*, pp. 95, 112, 118, 131, 140, 214.
6. Annie Proulx, Review of *The Cat's Table*: 'Journey from Childhood', *The Guardian Review* (3 September 2011), p. 10.
7. Pico Iyer, 'Kip and Kim: How Michael Ondaatje is Subtly Remaking the English Novel', *Times Literary Supplement* (23 September 2011): 14–15.
8. Adam Mars-Jones, 'Confusing Rites of Passage Tale', review of *The Cat's Table, Observer New Review* 5660 (25 September 2011), p. 38.
9. On the 'worlding' of cultural forms, see Elleke Boehmer, 'Circulating Forms: The Jingo Poem at the Height of Empire', *English Language Notes* 49.1 (Spring/Summer 2011): 11–28.
10. Cara Murray, *Victorian Narrative Technologies in the Middle East* (London and New York: Routledge, 2008).

11. Philip Hensher, Review of The Cat's Table, *The Telegraph* (5 September 2011). See <http://www.telegraph.co.uk/culture/books/bookreviews/8735345/The-Cats-Table-by-Michael-Ondaatje-review.html> (accessed 8 January 2015).
12. Lloyd Pratt, 'The Deprivation of Time in African American Life Writing', in *Archives of American Time: Literature and Modernity in the Nineteenth Century* (Philadelphia, PA: University of Pennsylvania Press, 2010), p. 168, gives an extended account of the contradictory temporalities that interrupt the progressive narrative of post-bellum America. See also Dipesh Chakrabarty, *Provincializing Europe* (Princeton, NJ: Princeton University Press, 2000), pp. 95–112, on 'the heterotemporality of the world'; Benedict Anderson, *Imagined Communities*, rev. edn (London: Verso, 1991), p. 24, on the 'homogeneous, empty time' of modernity; Dana D. Nelson, *National Manhood: Capitalist Citizenship and the Imagined Fraternity of White Men* (Durham, NC: Duke University Press, 1998), p. 46.
13. Barbara Harlow and Mia Carter, eds., *Imperialism and Orientalism: A Documentary Sourcebook* (Oxford: Blackwell, 1999) p. 59. See also Sukanya Banerjee, *Becoming Imperial Citizens: Indians in the Late-Victorian Empire* (Durham, NC, and London: Duke University Press, 2010).
14. Priya Joshi, *In Another Country: Colonialism, Culture and the English Novel in India* (New York, NY: Columbia University Press), p. xvii.
15. Lala Baijnath, *England and India: Being Impressions of Persons and Things, English and Indian, and Brief Notes of Visits to France, Switzerland, Italy and Ceylon* (Bombay: Jehangir B. Karani and Co., 1893), p. 1. The full quotation reads: 'It is now-a-days the ambition—the dream of every educated Indian, to pay a visit to the home of his rulers, to those lands of civilization and liberty of which he has read so much, or wishes his own country to come up to.'
16. Satadru Sen, *Migrant Races: Empire, Identity and K. S. Ranjitsinhji* (Manchester: Manchester University Press, 2004), pp. 16–17.
17. Amitav Ghosh, *In an Antique Land* (Delhi: Ravi Dayal Publishers, 1992), p. 236.
18. Sen, *Migrant Races*, especially pp. 24–5.
19. A relatively new town, founded in 1859 when the building of the Suez Canal began, Port Said struck many travellers from Europe in the same way, as a seedy, somewhat decadent 'Oriental' port city. For the Parsi traveller B. M. Malabari in *The Indian Eye on English Life; or, Rambles of a Pilgrim Reformer* (London: Archibald Constable, 1893), pp. 18–19, it was, typically, 'a mixture of European and Asiatic vices', 'dirty and woebegone'.
20. Cornelia Sorabji, Letter of 27 August 1889, *An Indian Portia: Selected Writings of Cornelia Sorabji, 1866–1954*, ed. Kusoom Vadgama (New Delhi: Blacker, 2011), p. 63.
21. Rabindranath Tagore, *An Anthology*, ed. Krishna Dutta and Andrew Robinson (London: Picador, 1997), pp. 136–7.
22. Edwin Arnold, *India Revisited* (London: Trübner and Co., 1886), pp. i–ii.
23. M. K. Gandhi, *An Autobiography; or the Story of my Experiments with Truth* (1927; Ahmedabad: Navajivan Publishing House, 1958), pp. 31–2. Judith

Brown, *Gandhi: Prisoner of Hope* (New Haven, CT and London: Yale University Press, 1989), pp. 22–3. As is seen at greater length in Chapter 2, in Gandhi's case it was not so much the journey as the arrival that mattered. His chapter recounting his voyage out is simply entitled 'In London at last'. The keynotes of his short description of the passage, which began on the day of leaving Bombay, 4 September 1888 (pp. 30–1), are loneliness and bewilderment. So shy was he, so self-conscious about his poor English and lack of English table manners, so isolated as one of only two Indians on board the *SS Clyde*, that he spent most of the journey in his cabin, and describes no passing features whatsoever. A single well-meaning conversation with an Englishman is recorded, but its import is worrying for the young man, as he gains the impression that in Britain vegetarianism will be impossible to sustain. In his unpublished 'London Diary', Gandhi went into more detail, remarking on the aridity of Aden, 'the genius of the man who invented [the Suez Canal]', and his sense from using British currency in Port Said that he had finally left his homeland behind him. See Ramachandra Guha, *Gandhi Before India* (London: Allen Lane, 2013), pp. 36–7. In short, the language of the wider world, at first incomprehensible and alarming to Gandhi, became clearer and more manageable to him only once he arrived in Britain. Interestingly, too, for Willie Chandran, the protagonist of Naipaul's novel of Indian migration, *Half a Life*, the passage to England passes in a Gandhi-like blur: 'everything about the journey frightened him into silence'. See V. S. Naipaul, *Half a Life* (London: Picador, 2001), p. 51.

24. Murray, *Victorian Narrative Technologies*, pp. 1–3. See also Deep Kanta Lahiri Choudhury, *Telegraphic Imperialism: Crisis and Panic in the Indian Empire, c. 1830–1920* (New York, NY: Palgrave Macmillan, 2010); Bruce J. Hunt, *Pursuing Power and Light: Technology and Physics from James Watt to Albert Einstein* (Baltimore, MD: The Johns Hopkins University Press, 2010), p. 85. The Suez Canal appeared as the summation of the world-enveloping technologies of the undersea cables and steamships which allowed Britain to rule the world, and whose production Britain dominated.
25. Moreover, it was a crossing point that screened out some of the vast complexities of the Indian Ocean and the east. See Sugata Bose, *A Hundred Horizons: The Indian Ocean in the Age of Global Empire* (Cambridge, MA: Harvard University Press, 2006); Isabel Hofmeyr, 'The Complicating Sea: The Indian Ocean as Method', in *Comparative Studies of South Asia, Africa and the Middle East*, 32:3 (2012): 584–90; Pamila Gupta, Isabel Hofmeyr, and Michael Pearson, eds., *Eyes Across the Water: Navigating the Indian Ocean* (Pretoria: Unisa Press, 2010); Charne Lavery, 'Writing the Indian Ocean in Selected Novels by Joseph Conrad, Amitav Ghosh, Abdulrazak Gurnah and Lindsey Collen', D.Phil. thesis, University of Oxford, 2013.
26. Lockwood Kipling letter. Bateman's Archive, Box 1, Item 7, Wimpole Papers, SxMs38/1/7. I am grateful to Alexander Bubb for this reference. Other references to heat-maddened lascars may be found in Rozina Visram, *Asians in Britain: 400 Years of History* (London: Pluto Press, 2002), pp. 54–7.

27. See Alfred, Lord Tennyson, 'To the Marquess of Dufferin and Ava', *The Poems of Tennyson*, ed. Christopher Ricks, 2nd edn, vol. 3 (Berkeley, CA: University of California Press, 1987), p. 200. See also Cornelia Pearsall, *Imperial Tennyson: Victorian Poetry and the Expansion of England* (forthcoming).
28. Arnold, *India Revisited*, p. 25.
29. Gandhi, *An Autobiography*, pp. 29–30, 65–6. See also Anderson, *Imagined Communities*, pp. 47–66, 114–40, on creole pioneers and pilgrimages.
30. The cricketer Shri Ranjitsinhji, for example, went to Cambridge from Rajkumar College, in his own state of Nawanagar. In many princely states Chief's Colleges modelled on British public schools had been set up as preparatory platforms for Oxbridge. See Sen, *Migrant Races*, pp. 44–5.
31. Mohammad Said-Pacha, 'Charter of Concession and Book of Charges for the Construction and Working of the Suez Grand Maritime Canal and Dependencies', in Harlow and Carter, eds., *Imperialism and Orientalism*, p. 26.
32. Harlow and Carter, eds., *Imperialism and Orientalism*, p. 111.
33. See Lord Kinross, *Between Two Seas: The Creation of the Suez Canal* (London: John Murray, 1968); T. K. Lynch, *A Visit to the Suez Canal* (London: Day and Son Ltd, 1866).
34. See Carol Zeman Rothkopf, *The Opening of the Suez Canal* (New York, NY: Franklin Watts, 1973), p. 8.
35. Niall Fergusson, *Empire: How Britain Made the Modern World* (London: Allen Lane, 2003).
36. Zachary Karabell, *Parting the Desert: The Creation of the Suez Canal* (London: John Murray, 2003), pp. 262–7.
37. As Murray, *Victorian Narrative Technologies in the Middle East*, also observes, the Canal promoted some of the core benefits of capitalism, in particular its space–time transformation and compression. See also David Harvey, *The Condition of Postmodernity: An Enquiry into the Origins of Cultural Change* (Oxford: Blackwell, 1990).
38. Kipling, 'A Song of the English', *Definitive Edition*, p. 170.
39. See Ailise Bulfin, 'The Fiction of Gothic Egypt and British Imperial Paranoia: The Curse of the Suez Canal', *English Literature in Transition* 54.4 (2011): 411–43; Emily Haddad, 'Digging to India: Modernity, Imperialism and the Suez Canal', *Victorian Studies* 47.5 (2005): 363–96.
40. Leonard Woolf, *An Autobiography 1: 1880–1911* (Oxford: Oxford University Press, 1980), p. 136.
41. Arnold, *India Revisited*, p. 33. See also Baron Samuel Selig de Kusel, *An Englishman's Recollections of Egypt 1863–1887* (London: John Lane, 1915).
42. Edward Carpenter, *From Adam's Peak to Elephanta: Sketches in Ceylon and India* (London: Swan Sonnenschein and Co., 1892), pp. 5–7.
43. See E. Ashmead Bartlett M.P., *The Conference and Mr Gladstone's Proposals* (London: The Patriotic Association, 1885), pp. 10–11. The pamphlet is interesting for its emphatic Tory views on the need for Britain to show greater assertiveness in her dealings with France over the control of the

Canal and hence impatience with Gladstone's Liberal prevarications in this regard.

44. Raja-i-Rajgan Jagatjit Singh of Kapurthala, *My Travels in Europe and America 1893* (London: George Routledge and Sons, 1895), pp. 7–8.
45. T. N. Mukharji, *A Visit to Europe* (Calcutta: W. Newman and Co./London: Edward Stainford, 1889), p. 3.
46. See Omar Khalidi, ed., *An Indian Passage to Europe: The Travels of Fath Nawaz Jung* (Karachi: Oxford University Press, 2006), pp. 18–19.
47. Malabari, *The Indian Eye on English Life*, pp. 18–19.
48. Visram, *Asians in Britain*, pp. 54–9.
49. Sarah Searight, *Steaming East: The Forging of Steamship and Rail Links Between Europe and Asia* (London: The Bodley Head, 1991), pp. 129, 131.
50. Kipling, *Definitive Edition*, p. 457.
51. Malabari, *The Indian Eye on English Life*, p. 9. The perceptive Anglo-Indian Sara Crewe in Frances Hodgson Burnett's *A Little Princess*, whom we will meet again in Chapter 4, carries with her to London vivid memories of 'the big ship' on which she sailed to England, and 'of the lascars passing silently to and fro on it, of the children playing about on the hot deck'. See Frances Hodgson Burnett, *A Little Princess* (1905; London: Penguin, 1970), p. 7.
52. Kipling, 'The Exiles' Line', *Definitive Edition*, pp. 162–4.
53. Arnold, *India Revisited*, p. 35.
54. Elizabeth Buettner, *Empire Families: Britons and Late Imperial India* (Oxford: Oxford University Press, 2004), pp. 1–3.
55. Arnold, *India Revisited*, p. 25.
56. Romesh Chunder Dutt, *Three Years in Europe 1868–71*, 4th edn (1872; Calcutta: SK Lahiri, 1896), p. 9.
57. Cited in Khalidi, *An Indian Passage to Europe*, pp. 18–19.
58. In the case of Arnold, despite his many apparent cross-cultural interests, the most elaborated image in his travelogue is of the social hierarchy that obtains on board ship: the ceremony of praying together on Sundays for 'the peace and welfare of the Queen' strikes him powerfully as a microcosm of the 'glorious British empire'. See Arnold, *India Revisited*, pp. 35–6.
59. Woolf, *An Autobiography 1*, pp. 135–40.
60. Victoria Glendinning, *Leonard Woolf* (London: Simon and Schuster, 2006), p. 79.
61. Alice Perrin, *East of Suez* (London: Anthony Treherne and Co., 1901).
62. Leonard Woolf, 'Pearls and Swine', in *Empire Writing*, ed. Elleke Boehmer (Oxford: Oxford University Press, 1998), p. 416. In an ephemeral English mystery story about Suez, Cpt Charles Hillcoat's 1896 *A Mystery of the Suez Canal*, the young bride-to-be Ida, travelling out to India, is abducted at Port Said. All the technologies of the agent's office, including its telegraph link, avail the British nothing against the predictably predatory behaviour of 'a dark, foreign-looking man' on board. See Charles H. Hillcoat, *A Mystery of the Suez Canal* (Glasgow: David Bryce and Son, 1896), especially pp. 29–33.

63. Leonard Woolf, *Letters*, ed. Frederic Spotts (London: Bloomsbury, 1990), p. 66. Similarly for Malabari, the Bombay to Aden leg of the journey was 'disagreeably smooth'. See Malabari, *The Indian Eye on English Life*, p. 15.
64. Woolf, Letter to Strachey of 4 December 1904, *Letters*, p. 67.
65. Leonard Woolf, *Growing: An Autobiography of the Years 1904–1911* (London: The Hogarth Press, 1964), p. 11.
66. Woolf, Letter to Strachey of 4 December 1904, *Letters*, p. 66.
67. E. M. Forster, *A Passage to India* (London: Penguin, 1967), pp. 204, 241–2. Citations will be included in the text.
68. The statue was razed at the time of the Suez Crisis in 1956, which ended the century of Anglo-French control over the Canal.
69. V. S. Naipaul, *The Enigma of Arrival: A Novel* (London: Penguin, 1987), pp. 140–1.
70. See the Introduction, Sections II and IV.
71. See Michel de Certeau, *The Practice of Everyday Life* (Berkeley, CA: University of California Press, 1984), pp. 99–100.
72. Paul Gilroy, *Between Camps: Nations, Cultures and the Allure of Race* (London and New York: Routledge, 2004), pp. 129–31.
73. Chapter 2 explores the symbolic interconnection of geographical and social pathways in more detail.
74. See Gauri Viswanathan, *Masks of Conquest: Literary Study and British Rule in India* (New York, NY: Columbia University Press, 1998).
75. Naipaul, *The Enigma of Arrival*, p. 52.
76. B. M. Malabari, Preface, *The Indian Muse in English Garb* (Bombay: Reporters' Press, 1879), pp. 1–5. The collection is largely made up of panegyrics to British royalty and the ideals of empire.
77. Malabari, Preface, *The Indian Muse in English Garb*, p. 4.
78. Joshi, *In Another Country*, especially pp. 41–2. Joshi draws from the 1881 census in India the interesting fact that at this time 6.6% of Indian males were literate, and 0.3% of females, which would have meant literate in English. The Indian travellers who move through the pages of this book would have come from this small literate minority. But, even if small in numbers, this group had global or world-enveloping literary imaginations if with a particular Anglocentric tendency, in the sense that their reading culture was shaped by books written in English, about England, and imported from England. In this period, a number of British publishers, Macmillan and Stanley Unwin among them, exported novels to India, and Indian readers duly claimed the English novel as their own, consuming authors like Dickens and G. M. W. Reynolds in large quantities. See also John Barnes, Bill Bell, Rimi B. Chatterjee, Wallace Kirsop, and Michael Winship, 'A Place in the World', *The Cambridge History of the Book in Britain*, Volume 6: 1830–1914 (Cambridge: Cambridge University Press, 2009), pp. 595–634; Rimi Chatterjee, 'Macmillan in India', in *Macmillan: A Publishing Tradition*, ed. Elizabeth James (Houndmills, Palgrave, 2001); Alexis Weedon, *Victorian Publishing: The Economics of Book Production for a Mass Market 1836–1916* (Aldershot: Ashgate, 2003), p. 39.

79. Dutt, *Three Years in Europe*, 1896.
80. Meenakshi Mukherjee, *An Indian for all Seasons: The Many Lives of R. C. Dutt* (New Delhi: Penguin, 2009), pp. 2–4.
81. Dutt, *Three Years in Europe 1868–71*, pp. 4–6.
82. In a later, equally pioneering travel book, *Rambles in India During Twenty-Four Years*, Dutt would again gloss key sites with a 'retelling of place legends'. See Meenakshi Mukherjee, *An Indian for All Seasons*, pp. 114–15.
83. Baijnath, *England and India: Being Impressions of Persons and Things*, pp. 1–2.
84. Baijnath, *England and India: Being Impressions of Persons and Things*, pp. 2–3.
85. Jagatjit Singh of Kapurthala, *My Travels in Europe and America 1893*, pp. 8–10.
86. N. L. Doss, *Reminiscences: English and Australasian* (Calcutta: M. C. Bhowmick, 1893), p. 21.
87. Malabari, *The Indian Eye*, pp. 15–17.
88. Baijnath, *England and India*, p. 2. Reciprocally, it was Baijnath who found the English on board less reserved and superior than in India.
89. Doss, *Reminiscences*, pp. 25–6.
90. Rev. T. B. Pandian, *England to an Indian Eye* or *English Pictures from an Indian Camera* (London: Elliot Stock, 1897), p. 2.
91. It is in this light that many Gulf city-states are perceived by Indian migrant workers, as Amitav Ghosh, for example, reflects in his first novel, *The Circle of Reason* (London: Hamish Hamilton, 1986). The similarities are in part geophysical: colonial Bombay was built on a cluster of offshore islands, whereas Aden, a smaller town, was located on an isthmus.
92. Searight, *Steaming East*, pp. 134–6.
93. Baijnath, *England and India*, p. 3. Aden was widely perceived to hold both Indian and imperial associations. Thomas R. Metcalf, *Imperial Connections: India in the Indian Ocean Arena, 1860–1920* (Berkeley, CA: University of California Press, 2007), notes that the port cities of the Indian Ocean rim, which include Aden, gave definitive shape to the nineteenth-century's India-centred imperial network.
94. Malabari, *The Indian Eye*, p. 17.
95. Malabari, *The Indian Eye*, p. 18.
96. Mukharji, *A Visit to Europe*, pp. 3–12.
97. Mukharji, *A Visit to Europe*, pp. 24–6.
98. Mukharji, *A Visit to Europe*, p. 25.
99. Malabari, *The Indian Eye*, p. 18.
100. The word is here adapted from Sugata Bose's reading of the Indian Ocean's very different (politically anti-colonial and religiously universalist) ecumene. See Sugata Bose, *A Hundred Horizons*.
101. Cornelia Sorabji, *India Calling*, ed. Elleke Boehmer and Naella Grew (1934; Nottingham: Trent Editions, 2004), p. 37.
102. Cornelia Sorabji's first journey to England was from Bombay to Liverpool on the *SS Asia*, bound for study at the University of Oxford.
103. Sorabji, *An Indian Portia*, pp. 56–65. The Suez Canal description is in a letter of 6 September 1889, p. 63.

104. Cornelia Sorabji, 'Love and Death', in *Love and Life Behind the Purdah* (London: Freemantle and Co., 1901), pp. 85–102.
105. The grip of orientalist language in the writing of east–west crossing of course remained tenacious. Nehru in his *Autobiography* observed, for example, that English words denoting self-government had different meanings depending on which side of Suez they were used. Jawarhal Nehru, 'Democracy in East and West', in *An Autobiography; with Musings on Recent Events in India* (London: Bodley Head, 1936), pp. 498–503.
106. See Tricia Lootens, 'Bengal, Britain, France: The Locations and Translations of Toru Dutt', *Victorian Literature and Culture* 34.2 (2006): 574–90.
107. Edmund Gosse, 'Toru Dutt: Introductory Memoir', in Toru Dutt, *Ancient Ballads and Legends of Hindustan* (London: Kegan, Paul, Trench and Co., 1882), pp. vii–xxvii.
108. Toru Dutt, Letter to Mary Martin of 19 December 1873, in Toru Dutt, *Collected Poetry and Prose*, ed. Chandani Lokugé (New Delhi: Oxford University Press, 2006), pp. 222–4.
109. For her careful reading of the layered and 'intransigent' ambiguities of the casuarina tree symbol, see Tricia Lootens, 'Alien Homelands: Rudyard Kipling, Toru Dutt, and the Poetry of Empire', in *The Fin-de-siècle Poem: English Literary Culture and the 1890s*, ed. Joseph Bristow (Athens, OH: Ohio University Press, 2007), pp. 284–310.
110. Gosse, 'Introductory Memoir', p. vii. Gosse himself had a considerable 'sympathetic imagination'—that 'dual individuality' that encouraged an individual to reach out to a relative cultural stranger, as he wrote in his memoir *Father and Son*. For all that Gosse carried a reputation among modernists like Virginia Woolf as a fusty old Victorian, this capacity for sympathy with others is a feature that marked many of his relations with others. See Edmund Gosse, *Father and Son*, ed. and intr. Michael Newton (1907; Oxford: Oxford University Press, 2004), pp. 5, 26–7, 41, 159–60; Ann Thwaite, *Edmund Gosse: A Literary Landscape, 1849–1928* (Oxford: Oxford University Press, 1985). However, as we saw, Thwaite fails to mention Gosse's interactions with either Naidu or Dutt.
111. This and the quotations which follow are all from Gosse, 'Toru Dutt: Introductory Memoir', pp. vii–xxvii.
112. Manuscript Poems and Letters of Sarojini Naidu, Index 15, National Archives of India, New Delhi.
113. 'Recent Verse', *Manchester Guardian* (20 December 1905), p. 5; 'An Indian Poetess', *Manchester Guardian* (27 January 1913), p. 7; J. D. W., 'Review of *The Bird of Time*', *The Indian Magazine and Review* 508 (April 1913), p. 89.
114. See in particular R/E/O 821.91 N 143a, and also R/E/O 821.91, vols. 1–3. Sarojini Naidu papers, Special Collections, National Library, Calcutta. The Nizam was a warm supporter of Naidu's work; several of her poems are dedicated to him. See also David Cannadine, *Ornamentalism: How the British Saw Their Empire* (London: Allen Lane, 2001), p. 42.
115. R/E/O 821.91 N 143a. Sarojini Naidu papers. For further discussion of the poems, see Chapter 3.

116. Swami Vivekananda, Letter to Mary Hale of 3 January 1897, in *The Complete Works of Swami Vivekananda*, vol. viii (Calcutta: Advaita Ashrama, 1991–92), p. 395.
117. Gilroy, *Between Camps*, pp. 55–6. Here it is appropriate to observe that Amitav Ghosh, too, refers to the shipboard journey as 'a striking metaphor . . . for how identity is fluid, movable, mobile, can be reinvented'. See Elleke Boehmer and Anshuman Mondal, 'Networks and Traces: Interview with Amitav Ghosh', *Wasafiri* 27.2 (June 2012): 30–5, especially 33.

2

The Spasm of the Familiar

Indians in Late Nineteenth-century London

> But the passenger, looking at the city in the morning haze, seeing the unremarkable city debris floating out on the sea, unremarkable though the city was so famous—rotten fruit, fresh branches, bits of timber, driftwood—the passenger had a spasm of fear . . . he didn't want to leave the ship . . . [there was] no route back to the home left behind . . . [he would] continue to travel versions of [his] old route.
>
> V. S. Naipaul, *The Enigma of Arrival* (1987)

> Nehru had to go to England to discover India. Things are clear only when looked at from a distance.
>
> A. K. Ramanujan, 'Annayya's Anthropology' (1992), p. 44[1]

I '. . . TO ENGLAND TO DISCOVER INDIA'

The compendious late nineteenth-century glossary of Anglo-Indian English, *Hobson-Jobson* (1886), compiled by the lexicographer Henry Yule, records under the entry for *bandow* a nicely turned anecdote. Yule's informant Keatinge heard the imperative *bandow!* (meaning 'tie' or 'make fast') used by two London lighter-men on the Thames docks as they shouted instructions to each other while working.[2] In that setting, the word *bandow* is likely to have been an expression brought to the East End by Indian lascars or seamen, and then naturalized as English speech on the London riverside. It is as telling an instance as might be found of how towards the end of the nineteenth century India was in myriad forms brought over to England, carried by both Indian visitors and British travellers moving along multiple different routes.

The incident is far from a one-off case, however. In *East in the West*, the reformer Joseph Salter of the London City Mission described the late 1800s east of the city as 'an Asiatic jungle of courts and alleys', so many Indian sailors and mendicants did he find milling in the streets.[3] In the same area, the Strangers' Home, a repatriation centre for 'Asiatic, African and South Sea islander' sailors, part-funded by the Maharaja Duleep Singh, processed around 4,000 cases a year. So, too, 1886 parish reports observed the presence of East Indians or 'Hindoos' in workhouses in St George's, Kensington, and Whitechapel, noting, for example, most Indians' refusal to eat anything 'but what he cooked himself'.[4] In the preface to his 1890s *Three Years in Europe*, R. C. Dutt wrote in matter-of-fact terms: 'It is an old story now... many of my country men have travelled in Europe.'[5] 'It is quite a common sight to meet Indians in all the principal thoroughfares of London', the Anglican clergyman S. Satthianandhan concurred in 1897, while other visitors to London noticed the number of Asian and African faces looking out of the windows of Bloomsbury boarding houses.[6] In his memoir *Father and Son* (1907), Edmund Gosse recalls being introduced as a child in the late 1850s or early 1860s to an Irish member of the Plymouth Brethren and his wife, an 'Asiatic' 'lady of colour' (to him somewhat unfamiliar and alarming).[7] And the 1901 census reveals numerous more and less anglicized Indian names, both Lalls and Lals, Alis and Allys, Das and Dasses, living around the London docks.[8]

'Asiatic' London comprised a multilayered urban underworld, the novelist Wilkie Collins agreed—one that interpenetrated the entire greater city. His prescient *The Moonstone* (1868), a sensation-cum-detective fiction, offers probably the most insightful observations of any novel of the period on the ways in which Indian presences thus wove through the great imperial metropolis. *The Moonstone* examines in detail how the intrigues and complications of empire impinge on domestic relations both in London and in Britain more widely, in such various forms as a gifted jewel, opium consumption, and the prevalence of musky odours, decorated manuscripts, and tell-tale stray gold threads, as well as in the shape of travelling Indian mendicants. Throughout, the novel is also deeply preoccupied with the gathering and decoding of information, sifting through a series of different possible interpretations for the disappearance of the eponymous South Asian stone. As the reader traces 'the devil's dance of the [mysteriously stolen] Indian diamond [that weaves] its way' through the plot, between India and Britain, but also between Yorkshire and London, repeated interpretative links are made between Indian presences and British domestic space—links that will prove pre-emptive and diagnostic also for this chapter's reading of India in metropolitan Britain in the late nineteenth century, as reflected in the writing and scholarship of Charles Dickens, Edwin Arnold, and F. Max Müller, as well as Swami Vivekananda, B. M. Malabari, and K. C. Sen, amongst many others.[9]

The chapter's four sections—of metropolitan scene setting, including literary mapping; India-in-Britain overview; contextual investigation, especially of cultural networks; and finally case study—take as their focus peripatetic Indians' cultural, political, and textual embedding, and, where salient, as in the section on metropolitan scene setting, British responses to them. Throughout, as in other chapters, the informing context is comprised of the networks, institutions, groupings, and partnerships by way of which Indian visitors and their British hosts and mentors drew closer together in this period. A key part of the Indians' process of embedding was the fact that they were in many cases self-conscious and articulate observers of their arrival, noting the subtle interplay of perceptions of difference and sameness that Britain presented. Their writing, whether published or private, gave them an important interpretative grasp of their experience. It allowed them to negotiate serviceable pathways through the frenetic modern world and to gain a critical distance on its social fluidities and cross-cultural intersections. Though they were by no means the first Asian visitors to visit England, or to write up their observations of European cultural and religious life as amateur ethnography, they did so in far greater numbers, and arguably with greater mutual awareness, than before.[10]

The important backdrop to these readings of Indians in Britain in the final decades of the nineteenth century is provided, first, by the Liberal 'Grand Old Man' W. E. Gladstone's four phases of premiership, beginning with his so-called 'Great' Liberal Ministry of 1868–74; and, second, by the large-scale imperial celebrations and festivals held in the metropolis in these and subsequent years, designed to demonstrate the penetration of British imperial power around the world. In his letters, the economic historian R. C. Dutt fondly evoked his early years in England as marking the highpoint of Liberal Britain. Not long after Dutt's first visit to Britain, his distant cousin the poet Toru Dutt and her father arrived and saw their poems published under the domestic-sounding and anglicizing title, *The Dutt Family Album* (1870), reflecting their sense that their creative productions as a family were accessible to a British readership.[11] Some twenty years later, in 1889, the same year that T. N. Mukharji published his lavish report on the Colonial and Indian Exhibition, with Gladstone still a force in Westminster, and Queen Victoria still on the throne, the 'Indian' Kipling arrived in London.[12] Like Mukharji or Malabari in their different milieus, Kipling styled himself as a modern citizen of several cultural worlds; and his work, too, like Mukharji's, would serve as a dynamic conduit of cultural perceptions between Britain and India, once again increasing the latter's visibility.[13] Throughout these years, the warp and weft of Indian–British networks was thickened by the many repeated east–west journeys of Indian as well as Anglo-Indian scholars, businessmen, lawyers, and civil servants, whose careers demanded such shuttling. 'Native' Indian Civil Service officers such as Dutt and W. C. Bonnerjee, like their British counterparts, were entitled to periodic 'home leave' with their families in London.

Particularly persuasive evidence for the involvement of Indians in London's social and political life came with the Liberal landslide election of 1892 when, after a concerted campaign waged by a group of British Liberals, Dadabhai Naoroji was elected as Liberal MP for Finsbury Central, albeit by a narrow margin.[14] He had stood for the first time in the 1886 election, for Deptford, along with Lal Mohun Ghose for Holborn, on which occasion the Tory Prime Minister Lord Salisbury had remarked that the English were not ready to elect a 'Blackman'. In 1895, Mancherjee Bhownaggree followed Naoroji's success with a Tory election win in Bethnal Green. Naoroji, an inveterate networker, also sometimes called the 'Grand Old Man', thus became the first Indian to represent a predominantly white constituency, yet, while doing so, persistently raised questions in Parliament pertaining to injustices meted out to India, as well as to Ireland. Across the years leading up to his election, Naoroji had been instrumental in the establishment of several interlinked proto-nationalist Indian groupings in London, including the East India Association, as will be seen later. The late 1880s also saw the formation of the Anjuman-e-Islam, a society for educated Indian Muslims (which became the Pan-Islamic Society from 1903).[15] It was on the shoulders of these organizations, their publications, and campaigns for Indian social and political reform that the rising prominence of India in Britain rested, as Section III of this chapter discusses.

With their way smoothed by such developments, various soon-to-be-prominent Indian students began to arrive in Britain from the 1880s, to follow the pathways laid down by pioneers like Dutt, Surendranath Banerjee, and Rabindranath Tagore (who briefly studied law at University College London in the late 1870s). The social reformer Pandita Ramabai attended Cheltenham Ladies College in 1883. M. K. Gandhi studied at the Bar from 1888 to 1891. From 1889, Cornelia Sorabji read first English and then law at Somerville College, Oxford, where she could well have bumped into Manmohan Ghose the poet, a student at Christ Church in the same period. She was certainly photographed with the Duleep Singh sisters, who also studied at Somerville. K. S. Ranjitsinhji, the gifted cricketer, attended Trinity College, Cambridge in 1892–93, neglecting his studies in favour of the sport at which he excelled.

II NATIVE AND FOREIGN IN ENGLAND

Wilkie Collins's *The Moonstone*, with its prescient focus on India's pervasive presence in Britain, is probably one of the first Victorian novels to expose the complicated involvement of imperial capital in the empire, and of metropolitan with colonial wealth.[16] From the opening scenes, which take place in late eighteenth-century India, the novel sets about undermining the conventional separation of capital and colony, where the one signifies order and control, and the other disorder and violence. In quest of the precious looted diamond, Collins's juggling Indian mendicants (in fact temple guardians) travel to Britain and manage English railway timetables and the geography of inner-city rooftops and hansom cab chases in London with a confidence and alacrity that is the marvel of the British characters, as are their 'elegant manners'. They are masters, too, of the social mores of London, 'employed in ministering to some of the multitudinous wants of this great city'.[17] Their being *au fait* in these ways powerfully offsets the standard-issue orientalist vocabulary with which they are, however, also represented, 'jabbering' in their own language.

Not insignificantly, it is given to Ezra Jennings, the opium-addict doctor, 'brought up in one of our colonies' with 'the mixture of some foreign race in his English blood', to unravel the mystery of how the moonstone, given as a birthday gift, disappears for a second time. And he is able to do so precisely because he understands how deeply British cultural and emotional life is imbued with the tincture of Indian ideas and dreams.[18] Like Yeats, and Dickens to an extent, as we will see, Collins thus demonstrates a clear awareness of the transformative potential of hosting Indians in Britain's midst. The Indians' presence in the novel encodes what was for the time a boundary-shifting world-view in which India is no mere satellite to the British centre but part, if not yet a major part, of the world-spanning network of Greater Britain.[19]

It was the India-interpenetrated world of Collins's *The Moonstone* that, some twenty-five years later, the peripatetic Indian seer Swami Vivekananda (Narendranath Datta), too, would map and help to mould—once again in indicative and form-giving ways for this chapter. Visiting Europe and America in the 1890s in order to propagate his doctrine of the Unity of the Divine, above and beyond the social divisions which empire embedded, the Swami, much like Collins's jugglers—indeed enabled by such earlier travellers—capably managed the metropolitan public world of lecture timetables, train and boat schedules, and publication deadlines, as his travel plans of the time show.[20] At the same time, in his talks to a range of audiences, including free-thinkers, 'orientalists', 'sceptical intellectuals', theosophists, and ex-colonial officers, on such subjects as 'The Eastern Doctrine of Love' and 'Indian Philosophy', he opened out, within the homes and the meeting halls of the capital, a widened, more ecumenical and integrated understanding of religious belief as interconnecting rather than dividing cultures. He propagated a vision of the world in which India, far from being in a subsidiary position, had a key role to play, due in part through its representation in the metropolis by individuals such as himself.

Sharing Collins's and to an extent Vivekananda's vision of the intricate relations that interlaced London, wider England, and the rest of the world, Charles Dickens in his last, unfinished, novel, the would-be twelve-part *The Mystery of Edwin Drood* (1870), also draws far-sighted attention to the multiple ways in which that wider British world, and in particular greater India (the entire subcontinent and Ceylon), had, in the final decades of the century, started to infiltrate English domestic worlds.[21] Arguably more so than in his other empire-aware novels, such as *Dombey and Son*, in *Edwin Drood* Dickens focuses on the fine material detail and the mutuality of this involvement. (That *Edwin Drood* was, like *The Moonstone*, a noir-ish mystery also suggests that gothic forms encouraged a more ambitious, if still coded, interrogation of colonial discourse than did the realist novel.) Although Cloisterham, the novel's primary setting, not unlike Dickens's native Rochester, is repeatedly represented as secluded from 'the noisy world', an ancient city where the express train does not stop, the shock-waves that move through the community with the disappearance and presumed murder of the young orphan–heir Edwin Drood mingle ties of blood, inheritance, business, habit, and life-style that nevertheless link the 'drowsy' town to that wider world.[22] Moreover, this wider world does not stop at London, but extends outwards to embrace China and Ceylon, the former home of Cloisterham's mysterious and aptly named orphan arrivants, Neville and Helena Landless: 'tigerish' and 'very dark . . . almost the gipsy type' (and strongly reminiscent of Ezra Jennings).[23] Though the novel's resolution must remain for ever obscure to its readers, the murder plot, driven by addiction, obsession, and betrayal, involves a constant mixing of English and eastern individuals, object-agents, and substances.[24]

A particularly significant aspect of this eastern-and-English mixing in *The Mystery of Edwin Drood*, at least in relation to this study, is that, as in *The Moonstone*, Indian persons and products in the novel are represented at one and the same time as out-of-the-ordinary and yet in the thick of public life. During the complicated goings-on on the night of the murder and in its aftermath, the exotic characters are interestingly regarded as neither more nor less threatening than the locals. Setting aside the bigoted

Mr Sapsea's association of 'un-English' darkness with danger, the narrative desists from attributing a greater blame to these conventionally less trustworthy presences than to the homegrown English.[25] Far greater suspicion is in fact directed at the Choir Master, John Jasper, the frequenter of Princess Puffer's opium den, than at the outsider Neville. It is an important new departure even for the author of *Great Expectations*—one that in part reflects the deep impression that Collins's mystery work had made on Dickens, but in part also conveys Dickens's deepening sense of the metropolis of London as a space accommodating the many varied journeys of both 'land customers and water customers', in Princess Puffer's words.[26] Both the migrant and the visitor in the two novels are, if not 'one of us' then 'one among us', and if not in place then certainly proximate to what is native and English.[27] If anything, in *Edwin Drood*, the tigerish and the gipsy are domesticated more thoroughly than they are in Collins.

In this context, perhaps the most symptomatic foreign object in the novel, far from being anything to be found in the Tartar's apartment with its many exotic wonders, is Neville Landless's heavy 'iron-shod' walking-stick, the weight and aspect of which lead his accusers to regard it as incriminating evidence.[28] Bearing no overt eastern connotations, the stick is an ordinary British walking accessory, which, by Neville's own admission, looks out of place on his person, yet it is exactly this lack of fit which is indicative. Most South Asians in Britain at this time would have been not only city residents but also city-dwellers by background, metropolitans who might not have been immediately comfortable in those areas that extended beyond Greater London—despite the evidence that exists, for instance, of Gandhi's country walks or Dutt's cross-Britain travels. Julian Barnes's novel *Arthur & George* (2006), discussed in Chapter 4, explores some of the deeper contradictions of Indians' relative unfamiliarity with the English countryside.[29] Or, as Neville himself remarks: 'I have not lived in a walking country, you know.' Neville's plans to go walking therefore represent an interesting attempt to take on a more English way of life than city-dwelling allowed, and his walking stick, though considered incongruous by his accusers, emerges as a metonym of his laying claim to England or of 'going native', in part by virtue of that very incongruity. The stick becomes a means for this allegedly 'tigerish' South Asian to plot a route both unexpected and determined along English cart-tracks and rutted paths, and hence provides a measuring rod for his seemingly 'un-English' yet self-anglicizing entry into England—that is, for the enigma of his arrival.[30]

Further literary elaboration of the economic and cultural proximity of India to London comes from the perhaps unlikely source of Anthony

Trollope's *The Eustace Diamonds* (1873).[31] Though the novel again carries echoes of Collins's *The Moonstone*, whose plot concerning disappearing jewellery it to some extent mimics, Trollope is not overtly interested, unlike Collins, in the presence or palpability of India and Indians in Britain. Even the precious jewels of the title, family diamonds 'worth £10,000', though they would have carried Indian connotations to most British readers, are not explicitly given Asian provenance. And when they disappear, irrevocably, it is to the diamond dealers of Vienna or Paris, not back to India. Yet Indian and colonial associations, including references to Irish estates, swirl between the characters of *The Eustace Diamonds* in at once binding and divisive ways, while the value of possessions with colonial provenance is repeatedly discussed. The difficult but sparky heroine Lizzie Eustace, who determinedly fights to keep hold of the precious diamond necklace her late husband gave her, turns into a magnet for 'all those evidences of a world beyond England', in particular when the 'Sawab of Mygawb's' official complaint concerning the restoration of his family fortune becomes the source of a dispute between Lizzie's love interests, Frank Greystock and Lord Fawn. Their differences reflect certain of the difficult arrangements in the late 1850s that accompanied the transfer of the government of India from the Company to the Crown, and the many land settlements this involved. The Sawab's 'question' itself, which is raised in Parliament, is especially reminiscent of the Maharajah Duleep Singh's grievances concerning the restoration of his vast Punjabi inheritance, including the priceless Koh-i-Noor diamond, as we will see, from which he was, however, to remain permanently alienated.[32] On this reading, Lizzie Eustace's failure to keep hold of her treasure to some extent equates with the Maharajah's, especially considering that she is the novel's catalyst of all that is invasive and disruptive.[33] In this least political of Trollope's political novels, therefore, imperial references not only form an intrinsic part of the fabric of everyday domestic life, but are also encoded in ways that suggest a significant extraction of wealth from India (and Ireland) to England.

Yet the novel was not the only literary genre to register the impact of Indian ideas, beliefs, and presences on British cultural life in this period. Here another Edwin steps into the mix—one who, like Rosa Bud's friend Tartar in *Edwin Drood*, was a British expatriate, a returnee from India (in which incarnation he appeared in Chapter 1). In 1879, the poet and translator Edwin Arnold made a particularly influential contribution to the India-infused networks already ramifying through the imperial metropolis with his remarkable epic poem *The Light of Asia*, a respectful rendition of the life of the Buddha, Prince Siddhartha: in the words of its preface, the 'noble hero and reformer, Prince Gautama' to whom 'a third of mankind' owes allegiance.[34] Throughout his time as principal of Government College in Poona in the late 1850s, Arnold had retained, like many British in India, 'an exile's sympathies' for his English home, even as he made an in-depth study of the languages of India and the Middle East.[35] Yet, on his return to England to embark on a new career as editor of the London *Daily Telegraph*, he experienced an equally characteristic switchback of emotions, pouring his nostalgia for his second home into several translations from Sanskrit and Pali.

Of these works, the most notable was Arnold's epic-scale life of the Buddha, which went into multiple editions, both tapping into, and itself nurturing, the widespread new interest in eastern texts and learning that the orientalist scholarship of the period had encouraged, as had the ongoing popularity of the *Arabian Nights*.[36] To Edwin Arnold can be attributed the first credible creation in English poetry of a timeless yet humanly conceived India, assimilated from different spiritual and aesthetic traditions. Plausibly cast in the voice of a 'Buddhist votary', *The Light of Asia* helped to shape the late nineteenth-century British and American understanding of Buddhism, to the extent that Arnold was charged with proselytizing for the religion, but the book also underpinned the increasing new openness to eastern wisdom in metropolitan culture at large, on the part of Britons (as exemplified also with the emergence of theosophy, as Section III will show).

III 'VERSIONS OF OUR OLD ROUTE': INDIA-IN-BRITAIN

Asiatic alleys threaded with a thin gold weave:[37] if these were the views of the British host—the novelist or poet—what of the Indian incomer? How did he—in those days rarely she—negotiate their way through England's, especially London's, streets? The 1890s metropolis, the social reformer B. M. Malabari magisterially observed in his *The Indian Eye on English Life* (1893), constituted a 'vortex of high-pressure civilization' that subjected everyone to 'the law of the survival of the fittest'.[38] M. K. Gandhi, a law student at the Inner Temple from 1888, was not so judgemental, finding the capital cold in temperature, but not inhospitable.[39] Moving within the spectrum described by these countervailing responses, this section traces some of the pathways Indian visitors to London forged, and explores their interaction with the city's streets and inhabitants. It considers, in other words, their incremental making of India-in-Britain.

In the final decades of the nineteenth century, travelling Indians—including traders, princes, political activists, ethnographers, students, entrepreneurs, curators, gurus, and artists of different descriptions—expressed a noticeable sense of cultural connection and even familiarity with the metropolis's meeting halls, salons, universities, parks, hostels, and eateries, as the records they left show. Their English addresses included places as far as apart as the Strangers' Home in West India Road, which is now in the London Docklands, through the Grosvenor Hotel and lodgings in Brompton Road and Oakley Street, among Toru Dutt's places of residence in central London, to Professor F. Max Müller's leafy Norham Gardens home in Oxford, through which Swami Vivekananda, K. C. Sen, and many other Indian visitors passed while in England. In their daily comings and goings between and around these spaces, and in their writing about their activities, these Indian travellers, as we will see, shaped their identities in response to the demands of metropolitan life.

To expand the concept of anticipatory familiarity introduced in Chapter 1, it is important to remind ourselves at this point that late nineteenth-century Indian travellers, in encountering the capital of the modern world, did not tend to see themselves as secondary or belated in relation to it. Rather, they mapped and decoded the city's streets with reference to a ready-made index of pre-existing images, geographical co-ordinates, and spatial terms acquired as part of a colonial education and from the pages of colonial newspapers. Urban dwellers themselves, citizens of Bombay, Calcutta, Lahore, or Delhi, self-consciously modern inhabitants of a rapidly expanding imperial world, they met the world's largest metropolis on relatively equal terms, even while conceding (as did Pandian and Dutt) that its bustle, traffic, and sheer scale were matched nowhere else on the planet. Far from being unintelligible, London to these colonial travellers was comprehensible and readable, in some cases *déjà vu*, even if those feelings of familiarity went along with a Naipaul-like 'spasm' of fear at the irretrievability, therefore, of origins or 'home'.[40]

In many 1880s and 1890s Indian travelogues, the writers explicitly style themselves as ethnographers of the capital, approaching the city as a site available for commentary and critique, and pronouncing authoritatively on its social and economic conditions.[41] As Antoinette Burton contends, nineteenth-century Indian visitors to the British heartland became 'exhibitors of Western mores'.[42] In some cases indeed, their travelogues were openly intended to serve as guides to the metropolis for the next generation of Indian visitors, and catered to an already established market in tourist guidebooks.[43] Though these writings may initially have been compiled in a haphazard way out of letters home and journalism, they were nonetheless seen as useful for Indian students of the future, by pointing out potential pitfalls, as well as sources of support and reassurance. Overall, even as travelling Indians' dress and manners inevitably remained objects of public scrutiny, in their writing they produced a spectacle of London that was a riposte to the city's own 'spectacular [imperial] gestures'.[44] The ocular references in the titles of several of these travelogues testify to the Indians' confident assumption of the city's visibility and legibility to their eyes (consider: *The Indian Eye on English Life*; *London and Paris Through Indian Spectacles*; *England to an Indian Eye*).

It is true, of course, that cross-empire exchange was not conventional for this period. Even as scholars make the case for intercultural encounter, it remains an incontrovertible fact of Indian–British relations at the end of the nineteenth century that considerable wariness beset attempts at reaching across the cultural divide, outside the privileged islands of hospitality provided by universities and literary salons. Imperial cosmopolitanism, we remember, was not cosmopolitanism *tout court*: it was always inflected by complex orientalist configurations; by a simultaneous attraction to and repulsion from those perceived as racially different and exotic. Therefore, no matter how determined the approaches of travelling Indian poets or politicians were to their British counterparts, and no matter how interested were their often liberal, open-minded hosts in reciprocating their overtures in principle—in practice, within the public arena, racial and cultural divisions pertained in the capital as they did on the colonial periphery, though not as starkly. In India, certainly, the 1857–58 Sepoy Rebellion (or Indian Mutiny) still cast a long shadow over opportunities for Indian–British interrelationship. Anglo-Indians in particular continued for decades to harbour a virulent hostility and mistrust towards Indians.[45] The matching of Indian with British cultural horizons that was to an extent possible in London, therefore, was in sharp contrast to the separation of the races in India.

Moreover, across mid-to-late nineteenth-century Europe, including Britain, as free trade idealism gave way to competitive efforts to secure colonial power through territorial possession, new theories of racial difference and superiority became more widely prevalent, underpinning and elaborating the already existing ethnographic vocabularies through which other races and cultures were categorized.[46] As colonial rivalries between Europe's great nations mounted, fears of invasion affected the wider British public for perhaps the first time since Napoleon. Individuals who looked other than English, whether in skin colour or physiognomy, were, as the century turned, increasingly singled out as subversive elements, forerunners of the ill-disciplined hordes who might at any point overrun the British Isles (as we will see in Chapter 4). This meant that, like Africans and South Sea Islanders, Indians in the press and popular literature, as well as in exhibition spaces, were often indiscriminately objectified, represented as either weird strangers or decadent Orientals.[47] Even as the empire was propagated through the outflow from Britain of manufactured goods, systems of administration, and technology, as well as settlers, at home empire operated in comparable ways to diversify the available sources of knowledge, information, entertainment, and bodily stimulation under a variety of exotic labels.[48]

Yet, in spite of these prevailing prejudices, late nineteenth-century Indian arrivants in various ways succeeded in making a place for themselves in the capital as well as in smaller British cities, especially university cities and towns—or, at worst, did not feel entirely out of place. In a word, as Ramachandra Guha writes of this period: 'the Englishman in England was less prejudiced than the Englishman abroad'.[49] As travelling colonials from around the world tended to discover, the interaction of Britain with its colonies on home ground, not least with its richest and most glamorous colonial possession, was livelier and more open than colonialist attitudes in the empire might have allowed them to expect. In nearly all cases, Indian visitors were welcomed and made to feel at home by one or more British mentor or friend: the UCL Professor Henry Morley in the case of R. C. Dutt, say, or Friedrich Max Müller in respect of K. C. Sen and a host of others.[50] On the British side, showing hospitality to Indians was regarded in both liberal and more radical circles as an important part of the work for social and religious reform.[51] Corroborating these overtures, racialized ideas concerning the hierarchical development of civilizations encouraged a view of South Asians as representatives of fallen yet ancient and sophisticated cultures and therefore as more culturally proximate to Europeans than other colonized races.[52]

In *The Indian Eye on English Life*, B. M. Malabari powerfully turns the tables on the orientalization of his countrymen with his observations that the city's 'feverish' mania for novelty and commercialism transformed its citizens into little more than primitive fetish worshippers, bowing themselves before their idols of 'Emperor Coal and King Iron'. This device of the knowing or 'civilized' put-down—a colonial judgement of others aimed to forestall judgement by them—is a trademark of the urbane Malabari's travelogue, one that he repeatedly uses to testify to his insider position in the metropolis, and which invites comparison with Collins and Dickens. Published in Bombay and London, Malabari's bullishly authoritative commentaries on English society were written up after an 1890 visit on a mission of social reform relating to Indian child marriage, and soon became paradigmatic for the many other Indian travelogues that appeared in the wake of the 1887 Golden Jubilee. The Reverend T. B. Pandian, in his *England to an Indian Eye*, subtitled *English Pictures from an Indian Camera*, published later in the same decade, for example, wrote in evident emulation of Malabari's commanding and judgemental stance, as his title reflects.[53] Gandhi, too, began in 1893 a 'Guide to London', 'the very centre of civilization', which was conceived as a way of assisting the many young Indians who bombarded him with requests for travel advice after his return to India.[54]

Throughout Malabari's now investigative, now ethnographic travelogue, he deftly styles himself as a perceptive eastern 'eye' within the west, playing the role of both observer and observed 'rambling in the field of [British] Humanity'.[55] As Burton persuasively suggests, he is particularly concerned to 'consolidate his position as the authoritative manly voice of Indian social reform', and, to do so, subscribes to several interrelated genres of self-fashioning, now as a metropolitan *flâneur*, now as a confident colonial traveller directing his masterful gaze across the city.[56] In the chapter 'Sex', for instance, this urbane self-fashioning, motivated always by his social crusade in the name of Indian women, is put to the test in public encounters with English women of different classes, so giving Malabari the opportunity to enlist those women who meet his standards of respectability to his reformist vision for India. As with Malabari, Pandian's travelogue, too, predicates its authority as a London guidebook above all on the writer's experience of *seeing* the city as an urban rambler or *flâneur*, and, relatedly, on his awareness of participating in a live tradition of writing about the metropolis from a campaigning (in this case, Christian) Indian's point of view.

One of the outstanding features of Malabari's self-projection as the Indian abroad, which Pandian amongst others emulates, is the supercilious tone he assumes in relation to his main subject, London life, which is expressive of his defensive concern to demonstrate competence in decoding the city. Standing back from the crowd 'at a safe distance' from 'the noise and bustle', sometimes in the elevated position the omnibus provides, he reports on matters ranging from the city's poor to 'British Pluck' with a brusque *savoir faire*, distilled into cutting put-downs.[57] A comparable claim to know-how from a distance marks the pages of a much earlier work of Malabari's, a collection of occasional verse, *An Indian Muse in English Garb* (1876), which is underscored in the parallelism of the two titles. Published to mark a visit of the Prince of Wales to India, the collection throws light on the tension Malabari maintained between two simultaneous but countervailing assertions in his work, that of his cultural difference (reflected in his ingratiating deference to the 'Heav'n-directed Sovereign'), and that of his familiarity with English poetry and the English language ('the current language of India—the soft, insinuating English', which 'bids fair, at no distant date, to be a world language').[58] In the same way as Malabari endeavoured with these poems to establish himself as an English-language poet, so, too, in *The Indian Eye on English Life*, did he subscribe to the ethnographic genre of investigative reportage, such as propagated in England by Henry Mayhew and others, a genre predicated on the all-seeing perspective of the reporting citizen-subject.

Yet, despite this more or less achieved magisterial position, the dominant impression Malabari's compressed prose style ultimately creates is of the ceaseless traffic of the London street, the 'hurry-scurry' and 'permanent motion' in which divisions and borderlines are constantly breached—between inside and outside, and east and west, certainly, but also between sexes and classes. Moreover, Malabari observes, Indians in London are not excluded from the endless mingling and moving. Far from it: Indian presences crop up in the text at various random intervals, as if whirled pell-mell into the Brownian motion of the crowd. There is, for instance, the '[Indian] stranger' or 'pilgrim from the East' 'rigged out' in English dress, who Malabari sees knocked down by weather and hurry. There are also the 'Indian dishes, rice and curry' that he notices feature on English menus; as well as his repeated recommendation to Indian students in London and Oxbridge to live in respectable family lodgings, which is presented as a not unattainable goal.[59] Even the scenes that do not include Indians elicit comparative remarks from Malabari, which switch deftly between British and Indian urban perspectives, as when he mishears London street cries as being spoken in Indian vernaculars. As this might suggest, Malabari's double-voiced point of view as an insider–outsider can itself be viewed, and used, as an interpretative measure of Britain's intercultural hodge-podge at this time—'great in varieties, great in contrarieties, unequalled in the power of contrasts and the wealth of extremes'—a hodge-podge which included Indian infusions, amongst many others.[60]

The form-giving influence of Indian travelogues like Malabari and Mukharji's is tellingly registered in an English novel of the same period, George Meredith's *One of Our Conquerors* (1891). One scene in particular in *One of Our Conquerors* underscores the involvement of India in British public life, confirming from a British point of view the knowledgeable and knowing position of the Indian abroad. The somewhat tortuous 'political jeremiad' of Meredith's late novel is directed at Britain's restrictive divorce laws and accompanying social hypocrisy, though satirical sideswipes are taken at nationalist bombast also.[61] The flawed hero Victor Radnor, a City of London speculator, is 'one of our conquerors', though not in a straightforward colonial sense, but rather of 'Old England's' economic sphere. Married in his youth to a moneyed older widow, Radnor wishes now to marry his mistress of twenty years' standing, Nataly, in order that their daughter Nesta might gain legitimacy. However, the novel's various frustrations concerning the ills of the English establishment, including its overtly anti-semitic aggravation at 'Hebrew' competition for 'the fruits of Commerce', are not directly at issue here.[62] For our purposes, *One of Our Conquerors* instead makes a single powerful contribution to the period's conceptualization of India-in-Britain with, close to its start, its remarkable view of the city of London, styled as if observed by a travelling Rajah.

Entitled 'The London Walk Westward', chapter 5 self-reflexively describes the London rush-hour—'the march of London citizens Eastward at morn, Westward at eve'—as Zoroastrian-type sun-worship, in the manner of a satirical ethnographic travelogue. The salient text is in fact named in the opening sentence as '*The Rajah in London* (London, Limbo and Sons, 1889)'.[63] Though the passage developing the travelogue conceit comprises a mere fraction of the novel, still it vividly conveys the extent to which, by the final decade of the nineteenth century, the Indian abroad had turned into something of a stock figure in guidebook-type overviews of city life. Even though the tone of Meredith's précis is sardonic, interspersed with tendentious quotations from a so-called 'Indian story' in verse, the rajah visitor is nonetheless regarded as a reliable vehicle for a description of 'this London, this England, Europe, world, but especially this London', in both its material 'immensity' and its moral 'hideousness'—one to rival Thomas Babington Macaulay's by now established trope of the future New Zealander's contemplation of London in ruins.[64] In contrast to the proverbial New Zealander, the Indian observer in this scene sees London in a state of sun-burnished splendour, even if raddled in many places: as the capital of his not yet ruined, yet clearly inadequate conquerors (the novel's titular irony thus becoming starkly apparent).

London is also a city the 'mysterious contrarieties' of which the Indian visitor is easily equal to analysing. Several of Meredith's devices in the passage—the framing of the Rajah's satire as a dialogue with 'his Minister'; their situation 'on board a departing vessel', tracing 'versions of the old routes', as Naipaul might say; and the self-reflexive references to their position as objective observers, including the ostentatious bibliographical reference already cited—suggest that the novelist had some knowledge of the emergent genre of the 'Indian abroad' travelogue, most probably of Mukharji's influential 1889 *A Visit to Europe*. But it also suggests, as powerfully, that the metropolitan overview delivered by the high-status Indian was one that by 1890 carried a certain literary recognizability, even a cultural caché. This quality of authoritativeness, couched in a spirit of 'sympathetic Conservatism' (associated in particular with the Rajah's Minister), would have been thrown into particular relief within the context in which the chapter was first published. *One of Our Conquerors* was first serialized in the *Fortnightly Review*, beginning in 1890. Appearing in the form of a lone-standing essay, 'The London Walk Westward' could very likely have struck a casual browser as an actual citation from an Indian travelogue. Therefore, if we accept, along with Edward Said, that literary texts were deployed in the management of colonial relationships, then the appearance of Meredith's Rajah and his Minister on the Thames in the pages first of the *Fortnightly Review* and then of the published novel, can be seen to underpin the legitimacy of the Indian visitor's role and perspective in pronouncing on London society.[65]

As the symptomatic link between the well-to-do Lizzie Eustace and the fabulously wealthy Maharajah Duleep Singh already anticipated, a key factor accounting for this relative acceptance of visiting Indians in late nineteenth-century imperial Britain was that, in sharp contrast with the racially stratified periphery, in the metropolis differences of race and ethnicity were mediated and to an extent suspended within a more dominant hierarchy of class (and to some extent of religious heterodoxy, as will be seen). This was especially the case when it came to encounters with Indians perceived to be of high status, as Martin Wainwright submits.[66] Apart from lascars, most travelling Indians from the 1870s tended to be members of elites, and hence educated in the colonial system. They were also by and large male, with the fellowship of gender in such cases also overriding, or in part bridging, racial distinctions. Far distant from the places in which authority was often brutally imposed, the British metropolis provided these male elites with a 'unique zone of encounter' where, in accordance with the ideals of the civilizing mission, British subjects of most ethnicities were given relative freedom to manipulate their status and secure recognition within an alternative hierarchy of class.[67] So it is no accident that a number of the Indians who feature in this study, including Mohini Chatterjee, Manmohan Ghose, the cousins Toru and R. C. Dutt, and Cornelia Sorabji, were either high-ranking Bengali Brahmins or Bombay Parsis, that is, stemmed from ethnic groups that had long since positioned themselves as imperial go-betweens.[68] Though a measure of racial and religious prejudice would have continued to mark their daily encounters with Londoners, as we saw, at the same time these individuals experienced the city's streets, hotels, lecture halls, and meeting rooms as relatively open and accessible public spaces, through which they were able to negotiate their way with relative confidence. With their social status effectively eliding or muting their racial difference, such travellers were, from the moment of arrival, in a reasonably good position to build bonds of amity and common purpose with their British interlocutors and hosts.[69]

Indian rajahs or princes in particular were not shy of standing upon their ceremonial rights and privileges in relation to their aristocratic counterparts in Britain. In a special case of shared status facilitating horizontal interaction, maharajahs and rajahs were received by Queen Victoria at court, with Indians from other high-ranking families also being welcomed. On such occasions, the wealthy rajahs played on and manipulated to their advantage in their dress, bearing, and manner, perceptions current in British culture of the fabulously opulent east. In related ways, T. N. Mukharji, as Government ethnographic assistant at the 1886 Indian and Colonial Exhibition, used extravagant displays of Indian arts, crafts, and traditional performances to showcase India as exotic and eastern, in this way corroborating British preconceptions of the subcontinent while also transmitting images of a unitary, culturally coherent India back to audiences at home.[70] As for the Queen, she delighted in her position as the Empress of the fabulous Raj. Arranging her décor to match her station, in 1890–91 Victoria oversaw Bhai Ram Singh's construction of the durbar room in the main wing of her private residence, Osborne House on the Isle of Wight, in an intricate Mughal style. In 1887, the year of her Golden Jubilee, as if to consolidate this domesticated Indianness (and to make up for the fact that she herself had never visited India), she took on two Indian servants, Abdul Karim and Mohammed Buksh. She famously grew particularly fond of Abdul Karim, promoting him from table waiter to clerk, taking lessons in Hindustani from him, building him a cottage, and spending much time with him in conversation.[71]

It is in one sense indubitably true, therefore, that a part-orientalized Crown presided over imperial Britain across its jubilee years, even though the rajahs' court appearances continued to pit the hierarchical differences contingent upon colonial defeat in subtle ways against the claims of aristocratic status held in common. For all the Indians' vaunted nobility, their submission to the mighty monarch at such ceremonies was always sharply dramatized by contrasting visual effects (as it also was at coronation durbars in India). One of the most pre-eminent among the later nineteenth-century Indian aristocrats, the Maharajah Duleep Singh, who arrived in Britain as a teenager after the 1849 annexation of the Punjab, lived the life of a British aristocrat at his orientalized country estate Elveden on an India Office pension, and was a frequent guest at Osborne House. However, the situation of seeming fellowship he enjoyed with his royal patron was always premised on asymmetrical power relations, as was clear from the moment when, in 1850, the young Maharajah was put under pressure to present the legendary Koh-i-Noor diamond, allegedly freely, to the Queen as a gift. (It is now set in the Crown of Queen Elizabeth II.) It was as emphatic a mark as could be of the Punjab's subservience to the British throne.[72]

As for the period's other, somewhat less privileged, though still elite, Indian arrivants, they negotiated their way through London and claimed their place in city life both through their actual exchanges with Britons on the street, in the university or meeting hall, and through various forms of cultural and literary expression, in exhibitions and performances, certainly, but also in writing, including in journalism. Across the 1880s, and until after the First World War, high-ranking Indian appearances were cited in such channels as published itineraries, court circulars, and a range of newspapers and periodicals: *The Times*, predictably, but also the *Indian Magazine and Review* and the *Illustrated London News*.[73] These channels worked in tandem with less ephemeral forms of expression such as published letters home and guidebooks (as we saw), political commentaries, and, eventually, literary sketches and poems. Embedding India-in-Britain in these different ways, the Indian writers along with English commentators like Collins or Meredith echoed and amplified the Indian comings and goings already on record elsewhere and, in so doing, at once invoked and modified some of the standard images of an exoticized India put about by the grand exhibitions. Willy-nilly they contributed to how cosmopolitan London would be viewed not only by Indians but also by its many other intercontinental visitors (as Meredith, for one, archly acknowledges).

Writing their way into the metropolis, peripatetic Indians joined in with an emergent discussion of what it meant to be a British (as against 'merely' an Indian) subject, that is, a part of Greater Britain and a citizen of empire, possessing certain political rights. At a time when a fully independent Indian nation was barely conceivable and Indian citizenship unobtainable, Indians in Britain became increasingly more involved in exploring, defining, and asserting what their broader citizenship might entail. Queen Victoria's 1858 Proclamation, and perhaps as powerfully the 1877 Proclamation of the Queen as Empress of India, energetically promoted at the time by Prime Minister Disraeli, had granted her Indian subjects, in principle, citizenship of the empire alongside and in equal measure to Britons. It was a political architecture designed to bridge the rigid bifurcation of Britain *versus* India following the 1857 Great Rebellion.[74] In the same period, historians and other commentators from the white 'brotherhood' of colonies used the pages of periodicals like the illustrated weekly *The Graphic*, W. T. Stead's *Review of Reviews* or the *Pall Mall Gazette* to explore the make-up of a 'Greater Britain' across the globe—one of the pre-eminent imperial topics of the day.[75] Greater Britain, as a global federal system linking Anglo-Saxon people, propagated in the work of Oxbridge historians like J. R. Seeley and J. A. Froude, was conceived especially by Liberals such as Seeley as a finely balanced political system, in which the lack of political representation for imperial citizens in one area, such as in India, was perceived to reduce the quality of freedom for all Greater Britain subjects.[76]

Indian opinion makers of the time took part in a linked set of discussions concerning the status of India in relation to a largely white Greater Britain; the concept of imperial citizenship 'in principle'; and, by extension, the nature of their Indian identity. These individuals included the entrepreneur Dadabhai Naoroji and the political economist R. C. Dutt, both of whom used the influential media of the pamphlet and specialist newspaper, like *India*. Logically projecting the implications of the Proclamations on to their being in Britain, they developed ideas of belonging to an expanded imperial community, a more ecumenical Greater Britain that would include both India and Britain—as opposed to Britain standing at the centre of the Greater British system.[77] For them, the Proclamations, informed by the underlying Roman concept of citizenship regardless of nationality or ethnicity, had created the sense of participating in a shared imperial subjectivity with Britons. This once again allowed them to put in suspension, at least for the period of their sojourn, certain burdens of colonial representation—as native, exotic, oriental, effeminate—and deploy the more fluid language of citizenship, and of the colonial cosmopolitan at large in the modern world, to describe themselves and their relations with the metropolis. It could even be said that their position as outsiders within, and as intercultural travellers around the empire, contributed to the production of a self-conscious 'Greater British' imperial culture. Staging their encounter with the imperial heartland, Indians' political writings and travelogues considered what it meant to be at once an Indian and a citizen of the British world.

Drawing from his knowledge as an entrepreneur in the worldwide cotton trade, the businessman-activist Dadabhai Naoroji was a particularly strong advocate for how Indian and British cultural horizons, already complicatedly knotted together by history and economics, might be more constructively interrelated, to the mutual benefit of both parties.[78] In his efforts to push Indian affairs to the centre-stage of British politics, and to protest against India's economic exploitation, Naoroji from the 1860s made contact with some of the leading Liberals and radical figures of the day, from Gladstone and Charles Dilke, through to more left-wing contacts such as Charles Bradlaugh, John Bright, and H. M. Hyndman. In tandem with Irish and radical British politicians like Michael Davitt and Wilfred Scawen Blunt, a central tenet of Naoroji's argument, expressed in work like *Poverty and Un-British Rule in India*, was that the lack of Indian political representation qualified the freedom of all imperial citizens, a claim that again highlighted the interdependence of Britain and

India.[79] M. K. Gandhi, too, drew on ideas of 'impartial' admission to 'office in our service' in the 1858 Proclamation to campaign for freer and more equal interaction between the Queen's Indian and English subjects, and the unfettered entitlement of Indians to imperial citizenship (despite legal restrictions on such entitlement).[80] Himself too shy to visit the 'Grand Old Man of India' while a student in London, Gandhi, like Naoroji, used the tool-kit of his colonial education—its language and liberal principles—in a lifelong struggle to plead for citizens' rights for diasporic Indians.[81] Some twenty years later, Jawaharlal Nehru, a student in Harrow and Cambridge (1905–12), would embark in turn on a path moulded by Gandhi's example.

In sum, the early decades of Indian migration to Britain forged 'Indian identity' from afar, positioned in relation to 'the ocean of human-life called London', as a British-made yet cosmopolitan and always open-ended concept.[82] As Wilhelm Halbfass wrote of Roy: 'in the act of presenting himself and his tradition to the foreigners, [the Indian] learns, as it were, to see himself with foreign eyes'.[83] Indianness, as well as Britishness, became something acquired and developed through the encounter with British society, both its inclusions and its discriminations, as an expression of what Ramachandra Guha calls diasporic nationalism.[84] It is small wonder therefore that the list of names of those who studied in Britain from the 1880s to the First World War read as a *Who's Who* of the nationalist movement in India.[85] At a time when most Britons failed to see any future possibility for a united India, Indians, even as they experienced England or Scotland as a unified cultural terrain, were able to transfer this field-vision of a nation eastwards, and project it onto the whole subcontinent.

IV CITY NETWORKS: 'NO ROUTE BACK'

Fundamental to an understanding of British–Indian relations in southern England in the later decades of the nineteenth century is the fact that the social and cultural worlds of both parties to the encounter had already undergone significant convergence in relation to one another. By the time they met, a degree of migration into one another's cultural zones had already taken place. To begin with, Indian visitors to Britain tended to come from cosmopolitan milieus and other in-between contexts in India, sewn together whether loosely or tightly by cross-regional and intercity groupings, movements, and organizations—which some worked to replicate abroad. This meant that they held cultural vocabularies in common with their British hosts—of citizenship, say, or civilized status, or theistic belief. Even at the time of initial contact, therefore, British hosts and their Indian guests were in a position to make a series of scalar adjustments to accommodate one another's perspectives, despite the exotic preconceptions they may mutually have entertained. For the Indian visitors, this meant that the direction of their travel was always towards Europe, as well as within the west: there was in this sense, too, as Naipaul writes in *The Enigma of Arrival*, 'no route back' to the India left behind.

Education represents an especially key factor in conceptualizing this Indian–British convergence, on both sides. Elite Indians in the period were in educational terms certainly already relative insiders to British culture. All who had passed through colonial schools and colleges had gathered an extensive knowledge of English literature and history. Nehru had read widely in the English classics by the time he came to England, as we saw earlier, and R. C. Dutt in India read out loud to his family from Walter Scott.[86] As Tapan Raychaudhuri observes in respect of the Bengali *bhadralok*, contrary to colonialist views of this intelligentsia's cultural cringe before the assumed superiority of the west, in fact Bengal's travelling intellectuals demonstrated 'a measure of self-confidence in relation to Europe', based on several decades of accumulated contact.[87]

Britons, for their part, had a more than rudimentary understanding of India due, of course, to India's longstanding colonial involvement with Britain. Radhika Mohanram writes in *Imperial White* that the interweaving of British culture by colonial cultures in this period changed how Britons saw themselves in relation to the rest of the world, shifting that self-image from an axis of separation to one of greater proximity.[88] And this meant that British cultural and spiritual departures for other shores, even if sometimes only in the imagination, in many cases moved in consort with, while also facilitating, Indian arrivals. On both sides, therefore, stood individuals who even before they encountered one another were median figures—middle men or cultural interpreters—and hence active participants in the process of making contact across the colonial divide. The Indian travellers in particular, distant from their home environments, often cut off, even if only temporarily, from their caste backgrounds, were in several ways receptive to new ideas and experiences. They were, by definition, modern in outlook.[89]

Gandhi's 'Experiments in Dietetics', chapter xiv of his *Autobiography*, offers a metonymic account of the reciprocal in-tandem exploration of the modern that characterized India-in-Britain. In his case, the convergence of his interests and perspectives with those he met in the metropolis grew out of the fortuitous coincidence of the 'new cult' of vegetarianism (in particular, a vigorous outreach campaign by the London Vegetarian Society), with his own concerted efforts to maintain caste conditions in respect of food.[90] The *Autobiography*'s sketch of Gandhi the questing vegetarian gives a vivid picture of the myriad pathways he traced through London searching for appropriate food and a suitable way of being:

> I would trot ten or twelve miles each day, go into a cheap restaurant and eat my fill of bread, but would never be satisfied. During these wanderings I once hit on a vegetarian restaurant in Farringdon Street. The sight of it filled me with the same joy that a child feels on getting a thing after its own heart. Before I entered I noticed books for sale exhibited under a glass window near the door. I saw among them Salt's *Plea for Vegetarianism*. This I purchased for a shilling and went straight to the dining room. This was my first hearty meal since my arrival in England.[91]

As the movement of Gandhi's syntax suggests, to this hungry Indian vegetarian the discovery of the book felt tantamount to being given a meal. From this point on, with Salt's scientific and moral manifesto in hand to guide his eating, he became certain he would be able to cope in England.

As Gandhi makes clear, it is England and not India that therefore 'converts' him into being a convinced vegetarian. And it is vegetarianism that gives him access to the energetic group of English reformers who would henceforth shape his political views, as well as providing him with reading materials, restaurant listings, and journalistic opportunities. Setting a seal on these new vegetarian associations, Gandhi would later become a member of the London Vegetarian Society Executive, and even went on to establish his own vegetarian club, with Sir Edwin Arnold as Vice-President. Vegetarianism provided him with a mode of ethical communion with the English that would foster deeper sympathies with India, while also 'facilitating the way of other Indians to England a great deal', as he wrote in *The Vegetarian* in 1894.[92] As his experience of theosophy also demonstrates, his exposure to eastern and western books standing side-by-side on the shelves of London's bookshops allowed him to develop a consolidated and increasingly radical sense of himself as an Indian as well as a citizen of the empire, as Hindu as well as cosmopolitan. Metropolitan London at once allowed him to reach beyond the confines of his provincial point of view, yet returned him to himself as an Indian. The same process of simultaneous opening out and self-consolidation was to be experienced by many other travelling Indians—students, poets, doctors, gurus—when they visited the capital.

Gandhi's picture of the dovetailing between English and Indian lifestyle choices and cultural interests is reflected in other contemporary reports on Indian–British encounters in the metropolis. The following short account in the London *Daily News* by an anonymous Ceylonese visitor to the 1886 Indian and Colonial Exhibition once again underlines in precise terms the perception on the part of visiting South Asians that their approach to Britain was on the basis of cultural proximity and recognition, even a perceived unique status. The Ceylonese correspondent registers his awareness of a new, yet not entirely unfamiliar or remote, cosmopolitan diversity, one which would be echoed in the slightly later travel writings of Lala Baijnath, B. M. Malabari, and others.[93]

> The Englishman here is very common. When he comes to Ceylon he is a great man; but a black man is a great man in England...
>
> Still a large number of people come to the Exhibition... Who thought when I first said I would come to England on account of the sea, that I would see peoples of all the world ['Africans, Maoris, Fijians, Cypriots, Rajpoots, Chinese, Japanese, Russians, French, Americans', he glosses elsewhere]?... It must be owing to this that everyone likes to see England.[94]

An immediately striking aspect of these lines is the way in which the Ceylonese participant draws explicatory analogies between home and abroad, Ceylon and London, while at the same time cross-hatching these with shifting ideas of relative scale: 'A black man is a great man in England.' As his remarks imply, social configurations existed whereby a South Asian traveller, who may well have experienced colonial discrimination on the subcontinent, might be made to feel welcome in the capital. Indeed, as when high-ranking Indians were presented at court, in certain cases his or her presence could be regarded as an enhancement of the high imperial and Greater British (even 'world') status of the host city.

The Ceylonese reporter's remarks make for an interesting comparison with B. M. Malabari's pointed response to London's at once enjoyable and enervating 'modern civilization' in *The Indian Eye on English Life*, introduced earlier—despite the obvious contrasts between the one's plain-spoken reportage, and the other's educated literary and biblical references. Reflecting on London's 'high pressure material progress', Malabari comments:

> Anyhow it is hopeless to stem the tide of this modern civilization. If it shortens life, does it not make it more enjoyable? *Better fifty years of Europe than a cycle of Cathay.* This artificial civilization, dominated by King Coal and Emperor Iron, and typified as Kaliyuga by the wise men of the East, has its price, which is paid every day in disease and death, in accident and crime. (p. 46)

There is in these lines, as before, a rapid shuttling between different scales of value, though the graduations of tone are more sophisticated than in the Ceylonese example, especially in so far as Malabari's admiration for the progress London embodies is cut across by his distress at its deleterious social consequences, as it is throughout *The Indian Eye on English Life*.[95] The weight of his indictment rests on the highlighted quotation from Tennyson's 'Locksley Hall', which at one level he uses to vaunt the achievements of the west (and his own cultural knowledge), in the tone of Thomas Babington Macaulay's praise for western books in his 1835 Minute. Yet, in relation to the juxtaposed references to poverty and crime, the knowing citation from Tennyson is simultaneously also undercut and exposed for the vainglorious cultural boasting it is. It is a notable instance of Malibari's double-voicing: fifty years of Europe resemble nothing so much as the dark period of civilizational chaos called the *Kaliyuga* in the Hindu scriptures. The convergence of bicultural reference points and actual geographical pathways that he accomplishes is extremely subtle. An Indian commentator here deploys his copious knowledge of English poetry, acquired as part of his colonial upbringing, in order to pronounce on the state of England, yet also to withdraw into a removed, if not countervailing position, that is sympathetic to India.

A key point of agreement between the extracts from Gandhi, the Ceylonese, and Malabari concerns their relative familiarity with city life. Despite predictable differences of context and perspective, it is evident that all three South Asian travellers came from similar urban domains, the great and growing cities of India, worlds that in many ways stood closer to metropolitan Britain than did England's towns and villages, and so could be conceptualized—and were experienced as—converging spaces. As was seen also with travellers' responses to the Suez Canal, their reports on their encounter with the west were profoundly informed by this relative cultural proximity—a proximity that intensified with colonial expansion and the ramification of the empire's communication networks. Indian cities like Calcutta and Bombay, which had grown up as trading ports, or Delhi, from 1911 the new imperial capital, were in many respects therefore not merely colonial, but transregional and intercultural environments, distinguished by their cosmopolitan character and heterogeneous social relations.

As Malabari's comparative remarks suggest, the large Indian cities, even when viewed in relation to a significantly larger London, could be regarded in this period not so much as extremes, but as points on a sliding scale of urban complexity. To some extent, these cities' structures—their civic architecture, market place layout, maidans and esplanades, and other aspects of urban planning—replicated one another, having been designed and built by similarly trained and educated planners and architects, in some cases as if in one another's image. So London may have been as familiar or unfamiliar to peripatetic Bombay or Calcutta citizens as their own home cities, not because these had been modelled on London *per se*, but because of the serial formation of social spaces and structures under empire famously described by Benedict Anderson.[96] Theorizing the multisited emergence of global modernity, Partha Mitter in *The Triumph of Modernism* explores in related terms how the 'hybrid cosmopolises' of the Indian colonial world, Bombay and Calcutta, operated as crucibles for peripheral or lateral modernist formations.[97] As his examples suggest, the vectors of such global city formations ran in multiple different directions, and did not merely radiate out from London: indeed, it was their complex seriality that shaped their modernity.[98]

By the time of Victoria's two Jubilee celebrations of 1887 and 1897, therefore, during that period when Indians were arriving in Britain in more significant numbers than had previously been the case, the interactive cultural worlds of the global city were being created and recreated across the empire on a daily basis, mainly through the operation of the print media, but also through the not unrelated spread of the imperial *lingua franca*, English. The unchanging format of the daily newspaper, in particular, whether produced in Bombay or London, often though not exclusively in English, replicated social imaginaries from one city to another, wherever in the world it was produced. A telling example of this at once formal and imaginary replication can be found in the way in which Malabari used the Bombay newspapers, in particular his own *Indian Spectator*, to agitate for sexual reform in India at more or less the same time that the journalist campaigner W. T. Stead was writing for the London media to the same ends—and no doubt with a sideways glance at the influential Stead's work.[99] Through their participation in the empire's burgeoning print cultures, therefore, elite inhabitants of Bombay, Calcutta, and London, amongst other colonial cities, can be seen to have shared in a loose corpus of ideas of the modern and the cosmopolitan that drew them into a global virtual community—a community that was in part fostered within the precincts of their own cities.

Equipped with these powerful city imaginaries, late nineteenth-century Indian travellers, when they reached the imperial metropolis, inevitably read its public spaces through a standardized vocabulary of the urban everyday acquired as part of their city experience in India, which included their newspaper reading. And though London was generally seen to be far larger and more crowded than their home cities, still it was the case that the features these travellers singled out for comment had already been formalized as synecdoches or codes of a global city life drawn from what they knew of Indian cities, or what Mitter might term their 'virtual cosmopolitan' know-how. So when Malabari in his travelogue picks out such noteworthy features of London life as its many modes of public transport, or its 'circulars and advertisements', he is reading these not *ex nihilo*, but against an already existing index of city experience.

The replication of an urban imaginary through print technology is persuasively illustrated in the example offered by the relatively unknown, yet for all that representative provincial paper, the *Indian Mirror*, the weekly journal of the Calcutta Brahmo Samaj.[100] Like the later *Modern Review* (1907), the Calcutta monthly associated with Bengal's modernist art movement, the *Indian Mirror* was broadly liberal nationalist and reformist, much concerned with the measure of 'Indian loyalty to the Crown'. Its four-page broadsheet featured short reports on foreign news (often relating to India, such as Irish Home Rule developments) and civic notices (concerning temporary closures of the Hooghly Bridge, for example), alongside reviews of local cultural events: a performance of the *Mahasheta* at the Opera House, for instance, where 'a well-written English synopsis of the piece' was 'placed into the hands of those who could not follow it in the original'. As in other metropolitan as well as regional newspapers of the day, these notices and reviews were juxtaposed with advertisements concentrated in the side columns and on the back page. Some of the advertisements interestingly featured businesses (publishers, opticians) with outlets in London and Bombay, as well as Calcutta. Lawrence and Mayo opticians, who advertised their 'perfect pebble' spectacles in the *Indian Mirror*'s pages, boasted of offices at 1A Old Bond Street in London, Rampart Row, Bombay, and 3–4 Hare Street, Calcutta.[101]

In respect of virtual cosmopolitanism, perhaps the most interesting articles in the 1886 *Indian Mirror* were its almost daily reports on the Government of India's Colonial and Indian Exhibition in London, which highlighted both insignificant and important features and events. The detail lavished on a description of the installation of the display cases, or an address by the Prince of Wales, created a striking effect of close yet transnational focus, certainly when compared to the same paper's far briefer, broad-brush reports on Calcutta-based events. From the point of view of the *Indian Mirror* (or indeed other of India's regional newspapers, such as the *Bombay Gazette*), it is as if the Exhibition were taking place, not thousands of miles away, but in a parallel world proximate to Calcutta. As this suggests, the imperial communications networks that sustained the newspapers created so dynamic a connectivity between the empire's cities that, in local readers' imaginations at least, the peripheries could be regarded as less distant from the metropolis than the latter's elevated status implied. Within these lively networks, Indian tourists writing on the Exhibition in London might overnight convert their travel notes into newspaper columns for Calcutta or Colombo newspapers (and subsequently, as we saw, into guidebooks for later travellers), and Thomas Cook and Sons set out to reinforce existing intercultural links by arranging regular tours from India to the Exhibition via the Suez Canal. Within the 'mirror' worlds of the *Indian Mirror*, therefore, the India being staged abroad could be placed cheek-by-jowl with the India being lived at home, within the time frame of a single day. The interconnected narrative world implied in the repackaged and juxtaposed reports found no suture between these different Indias, just as the London-based newspapers, too, were conjuring into being an increasingly globalized world through intersplicing stories from the colonies with reports on Britain.

From the perspective of the individual Indian traveller, somewhat smaller-scale channels also facilitated important interactions between the distant geographies he or she straddled. Another vital element within the networked landscape that connected Indians and Britons in this period, which served as the underlay or infrastructure, as it were, to its intercultural relations, comprised the many organizations and fraternities in which they were involved. Indians abroad often belonged to a number of these at times overlapping political and religious, nationalist and philanthropic, reformist and cosmopolitan groupings. For those who were students, the institutions and colleges they attended also formed an important part of this underlay, especially as these educational sites were relatively small in number, which meant that their pathways there often crossed. The opportunities for fostering social relations and moulding reading experiences that these groups and institutions created were extremely significant, as were the meeting- or crossing-points that existed within the networks, sites where Indians and their British hosts could meet and socialize. These ranged from places of worship such as temples, mosques, Unitarian meeting halls, and Theosophical Lodges, to Tottenham Court Road curry houses, hotel lobbies, and private homes, including Naoroji's Bloomsbury home or 'Kidderpore' in Croydon, home of the prominent Indian advocate W. C. Bonnerjee. As did the newspaper, but in more concrete, immediate ways, these political groups, religious organizations, educational institutions and weekend 'at homes' drew Indian visitors to Britain together, and drew them closer to their British hosts. Through these networks they were able to juxtapose English and Indian cultural worlds, as well as different ideas of India and ways of being Indian. It is this pell-mell and interwoven sense of the world that Meredith's travelling Rajah represents in *One of Our Conquerors*. And it is a related syncretic view of the world or 'Anima Mundi' that W. B. Yeats's 1880s involvement with the Theosophical Society in Dublin and the Hermetic Society of the Golden Dawn in London allowed him to create in order to begin to shape a mythology for his poetry.

One of the more prominent and long-lasting formal organizations set up in Britain for Indians was probably the National Indian Association (NIA). First founded in 1867 in Bristol by Mary Carpenter, a friend to Rammohan Roy and K. C. Sen, the organization operated from 1877 out of the Maida Vale home of the social reformer Elizabeth Adelaide Manning. The NIA offered pastoral care and advice to Indian students, and organized lectures and soirées where they could meet. Its monthly, the *Indian Magazine and Review*, along with its *Handbook of Information*, served as a useful information hub for most, if not all, Indian visitors to London. In the early twentieth century, the NIA re-formed as the aptly named, apparently apolitically constituted Bureau of Information for Indian Students. Though prominent however, the NIA was by no means the only organization dedicated to superintending and connecting Indians in Britain. Anjuman-e-Islam, a related group with a Muslim focus, was formed in 1886 by Abdullah Al-Mamoon Sohraworthy, and its meetings were attended by Gandhi. In the political sphere, the London India Society, first established in 1865, was in 1867 formally reconstituted as the East India Association (EIA) by influential Indians including Naoroji and W. C. Bonnerjee. Its campaigning agenda brought Britons and Indians together to seek political reform within the Raj. In 1889, the British Committee of the Indian National Congress (BC INC) emerged out of the EIA, once again steered by Naoroji. Its journal *India* (1900) aimed to put the Indian point of view on responsible government and self-determination before an interested British public. In contrast to the EIA and the BC INC's political focus, the Northbrook Indian Society followed a pastoral programme of guardianship especially for Indians boarding with English families, not unlike the NIA. Established in 1879, the Northbrook Society met first in Bedford Row and then at 3 Whitehall Gardens, and endeavoured to involve both Indian and English gentlemen in welcoming Indians to London, using funds drawn from India. As this strongly suggests, the underlying connective tissue of these groups, their make-up, agendas, and wider support networks, repeatedly crossed, diverged, and again intertwined, returning always to an ongoing concern with Indian well-being, identity, and citizenship. When, some decades later, as will be seen, the India Society (1910) was founded, its interest in questions of Indian art and self-definition overlapped with the aims of these early organizations, though the India Society's agenda in respect of self-representation was explicitly cultural rather than political.

From the mid-1800s, Britain's older established universities, Cambridge and Oxford (despite continuing confessional and subject-area restrictions), and Edinburgh and University College London (secular and non-sectarian to varying degrees), were the preferred institutions of higher learning for Indian students, as were London's Inns of Court for would-be lawyers.[102] Where universities like Oxford and Cambridge had long looked to India for philological and historical understanding, India now, in its turn, approached these institutions in pursuit of higher learning and a deeper knowledge of the west, as well as professional qualifications and career advancement. By the final third of the nineteenth century, therefore, these bedrock British institutions were variously marked by their contact with India—by the presence of Indian students first and foremost, but also of Indian studies (philological, legal, and religious), as well as of forums for political debate, most notably the Cambridge and Oxford Majlis societies. Founded in 1891 and 1896, respectively, and modelled on the University Unions, the Majlis societies gave the opportunity to Indians from different regional, political, and cultural backgrounds to come together to debate and socialize, encouraging its members to see themselves, perhaps for the first time, as Indians first and foremost (and so to begin to imagine how India might be constituted as a nation).[103] When the number of Indians at Oxford in the first half of the twentieth century peaked in 1922, with 149 students enrolled, nearly all were in the Majlis. In 1887, a University of Oxford statute allowed a number of named universities within the empire 'affiliated status', which gave exemption from matriculation requirements, permitting students from these universities to take the three-year Oxford undergraduate degree in just two years. This immediately increased the number of Indians able to study at Oxford, though academic positions in 'Indian' subjects like Sanskrit tended until later on to be held by Europeans. As for London's Inns of Court, including the Inner Temple, where both Gandhi and Nehru studied for the Bar, from the 1880s these formed a destination of choice for Indians, as well as other colonial students seeking entry into this most prestigious branch of the legal profession. A 1907 India Office study reported that of the 700 Indian students then in Britain, nearly half were enrolled in the Inns of Court.[104]

Oxford, with its Indian Institute, formed a particularly important lodestone for Indian students throughout the period in question, over and above even Cambridge. Though Oxford University retained the requirement that all students affirm the Church of England's 39 Articles of Faith on matriculating and graduating longer than did Cambridge, under the Vice-Chancellorship of Benjamin Jowett (from 1883), a number of the more prominent colleges, including his own Balliol, began to build stronger imperial links and to show a new openness to colonial, and specifically Indian, interests and concerns. In Jowett's view, the university should rise to and consolidate its central position as a place of imperial knowledge gathering and dissemination, and do so in particular by educating its administrative elites. The ICS examinations were accordingly reshaped to attract graduates in the Literae Humaniores or 'Greats', with the result that the study of the Classics at Oxford was turned into a secular training ground for colonial officers. Already, in the 1860s, a teacher of Hindustani and a Reader in Indian Law and History had been appointed to stand alongside the Boden Professor of Sanskrit in training up ICS officers. In the period 1892–1914, Oxford duly produced more ICS officers than any other university, a small proportion of whom were Indian.[105] Between 1871 and 1893, forty-nine Indian students matriculated at Oxford, including Manmohan Ghose. Thirty-two were present in 1907.[106]

Many Indian students were especially attracted by Oxford because of its Indian Institute (1884), the brainchild of Sanskrit Professor Monier Monier-Williams, which rapidly turned into a dynamic and influential zone of encounter between Indians and Britons. From the 1870s, all ICS candidates, both British and Indian, were required to take a probationary year of language learning and general administrative training after passing their final university examinations. It was Monier-Williams's idea that these activities best be housed in a properly constituted study centre, with its own library and museum, which could become a place of interaction for all who were engaged in Indian and Oriental Studies. With an Indian Institute in place, he believed, Oxford would assume the vital role not merely of bringing eastern knowledge to the west but, as part of the imperial civilizing mission, of representing western knowledge to the east. To give concrete shape to this idea he travelled several times to India to secure moral and financial support for the centre from among the Indian Princes. Opened by Vice-Chancellor Jowett, the Institute over the years played host to a wide range of students, visiting scholars, and academics, one of the first and most prominent of which was the later radical nationalist Shyamaji Krishnavarma (1857–1930), who worked as Monier-Williams's assistant from 1879 to 1883.[107] Founded on assumptions of western cultural superiority, the Institute turned into an interesting example of a colonial structure that in practice produced levelling and even radicalizing effects, especially within the dimension of interpersonal relations. Within the four walls of the Indian Institute, Indian students and their British counterparts, many among them future civil servants of the empire, came together in a wide-ranging discussion about the make-up of a Greater Britain across the globe, and the place of India within that imagined federation. The traffic of Indians and friends to India through the Indian Institute continued across the ensuing decades to feature many prominent names, from the visitors that Professor Max Müller hosted in the 1880s and 1890s, as will be seen, to the visit of a garlanded Rabindranath Tagore in 1913.

Yet the Institute was not the only venue for Indian–British interaction within the universities, though it may have been one of the best known. The college environment, too, with its clubs, societies, and sports teams, created strong and lasting bonds between Indian and British students, tutors, and alumni. From this period, the pages of College Registers unostentatiously, if indelibly, list Indian names alongside their British counterparts: they are seen to participate side-by-side in the matriculation ceremony and to take their tutorials together.[108] In due course, Indian students were also invited to take part in the different societies, or at least befriended British students who were members, as is instanced in the 1910s collaboration between the Cambridge Apostle and mathematician G. H. Hardy and the Indian mathematical genius Ramanujan (see the Coda). Outside tutorial and society hours, the university context, whether in Oxbridge or elsewhere, fostered many other informal, extra-curricular relations, such as the friendship between Jowett, then Master of Balliol, and the Parsi law student Cornelia Sorabji, and between Sorabji and the Sanskrit scholar Professor Max Müller, which developed while she was a student at Somerville College.

Victorian interests in alternative forms of religious belief provided other important stimuli to late nineteenth-century British webs of interconnection, not only with India or other parts of the wider British world, but also between different social groups in Britain. Indeed, the reception of India and Indians in the late 1800s is hardly explicable without reference to the ongoing crisis of established faith and the new climate of religious seeking and experimentation for which Hinduism and Buddhism both supplied rich treasure troves. The popular acclaim and interest that greeted Edwin Arnold's *The Light of Asia* offers a particularly strong indication, as was seen, of the new appeal in western society at large of eastern religious ideas. To the same extent that spiritualist, revivalist, and evangelical groups offered vocational and status opportunities to women, so too were visitors from other cultures made to feel welcome within these groups' progressive and relatively democratic structures. It is no accident therefore that the receptivity of Britons to Indian philosophy and beliefs from the late 1870s onwards, and at an everyday level the influx of Indians into British boarding houses and guest homes, coincided with what Alex Owen calls the golden age of spiritualism.[109]

Unitarianism and theosophy in particular stand out in these years as religious or spiritualist formations that provided important intellectual zones of encounter for Indians with Britain, where they were assured of hospitality and had access to a relatively free and open exchange of ideas. The pioneering utopian poet and socialist philosopher Edward Carpenter, for example, was one of those strongly drawn to the Hindu ideas of spiritual enlightenment that had in part been introduced to western audiences by theosophy, though he would remain dubious about theosophy's exclusive claims to eastern truth. Capturing these complexities of allegiance, he observed in his memoir *My Days and Dreams* (1916):

> ...during the years '80 to '90 there was a great deal of Theosophy and Oriental philosophy of various sorts current in England and much talk and speculation, sometimes very ill-founded, about 'adepts', 'mahatmas' and 'gurus'. I too felt a desire to see for myself one of these representatives of the ancient wisdom.[110]

Carpenter's quickened interest in the ideas brought to Europe by visiting Indian seers, who themselves moved within the travelling belief-system that was theosophy, is highly characteristic of Indian–British contact in this period: a search for authenticity by way of an 'ancient wisdom' that was already transplanted and reinvented.[111] Just as the Theosophical Society opened avenues of spiritual exploration to Indians like Gandhi, so, too, for Britons, the Indian mystical and philosophical ideas to which theosophy exposed western seekers offered ways of conceiving a more egalitarian society.

Edward Carpenter first came into contact with Buddhist and Hindu religious thought as a student at Christ's College, Cambridge, in the late 1860s, beginning with his reading of the *Bhagavad-gita*, a text that his Ceylonese friend and fellow Cambridge student Arunachalam had recommended.[112] Arunachalam, the first from his island to pass the Civil Service examinations and later a District Judge and social reformer, worked hard, like many of his South Asian counterparts, to keep his admiration for the west's modern energy in balance with his Hindu beliefs, and frequently dispensed advice to his friend in England from his vantage point in Ceylon.[113] Yet the Vedantic ideas Carpenter derived from his reading, in particular of the soul's passionate encounter with God, were also ignited by his close study of both the American transcendentalists and the radical poet Walt Whitman, who likewise acknowledged Indian influences on their thinking.[114] In Carpenter's view, Whitman's celebration of the interconnection of body and spirit, and of nature and engineering, laid down possibilities for a transformation of consciousness without which social and political change could not be achieved. Through this mix of Whitman and 'theosophized' Vedantic philosophy, Carpenter charted his own 'passage to India', in Whitman's signature phrase, advocating ideas of comradeship, brotherhood, and cultural interrelationship that fostered his disaffection with colonialism, and extended an eastern gloss across his oeuvre. Though he never entirely lost his Eurocentric cultural preconceptions regarding the natural hierarchy of civilizations, Carpenter enlarged his faith in 'the essential oneness of humanity everywhere' by travelling through Ceylon and the Indian subcontinent in 1890, a journey described in *From Adam's Peak to Elephanta* (1892).[115] Believing in a radical simplification and purification of life, he was an advocate for vegetarianism and naturalism, and had links with Henry Salt of the Humanitarian League, whom Gandhi also knew, as well as with the reformers Annie Besant, Olive Schreiner, and Sarojini Naidu. In a vivid illustration of the conceptual feedback loop or 'world-wide circle' in which some of the alternative thinkers of the day, both Indian and British, were engaged, Carpenter's view of western 'civilization' (or, to him, capitalist competition) as a pollution to be abandoned, that he expounded in *Civilization: Its Cause and Cure* (1889), imprinted noticeably on Gandhi's 1910 *Hind Swaraj*, the Indian leader having read Carpenter while a student in London.

The Unitarian movement, a denomination of Christianity based in Bristol and the West Country, enjoyed an especially longstanding bond with India, one that stemmed from the 1830s, when it hosted the Indian theist Rammohun Roy (1772–1833), and from its subsequent custodianship of his grave. Following the appointment of the Reverend James Drummond as Principal in 1885, Manchester College in Oxford offered an institutional home to Unitarian and other free religious thought, and welcomed a long line of Indian visitors and students through its doors.[116] The Unitarians' rational approach to religion, and view of Jesus Christ as a messenger, not God incarnate, rested on a commitment to civil and religious liberty, and an effort to accommodate the discoveries of science to religious belief. Even in Roy's time, its monotheistic tendency, which involved a rejection of the Anglican doctrine of the Trinity, provided a particularly hospitable venue for reformist Hindu groups as they developed their own forms of monotheism—most notably, the Brahmo Samaj.[117] Roy's death on his visit to the Bristol Unitarians in 1833 if anything embedded such patterns of intellectual exchange more deeply in the future development of Unitarian thought.[118] Many of Roy's successors on his journey into the west, not least K. C. Sen, discussed at the end of this chapter, had the sense of walking in Roy's spiritual company. He was the first, wrote Professor Max Müller, deploying a striking image of circuitry, 'who came from East to West, the first to join hands and to complete that world-wide circle through which henceforth, like an electric current, Oriental thought could run to the West and Western thought return to the East'.[119] Acting always with the example of Roy in mind, the Unitarian group around Mary Carpenter, Sen's Bristol host, developed those strong and lasting links between British feminists and Indian social reformers that were to prove binding in other related groups also, including the Theosophical Society.

The Theosophical Society was founded in 1875 in New York by the Russian clairvoyant Madame H. P. Blavatsky and her collaborator Colonel Olcott, and provided the first, and certainly one of the most influential, western platforms for the exploration of eastern mysticism and the study of the Sanskrit classics. Within the wider landscape of nineteenth-century religious seeking, where Christianity was coming under pressure from new explorations in evolutionary science, the Theosophical Society's esoteric philosophy accommodated Hindu and Buddhist motifs to western religious expectations in spiritually compelling and emotionally convincing ways. Theosophy not only addressed prevalent concerns and questions about the nature of god and the godliness of man; it also projected topical ideas of human evolution on to the plane of consciousness, rather than biology alone.[120] Though theosophy rested on orientalist underpinnings that represented the east as fallen from a Vedic golden age (and so bears the imprint of Max Müller's scholarship), theosophical allegiances at the same time involved a respectful consideration of non-western religious and cultural traditions and, as such, laid the ground for a countervailing critique of western society—something that Annie Besant, for example, achieved in her life and work. With its emphasis on scientific system and method, and its harmonization of religious ideas with the claims of modern science, the Society excited interest among many different alternative thinkers, and rapidly branched into several European cities. An eastern headquarters was set up in Adjar, in Madras, thus linking this Indian city, as the European cities had also been, into theosophical networks.

Even though its interpretation of Hindu spirituality always retained recognizable western aspects (not least in linguistic terms), the Theosophical Society supplied a rich context in the late nineteenth century for the exploration and cross-fertilization of religious, mystical, philosophical, and philological ideas. Especially from the vantage point of Indian visitors to the west, the Theosophical Society was of crucial importance for situating ancient India as the heartland of ancient wisdom, rather than the more conventional occult centre of Egypt, and therefore provided opportunities for Indians to reconcile their modern aspirations to scientific understanding with traditional ideas of the soul (as in Vivekananda's thinking). Moreover, predicated on an ideal of universal brotherhood as it was, the Society saw no barrier to integration and exchange in other domains also, including the social. As such, theosophy opened an inviting door to many individuals seeking new ways of being in an interconnected modern society, not least travelling Indians new to Britain. Nationalists and New Women, socialists and aesthetes, celebrity gurus from India, as well as more everyday voyagers found in the Society open avenues through which to articulate new questions about the world and the self that bore little relationship to the hierarchies of the past. With the conversion to theosophy in May 1889 of the prominent feminist and socialist Annie Besant, who rapidly established herself also as a friend to Indians, the 'new message' of the Society became firmly embedded in the migrant Indian imagination.

As the pages of the theosophical magazine *Lucifer* (1887–97) record, by the late 1880s, the time when Gandhi first came into contact with the Society, theosophical meetings in London had already become a lively hub of traffic between India and Britain.[121] At these meetings, Indian spiritual experts, gurus, and seers socialized, gave addresses, and dispensed advice. In many cases, they then went on to perform similar functions elsewhere, in America or Europe, such as, most notably, at the vast junction of spiritual exchange that was the 1893 Chicago World Parliament of Religions. On 4 August 1889, for example, *Lucifer* reported that Besant gave the first of two lectures at the Hall of Science, Old Street, about the process of truth seeking that led her from free-thinking Fabianism to theosophy, and met with 'vociferous and prolonged applause' from the audience of Free Thought Party members, while 'the Hindu gentlemen who were present, conspicuous by their quiet mien, nodded their frequent approval in silent but significant manner'.[122] These guru-figures, regarded as tantamount to theosophical VIPs, contrasted in powerful ways with the stereotype of the exotic oriental, the standard-issue snake charmer, current in the British media, including periodicals like the *Strand Magazine* or the *Nineteenth Century*.[123] Gandhi, who is known to have heard Besant speak, can be imagined as part of this company. In October 1889, a couple of months after Besant's talk, another Society lecture, 'The Theosophical Society and its Work', given by the President Colonel Olcott at the South Place Institute, once again drew an audience of 'all sorts and conditions of men,' including: 'the dark-skinned children of India and of Japan. Keen-eyed thinker jostled against dreamy-eyed enthusiast, poet rubbed shoulders with doctor, and women were as eager and earnest as men.'[124] As these examples suggest, the Theosophical Society's many lectures, meetings, and charity events (including a November 1892 'Indian bazaar' exhibiting 'the best of Eastern art and industry'), held in community halls and institutes, as well as at its base at 19 Avenue Road, brought Indians and Britons together in a constantly shifting and amiable proximity.[125] Yeats, too, as we will shortly see, first encountered both Indians and Indian philosophy at theosophical meetings in Dublin.

In assessing the almost immeasurable influence of theosophy on the reception of Indians in Britain, Gandhi's example is instructive. For Gandhi, theosophy served as the ecumenical umbrella under which he felt able to approach certain aspects of Hindu as well as Christian belief, in both cases for the first time. As he narrates in his *Autobiography*, he traced a pathway back from London to Hindu and then Buddhist thought via his reading of Edwin Arnold's *The Light of Asia* (1879), his life of the Buddha, and *The Song Celestial*, Arnold's translation of the *Bhagavad-gita*, books that were introduced to him in 1891 by 'two Theosophist brothers', most likely Bertram and Archibald Keightley (in fact uncle and nephew), whose Notting Hill home was placed at the Society's disposal. Though Gandhi may have become an associate member, he did not himself formally join the Society, partly because he believed his meagre knowledge of Hinduism would be shown up if he did so. At the same time, he openly acknowledged that Blavatsky's syncretic *The Secret Doctrine* (1888), along with Arnold's work dismantled many of his long-held prejudices about Hinduism. Reading *The Light of Asia*, like reading Salt, in effect helped Gandhi to become, while in London, more of an Indian. So, too, Arunachalam, the Ceylonese mystic and friend to Edward Carpenter, found his way to Buddhism through theosophy while a student in Cambridge. For these and many other South Asians, as the nationalist B. C. Pal was later to write, theosophy played the crucial role of overturning stereotypes of Indian degradation and so '[raising Indians] in their own estimation'.[126] It was in this way that the Society laid the ground for the Hindu religious revival that from the 1890s brought a new wave of Indian visitors to Britain, including the Swami Vivekananda. Not surprisingly, as the Swami's itineraries show, many of his talks and presentations in England were facilitated and hosted by the Theosophical Society.[127]

V A POETICS OF CROSSING: 'THAT WORLD-WIDE CIRCLE . . . LIKE AN ELECTRIC CURRENT'

The connectivity or call-and-response between India and Britain, here necessarily including Ireland, that had such diffuse and intriguing effects on metropolitan letters and culture in the decades from 1870 can be reconnoitred not only through encounters recorded in diaries and memoirs. Interconnectedness also imprints on the textual matter itself, the correspondence, poetry, and other writing that emerged out of these Indian–British relations. In some cases—as here with the letters from the Brahmo Samaj reformer K. C. Sen to Professor Friedrich Max Müller—the correspondence remained private and remote from the public record, though the correspondents' public lives and interests shaped its contours. In other cases—as with W. B. Yeats's early poems infused with images from Indian legends—the interaction with India was deliberately attention seeking, an expression of the poet's quest for an authoritative esoteric voice—though one that in due course led him back to developing closer connections with a mythologized ancient Ireland. In both instances, however, the wrought expressions of interest in and identification with India that emerge from these writings highlight once again the convergence of social, cultural, and formal perspectives that Indian visits to Britain brought about, and begin to outline the dimensions of what might be called a poetics of intercultural crossing.

An eloquent instance of late Victorian inscription linking India and Britain may be found in the many papers held under the name Friedrich Max Müller in Oxford's Bodleian library—which also throws light once again on Oxford's special position as a zone of Indian–British encounter. Unlike the many published books and lectures on ancient Hindu texts and religious traditions the great Indianist produced across his career, this document is a bound book of letters from Indian friends and contacts in India, addressed to the eminent Professor of Comparative Philology in Oxford.[128] Collected by him across the 1880s, the 'text', such as it is, is marked throughout by that 'vast and sincere regard' for Hinduism (his phrase) that the Professor evidently shared with his Indian correspondents, many of them linked to the reformist Brahmo Samaj. This regard is palpable from the letters' content: from the professional approval they seek, or the advice they either offer or solicit on questions of philological or religious interpretation—questions which, significantly, are often picked up from reports in the Indian press, as well as from the scholar's own publications. But the sense of mutual regard for each other's traditions is palpable, too, in Max Müller's marginal instructions to himself, mainly in pencil, to keep certain letters, marking them up for binding in book form (as they then were by his wife after his death, though his own letters to his Indian friends have been lost).

Though F. Max Müller himself never visited India, he made a career of his study of the ancient Indo-European languages, especially Sanskrit, believing these tongues to be closely tied to the cultural and religious systems of the peoples from which they sprang. Though his comparative Romantic approach to the study of religion (as nature worship rather than divine revelation) created controversy both within Oxford and far beyond, he persisted in his advocacy of a greater openness towards Indian religious and mythic traditions on the part of the university's orientalists, and consistently sought a deeper understanding of Indian thought through his intercourse with Indian scholars. As he asserted in *Ramakrishna: His Life and Sayings*: 'behind such strange names as Indian Theosophy, and Esoteric Buddhism and all the rest, there was something real, something worth knowing'.[129] Even in their heterogeneity and inadvertent juxtapositions, therefore, these letters, or traces of contact, can be read both as symptomatic of the connectivity in which the circle of interlocutors was engaged, and, more broadly, as metonymic of the shaping of British intellectual and cultural life by translated and migrant Indian presences.

The letters in the book are from divers hands, including from Indians who had physically met the great Oxford Sanskritist, and those who had never travelled to Britain, yet who sought contact or offered information because of his reputation as a scholar of ancient India. However, one hand or voice in particular stands out, as its primary objective is not to solicit advice. Instead, it records in fond, if not nostalgic terms, time spent together in Oxford, the views that were exchanged, the communion enjoyed. The voice is that of the social reformer, universalist thinker, and friend to Unitarians, Keshab Chandra Sen, who toured in England in the summer of 1870 as a representative of the Brahmo Samaj. Widely acclaimed as a worthy successor to Rammohan Roy, Sen became for a brief period, in Max Müller's words, a 'household name' in England, and was recognized to be, in his monism, a dynamic crosser of boundaries, as is captured in the quotation from Max Müller's pen-portrait cited in the subheading above.[130]

As for Friedrich Max Müller himself, the reputation of the German-born, Paris-educated Professor of Philology rested in particular on his multivolume translation of the *Rig Veda*, the ancient Vedic scriptures, published by Oxford University Press, to which he devoted many years of his working life. Arriving in Oxford in 1851, first as a member of Christ Church, then as Fellow of All Souls (1858), he held various positions in the university including the Taylorian Professorship of Modern European Languages. Losing out to his conservative rival Monier-Williams, later founder of the Indian Institute, in the election to the Boden Professorship of Sanskrit in 1860, Max Müller continued to pursue his studies in the Vedas, and in 1868 became Oxford's first Professor of Comparative Philology. Across his career, he cultivated friendships with Indian scholars both directly and through correspondence, and invited many Indian visitors to the university, the loss of the Boden election if anything driving him more energetically in the direction of his Indian interlocutors, while also drawing India more closely into his own scholarly purview.

Keen to build bridges of religious understanding between Hinduism and other religious traditions, K. C. Sen made his 1870 trip to England at the invitation of the British and Foreign Unitarian Association and was frequently hosted by Unitarian groups while in England.[131] He was first introduced to an English audience by James Martineau at a Unitarian 'welcome soirée', held in London's Hanover Square Rooms on 12 April

1870, and in Bristol encouraged Mary Carpenter to found her National Indian Association for the promotion of women's education in India. A young assistant, Pratap Majumdar, accompanied Sen on the trip: along with Vivekananda, he would later represent Indian religious thought at the 1893 World Parliament of Religions in Chicago.[132]

Firing English imaginations with visions of Indian social change, Sen's visit was a public relations success in circles far above and beyond the Unitarians. Though his period of stardom was to be short-lived, ending a few years later when he sanctioned the marriage of his thirteen-year-old daughter to the Maharaja of Cooch Behar (though in the same period ensuring the passage of the Native Marriage Bill), the more diffuse social impact of his visit did not so easily wash away. Sen addressed many different groups across southern England, including temperance societies, and theistic and philosophical societies, as well as the Unitarians. He visited the Queen at Osborne House and met Gladstone, the Dean of Westminster, and Prince Leopold, one of Victoria's sons, among other well-known Britons. In Oxford, as well as speaking to Unitarians and attending the boat races, as the letters show, he memorably conversed with Professor Max Müller in the summer shade. Wherever he went, posters and handbills publicized his tour route, prominently marking his pathway through Britain. Audience numbers at his talks suggest that he was seen and heard by thousands of people.

By the time K. C. Sen and Max Müller met in 1870, word had already got through from England to India that Indian scholars and scholarship might find a particular welcome in the eminent philologist's study. Many philosophical and epistemological bridges had been, and continued to be built between India and England in the second half of the nineteenth century on the back of Max Müller's open-minded and generously framed comparative work, not least in the form of his links with the monotheistic Brahmo Samaj. Though he continued throughout his career to find points of resolution for his cross-cultural investigation of divinity in his own Lutheran Christianity, his work in this era of religious crisis was of keen interest to non-Christian seekers such as Madame Blavatsky and the folklorist Charles Godfrey Leland. As Sen observes in one of his letters, Max Müller's family home at 12 Norham Gardens was a fixed destination on the map of any Indian visiting Oxford. South Parks Road and Banbury Road became well known as 'Indian' thoroughfares where gurus of different stripes and other learned men (and some women) might be seen plying back and forth to enjoy his legendary hospitality. Cornelia Sorabji regularly dropped in as a student in the late 1880s, and Swami Vivekananda visited in 1896. In a 1900 memorial address, R. C. Dutt, another Norham Gardens pilgrim, observed that: 'For a period of half a century, my countrymen have looked upon Professor Max Müller not only as the best interpreter of ancient Indian literature and philosophy and thought in Europe, [but] also the truest friend of the people of modern India.'[133] Had the Professor still been alive when Rabindranath Tagore visited Oxford in 1913, the poet, too, would certainly have been a guest at Norham Gardens.

The sense of communion that Max Müller felt with India was thus imprinted in a very real, physical way on university life while, at another level, his correspondence, as reflected in the rough-edged Bodleian book of letters, reiterated and reinforced these Indian exchanges. In its woven-together form, the book tangibly captures how Indian and British scholars were tied by common religious, cultural, and political interests and energies into forging now close and now transitory cross-continental relations. These interests rested in particular on ideas of underlying religious unity and the sense of an 'all-ruling Providence', as Brahmo Samaj founder Debendranath Tagore writes in his letter in the correspondence book—ideas which had, of course, been substantially fostered by Max Müller's translation work. As Debendranath Tagore's letter has it:

> By the publication of the Rg Veda and the Upanishads you [Max Müller] have brought within easy reach of European scholars the thoughts and aspirations of our ancient Ritchis, hitherto hidden in inaccessible manuscripts, and it is to be hoped that the dissemination of the knowledge of our ancient literature will help to cement the bonds of union between the two people who, brought up under a common roof, parted from each other and scattered over distant quarters of the globe, [are] again to be brought together under the mysterious decree of an all-ruling Providence.[134]

As Tagore's words suggest, there was that in Max Müller's work which prompted some Indians to view this friend to India as himself an embodiment of the ideal of spiritual oneness, similar to how figures such as Sri Ramakrishna and Swami Vivekananda, both promoted by Max Müller, were also regarded. The correspondent V. S. Mitra in an 1887 letter, for example, speaks of MM's 'genial sympathy with the natives of this land in every matter connected with their welfare'.[135]

Regardless even of the inevitable one-sidedness of the letters book, it is clearly apparent from the correspondence that both Max Müller and K. C. Sen were animated by their concern to find points of synthesis between the different religions of the world—a synthesis that had been actively promoted by the Brahmo Samaj movement and which they both in their different ways supported. Meeting Max Müller for the first time in London, at the gathering with the Dean of Westminster, Sen soon thereafter came to Oxford to engage in a public debate about salvation with Dr Pusey of the Oxford Movement and to stay with the Müller family. In their later correspondence, Sen and Max Müller, while discussing controversies within the Brahmo Samaj, hark back to these happy summer days. As a later pen-portrait the Professor made of Sen shows, his hope in meeting and hosting him was that the Indian's belief in love as an underlying spiritual culture connecting societies might bring him in time to convert to Christianity. Sen's views on that religion were in fact far more ambivalent than Max Müller's hopes gave him credit for, yet a preoccupation with what might be termed intercultural spiritual communion streams through Sen's three letters in the correspondence book. Perhaps the most suggestive letter is that of 2 May 1881, in which the writer refers obliquely to the controversy unleashed by his daughter's marriage, yet expresses at the same time his appreciation of Max Müller's friendship and his own openness to everything his correspondent might have to say to him, including reproof. Sen's memory of the time spent with the Professor in Oxford has not faded with the passing years, he urges:

> In writing to me you need not conceal your real feelings. Discriminating criticism cannot pain me. Even the reprimands of a true friend are acceptable and must prove beneficial. I have read your letters with the deepest interest, and I only wish I could sit with you under one of those shady trees in Oxford which I saw during my short visit, and talk over the many important subjects referred to therein, for hours together. My heart is full.

If the amity between Sen and Max Müller that is captured in this letter grew out of mutual efforts of cultural identification, W. B. Yeats's experimental citation of figures from Indian myth in some of his early poems, represents by contrast a more transient and uneven exchange of influence. Yet, as with Max Müller, the Irish poet's precocious interest in the east was quickened both by his actual contact with Indians, and by his spiritual involvements, most notably with theosophy (especially one of its inner circles, the Society of the Golden Dawn).[136] Though these contacts may now come across as somewhat opportunistic and even self-aggrandizing on the part of the career-driven young poet, his studies in eastern lore were, for all that, remarkably intense and serious. His interest illustrates in a vivid way the degree to which theosophy served not merely as a channel of contact but also as a transcontinental network opening out new perceptions and understanding between Britain and Ireland, on the one hand, and India on the other.

By the mid-1880s, Yeats's spiritual seeking had led him into an involvement with the Dublin Hermetic Society, the first Irish incarnation of the Theosophical Society, founded in June 1885. He would retain connections with the group until at least 1889. For a young man who had not had a formal education, his biographer Roy Foster observes, theosophy, as a western amalgam of eastern ideas, became the equivalent of Yeats's 'university', introducing him to ancient Indian philosophy, books, and beliefs which 'confirmed [his] vague speculations and seemed at once logical and boundless'.[137] Even in 1886 he was reading Kalidasa.

But Yeats's involvement in the Society was not confined to esoteric contact alone. It also brought the Irish poet into contact with visiting and migrant Indians, one of the first being theosophy's charismatic envoy to the west, Mohini Chatterjee, whom Yeats in his *Autobiographies* calls 'a Brahmin philosopher'.[138] Chatterjee was at the time, in the Theosophical Society's early heyday, among the more publicly feted Indian travellers in the west. Indeed, Yeats was intrigued by his contact with Chatterjee to the extent that he developed a lasting receptiveness to Indian contacts and acquaintance, also befriending across his long career Sarojini Naidu, Rabindranath Tagore (as will be seen), and Shri Purohit Swami. Yeats himself never made it to India, despite being keen to visit (Tagore, amongst others, later encouraging him[139]), but, in the first flush of his newly awakened sympathy for its beliefs and ideas, he did set about evoking in his early poems something of the dynamic intercultural circuit with India to which theosophy had exposed him.

From this vantage point it is almost impossible to speculate on the nature of the encounters that took place in Dublin in 1885 between the two young theosophists, Mohini Chatterjee and W. B. Yeats, the one a travelling teacher and guru, the other a self-proclaimed seeker. Theosophical Society meetings were necessarily veiled in secrecy, and Chatterjee, for his part, left no written travelogue of his time in England and Ireland helping to establish the still-emergent transcultural hub of the Theosophical Society. In both cases, as for all the encounters examined in this book, there was perhaps some mutual stereotyping, the predictable perceptions of us-against-them that the public spectacles and media of the period made available. Even so, eyewitness reports from fellow theosophists suggest that Chatterjee found European society congenial and made himself amenable especially to European women in ways that would have helped to allay the racial or cultural concerns that might otherwise have obtained. As for the shy and socially gauche Yeats, he was no doubt intrigued by Chatterjee's easy manner, charming talk, exotic looks, and (to Yeats) dynamic Vedantic message, to the extent that he recalled some of these features in his much later 1929 poem 'Mohini Chatterjee'.[140] Yet, even in the early poems, as Foster recognizes, these different powerful elements, in particular the tenets of Chatterjee's Hindu beliefs, mediated through theosophy, were powerfully 'recapitulated' by Yeats. To effect the recapitulation he took on, remarkably for the time, Chatterjee's perspective as 'the Indian'.[141]

Yeats's three most distinctive Indian poems, 'Anashuya and Vijaya', 'The Indian upon God', and 'The Indian to his Love', were among the first poems he published. They were later brought together in the opening section of his *Collected Poems*, (significantly) entitled 'Crossways'.[142] The majority of these early poems, including the long poem 'The Wanderings of Oisin' with which they were first published, are characterized by a running together or zigzagging between different cultural and mythic resources (Irish and Indian, especially), as well as by a striving for a heightened poetic emotion concocted out of this mix—something that in retrospect can be seen to anticipate the decadent mood associated with 1890s verse. India was in some sense then the catalyst for an attitude that would soon become highly characteristic of Yeats. All three poems stage an exhibition of faraway sites and exotic landscapes, through which the poet tests his belief, as expressed in another poem of the time, 'The Song of the Happy Shepherd', that language and the images conjured by language alone have imaginative conviction.

In 'Anashuya and Vijaya', the main speaker, the temple attendant Anashuya (or the Uncomplaining), engages in a dialogue about fidelity with her love, Vijaya, who, it appears, has another lover, one who sleeps when she is awake. Pleading with Vijaya to swear his fidelity upon 'the parents of the gods' 'who dwell on sacred Himalay' (and bear some similarity with Keats's Titans), Anashuya offers the first articulation in Yeats's poetic work of what would become his theory of antitheses, of the self defined in contradistinction to its anti-self. In the second poem, 'The Indian upon God', godhead or divinity is conceived by the speaker, a wandering Indian, in a highly personal Vedantic way. In this poem, it is as if Chatterjee's ideas had been channelled, more or less unprocessed, into Yeats's thought. In the third and most ambiguous of the poems, 'The Indian to his Love', a pair of lovers seek a refuge away from 'unquiet lands' on an island featuring verdant grass, peahens, and a parrot, a shadowing forth of Yeats's later isle of Innisfree. Their coming together is represented in the image of an 'Indian star' or meteor approaching its reflection in the tide. The Indianness of the 'star' perhaps refers to its paisley shape as well as its evanescence, but is then embosomed within the poem as a symbol of mutual love. Indianness, therefore, is acknowledged as being both exotic and proximate. Although by the decade's turn Yeats was to return to Irish mythic materials as more immediately credible ingredients for his work, the most notable feature of these early poems is how images drawn from Indian story and legend, transmitted to Dublin and London by Chatterjee, allowed Yeats to begin to test out some of his core ideas and techniques at this formative stage; in short, to explore the theme of cultural interconnection with India.

When read in the context of his oeuvre, even its early phases, there is that in Yeats's adoption of an Indian persona in 'The Indian upon God' that is extremely unusual and anomalous, and hence the more culturally remarkable, even if at the same time recognizably orientalist. It demanded an effort of imaginative sympathy to make the poetic leap into the remote mythic world of India that he forges with these lyrics, even if references to such worlds may have been introduced to Dublin's streets on a regular basis by theosophical talks and activities. The only immediately comparable instance of such sympathy is found in the slightly later 1890s friendship between the poets Laurence Binyon and Manmohan Ghose, though in their case the contact was mutual and more lasting (as Chapter 3 explores). In both situations, a transformative energy emerges from the willingness to reach across the cultural gulf and forge a cross-border poetics. Granted, the poets' generative sympathy bore all the complex marks of orientalism (even in respect of Binyon), its simultaneous objectification and sense of ownership of the east. Yet, as we will see, that reaching across also offered something more again: a genuine openness in spite of such distance; a desire not only to embrace but to internalize the other; an ambition on the part of the westerner to assume the voice of the east as being in some sense more spiritually true than his own.

*

Late nineteenth-century Indian visitors in London, ranging from students to politicians, and servants to maharajahs, not only responded to but also integrated with its frenetic modernity, as the examples given in this chapter suggest. Though they may at times have felt apprehensive or unnerved, they were by and large city-dwellers, and therefore represented themselves in their memoirs and letters as adaptive participants in the city's hubbub, as Wilkie Collins, for one, depicted them. In these various ways, all the Indian figures cited here interrogated the east–west divides that organized the British metropolitan imagination. A traveller like Malabari felt *au fait* enough with London city life to criticize its more socially derelict aspects, while Mukharji self-consciously choreographed an Indian oriental identity for metropolitan consumption. After R. C. Dutt's early retirement from the ICS he confidently envisaged that the next stage of his career, whether as scholar or academic, would be set in southern England—and he did in fact return to London to take up a lectureship in Indian history and to write.[143]

If, as Joseph McLaughlin argues, many late nineteenth-century writers, including A. Conan Doyle in *A Study in Scarlet*, saw the imperial metropolis as dangerously contaminated and reshaped by its peripheries, Indian visitors to London, by contrast, on several levels related to its crowdedness, noise, and heterogeneous traffic. Far from seeing the city as an uncivilized periphery or jungle (though they were not immune from such representations), London to them appeared in the main as a space of global interchange, 'an amalgam of multiple frontiers', whose heterogeneity in several ways anticipated the cityscapes of Eliot's great modernist poem *The Waste Land*.[144]

NOTES

1. A. K. Ramanujan, 'Annayya's Anthropology', trans. Narayan Hegde, in Ramachandra Sharma, ed., *From Cauvery to Godavari: Modern Kannada Short Stories* (New Delhi: Penguin, 1992), p. 44. For the Naipaul epigraph, see again *The Enigma of Arrival: A Novel* (London: Penguin, 1987), pp. 156, 162.
2. The entry reads: 'BANDO! [Hindustani] imperative bāndho, "tie or make fast." "This and probably other Indian words have been naturalised in the docks on the Thames frequented by Lascar crews. I have heard a London lighter-man, in the Victoria Docks, throw a rope ashore to another Londoner, calling out, Bando!"—(M.-Gen. Keatinge.)' See Henry Yule, *Hobson-Jobson*, ed. Kate Teltscher (Oxford: Oxford University Press, 2013), p. 78. In a personal communication, *Hobson-Jobson* editor Kate Teltscher observes: 'The entry is unusual in that it has no gloss from Yule, just the note from Keatinge.' Major-General Richard Harte Keatinge (1825–1904) was a friend and correspondent of Yule's, and a former Chief Commissioner of Assam (1874–78).
3. Antoinette Burton, *At the Heart of the Empire: Indians and the Colonial Encounter in Late Victorian Britain* (Berkeley, CA: University of California Press, 1998), p. 55.
4. IOR: L/PJ/6/209, f.1299. 'Pauper Natives of India and Other Countries Relieved by Certain Workhouses' (6 August 1887). Relatedly, in her *In Darkest London*, the reforming journalist Margaret Harkness reported seeing on Whitechapel Road, Polish Jews and German Gentiles mingle with the 'grinning Hottentot' and an 'Algerian merchant [walking] arm-in-arm with a native of Calcutta'. See Joseph McLaughlin, *Writing the Urban Jungle: Reading Empire in London from Doyle to Eliot* (Charlottesville, VA, and London: University Press of Virginia, 2000), in particular pp. 2–6, 176; Jonathan Schneer, *London 1900* (New Haven, CT: Yale University Press, 1999), especially pp. 184–7, 197–201; Rozina Visram, *Asians in Britain: 400 Years of History* (London: Pluto Press, 2002), especially pp. 54–62.
5. Meenakshi Mukherjee, *An Indian for all Seasons: The Many Lives of R. C. Dutt* (New Delhi: Penguin, 2009), p. 47.
6. S. Satthianandhan, *A Holiday Trip to Europe and America* (Madras: Srinivasa, Varadachari & Co., 1897), p. 61; cited in Antoinette Burton, 'Making a

Spectacle of Empire: Indian Travellers in Fin-de-siècle London', *History Workshop Journal* 42 (1996): 131.

7. Edmund Gosse, *Father and Son*, ed. and intr. Michael Newton (Oxford: Oxford University Press, 2004), pp. 30–1.
8. <http://search.ancestry.co.uk/search/group/1901uki> (accessed 7 January 2015). Also see Herman Melville's semi-autobiographical novel *Redburn,* in which he describes the globalized port of Liverpool and an illuminating conversation with a lascar seaman from the *Irrawaddy,* a 'country ship' crewed by 'Malays, Mahrattas, Burmese, Siamese, and Cingalese'. Herman Melville, *Redburn: His First Voyage* (New York, NY: Harper and Brothers, 1850), p. 217.
9. Wilkie Collins, *The Moonstone*, ed. and intr. Sarah Kemp (1868/1871; Oxford: Oxford World's Classics, 2008), pp. 83, 206.
10. This privilege is reserved for travellers like the 1820s political and social commentator Rammohun Roy earlier in the century. See Michael H. Fisher, *Counterflows to Colonialism: Indian Travellers and Settlers in Britain, 1600–1857* (Delhi: Permanent Black, 2004). It is worth noting that the Regency 'Good Food Guide' to London, by Ralph Rylance (1815), points to what may have been the first Indian eatery in the capital, the Hindoostanee Coffee House, in George Street, on the Edgware Road, where the dishes were notable for being 'dressed' with spices and rice. See Ralph Rylance, *The Epicure's Almanac: Eating and Drinking in Regency London—The Original 1815 Guidebook*, ed. Janet Ing Freeman (1815; London: British Library, 2012); Norma Clarke, 'Excellent Larders', *Times Literary Supplement* 5705 (3 August 2012): 3–4.
11. These included the extravagant 1886 Colonial and Indian Exhibition, held in South Kensington, the events surrounding Queen Victoria's Golden Jubilee in 1887, and the Glasgow Exhibition in 1888. Studded with displays of Indian wares, industry, wealth, and finery, the exhibitions were widely reported in the press and massively enhanced India's visibility in the British public sphere, as they did that of other cultures. See, for example, Burton, 'Making a Spectacle of Empire', pp. 126–46; Anonymous, 'India in London', *Pall Mall Gazette* (6 Feb 1888); Anonymous, 'A Lady's Day at the Glasgow Exhibition', *The Indian Magazine* 214 (October 1888): 540–6.
12. Kipling's striking short-story portraits of Anglo-Indian life, as we find in *Life's Handicap* (1891), were introduced by literary impresarios like Andrew Lang and Edmund Gosse (Dutt's advocate as well as Naidu's). See Robert H. MacDonald, *The Language of Empire: Myths and Metaphors of Popular Imperialism, 1880–1918* (Manchester: Manchester University Press, 1994), pp. 145–73.
13. N. N. Ghose, in his preface to Mukharji's *A Visit to Europe*, styles the work as 'an interpreter, of the government [of India] to the people'. See N. N. Ghose, 'Preface', in T. N. Mukharji, *A Visit to Europe* (Calcutta: W. Newman, 1889), n. p.
14. Schneer, *London 1900*, pp. 186–9.

15. In the same year, the Woking Mosque, Britain's second mosque after Liverpool, was built by Dr Gottlieb Leitner, who in 1883 had also established the Woking Oriental Institute.
16. As it is, though not as disruptively, in Anthony Trollope's *The Eustace Diamonds* (1873; Oxford: Oxford World's Classics, 1982), which, as will be seen, reads as a partial response to *The Moonstone*. See also Pablo Mukherjee, *Crime and Empire: The Colony in Nineteenth-Century Fictions of Crime* (Oxford: Oxford University Press, 2003), especially the discussion of 'destabiliz[ing] messages' of 'British moral and ideological supremacy', pp. 15–16, 158–87.
17. Collins, *The Moonstone*, pp. 83, 289.
18. Collins, *The Moonstone*, pp. 31, 371, 441, 461. Mukherjee, *Crime and Empire*, p. 180, writes: 'The solution to the mystery of the theft . . . is only achieved by recognizing the oppressive structure of the metropolitan society that marginalized a figure [like Ezra Jennings].' Interestingly, Jennings dies saying 'Peace! Peace! Peace!', which is reminiscent of the devotional invocation 'Shantih! Shantih! Shantih!'
19. This reading takes a significantly different direction to Deirdre David's influential account in *Rule Britannia* (1995) of the 'foreign Indians' as invaders who 'fracture the domestic social harmony secured by half a century of British colonial conquest', and of the 'gipsy dark' Jennings as a fully assimilated subaltern figure. As is seen in Jennings's greater appreciation of the English countryside (and English psychology) than anything found among the English, Collins allowed a far more mobile, uneven set of exchanges between India and Britain than David's tidy description admits. The babu-figure or mimic man, like Jennings, or like the many Indian visitors reviewed in this chapter, was not so acquiescent or passive an observer of English life. See Deirdre David, *Rule Britannia: Women, Empire and Victorian Writing* (Ithaca, NY, and London: Cornell University Press, 1995), pp. 17, 143–7.
20. Terrance D. Höhner and Carolyn B. Kenny, *Chronology of Swami Vivekananda in the West* (Portland, OR: Prana Press, 2000). A pioneer of neo-Hinduism, Swami Vivekananda was a member of the Brahmo Samaj as a young man, later becoming a follower of Sri Ramakrishna Paramahamsa, founder of the Ramakrishna Mission.
21. Charles Dickens, *The Mystery of Edwin Drood*, ed. Margaret Cardwell (1870; Oxford: Oxford World's Classics, 1992).
22. Dickens, *Edwin Drood*, pp. 12, 41, 107.
23. The Landless twins also bear a certain air of 'being objects of the chase'. Predictably, therefore, suspicion for the murder of Edwin Drood falls straightaway on the 'inflammable' Neville. Dickens, *Edwin Drood*, pp. 43, 61, 128.
24. This is to the extent that the orientalist associations of eastern characters and substances in the novel are, as in Collins, subtly questioned, in a way that contrasts with their more stereotypical representation in work from earlier in the century, such as Thomas de Quincey's *Confessions of an English Opium*

Eater (1821). So Cloisterham's residents are referred to as 'natives', according to convention yet resonantly, in the same scene as Neville and Helena Landless, recently arrived, are described as 'untamed' 'barbaric captives' (Dickens, *Edwin Drood*, pp. 42–3, 146). The mysterious stranger Mr Datchery, by contrast again, is called a 'settler in Cloisterham'.

25. Dickens, *Edwin Drood*, p. 128.
26. Dickens, *Edwin Drood*, p. 206. The opium den scene on which the novel opens (and, in its unfinished state, closes), with the Chinese, 'Lascar', and English bodies lying side-by-side on a 'large unseemly bed', vividly sets the scene of confused and confusing closeness which is then developed throughout (see pp. 1–2).
27. The novel's intercutting of the foreign and the familiar shapes Edwin himself, written down for a career as an engineer 'waking up' 'undeveloped' Egypt (Dickens, *Edwin Drood*, pp. 19, 54); Rosa Bud, his fiancée, an English-rose lover of Turkish delight; and the xenophobe Mr Sapsea, who boasts: 'If I have not gone to foreign countries . . . foreign countries have come to me' (p. 26). Other examples of cultural syncretism include Jasper's opium 'Spectres' (p. 36), Reverend Crisparkle's Souchong tea-drinking habit (p. 40), his mother's dining-room closet with its 'luscious lodgings of preserved tamarinds and ginger' alongside English pickles and jams (p. 78), and the tanned sailor Tartar's apartment full of curiosities (pp. 188–9).
28. Dickens, *Edwin Drood*, pp. 122–3, 146.
29. The higher concentration of Indian visitors in Britain's cities as compared to towns and the countryside should not be taken to imply, however, that Indians were simply absent from the quintessentially English domain of the countryside, or from the Scottish hills. Gandhi, by his own admission, regarded walks with his landladies' daughters as excellent opportunities for flirtation, as they seem also to have done. And many Indian scholars and seers at least travelled *between* Britain's cities, on the London–Bristol route first plied by Rammohan Roy, for instance, or between Cambridge and London, as well as between England and Scotland, on their way to the University of Edinburgh, at whose medical school many Indians studied in these years. R. C. Dutt was a particularly energetic student traveller, going as far afield as Devon and the West County, as well as Scotland, Ireland, and Wales, as he describes in *Three Years in Europe 1868–71*, 4th edn, (1872; Calcutta: S. K. Lahiri, 1896), pp. 27–50, 69–78 and 78–80, respectively. Tamson Pietsch, *Empire of Scholars* (Manchester: Manchester University Press, 2013), p. 48, notes that already in 1868 16% of students at the Edinburgh Medical School came from the different regions of the Empire.
30. Dickens, *Edwin Drood*, pp. 132–3.
31. Trollope, *The Eustace Diamonds*. The references that follow are to pp. 66, 15, and 25, respectively.
32. Trollope, *The Eustace Diamonds*, p. 66.
33. When Lizzie wears the necklace in public, she is equated with her diamonds: 'She was made to sparkle, to be bright with outside garniture' (*The Eustace*

Diamonds, p. 159). Along with her feminine wiles, Romantic interests and remote Scottish castle, Lizzie also has the tendency to consort with various disreputable characters (including uncultured Americans and untrustworthy Jews, especially the jeweller Mr Benjamin and her second husband the Christianized Mr Emilius). Unlike in *The Moonstone*, in *The Eustace Diamonds* the establishment loses its diamonds, due in part to Lizzie's machinations.

34. Edwin Arnold, Preface, in *The Light of Asia* (1879; London: Senate, 1998), pp. vii–xi.
35. Mukherjee, *An Indian for All Seasons*, p. 40.
36. Rosinka Chaudhuri, *Gentlemen Poets in Colonial Bengal: Emergent Nationalism and the Orientalist Project* (Calcutta: Seagull, 2002), pp. 170–3.
37. Zerbanoo Gifford, *The Golden Thread: Asian Experiences of Post-Raj Britain* (London: Pandora, 1990), develops a similar Collinsesque metaphor in relation to post-1948 South Asian migration to Britain.
38. B. M. Malabari, *The Indian Eye on English Life; or, Rambles of an Indian Reformer* (London: Archibald Constable, 1893); 2nd edn (Bombay: Apollo Printing Works 1895), pp. 41, 46.
39. Ramachandra Guha, *Gandhi Before India* (London: Allen Lane, 2013), pp. 38–47.
40. See Sumit Sarkar, 'Rammohun Roy and the Break with the Past', in V. C. Joshi, ed., *Rammohun Roy and the Process of Modernization in India* (New Delhi: Vikas, 1975), p. 63.
41. Burton, *At the Heart of the Empire*, pp. 128–31, 133.
42. Burton, *At the Heart of the Empire*, pp. 3, 10. In terms of Michel de Certeau's theory of modern urban space, as Burton also recognizes, late nineteenth- and early twentieth-century Indian commentators subscribed, though with local modifications, to the quintessentially modern position of the 'subject who sees': the shifting viewpoint of the indubitably masculine 'practitioner of everyday [city] life', viewing the city both as cosmopolitan traveller, and as Indian. See Michel de Certeau, *The Practice of Everyday Life*, trans. Steven F. Rendall (Berkeley, CA: University of California Press, 1984), pp. 92–3; Deborah Epstein Nord, *Walking the Victorian Streets* (Ithaca, NY, and London: Cornell University Press, 1995). In respect of Afro-Caribbeans in colonial London, see also Mary Lou Emery, *Modernism, the Visual, and Caribbean Literature* (Cambridge: Cambridge University Press, 2007), pp. 10 and 15.
43. See Burton, 'Making a Spectacle of Empire', p. 128.
44. Paul Greenhalgh, *Ephemeral Visits: The Expositions Universelles, Great Exhibitions and World's Fairs, 1851–1939* (Manchester: Manchester University Press, 1988), p. 1.
45. See Bill Schwarz, *The White Man's World*, vol.1: *Memories of Empire* (Oxford: Oxford University Press), especially pp. 73–4 and 86, in which Schwarz notes that it was after the Sepoy Rebellion that the word 'nigger' became common currency on the streets of London.
46. See Robert Young, *Colonial Desire: Hybridity in Theory, Culture, and Race* (New York and London: Routledge, 1995). As scientific racism became

compounded by commodity racism, advertising, photography, museums, and imperial exhibitions all took the imprint of racialized ideas and became saturated with nationalist and imperialist conceit, as Anne McClintock, Robert H. MacDonald, and John MacKenzie have variously observed. In Britain, Indians encountered a world inflated with a sense of its own self-importance and on many levels closed to them. It is indicative, for example, that Monier Monier-Williams, Oxford Professor of Sanskrit in the 1880s, pursued his academic interests in India for explicitly imperialist reasons, to promote the better governance of the Raj. See Anne McClintock, *Imperial Leather: Race, Gender and Sexuality in the Colonial Contest* (London and New York: Routledge, 1995), p. 33; MacDonald, *The Language of Empire*, especially pp. 2–17; John MacKenzie, *Imperialism and Popular Culture* (Manchester: Manchester University Press, 1986), especially pp. 3–9. See also Patrick Brantlinger, *Rule of Darkness: British Literature and Imperialism, 1830–1914* (Ithaca, NY, and London: Cornell University Press, 1988); Joseph Plotz, *Portable Property: Victorian Culture on the Move* (Princeton, NJ, and Oxford: Princeton University Press, 2008).

47. Tellingly, two of the first four Indians to sit the Indian Civil Service examination in the 1870s were at first disqualified, on dubious and possibly racist grounds. See Mukherjee, *An Indian for All Seasons*, pp. 10–11.
48. As Edward Said, *Culture and Imperialism* (London: Jonathan Cape, 1993) famously recognizes. See also McClintock, *Imperial Leather*. In this period of high imperialism, not only public thoroughfares, but also more secluded domestic spaces, were infused with Indian cultural influences in the form, first, of commodities like furnishings, fabrics, shawls, spices, and tea, as was predictable in an age of commodity capitalism, but also, as is seen again in Chapter 3, of more numinous presences like Indian images, designs, and religious ideas, not excluding also the colouring and arrangement of domestic interiors. For John Jasper in *Edwin Drood*, as for Franklin Blake and Ezra Jennings in *The Moonstone*, the frontiers of the everyday world of the senses dramatically dissolve under the influence of such colonial stimuli.
49. Guha, *Gandhi Before India*, p. 47.
50. On Indian unfamiliarity with the English life-style, see James D. Hunt, *Gandhi in London*, rev. edn (1978; New Delhi: Promilla and Co., 1993), pp. 9–10.
51. Shompa Lahiri, *Indians in Britain: Anglo-Indian Encounters, Race and Identity, 1880–1930* (London: Frank Cass, 2000), p. 194, makes the assessment that compared to the hostility that 'the host population' showed Indians some five decades later, Indians in Britain at this point in time were made relatively welcome. Satadru Sen, *Migrant Races: Empire, Identity and K. S. Ranjitsinjhi* (Manchester: Manchester University Press, 2005), p. 4, suggests that when the Indian minor aristocrat and world-class cricketer Ranjitsinjhi played for England, his exceptionality in many ways endeared him to 'the metropolitan observer'.

52. See Young, *Colonial Desire*; and *The Idea of English Ethnicity* (Oxford: Blackwell, 2008). The perceived cultural proximity of South Asians to Europeans was further reinforced by newly ascendant philological and ethnographic theories concerning the Indo-European or Aryan continuum of language and civilization that was held to connect the Indian subcontinent to Europe. The philological research of Oxford Professor Friedrich Max Müller, amongst others, was instrumental in developing these ideas: see, for example, his *Biographies of Words and the Home of the Aryas* (London: Longmans, Green and Co., 1898). As Indian travellers in Britain combined in their own person the antonymic connotations of the exotic and the familiar, they provide important countervailing instances with which we might interrogate Fredric Jameson's controversial contention that the life worlds of the empire remained 'unimaginable for the [metropolitan] subjects of the imperial power', given how far they were located from 'the daily life and existential experience of the home country'. See Fredric Jameson, 'Modernism and Imperialism', in *Nationalism, Colonialism and Literature* (Minneapolis, MN: University of Minnesota Press, 1990), pp. 60–4.
53. Rev. T. B. Pandian, *England to an Indian Eye* or *English Pictures from an Indian Camera* (London: Elliot Stock, 1897). Malabari's influence is apparent both in Pandian's choice of title and his dedication to the women of England who supported him in his own proselytizing work for social reform: the 'Enlightened Daughters of Great Britain'. Malabari's campaign on child marriage and widow remarriage culminated in the successful passage of the Indian Age of Consent Bill in 1892: it is a clear illustration of how India-specific debates were often resolved in London.
54. Hunt, *Gandhi in London*, pp. 6–7.
55. Malabari, *The Indian Eye on English Life*, p. vii.
56. Burton, *At the Heart of the Empire*, pp. 152–87, especially p. 165.
57. Malabari, *The Indian Eye on English Life*, p. 245.
58. B. M. Malabari, *The Indian Muse in English Garb* (Bombay: Merwanjee Nowrojee Daboo/Reporters' Press, 1876), pp. iv, 4. Malabari had hoped to dedicate the book to the Prince of Wales, but, in the event, laid it at the feet of the social reformer and Unitarian, Mary Carpenter. Though most of the verse is unmistakenly colonialist in manner and subject, fulsomely hailing 'the Lord's elect' (the representatives of British power in India), some of the later poems mark the splendours of ancient Indian history also.
59. Malabari, *The Indian Eye*, pp. 38–9, 47–9, 61–5, 239–40.
60. Malabari, *The Indian Eye*, p. 245.
61. Gayla S. McGlamery, '"The Malady Afflicting England": *One of Our Conquerors* as Cautionary Tale', *Nineteenth-Century Literature* 46.3 (December 1991): 327–50, especially p. 327.
62. George Meredith, *One of Our Conquerors* (London: Chapman and Hall, 1892), pp. 5, 7.
63. Meredith, *One of Our Conquerors*, pp. 30–4.

64. Thomas Babington Macaulay, 'Von Ranke's History of the Popes', in *Critical and Historical Essays* (1840: London: Dent, 1907), p. 65.
65. David, *Rule Britannia*, p. 4.
66. Martin Wainwright, *'The Better Class of Indians': Social Rank, Imperial Identity, and South Asians in Britain, 1858–1914* (Manchester: Manchester University Press, 2008). See also David Cannadine, *Ornamentalism: How the British Saw their Empire* (London: Allen Lane, 2001). Wainwright's analysis of differences of race trumping those of rank within Britain's idealized hierarchy of class complicates some of the homogenizing implications of David Cannadine's thesis of class-to-class bonding or 'ornamentalism' across cultural borders.
67. Wainwright, *'The Better Class of Indians'*, pp. 5–9.
68. See Peter Marshall, *Bengal: The British Bridgehead: Eastern India, 1740–1828* (Cambridge: Cambridge University Press, 1987); Mrinalini Sinha, *Colonial Masculinity: The 'Manly Englishman' and the 'Effeminate Bengali' in the Late Nineteenth Century* (Manchester: Manchester University Press, 1995).
69. Claude Levi-Strauss, *Tristes Tropiques*, trans. John and Doreen Weightman (New York, NY: Atheneum, 1973), p. 85, proposes that travel be held to mean also movement within social hierarchies, or, we might add, movement *between* and *across* social hierarchies. See Nile Green, 'Among the Dissenters: Reciprocal Ethnography in Nineteenth-century Inglistan', *Journal of Global History* 4 (2009): 293–395, especially pp. 313–14.
70. The 1886 Exhibition, with its Jaipur, Punjab, and Bombay courts, and displays of India's 'ancient arts', viewed by 4 million visitors, categorized and interpreted the lives of others, whether metropolitan or Indian, in much the same way as Britons were doing in India. See Burton, *At the Heart of the Empire*, pp. 44–6; Paul Greenhalgh, *Ephemeral Visits: the Expositions Universelles, Great Exhibitions and World's Fairs, 1851–1939* (Manchester: Manchester University Press, 1988); Peter H. Hoffenberg, *An Empire on Display* (Berkeley, CA: University of California Press, 2001); and Mukharji, *A Visit to Europe*. Hoffenberg, *An Empire on Display*, pp. 55–6, helpfully enlarges: 'Mukharji's activities at the exhibitions contributed to the development of Indian national institutions and public culture. By participating in these shows as commissioners, experts, and exhibitors, [South Asian experts like] Mukharji and the Indian princes became active agents in the invention of Indian art, and in its systematic classification, promotion, and public presentation... To some degree, Mukharji's exhibition projects nationalised Indian arts.' For the 1886 exhibition, as well as other exhibitions on which he worked, such as the Calcutta International, Mukharji prepared 'Indexes' 'to the manufactures and raw materials of the great continent of India'. His descriptions laid emphasis on both raw materials and cultivated design, showing how these together might produce an intellectual and commercial rebirth for India.
71. A. Martin Wainwright, 'Royal Relationships as a Form of Resistance: The Cases of Duleep Singh and Abdul Karim', in *South Asian Resistances in*

Britain, 1858–1947, ed. Rehana Ahmed and Sumita Mukherjee (London: Continuum, 2012); Michael Alexander and Sushila Anand, *Queen Victoria's Maharajah: Duleep Singh 1838–93*, 2nd edn (1980; London: Phoenix Press, 2001).

72. See Anand and Alexander, *Queen Victoria's Maharajah;* Visram, *Asians in Britain*, pp. 99–103. Queen Victoria later became the godmother of several of the Maharajah's children.
73. Burton, *At the Heart of the Empire*, pp. 32, 189.
74. The 1 January 1877 Proclamation of Queen Victoria as Empress of India, as engraved into a marble tablet inset within the central domed rotunda of the Victoria Memorial in Kolkata, reads:

    that from the highest to the humblest,
    all may feel that under our rule the
    great principles of liberty, equity,
    and justice are secured to them; and
    to promote their happiness, to add to
    their prosperity, and advance their
    welfare, are the ever present aims and
    objects of our Empire.

    Observed 24 March 2009.

75. See Duncan Bell, *The Idea of Greater Britain: Empire and the Future of World Order* (Princeton, NJ, and Oxford: Princeton University Press, 2007).
76. Elleke Boehmer, ed., *Empire Writing: An Anthology of Colonial Literature 1870–1920* (Oxford: Oxford University Press, 1998), pp. 72–9, 212, 493–4.
77. See Sukanya Banerjee, *Becoming Imperial Citizens: Indians in the Late Victorian Empire* (Durham, NC, and London: Duke University Press, 2010).
78. On Naoroji, see Banerjee, *Becoming Imperial Citizens*, pp. 36–74; Visram, *Asians in Britain*, pp. 146–62. See also Burton, 'Making a Spectacle', p. 126; and, *At the Heart of the Empire*, p. 62.
79. See Dadabhai Naoroji, *Poverty and Un-British Rule in India* (London: Swan Sonnenschein and Co., 1901); and *The Poverty of India* (London: Vincent Brooks, Day and Son, 1878).
80. Elleke Boehmer, *Empire, the National, and the Postcolonial: Resistance in Interaction* (Oxford: Oxford University Press, 2002), p. 20.
81. Hunt, *Gandhi in London*, p. 12.
82. Pandian, *England to an Indian Eye*, p. 19; Dutt, *Three Years in Europe*, p. 132.
83. Wilhelm Halbfass, *India and Europe: An Essay in Understanding* (New York, NY: SUNY Press, 1988), pp. 207–8.
84. The nationalism of the Indian National Congress was distinctively 'diasporic'. Due to this migrant understanding of Britain from within and India from without, for example, the potency of the INC's message lay in its efforts to persuade the British into governing India in a more 'British' fashion. See, for example, Dadabhai Naoroji, *Poverty and Un-British Rule in India*.
85. Burton, *At the Heart of the Empire*, p. 19.

86. Mukherjee, *An Indian for all Seasons*, p. 54. See also A. Rahman, 'The Burden of Imagination: Mapping the Centre Through the Colonised Gaze', *SACS* 3.1 (October 2011): 1–16: <http://blogs.edgehill.ac.uk/sacs/files/2012/05/Document-2-A.-Rahman-The-burden-of-imagination-FINAL.pdf> (accessed 7 January 2015).
87. Tapan Raychaudhuri, *Europe Reconsidered: Perceptions of the West in Nineteenth-century Bengal*, 2nd edn (New Delhi: Oxford University Press, 2002), p. 1.
88. Radhika Mohanram, *Imperial White: Race, Diaspora and the British Empire* (London: University of Minnesota Press, 2007), pp. xiv–xx.
89. As Susan Buck-Morss, *The Dialectics of Seeing: Walter Benjamin and the Arcades Project* (Cambridge, Mass., MIT Press, 1997), p. 210, observes in relation to Walter Benjamin's modernist dialectics, the modern emerges from the interplay of continuity and discontinuity; from what is 'new in connection with that which has always already been there'.
90. See M. K. Gandhi, *An Autobiography; or the Story of My Experiments with Truth* (1927; Ahmedabad: Navajivan Publishing House, 1958). Gandhi offers various different possible readings of the word 'experiments' in his title which are salient to the case being made here. Experimentation, he suggests, involves changes to life-style, as in the chapters on vegetarianism and his acquaintance with modes of religious thought. It also points to how one conducts oneself in society, as in the chapter 'The Canker of Untruth', in which he confesses to flirting with his landlady's daughter without informing the family that he was married (pp. 45–8). See also Guha, *Gandhi Before India*, pp. 36–54.
91. Gandhi, *An Autobiography*, pp. 35, 42.
92. Quoted in Hunt, *Gandhi in London*, p. 28.
93. Lala Baijnath, *England and India: Being Impressions of Persons, Things, English and Indian* (Bombay: Jehangir B. Karani & Co., 1893), p. 38; Malabari, *The Indian Eye on English Life*.
94. Anonymous [Ceylonese participant in 1886 Exhibition], 'A Stranger Within Our Gates', *Daily News* (8 and 9 October 1886).
95. As in the texts that followed it, like Pandian's *England to an Indian Eye*. Pandian's descriptions often coincide with Malabari's in respect of the particular urban features the writer chooses to foreground: the relative cleanliness of the city; the reassurance provided by the bobby's presence; the social malaise rising from widespread inebriation and prostitution; and, above all, the galvanizing yet also enervating effects of modernity, its commercialism, and its overpopulation. See Pandian, *England to an Indian Eye*, p. 43.
96. As Benedict Anderson, *Imagined Communities*, rev. edn (London: Verso, 1991), p. 192, suggests. Under colonialism, the creole or colonial elites of the New World developed a 'capacity to imagine themselves as communities *parallel and comparable* to those in Europe'—a thesis he further develops in *The Spectre of Comparisons: Nationalism, South-East Asia and the World* (London: Verso, 1998).

97. Partha Mitter, *The Triumph of Modernism* (London: Reaktion, 2009), in particular pp. 10–11, 229. Indian cities, Mitter writes, were dynamic sites where western capital and the forces of global modernity most forcefully impacted on the subcontinent, and where, in consequence, fruitful interactions between near and far, global and local, the western avant-garde and home-grown anti-colonialists, took place. Bombay, in particular, was from its outset a cosmopolitan even more than an imperial city, its early settlement in the late 1660s having involved different diasporic communities seeking commercial opportunities, not least Gujerati Parsis, Malabari's community, and Baghdadi Jews such as the Sassoon family. Bombay's Sarasenic Gothic architecture, for example, drew influences from several different cultural sources, most prominently the Mughal empire and the Victorian neo-Gothic. See also Preeti Chopra, *A Joint Enterprise: Indian Elites and the Making of British Bombay* (Minneapolis, MN: University of Minnesota Press, 2011); Guha, *Gandhi Before India*, pp. 60–1.
98. See Felix Driver and David Gilbert, eds., *Imperial Cities: Landscape, Display and Identity* (Manchester: Manchester University Press, 1999).
99. Burton, *At the Heart of the Empire*, pp. 60–1.
100. The following commentary is based on the 1886 copies of the *Indian Mirror* held in the Sir Asutosh Collection, National Library of India, Kolkata, read in March 2009. With its Brahmo Samaj sympathies, the *Indian Mirror* was at the time of the 1911 Durbar still going strong, at which point Satyendra Nath Sen, sub-editor from 1886, became chief editor.
101. The 4 May 1886 issue carried an advertisement for Thacker, Spink and Co., now perhaps better known as the publishers of Charlotte Bronte's *Jane Eyre* in India. See Josephine McDonagh, 'Rethinking Provincialism in Mid-nineteenth-century Fiction: *Our Village* to *Villette*', *Victorian Studies* 55.3 (Spring 2013): 399–424.
102. Sumita Mukherjee, *Nationalism, Education and Migrant Identities: The England-Returned* (London: Routledge, 2010), gives an in-depth account of the first generations of Indian students in England. See also Pietsch, *Empire of Scholars* on the fluid academic interchanges between British and colonial settler universities in the period from 1850.
103. Mukherjee, *Nationalism, Education and Migrant Identities.*
104. Hunt, *Gandhi in London*, pp. 15–16.
105. Richard Symonds, *Oxford and Empire: The Last Lost Cause?* (New York, NY: St Martin's Press, 1986), pp. 11, 306. *Oxford Magazine* in the period was consistently preoccupied with the entry of 'Oxford men' into the ICS. Across the period of formal imperialism, Oxford produced fifteen viceroys of India to Cambridge's five.
106. See Symonds, *Oxford and Empire*, in particular pp. 11–12, 27–9, 105–6.
107. Though the Institute library has long since moved away, and no longer exists as a discrete collection, the Indian Institute building with its distinctive gold-coloured elephant-and-howdah weather vane, and its foundation stone in Devanagri script, remains a reminder of how a small piece of India was, as it were, embedded within Oxford at this early date.

108. J. M. Brown, *Windows into the Past: Life Histories and the Historian of South Asia* (Notre Dame, IN: Notre Dame Press, 2009).
109. Alex Owen, *The Darkened Room: Women, Power and Spiritualism in Late Victorian England* (London: Virago, 1989), pp. 4–5.
110. Edward Carpenter, *My Days and Dreams* (London: Allen and Unwin, 1916), pp. 45, 143.
111. Sheila Rowbotham, *Edward Carpenter: A Life of Liberty and Love* (London and New York: Verso, 2008), especially pp. 149–60.
112. See Antony Copley, *A Spiritual Bloomsbury: Hinduism and Homosexuality in the Lives and Writings of Edward Carpenter, E. M. Forster and Christopher Isherwood* (Lanham, MD, and Oxford: Lexington Books, 2006), pp. 10, 22, 27, 40, 45.
113. Arunachalam was also a cousin of the art critic Ananda Coomaraswamy (see Chapter 4), and shared with him a commitment to social reform and the preservation of traditional crafts, as well as a conservative position on women's rights.
114. Ralph Waldo Emerson, for example, translated the *Upanishads* and expressed interest in the work and career of Rammohan Roy.
115. Edward Carpenter, *From Adam's Peak to Elephanta: Sketches in Ceylon and India* (London: Swan Sonnenschein and Co., 1892), p. vi; Rowbotham, *Edward Carpenter*, pp. 50–7, 149–61, 350–1, 445.
116. Victor Lal, 'Encounter and Response: The British Unitarians and Brahmo Samajees at Manchester College, Oxford, 1896–1948', *Faith and Freedom: Journal of Progressive Religion*, 2 parts, 68.1 (Spring/Summer 2015) and 68.2 (Autumn/Winter 2015) (forthcoming). I am grateful to Victor Lal for sharing his article MS with me.
117. In 1843, the Brahmo Sabha became the Brahmo Samaj under Debendranath Tagore, Rabindranath's father.
118. Green, 'Among the Dissenters', pp. 312–13.
119. Friedrich Max Müller, *Biographical Essays* (London: Longmans, Green and Co., 1884), p. 13. See also Halbfass, *India and Europe*, p. 199.
120. Owen, *The Darkened Room*; Ken Monteith, *Yeats and Theosophy* (London and New York: Routledge, 2008); Rudolf Steiner, *Spiritualism, Madame Blavatsky and Theosophy: Lectures*, ed. Christopher Bamforth (Great Barringon, MA: Anthroposophic Press, 2001). See also Gauri Viswanathan's work on theosophy, particularly 'The Ordinary Business of Occultism', *Critical Inquiry* 27:1 (2000): 1–20.
121. *Lucifer* was co-edited by Helena Blavatsky and Mabel Collins 1887–1889; by Blavatsky and Annie Besant from September 1889, and solely by Besant from June 1891, along with sub-editor G. R. S. Mead. In 1897, it appears to have been incorporated into *The Theosophist*.
122. As Besant explained in the paper, published as *Why I Became a Theosophist* (London: Freethought Publishing, 1889), she turned to theosophy in the main because of the Society's recognition of the material body's spiritual powers.

123. 'Annie Besant and Theosophy', *Lucifer* iv.24 (15 August 1889): 486–99, in particular p. 487. The lectures were later collected and published as *Why I Became a Theosophist*. See Alex Tickell, *Terrorism, Insurgency and Indian-English Literature, 1830–1947* (London: Routledge, 2012), pp. 68–94. In contrast, a report 'Theosophical Activities', in *Lucifer* xiii.73 (15 September 1893): 71, is worth citing for what it records of the traffic of Indian seers between India, Britain, and the United States in this year of the World Parliament, and the enthusiasm with which contact with these men was sought by British theosophists:

    During the last months the members have had the pleasure of becoming acquainted with Bros. Chakravarti and Dhammapala [at Blavatsky Lodge] who were staying in London for a short time on their way to attend the Parliament of Religions at Chicago. On each occasion of his presence at the Lodge, Br. Chakravarti spoke. The first time was when Bertram Keightley lectured on *India and the Theosophical Society* and again when Dr Archibald Keightley spoke on *Devotion as Cause and Effect*. It was with real pleasure that the members listened to their eloquent Indian brother, and it goes without saying that they will be glad to hear that there is every prospect of Bro. Chakravarti giving a lecture early in October, as he will be staying at Headquarters in the interval between his arrival from America and his departure for India. A pleasant evening was passed on August 22nd, when a good many members assembled at the Library, 17 Avenue Road, in order to avail themselves of the opportunity of making the personal acquaintance of our two Eastern visitors.

124. Reported in *Lucifer*, v.26 (15 October 1889): 147.
125. *Lucifer* xi.63 (15 November 1892): 257.
126. Hunt, *Gandhi in London*, pp. 29–32.
127. See Höhner and Kenny, *Chronology of Swami Vivekananda in the West*. Vivekananda's classes and talks that took place in various 'lodgings' in November 1895, for example, or the lectures that 'won disciples' in June 1896, following his return from New York, which members of the royal household allegedly attended incognito, were all organized under the auspices of the Theosophical Society.
128. MS. Eng. d. 2352. F. Max Müller, Correspondence book, Bodleian Library, Oxford. I am grateful to Sumita Mukherjee for first drawing this document to my attention.
129. F. Max Müller, *Ramakrishna: His Life and Sayings* (London: Longmans, Green and Co., 1898), p. 2.
130. Meredith Borthwick, *Keshub Chunder Sen: A Search for Cultural Synthesis* (Calcutta: Minerva Associates, 1977), p. 100: quoted in Burton, *At the Heart of the Empire*, p. 37. Friedrich Max Müller, *Biographical Essays* (London: Longmans, Green & Co., 1884), p. 74.
131. Michael Collins, *Empire, Nationalism and the Postcolonial World: Rabindranath Tagore's Writings on History, Politics and Society* (London and New

York: Routledge, 2011), pp. 31–3, 62–4; Halbfass, *India and Europe*, p. 225; Keshub Chunder Sen, *Keshub Chunder Sen in England: Diary, Sermons, Addresses & Epistles* (Calcutta: Navavidhan Publication Committee, 1938), p. 79.

132. Pratap Majumdar wrote to Max Müller on 29 August 1881, regarding the 'science of comparative theology', that 'the unity of truth in all lands and nations' depended on the 'recognition of the services which the great peoples of earth have rendered unto each other'. See Max Müller, *Biographical Essays*, pp. 145–6.
133. Mukherjee, *An Indian for All Seasons*, p. 165.
134. Max Müller, Correspondence book, letter 27, n. d., p. 3.
135. Max Müller, Correspondence book, letter 7.
136. See R. F. Foster, *W. B. Yeats: A Life*, vol. 1: *The Apprentice Mage* (Oxford: Oxford University Press, 1997), pp. 45–8, 85, 99, 101–3, 306–73, 469–73; Monteith, *Yeats and Theosophy*, pp. 23–5.
137. Foster, *W. B. Yeats: A Life*, vol. 1: *The Apprentice Mage*, pp. 47–8.
138. W. B. Yeats, 'Reveries Over Childhood and Youth', in *Autobiographies* (1955; London: Macmillan, 1979), pp. 91–2. The Trinity College Professor of Persian, Mir Alaud Ali, too, was a member of the Society.
139. But the First World War, in particular, withheld him from travel.
140. In 'Mohini Chatterjee' the Brahmin seer is cast in a sympathetic light as an icon of reincarnation. See A. Raghu, 'Yeats's "Mohini Chatterjee"', *Explicator* 51:3 (Spring 1993): 170–2.
141. Open to Indian cultural influences across his career, Yeats cannot be regarded as an orientalist in any straightforward way, as he sometimes is represented. See, for example, Collins, *Empire, Nationalism and the Postcolonial World*, pp. 120–1.
142. W. B. Yeats, *The Poems*, ed. and intr. Daniel Albright (London: Everyman, 1992), pp. 36–41.
143. Mukherjee, *An Indian for All Seasons*, pp. 128–9, 134–5.
144. McLaughlin, *Writing the Urban Jungle*, pp. 2–6, 176.

3

Lotus Artists

Self-orientalism and Decadence

Oh mother mine, I cannot stay, the faery-folk are calling

Sarojini Naidu, from 'Village-Song',
The Golden Threshold (1905)

... from the storied, sacred East afar,
Down Indian gorges clothed in green,
With flower-rein'd tigers and with ivory car
He came, the youthful god;
Beautiful Bacchus...

Laurence Binyon, from 'Youth',
Primavera (1890)

Here sense with apathy seems gently wed
The gloom is starr'd with flowers, the unseen trees
Spread thick and softly real above my head;
And the far birds add music to the peace,
In this dark place of sleep, where whispers never cease.

Manmohan Ghose, from 'XII',
Primavera (1890)

I want to glance back over my shoulder and savour it... patches of dappled sunshine lying all along [my] road from the very beginning—sunlight scented with rosemary and lavender. I inhale the Past in great whiffs... Sunsets—flaming gold and red-gold; or bruised and blue: or pale mauve and primrose: the deep shadows on the hills, folds in the broidered mantle of God: gold mohur trees trailing bloom, the green paroquets at Budh Gaya: the blue smoke in an Indian village... and always and always the Earth springing flowers.

Cornelia Sorabji, from 'Introduction', *India Calling* (1934)

I 'CATCHING THE NEARING ECHO': 1890s POETIC ENCOUNTERS BETWEEN INDIA AND BRITAIN

In 1896, a young Indian student in London, Sarojini Naidu, then Chattopadhyay (1879–1949), published in the *Savoy*, one of the tone-giving magazines of the decade of Decadence, a poem entitled 'Eastern Dancers'. (It was later published in her collection *The Golden Threshold* under the marginally less exotic title 'Indian Dancers'). Even to contemporary audiences acquainted with the 1890s devotion to high artifice and extravagant sensuality that preoccupied the London avant-garde, the hectic excesses of Naidu's poem and its charged evocation of an erotic 'eastern' dance, would have appeared remarkable, even if characteristic of the times.[1]

From its opening hyperbolic invocation to the dancers' 'Eyes ravished with rapture', immediately followed by the image of 'bosoms aflaming with fire', the poem presses a sustained chord of sensual abandon. For the editors of the *Savoy*, however, who stood 'boldly for the modern [or decadent] note without fear and without any wavering of purpose', Sarojini's lavish empurpled poem was cut to the right cloth.[2] Across its three long-lined quatrains with the loose rhyme scheme *abab cdcd* the poem is unremittingly hazy, breathy, and alliterative. There is no clear setting or action, other than a vaguely generalized Mughal court (evoked in the references to opiates, tinkling feet, 'jewel-girt arms' and 'houri-like faces') and the generic motions of the (presumably temple) dancers, captured in repeated 'winding' and 'lingering' poses as if viewed under intermittent light. The poem's lighting itself is fittingly hectic and empurpled: 'glittering garments of purple' burn along with enflamed bosoms under 'the hush of hyacinth heavens'. The lyric moves tortuously through an accumulation of adjectives and mixed metaphors (smiles '[entwine] like magical serpents/ the poppies of lips') till the final line of the third quatrain bring the heady build-up to a fairly abrupt close. Yet, far from marshalling the overwhelming sinuosity of the whole, the final panting repetition of the apostrophe to the dancers' ravished eyes and flaming bosoms rather accentuates what Makarand Paranjape, an editor of Naidu's work, calls the poem's 'hedonistic glut'.[3] Openly drawn to this kind of display, the glut-savouring *Savoy* magazine had been started in the same year it published the poem, 1896, by an influential troika, the critic of French symbolism Arthur Symons, the illustrator Aubrey Beardsley, whose work would become prototypical of *fin-de-siècle* perversity, and Leonard Smithers, known as a publisher of pornography. The magazine ran to only eight issues. The appearance of Naidu in the second issue gave a clear signal that, in the editors' opinion, this formally conventional lyric staging a display of decadent excess in both aroused and arousing tones captured the mood of both the magazine and the times.

In spite of her youth and her foreign background—indeed perhaps because of these things, as will be seen—Sarojini Naidu stood for qualities that London's avant-garde admired: poetic ardour, responsiveness, delight in beauty. She was the friend and student of two key figures who presided over this world: Edmund Gosse, the Victorian man of letters and literary impresario already known as a friend to India through his encouragement of Toru Dutt; and the younger but no less influential Arthur Symons, café poet and *demi-monde* critic. Both men befriended and supported Naidu. Gosse, himself a contributor to the 1890s publication *The Yellow Book*, famously gave Naidu instruction in the art of writing as an Oriental ('a genuine Indian poet of the Deccan, not a clever, machine-made imitator of the English classics')—that is, not naturally but *as if* naturally, in a self-conscious eastern mode.[4] It was his entreaty that she 'introduce us to the vivid populations of her own voluptuous and unfamiliar province'. And Symons, who was equally captivated by Naidu's inspired easternness—encapsulated in his Conradian observation 'Through that soul I seemed to touch and take hold upon the East'—found in her poetry qualities that cohered with his own avant-garde sensibility, not to say also with the dreamy, passionate poetics that he considered definitive of the age. He enthusiastically introduced Naidu, his 'personal link with the exotic', to the circle of poets around Yeats, in which she was again feted; and she, in turn, was happy to play to the 'un-English, Oriental' 'vehement sincerity of emotion' which he found in her work.[5]

As the fourth section of this chapter shows in detail, Symons and others' interest in Naidu's poetry grew from a star-struck admiration of her 'Oriental' persona—a persona that appeared itself to harmonize with the new movements in the arts. True, many features of her poems, such as her liberal use of such apparently 'eastern' devices as song-like cadences, anapestic dancing rhythms, and sinuous run-on effects suggest that she did in many ways play to the image that her friends, supporters, and readers were ready to ascribe to her; or, more forcefully, that she wrote a part for herself into the decadent script that London wove around her. In particular, her friends were enchanted with the almost choreographed, as if pre-planned, fit between that oriental, part-veiled, and bejewelled persona and her ornate, sinuous, and multihued verse. Symons as well as Gosse worked to encourage and promote this match in ways that can be described as a double colonial mimicry (in that Naidu incrementally sought to imitate *both* an English poetic voice and an eastern style acceptable to the west). However, as I will elaborate further, such complicated mimicry might equally be seen as a reverse orientalism, which arguably allowed the Indian poet, through the exercise of her dramatic and technical skills, to take some charge of how she was represented. This is different from, yet related to, the 'reverse colonization' described by Marina Warner in her analysis of how the myriad, fantastical cultural effects of the *Arabian Nights* were amplified in the work's European interpretations due to its audiences' 'fascination of the Other', in which the orientalism concerned was the western observer's.[6] A question that will be left for Chapter 4 is whether such reverse orientalism is to be distinguished from 'wise imperialism'—Yeats's seemingly contradictory term for the fawning but ultimately self-serving reception Rabindranath Tagore was accorded by avant-garde circles in 1910s London.[7]

A visual 'text' that evocatively stands alongside 'Eastern Dancers' as a window onto the chapter's core preoccupations, and onto Naidu as one of its key 1890s protagonists, is provided by a sketch of the young poet Sarojini Chattopadhyay, also from 1896, which is related to the publication of 'Eastern Dancers' (Figure 1). This image, too, is intriguingly reflective of some of the prevailing perceptions of India in avant-garde London. Following her publication in the *Savoy*, the doors of literary salons had opened to the young Sarojini Chattopadhyay and her circle of poetic acquaintance widened. W. B. Yeats—already interested in India—invited her to attend his evenings at Woburn Buildings, where his muse Maud Gonne remembered her in the guise of a 'little Indian princess', a description that Yeats seems himself to have used.[8] In July of that year, Yeats's brother Jack made the sketch in question, a pencil drawing of a girlish Naidu, which appears as the frontispiece to her 1905 *The Golden Threshold* collection with its 'Introduction' by Symons.

In the sketch, which is composed of strongly contrasting dark and light areas, Naidu is pictured sitting on a pale settee, facing forward and bare-faced, her legs angled to the left. She is wearing a light-coloured dress or sari with a border over a western-style bodice (the dress may or may not be draped and seems to have puffed sleeves). There is a dark brooch at her throat, again positioned slightly to the left. The dense cross-hatching of the surrounding background shapes in a suggestive way the central figure of the young poet, which appears to glow out of the shadows. Jack Yeats nicely captures the ethereal, elfin qualities for which Naidu was becoming well known. The same features are evoked in Symons's heated description of her in his Introduction, which touches in particular on her child-like tininess and nervous tremulousness, and the great eyes that dominated her face (as also in the portrait).[9]

Both Naidu's *Savoy* poem and the image that some of her artistic connections had of her, suggest that, far from being merely imposed,

Figure 1. Frontispiece sketch to Sarojini Naidu, *The Golden Threshold* (1905), by J. B. Yeats

her eastern persona in fact involved a certain amount of projection and manipulation on Naidu's part. Her self-presentation, though it played on orientalist connotations of the seductive yet inaccessible exotic, also entailed discriminating as to which elements of the imperialist script to adopt and act out, and which to discard. Moreover, this discrimination was geared to achieving certain objectives, including a platform for her

Figure 2. First edition of Sarojini Naidu's *The Bird of Time* (1912); image of the author as frontispiece

© British Library Board, (V 10326).

work, and, later, a voice for India, and therefore involved considerable planning and strategizing.[10] In turn, Naidu's self-projection shaped 1890s understandings of what a new, alternative (non-western, non-degenerate) culture might comprise—yet this alternative, happily, rather than being confined to faraway India, was found to be in this key instance relatively familiar and close to hand, dressed in ambiguous part-eastern, part-western clothes.

Interestingly, by 1912, when her reputation was established and her second British collection *The Bird of Time: Songs of Life, Death & the Spring* published, Naidu's image was rendered as less obviously mixed or hybrid in its cultural influences, which is to say, less western and more overtly Indian.[11] The frontispiece portrait in this case was a black-and-white photograph of Naidu in profile, wearing traditional (South) Indian dress, draped, patterned, layered, silken, and again with a brooch at the shoulder (Figure 2). Though the young woman in this image is again very young (the photograph in all likelihood dates from the same period as the sketch), the position of her head, with her chin slightly raised, and her eyes appropriately large, is bolder. And, though she remains situated in an unambiguously British context, in a book published by William Heinemann of London, she presents herself as a limpid-eyed, somewhat vulnerable yet still self-possessed eastern woman, confidently presenting her fine profile to her western audience.

Yet Naidu was far from the first Indian poet to gain entry to British literary circles in the last quarter of the nineteenth century. Within the same period she was narrowly preceded by her equally if differently decadent compatriot Manmohan Ghose, the elder brother of the radical nationalist and later guru Sri Aurobindo. He, too, published in collaboration with fellow British poets (including Laurence Binyon), and like Naidu would sound the aestheticist note in ways that his British audiences found resonant and true. Yet both 1890s Indian poets had themselves been preceded by Toru Dutt, as we saw in Chapter 1, as well as by their Bengali compatriot—and distant relative of Toru's—Michael Madhusudan Dutt (1824–73). The Christianized M. M. Dutt, despite his 'British style education' in the western Classics at Hindu College and Bishop's College, Calcutta, and his deep-seated faith in western enlightenment, had turned to Bengali as his medium of expression when his poetry in English, published in Calcutta, met with an indifferent reception.[12]

Like M. M. Dutt, Manmohan Ghose was a Classics scholar, yet his education was metropolitan rather than colonial, at St Paul's School and the University of Oxford. His familiarity with English thought and the English language meant that he did not have to bridge the same cultural distances as Dutt; some of his friends indeed regarded him as a fellow countryman, as Section III of this chapter shows. With his period of greatest poetic activity falling about six years before Naidu's debut, at the end of the 1880s, Ghose joined Naidu in embracing an orientalist tradition of poetry about India. This was a tradition to which Edwin Arnold was among the first English poets to contribute, as Rosinka Chaudhuri has discussed, and which Edward Fitzgerald's poetic translation, the *Rubáiyát of Omar Khayyám* (1859), set in Persia, also influentially shaped.[13] Both Ghose and Naidu subscribed to the mystical yearnings, exotic settings, and ornamental detail (including lotus references), which characterized this kind of verse, which in its turn bore the imprint of influences from the *Arabian Nights*. However, whereas Ghose's interpretation of the tradition chimed in more obviously than Naidu's with the aestheticist mode in British poetry ('I am prone to luxuriance and poeticism', he wrote), Naidu took up with some energy the impassioned romanticism and poetics of excess closely associated with Decadence.[14]

From this confluence of effects rises the suggestive subheading to this section, taken from Naidu's 'An Anthem of Love', a hymn of nationalist self-dedication that fixes its attention on future promise and dawning light. Transposing that sense of anticipation of the coming times, the consonance of Naidu's work and that of her compatriot Ghose with the dominant cultural mood indeed captured a 'nearing echo': it fulfilled an image of the Orient that London produced but to which the Indian poets were happy to approximate and to help manufacture in order to secure certain advantages; to approach or to near their own echo in the ears of Europe. Therefore, even while complying with the textual and artistic constructions of the east that Edward Said analysed as almost wholly a creation of Europe in *Orientalism*, they importantly also worked with forethought and exercised agency in respect of these constructions.[15] Hence their designation here as 'lotus artists', suggesting an attribution in part made to them, but which their imagery and style in part also consciously invited.

Both poets, Ghose and Naidu (as well as Toru Dutt), stood at the forefront of that long line of South Asian writers abroad in the twentieth century who were regarded as native informants and hence as outstanding but at the same time authentic representatives of India, based on the ongoing assumption that, as Ranasinha writes, 'migrant or minority artists [are often held to] speak for the entire culture or community from which they come'; as 'authoritative mediators'.[16] So Oscar Wilde, in his 24 May 1890 *Pall Mall Gazette* review of the poems of Ghose and his friends, focused on Ghose's 'lovely' lines in particular, and saw his 'high literary attainments' as reflecting something of the subtle 'Oriental mind', as well as imparting culture to Christ Church (though the tease is mainly at that college's expense).[17] Or, to take another example that will be explored in Section V, in the same period that Ghose enjoyed his greatest success as a poet, an all-male Oxford University elite championed the student Cornelia Sorabji—the first woman to sit Oxford University's BCL examination—both as an *Indian* woman and a person of exceptional character and talent.[18] Naidu, too, was consistently singled out by her supporters as a definitive voice of the age and of her culture. Indeed, her particular ability to capture if not typify some of the decade's core moods and gestures illustrates in very specific ways this book's central themes—that India and Indian voices became not merely one channel amongst others of British self-definition in this period, but one of its more prominent.[19] The generalized loveliness and hypnotic rhythms of Naidu's lines certainly helped give the anxieties about civilizational exhaustion that Decadence evoked a less threatening face. The oriental persona she projected came across as malleable and hence manageable, and her deft sound patterns as infinitely lulling.[20]

The consonance between the poetic vision and endeavours of these Indian writers, and that of their British friends, to a noticeable degree goes against what David Spurr has called 'the rhetoric of empire' with its keynotes of nationalist bombast and race superiority. It asks us, therefore, whether we are, even if only to an extent, mishearing that rhetoric, or at least missing some of its subtler undertones. Indeed, Mary Hobhouse, the reviewer of Ghose et al's *Primavera* for the *Indian Magazine*, went so far as to wonder whether the Indian poet's familiarity with English habits and verse did not qualify him to be regarded as a 'fellow countryman' rather than an Indian fellow subject.[21] Throughout, however, the question concerning imperial rhetoric must be weighed alongside the realization that even as these writers were participants in certain dominant cultural and intellectual trends that shaped the volatile end of the nineteenth century, their presentations and performances were orchestrated by those trends—trends which remained colonialist and racially founded. They were at times treated inclusively, but yet on exclusivist terms: as exceptions to the rule they were nonetheless seen to embody. However, they did exercise agency in this process—this is the crucial point. It was to achieve certain professional, cultural, and political goals that they co-operated with an aestheticized understanding of the east and, in so doing, participated in the creation of their own extraordinary status as figurehead Indians. In many ways, Naidu and Ghose (and to a lesser extent Sorabji) were following in the footsteps of T. N. Mukharji when he stage-managed and showcased 'India' for the British public in the London 1886 Indian and Colonial Exhibition. In form-giving ways they took a part in shaping how India—and in particular India-in-Britain—was perceived, and therefore must be seen to contribute to a more textured understanding of late-century Britishness itself.

II THE FANTASTICAL 1890s

The turn-of-the-century period running from the late 1880s and across the 1890s in British culture is generally characterized, as it is in Europe more broadly, as a time of social, religious, and moral uncertainty. It was marked, too, by a profound sense, pervasive at many levels, of world-weariness and malaise; a feeling of oncoming crisis, decline, and doom, encapsulated in the phrase *fin de siècle*, which was current from the 1880s. In his definitive 1893 essay, 'The Decadent Movement in Literature', Arthur Symons collectively designated the qualities that 'mark the end of [a] great period' as 'decadent': qualities that also included 'intense self-consciousness', the interrogation of all settled truths, over-refinement and 'spiritual and moral perversity'; in short, the symptoms of a society in the throes of 'a new and beautiful and interesting disease'.[22] In this he was speaking of French culture as much as English, and primarily of style, 'the ingenious deformation of the language'. For him, Decadence meant a concern with subjective impressions over fixed, God-given principles, and with sensation over morality, such as had also been extolled by the Oxford scholar Walter Pater in his influential book of art criticism, *Studies in the History of the Renaissance* (1873; from 1877 called *The Renaissance*). In its humid and controversial conclusion (suppressed in the second edition), Pater advocated the making of life into art through the heightening of fine emotion and hence of the moment in which that emotion was experienced to its fullest extent: 'to burn always with this hard gemlike flame [of fine emotion]', he resonantly wrote, 'is success in life.'[23] Along with J.-K. Huysmans *À rebours* (or *Against Nature*, 1884), the French experimental novel that holds such an abiding fascination for Oscar Wilde's Dorian Gray, *The Renaissance* can be seen to have written the motivating script of the *fin de siècle*'s obsessions and fascinations.[24]

As this suggests, Decadence presented the artist with the injunction to forge in the medium of their art and through the ecstasies it evoked the sensory and even spiritual plenitude that was believed to be lacking in the culture at large. Therefore, if the aestheticism of the previous decade had entailed a demanding commitment to the wrought forms of art over its content, Decadence, ringing fine changes on this commitment, involved a heightening of the emotions through concentrated sensory experience, such as might be most successfully achieved in the contemplation of high art. As in the case of the Irish poet and London resident Yeats, this struggle for cohesion could involve a return to more traditional or 'primitive' and hence (it was believed) truer modes of artistic expression, such as might be found in Irish folklore, including its aural and balladic traditions—or, in the case of Naidu, in Indian dance and song. Yet a devotion to the beautiful and the elevated could also lead to posturing and attitudinizing. This is typified in the character and manner of the dandyish aristocrat Lord Henry Wotton in Oscar Wilde's definitive *The Picture of Dorian Gray* (1890), who fascinates his protégé Dorian Gray with his alluringly crafted aphorisms. At another level, therefore, aestheticism promoted mannered display and a high camp imitativeness—categories of expression that embraced the arch, exaggerated mimicry of both eastern and western cultural forms at which Naidu excelled.[25]

Inevitably, the pervasive sense of internal cultural decline and fall carried wider imperial connotations (as it also did in France). Though the British Empire at this point was at once more extensive and more consolidated than it had ever been before in its history, it was also perceived as more vulnerable than at any other time, both from the threat of racial degeneration and peril from its margins, and of social and sexual disruption from within. Bram Stoker's *Dracula* (1897), in which the threat of the vampire is mounted from outside the island nation, yet also from within vulnerable female bodies, is another quintessential expression of the time. 'Mankind', agreed Max Nordau in his brooding and influential *Degeneration* (1892), 'and all his institutions and creations is perishing in the midst of a dying world.'[26] In this out-of-kilter situation, artifice would almost inevitably be valued over the natural, dreams over the everyday, the freak over the conventional, the heterodox over the orthodox, the coterie over the mass, and (metropolitan) *ennui* over (colonial) energy.

Yet, to cite from Holbrook Jackson's still-evocative account of the 1890s, 'fantastical attenuations of weariness' went hand-in-hand with 'fantastic anticipations of a new vitality'—as befitted a dichotomous age.[27] British society's widespread apprehensions of degeneration, in which it fatalistically revelled on some levels, could also signify transition and possibility, including possibility that came from without. The hostility to conventional values in certain situations produced a release of energy; an emphasis on the regenerated and renewed rather than the degenerate and wasted.[28] As this suggests, the *fin de siècle* was also widely recognized as an epoch of revolutionary new ideas about art and society, as reflected, for example, in the New Women movement and in the hedonistic and esoteric life-styles that attracted reformers and spiritual seekers, and were highly receptive to cultural influences from beyond Europe.

Ornate patterning, strangeness, diversity, languor, posturing: how 1890s—and how 'eastern'. It will already have struck readers of this book that many of the predominant features and moods of the last decades of the nineteenth century outlined here bore stereotypically orientalist as well as in some cases specifically Indian associations. For Oscar Wilde, certainly, a devotion to the sensations that beauty aroused was bound up with an excitement about refined and beautiful oriental things. Dorian Gray's interior is a display case of mixed European medieval and 'eastern' adornments and curiosities, the latter category including Persian saddlebags, globe-shaped china dishes, an Egyptian octagonal stand, and a lacquered Chinese opium box.[29] An intense curiosity about the east had long possessed Europe, which had been from the beginning of the eighteenth century stimulated in particular by travellers' tales, and the many variegated translations of the *Arabian Nights*.[30] More recently, these fascinations had been requickened by publications such as Edward Fitzgerald's *Omar Khayyám*, as we saw, and in the visual arts by the new vogue for Japanese prints and fabrics, which gave these eastern excitements specific Persian and Japanese shapes: the east was always an extensive and culturally capacious zone. Orientalism, as Edward Said's eponymous study persuasively contends, could take on oppositional significations—referring not only to the Far East and the Middle East, but also to high culture and to low, to the refined and the grotesque—significations in almost all cases defined from the position of the west.

With its glittering maharajahs and its teeming masses, India, too, connoted diametrical opposites and so harmonized with these broad patterns: of splendour set against decline, of immense wealth juxtaposed with abject poverty. India, at once colonized yet other, contained yet untamed, could signify both the effete beauty of Decadence, *and* its wild freakishness; not only the decayed sophistication but also the primitive intensity of a culture that had completed its full evolutionary cycle of ascent and decline. Exotic land of silks, spices, perfumes, and worked metals, India was widely perceived as a once-gilded civilization fallen into desuetude—far more deeply than any European culture could ever descend. As we have seen, such narratives of decline not only undergirded justifications for colonial penetration (and efforts to ward off imperial anxiety), but supported orientalist study as well. India fallen, exquisite in form yet drooping, its Vedic 'golden age' in irreparable ruin, presented to western eyes an almost enviable richness of decadent effects.[31] Among the most exquisite specimens in Dorian Gray's collection of textiles are, aptly, 'Delhi muslins' and 'Dacca gauzes'.[32] It is small wonder then that one of the most prevalent orientalist figures of the time, of the veiled, obscured, or hidden exotic woman, as is typified in H. Rider Haggard's *She* (1887) and Oscar Wilde's *Salome* (1891), also came to bear distinct Indian points of reference, in respect both of her implied waywardness and yet her ultimate submission.[33] Kipling plays on these traditional associations in his stories featuring Indian courtesans and secluded, veiled women, such as 'On the City Wall' and 'Without Benefit of Clergy'. Both Naidu and Sorabji certainly demonstrated an astute awareness of the western significance of the figure in their self-presentation as richly swathed (and in Naidu's case bejewelled) Indian women.

India also offered refreshing sources of spiritual wisdom to a society held in the grip of both materialism and religious doubt, as is crystallized in the widespread admiration for Arnold's *The Light of Asia* (1879). Both Naidu and Kipling had read Edwin Arnold, Kipling while still at school. As we saw, the Bombay-born Kipling—whose pathway as a journalist in India frequently crossed with those of theosophists, spiritualists, and Arts and Crafts devotees, as well as, of course, with the Anglo-Indian establishment—burst upon the London literary stage in 1889, at the very time that aestheticism was fading into Decadence. His work brought with it 'the scent and heat, the colour and passion of the East in all its splendours and seductiveness', as Holbrook Jackson put it in distinctly orientalist fashion, and it duly sparked a rage in the capital for all things Indian, colonial, and robust.[34] Yet, despite his imperialist attitudes, Kipling retained, very like Edwin Arnold, a profound appreciation for the contemplative aspects of Indian religions, Buddhism in particular—something that often imbues his work, most prominently *Kim* (1901).[35] As for Naidu, she based an early work, 'Mehir Muneer', on a story taken from Edwin Arnold's poems, dedicated a poem to him of her own, and continued throughout her poetic career to feel drawn to the meditative and languorous features of his work.[36]

The high-imperial capital London, both its grand public places, like Trafalgar Square or Regent Street, and the seclusion of its drawing rooms and galleries, presented scenes of pomp, luxuriance, and grandeur, which, again, bore multiple Indian—and orientalist—points of reference. The streets and parks of the metropolis were full of magniloquent monuments to victories and heroes.[37] Yet, as Watson opines in Arthur Conan Doyle's *A Study in Scarlet* (1887), London was also 'that great cesspool into which all the loungers and idlers of the Empire are irresistibly drained'. 'This grey, monstrous London of ours, with its myriads of people, its sordid sinners, and its splendid sins', according to Oscar Wilde, had something to stimulate every 'passion for sensation', however dangerous.[38] Though an Indian traveller might have pointed out to Watson or Wilde's Gray how the mixed cesspool of London was replicated also in other cities of the empire, like Calcutta or Lahore, it was true that from London's rich and populous mire there seemed to grow in more luxuriant fashion strange and exotic plants: sexual dissidents, Malays playing mah-jong outside 'ill-famed' Docklands taverns, a vast variety of hedonistic caprices and opiates, which were all captured in exaggerated form in Aubrey Beardsley's disturbing drawings.[39] 'Foreigners' were themselves strange blooms, in whom dandies and other eccentrics of the time revelled, as presenting modern alternatives to bourgeois materialism. Lady Henry in *The Picture of Dorian Gray* piquantly opines: 'I can't afford orchids, but I spare no expense in foreigners. They make one's rooms look so picturesque.'[40] As with the piling up of sensory stimulants in Dorian Gray's own hedonistic experiments, the cleaving together of diverse forms of strangeness was believed to bring forth new kinds of artistic stimulation and excitement. Not for nothing therefore did Yeats—in this matter, too, a key spokesman of the age—characterize Sarojini Naidu as the little Indian princess—though she was not a princess and her Indian manners and attire were choreographed, as we saw. In her orientalist guise, she represented a crossover between an opulent symbolism drawn from Europe's own aristocratic and medieval history, and a distant yet contemporary exotic. The crossover worked in harmony with Yeats's other experiments of the time—in developing a passionate and dramatic voice, tapping organic rhythms, and bringing the infinite into his poetry.[41]

After the discussion in Chapter 2, the *fin de siècle*'s Indian associations will not unduly surprise readers, especially if we bear in mind the Indian social and cultural influences that had migrated 'home' both with Indian arrivants and Anglo-Indian returnees. Indian visitors to the metropolis had for some decades encouraged impressions of the social, historical, and even moral proximity to the subcontinent that the late Victorian 'mystical revival' had fostered, as had political reform movements and new developments in the law. For example, Malabari in *The Times* in 1890, the medical student and reformer Rukhmabai in the *New Review* in the same year, and Sorabji in the *Nineteenth Century* in 1891, all joined the contentious debate about Indian child marriage and the reform of age-of-consent laws that raged in both Britain and the Indian Empire.[42] Decadence, if nothing else, intensified these links, in particular perhaps those relating to mysticism and the occult. As Alex Owen summarizes in her magisterial study of *fin-de-siècle* occultism, *The Place of Enchantment*:

> The Victorian fascination with the Orient owed a great deal to the exposure of an educated public to the ethnological work of colonial administrators, missionaries and explorers; the translation of sacred texts by scholars [such as Max Müller] and missionaries with linguistic expertise; and the emergence of a serious and professional study of language and culture as new academic specialties. By the late-Victorian period these various endeavors had raised public awareness of pan-Asian cultures and geographies, and engendered a conversation about the relative merits of non-Christian religious traditions.[43]

This prevalence of Asian cultural and religious influences in the metropolis strongly contributed to the *fin-de-siècle*'s orientalist patina—a contribution that the widespread fascination with ornate modes of eastern decoration only heightened. As we saw, the particular focus that 1880s occult interests and especially theosophy added to this mix was an eastward shift in the location of Europe's mystical Orient from Egypt and Persia to India, now perceived as the heartland of Buddhist and Hindu teaching. Motivated by interests both academic and spiritual, a significant number of writers and intellectuals followed in the footsteps of Carpenter and Yeats, and sought exposure to Indian religions, most often through theosophy, which continued to provide the most readily available channel. The 1890s poet Lionel Johnson, for example, encountered a 'theosophized' form of Buddhism at Westminster school, while fellow poet Laurence Binyon, whom Johnson met at Oxford, first came into contact with eastern philosophy in a rather less mediated form, through classroom conversations with Manmohan Ghose.

Contained within the domesticated orientalist panoply, India again signified both the high and the low, in both social and religious senses. The most elevated echelons of society, associated with 'jewel-girt' rajahs, as well as the higher spiritual realms occupied by teachers of Victorian occultism, such as theosophy's Mahatmas, were set against the seedier quarters of East End streets where Wilkie Collins's lascars and Oscar Wilde's foreign sailors and brawlers resided, or the darkened backrooms where séances might be held. The 1890s fad in some British cities for so-called Indian oculists, or eye-doctors, some (though not all) of whom turned out to be charlatans, neatly brought out this dichotomy of high versus low, or clear obscure. Contemporary advertisements in local papers of the time show that self-proclaimed Indian oculists practiced in several British port cities at this time, including Swansea and London. Some may have been lascars or abandoned servants who endeavoured by way of this alternative work to earn a passage home, though their inadequate know-how landed them not infrequently in court or homes for the destitute. In 1893, four Indian oculists were tried at the Old Bailey for fraud; a local Swansea MP alerted Naoroji in Parliament about the ill-fated plight of five others.[44] Yet, even as these oculists were trying and failing to improve their patients' vision, scientific organizations like the London Dialectical Society, often in association with leading spiritualists and theosophists, were investigating the truth or clarity of esoteric phenomena, which often carried non-Christian and, at times, Indian religious and philosophical associations.

Indian motifs of seclusion, screening, veiling, and the like, harmonized also with that inward-turning tendency of 1890s decadent poetry which provided such a strong contrast with the other dominant note in the poetry of the period—jingoist bombast. Several commentators at the time discerned a split in British poetry between that addressed to a public world of action on the one hand, and a dreamy verse of interiors and introversion on the other.[45] The dense concentration of nocturnal and zenana motifs in Naidu's work and the prevalence of secluded sylvan scenes in Ghose (as captured in this chapter's third epigraph)—as well as his persistent yearning for retreat—may therefore account to some degree for the interest that was shown in both poets' work among 1890s coteries of artists in London. Yeats's efforts in collaboration with musicians like Florence Farr to 'return the poetic voice to the centre of culture' were dedicated to resisting the materialism and commercialism of mainstream British and Irish society, and hence shared the tendency to withdraw from the public sphere.[46] Indeed, Yeats may well have favoured Naidu's work in the 1890s, and Tagore's in the 1910s, because of the poets' willingness to present as traditional balladeers. Interestingly, the Rhymers' Club, whose meetings at the Cheshire Cheese Yeats dominated with his experiments in heightening emotion through chanting, was also the group that welcomed Ghose and feted Naidu.

The two Indian poets, Sarojini Naidu and Manmohan Ghose, therefore, supplied the *fin de siecle* with a seemingly authentic oriental music that at once easternized their own work (perhaps in part self-consciously), yet also participated willy-nilly in the modern and metropolitan vogue for orientalist effects. Although it is impossible to say to what extent the culturally anglicized Naidu was aware of polishing the orientalist glosses in her work, her decadent-yet-eastern associations, especially the emphasis on artifice and sensuality in her poems, are so prominent that some measure of manipulation can surely be assumed. Ghose, too, even more anglicized than Naidu, adopted decadent affectations that were perceived (certainly in a native Indian poet) as both oriental and yet of the moment. Even Sorabji, though an altogether more matter-of-fact writer, not given to flights of fancy, subscribed to a Paterian, or at least Oxford-derived aesthetic, that celebrated crafted medieval beauty. Her evocations of India, in *Love and Life Behind the Purdah* (1901), *Between the Twilights* (1908), and *Sun-babies: Studies in the Child Life of India* (1904), as well as in the memoir *India Calling* (1934), accentuate the mysteries and gracefulness, if also the strange distortions of life behind the veil, alongside the hazy magic of India's 'twilight hour'. Though their paths in the 1890s did not cross (Naidu and Sorabji were to meet several times from 1904), all three writers in their different ways shared interests in exotic display and folk or classical traditions, and in an aesthetic of sinuous lines and decorative effects—interests that connected them with other avant-garde and modern writers and artists working in London and Hyderabad, in Dublin and Calcutta.

III 'LOTUS-EYED' GHOSE 'THE PRIMAVERA POET'

Sections III and IV of this chapter examine the work of these Indian-English poets in more detail, beginning with Manmohan Ghose (1867–1924), whose poetry forms the focus of this section.[47] Although Ghose's standing as a poet was more marginal than Naidu's, and his outlook more acculturated, in order to establish a poetic voice, he, too, like his younger countrywoman, struck distinctive *fin-de-siècle* poses and shared decadent and orientalist preoccupations. Both poets, for example, expressed a sense of lost cultural coherence, which for both carried nationalist overtones, as well as a strong yearning for a more customary, ordered world to be restored. Like Naidu, too, Ghose developed his poetic craft in collaboration with like-minded British poets, though the intercultural dialogues he enjoyed were arguably closer and more fraternal even than Naidu's.

In the mid-to-late 1880s, Manmohan Ghose's friendship with the turn-of-the-century British art historian, translator, and poet Laurence Binyon (1869–1943) in particular, became the alembic of his best work.[48] Significantly for the purposes of this study, the relationship was by no means one-sided. Binyon's encounter with the Bengali Ghose and their shared discussions about poetry, art, and religious belief also had shaping effects on the Englishman's early writing, as well as on his career as a commentator on eastern art; specifically, as the curator of eastern manuscripts in the British Museum.[49] Many decades later, in the 1920s, Binyon spoke of his friendship with Ghose as 'decisive' for a career that had been devoted to studying Asian art and philosophy.[50] On both sides, the relationship was nurtured in the rich cultural soil of a still-Paterian Oxford where, in the same heady summer term of 1890, the two youthful poets published a collection together with two other poet friends, and Binyon won the Newdigate Prize for Poetry. (It was also in that year that Wilde published *The Picture of Dorian Gray*.) Their collaboration, and the work that emerged from it, can therefore be seen to have contributed in modest, if also suggestive ways, to how aestheticist Oxford and decadent London were at the time perceived.

The friendship of the two poet-novices Manmohan Ghose and Laurence Binyon began at St Paul's School in London in the mid-to-later 1880s, where they were both dedicated Classics scholars. It matured at Oxford University in the short period 1887–90, Ghose arriving at Christ Church on an open scholarship the year before Binyon matriculated at Trinity.[51] Even during their school days, Binyon later remembered in his 'Introductory Memoir' to his friend's work, Ghose had shown himself to be better read than he in the Elizabethan poets, and also gifted with a sympathetic appreciation for the 'limpid and severe' Greeks, something seemingly far removed from an oriental's assumed 'luxuriant and ornate' taste.[52] Yet, Binyon also perceptively wrote, 'many of us are attracted to arts and literatures remote from our own traditions and just because of qualities in them which these have not. Why should not an Indian feel a parallel attraction?' Both young men explored questions of religious belief both in this period and at university: Binyon came through a personal crisis of faith to espouse a 'quasi-Platonic humanism', as described by his biographer John Hatcher, and Ghose drew closer to his father's Buddhism and what he called his own native paganism. If for Binyon the divine was 'the sum of all good', Ghose saw God as Nature, the sum of all existence: neither were conventional pathways of belief.[53] At the same time, to Ghose, the 'glory of the classics of Europe', his abiding interest, would always remain 'mingled in memory' with 'the whole hurried stream of western life'.[54] The western classical world and its literature served as an interface for him between his western experiences and his eastern origins. For both aspirant poets, too, the western classics provided strong formal models. At school, Binyon tried out different lyric forms and metrical patterns in his notebook; Ghose, his interlocutor, no doubt did so too. In his holiday letters to Binyon, Ghose begged repeatedly for robust criticism, and wrote of his experimentation with different lines and metrical structures, as Binyon presumably also did in respect of Ghose. (Binyon's letters to Ghose are now unfortunately lost.) Binyon, Ghose wrote in April 1887, had instructed him to avoid excessive 'Matthew-Arnoldism', despite their mutual admiration for his 'muse of marble'; in a later letter he admitted of an 'unconscious' influence from Arnold's calm sanity and architectonic shapes. As in his efforts to transpose 'Scenes from Indian Drama' 'into a Greek mould', Ghose appears to have avoided overt orientalism and, again like Binyon, did not find much of interest in Edwin Arnold.[55]

As these intertwined strands of influence suggest, Ghose and Binyon across the years of their closest contact demonstrated an untiring capacity to be open to the other's perspective. Until Ghose's period of 'infatuation' with his London life distanced them for a period of years, they also worked hard to talk through and mediate any differences of opinion they encountered.[56] Their friendship, captured in the responsive, at times almost dialogic letters Ghose sent to Binyon 1887 to 1890, and then again in the sadder and wiser letters from India 1893 to 1904, vividly dramatizes the give and take of ideas that is fundamental to cosmopolitanism, in Kwame Appiah's idealist terms, even if their exchange does at times snag on inevitable cultural and imperialist tensions. Many of the Indian–British relations featured in this book likewise reflect instances of such give and take but, within the 1870–1915 period, it was never so fully expressed as by these two writers in their youth.[57]

For Appiah, an ethical position informed by cosmopolitanism is based on a regard for the difference represented by another's values, yet a regard also worked out on the common ground of shared interests and desires. This common ground in respect of Ghose and Binyon I will shortly go on to read as an aesthetic of reciprocity that they developed *in unison*; a nuanced mode of critical negotiation that was worked out recursively *between* the east and the west. Importantly, Appiah further contends, a cosmopolitan respect for difference is negotiated through the 'imaginative engagement' supplied within the flow and counterflow, the candid exchange, entailed by conversation.[58] True, as we saw, Appiah's theory can tend to overlook the pressures that an unequal social context can bring to bear on cosmopolitan relations. The posturing in Ghose's letters certainly points to profound feelings of self-hatred and alienation rising from colonial inequality, wherever he found himself—feelings that complicated his friendship with Binyon. Even so, candid exchange is very much a constant feature of Ghose and Binyon's unique poetic dialogue as student poets, which was strengthened by their ability to meet at the interface supplied by their shared Classical interests. Their dialogue is most strikingly captured perhaps in the pages of *Primavera*, the collection they published with Oxford's Basil Blackwell in 1890, in collaboration with two other young poets.[59] The remarkable, sometimes seamless interleaving of sixteen poems by these four pairs of hands, English and Bengali, dramatizes on the page the active cultural interchange between India and Britain to which Oxford paid host at more or less the charged moment when aestheticism began to turn into Decadence.

With *Primavera*, the four young poet contributors, Ghose, Binyon, Arthur C. Cripps, and the actor Stephen Phillips (Binyon's cousin), '[submerged] their poetic identities in an ensemble [lyric] performance' that was also a publishing success, soon coming out in a second edition.[60] It was a groundbreaking intercultural exercise that would have no parallel for over twenty years, until the 1912 publication of Tagore's *Gitanjali*, edited by Yeats, and promoted by Pound and William Rothenstein, among others (as Chapter 4 explores). Throughout, the *Primavera* ensemble is intriguingly animated both by a spirit of Arnoldian self-effacement and the somewhat affected aestheticist devotion to beauty associated with the still influential Pater.[61] Botticelli's atmospheric painting *Primavera*, much admired by Pater, gave the collection its title. A print hung in Binyon's Trinity College room. Across the collection's pages, the poets' individual voices merge, mingle, diverge, and again intertwine, participating in shared yearnings and musings, as will shortly be seen. Yet, even so, for all its interactive aspects, the making of *Primavera* rested at base on Ghose and Binyon's collaborative friendship and their intense conversations across several years about Classical literature, modern English works, and their own poetry. The polysyllabic strands of decorative 'nineties devices that run through and across the poems can therefore be seen to make up a kind of brocade, wrought by both English and Indian hands. Its dense warp and weft provides one of the most persuasive reasons I can put forward to support the contention that the decadent poetry that emerged out of the 1890s, and defined turn-of-the-century art, bore Indian as well as European threads and traces.

The life of Manmohan Ghose, the older brother of Aurobindo Ghose (later the radical nationalist and then guru Sri Aurobindo), was quintessentially a product of the cultural and educational pathways through which Indians began arriving in Britain in increasing numbers in the late nineteenth century. Manmohan and Aurobindo's father Krishna Dhan Ghose, who had studied medicine at Aberdeen, brought his three sons (including also Binoy Bhushan) to England for their schooling in 1879. The fifteen years which Manmohan then spent studying in Britain, first with private tutors, then at Manchester Grammar School, St Paul's, and finally Oxford University, transformed him into 'four-fifths an Englishman, if not entirely one', as he wrote to Binyon in a tonally complicated March 1889 letter.[62] Across their school years, the Ghose brothers lodged together, with Binyon occasionally also meeting the younger Ghose boys when he visited Manmohan in order to talk about Greek translations and poetry. University vacations were spent, at first, in Keswick in the Lake District, and later in St Stephen's Road in Uxbridge, or at the South Kensington Liberal Club at 128 Cromwell Road.[63]

In Laurence Binyon's memoir essay about Ghose, which appears as the introduction to his 1926 *Songs of Love and Death*, he described how at St Paul's Ghose's recitations from Shakespeare disturbed 'our little world of everyday things and humdrum studies' 'with colours, mystery, romance'.[64] The two aspirant poets met in the Seventh Form *Aeneid* reading class, where Binyon felt 'immediate sympathy' for the Indian's 'low and [thrilling]' voice, whose 'dramatic emotion' seemed to suggest someone 'intoxicated' by poetry. Orientalizing though Binyon's sketch of Ghose as a 'fragment' of 'the legendary East' may appear, it is counterbalanced by his accompanying admission of outright fascination: 'anyone foreign who brought a breath from a world outside the world of habit ever attracted me'. Both young men felt at this point unmoored from their family and school contexts, where they encountered few like-minded companions, and few who were as passionately dedicated to poetry.

Their initial meetings represented on both sides therefore an encounter with spiritual kindred.

As Laurence Binyon's mature work as a poet and art critic shows, across his career he remained keenly attuned to what he described as 'the ever-moving, ever-changing, eternal and universal rhythm of life' (in a 1912 essay appropriately for the modernist magazine *Rhythm*).[65] It is likely that this sensitivity, as well as his Quaker background, quickened his openness and hospitality to other arts and forms of cultural understanding, an openness that his friendship with Ghose, however westernized the Indian may have been, clearly also stimulated. Ghose in effect represented Binyon's first guide into the oriental worlds—'the storied, sacred East... clothed in green'—on which he would continue to work across his long career. He also remained attracted to what can best be termed critical work across the borderlines between disciplines and cultures—something that also marked the syncretic arts of the 1890s. While the understanding that he formed with the Indian-born Classicist Ghose at school represented a living out of these interests and attractions, their collaborative interaction at the same time also supported and reinforced the east–west rapprochements taking place in the culture at large (as also with Japan, reflected in the vogue for Japanese arts and crafts). Capturing something of this closeness, Ghose, in a letter to Binyon of 28 July 1887, included a sonnet 'To Robert Laurence Binyon', in which he acclaimed the healing powers of his friend's work and his ability to inspire devotion: 'the whole love of a friend'.[66]

Manmohan Ghose left St Paul's in July 1887 after winning an open scholarship to Christ Church, where he pursued studies in Greek, mathematics, and also Sanskrit. A letter of October 1887 suggests that he was recommended by F. Max Müller, who would shortly also welcome Sorabji, though they had not met prior to his arrival. He was aware of the presence in Oxford of other Indian students, including a 'Mukherjee' at Christ Church and two senior Government scholars at Balliol, but he felt he lacked true 'appreciative and intimate friends' (147–9). He nailed Binyon's portrait to the wall of his Christ Church room and in several letters spoke of his isolation and his desire to set up, with Binyon 'when you come', 'a small fraternity of letters', 'a sphere in which to act'.[67] In October 1888, Laurence Binyon duly followed Ghose's path to Oxford, as he later would in respect of London, though he chose Trinity College. (Trinity at this point did not accept Indians on religious grounds). Across their times apart, including when Ghose left for London, up until about 1905, Ghose and Binyon kept up an active epistolary exchange in which they discussed their work and explored radical and avant-garde thought, not excluding controversial political approaches such as republicanism.[68]

It was in this same period that Manmohan's brother Aurobindo was becoming radicalized, not least by the effect of newspaper cuttings sent over by their father about political developments in India, as well as by his experiences of racial inequality. Though Manmohan, by contrast, favoured poetry over politics as a means of self-expression, he, too, in dialogue with Binyon, confronted the 'tyrannical' nature of British rule in India. Binyon, alone of Ghose's acquaintance, he wrote, would not meet him with 'unbelief' in pursuing these investigations.[69]

In mid-1889, against Binyon's 'entreaties', Ghose left Christ Church for London after eight terms of residence, without a degree. Under the pressure of debts and dwindling remittances from his father, as well as what he called the 'slavery of study', it had become difficult to continue as a student. In 1893, he returned to Oxford, living east of the city centre, in order to sit for a Pass Final. In the intervening years he had been involved in a desultory way on the fringes of *fin-de-siècle* literary London, enjoying some celebrity as the *Primavera* poet whom Oscar Wilde had singled out in his review of the collection: 'Mr Ghose ought some day to make a name in our literature.'[70] Wilde—Ghose told Binyon in a letter—had not only given time to penning the review despite being involved in writing *Dorian Gray*, but had also taken 'an immense liking to me; and now I know him well I love him very much . . . [he is] one of the most wonderful personalities of our age'.[71] Beneath Oscar's 'delightful mask of paradox and irony and perversity', he also wrote, his personality revealed depths of character and sagacity.[72] Ernest Dowson, another close friend, if not lover of Wilde, described Ghose in his letters as 'a divinely mad person' and as 'beautiful lotus-eyed Ghose', and referred also to spending long, drunken nights in their joint company. If Ghose knew Wilde well enough to speak of him in these terms (and Dowson Ghose), it is safe to conclude that Ghose must have enjoyed some intimacy within the 'decadent, aestheticist' circles around Wilde. First Ghose and then Binyon therefore approached Wilde and his friends under the aegis of what Leela Gandhi calls a fractured 'homoerotic dispensation'. At stake here, however, is that, as regards the Ghose–Binyon friendship, it was Ghose who preceded Binyon into London's cosmopolitan world. Setting aside for a moment the shaping effects of Ghose's anglicization, Indian arrivant here led British friend.

Ghose's star-struck London days also featured regular contact with the Arts and Crafts Century Guild association (1882) on Fitzroy Street, home of its *Hobby Horse* quarterly (which published Lionel Johnson, Dowson, Michael Field, and the radical W. S. Blunt, amongst others). He knew Charles Ricketts the illustrator and his partner Charles Shannon, editors of another aestheticist journal, the *Dial*. Evenings at the *Hobby Horse* featured many prominent names on the London arts scene, including Richard Le Gallienne, Walter Sickert and, once again, Arthur Symons. Ghose also met and mingled with members of the Rhymers' Club, including Lionel Johnson and Yeats, a number of whom had *Hobby Horse* associations. The Club gathered at the soon-to-be-renowned Cheshire Cheese public house in Fleet Street where, as Yeats records, within half a decade or so, the same group would fete Naidu.[73] In June 1891, Ghose's name appeared on the provisional list of contributors to *The Book of the Rhymers' Club*, but he was unable to participate due to a lack of funds. Binyon, for his part, first visited the *Hobby Horse* in 1890 and, on the same night, met for the first time both Wilde (who was performing) and Yeats. For both friends, Ghose and Binyon, the contrast between this culturally charged world and the scholarly seclusion of Oxford must have been staggering. Readers can imagine that when Ghose was invited into these different circles he may to some extent have been tolerated or even patronized due to his exotic appearance and eccentric behaviour. Yet what remains striking to us today about his time in literary London is the degree to which he was drawn into its different circles—much as this would have meant a measure of playing along on his part, tempered by his own 'passion for beauty' (as he says in a September 1890 letter). Donned in velvet (his brother reported), much like Wilde, he again appears not to have felt overly impeded by his foreignness.[74] Indeed, if Wilde's charmed tones in his *Primavera* review are anything to go by, far from undermining his presence and status in literary London, Ghose's oriental, yet assimilated aspect seems to have facilitated his entry to avant-garde circles, as it did Naidu's.

Throughout Ghose's heady time in the city, he continued to depend on Binyon as his interlocutor and confidante. He did, however, begin regularly to berate his university friend for his unwillingness to tolerate his 'wickedness' and to embrace the London attitudes that Ghose now found *de rigueur*, including what he called paganism. Tiring of the 'small' and 'worthy' world of the *Hobby Horse* and its eternal 'theorizing . . . about art and life', Ghose announced to Binyon a compulsion towards a new and dangerous individuality: 'Never before have I been throbbing so with strange desires, the exquisite temptations of youth'; 'I am brimming with youth and passion, sweet and dangerous things; how sweet and dangerous those only know who yield themselves wholly to their crimson fascination!'[75] Ghose's wilful archness and note of abandon, a tone no doubt struck in imitation of Wilde's circle, in particular the evocative stagey phrase 'crimson fascination', gives some sense of the transgressive pastimes with which London presented him. They were transgressions about which Binyon had undoubtedly warned him across the summer's correspondence of 1890, if Ghose's defensiveness is anything to go by. The key impression that the London letters give, however, is the association of perilous fascination with a somewhat attitudinizing passion—an association that is captured in the underlying references to Blake's poem 'The Sick Rose' with its destroyed 'bed of crimson joy'. The very real love that Binyon and Ghose shared—with Ghose writing to Binyon on 18 February 1888 'You are the only company to me'—was now being distributed across other interests and parties, though it remained an anchor on which both friends occasionally still depended. Indeed, until 1890, Binyon planned to write an 'Indian tale' in collaboration with Ghose. Reviewing *Primavera* for the *Hobby Horse*, Lionel Johnson, whom Binyon had first met in Oxford, inscribed on its flyleaf a poem celebrating Binyon and Ghose's poetic friendship. In it, he wished that these 'True sons of Arnold' would remain 'Friends in one art', linked together by the grace of their shared lyricism.[76]

Ghose returned to India in 1894, on a liner appropriately named (Binyon noted) the *Patroclus*, after Achilles's friend in the *Iliad*, his efforts 'to cramp and screw' his remaining funds having failed at last. He and Binyon continued intermittently to correspond with each other until the Indian poet's death in 1924, though from 1904 infrequently so. Ghose proceeded to hold a series of appointments in government colleges in India, beginning with Bankipore and then Dacca College, and finally Presidency College in Calcutta. Finding that his social conditioning in England had distanced him from most Indian people, whom he awkwardly referred to as 'brown things', Ghose embodied the malaise of the anglicized Indian doomed to spend his days living a vicarious existence, out of place. In his letters, he closely followed the cultural news from Britain with which Binyon was able to supply him, including reports of the trial and death of Oscar Wilde, and continued to discuss poetry and paintings. He mentally traced Binyon's visits to different picture galleries in Europe, and several times requested from him copies of Italian Renaissance paintings through which he might imagine, though at several removes, the art works to which his friend was responding—again, a telling admission of his sense of cultural alienation. As this suggests, Binyon's friendship remained to the end something fundamental and formative to Ghose's emotional and aestheticist make-up.

Laurence Binyon, the junior partner in the friendship, began studying Greats at Oxford in 1888, the same year that the third edition of Pater's *Renaissance* was published, with its controversial conclusion restored. Binyon's biographer John Hatcher appropriately describes him as a 'citizen' of Pater's Oxford of the 1880s. Yet, though he may have delighted in aestheticist involvements at Oxford, he did not meet Pater until after university, dining with him on two occasions in 1892. This suggests that his friend Ghose, too, may not have had the pleasure of making Pater's acquaintance—though Sorabji, interestingly, did. At Trinity, Binyon quickly established himself as one of the leading poets of his generation. In early 1890, he not only arranged for Basil Blackwell publishers in Broad Street to take *Primavera*, but also won the Newdigate Prize for poetry, with a still noticeably Arnoldian poem entitled 'Persephone'. The two events produced excellent mutual publicity. As was customary, Binyon read his Newdigate prize-winning poem at the annual graduation ceremony called Encaenia, on the occasion that the African explorer H. M. Stanley was awarded an honorary degree by the university.

After graduating, Binyon pursued his already well-cultivated Arts and Crafts interests, especially as these were given manual and synergistic expression by artists—by engravers in different media, for example, or those who combined the visual arts and poetry. In 1893, he began working for the British Museum, first for the Department of Printed Books, and later for Prints and Drawings, in 1913 eventually becoming the Keeper of the new Sub-department of Oriental Prints and Drawings. In 1898, he studied wood-engraving with the Scottish artist William Strang, so developing familiarity with one of the techniques fundamental to eastern plastic arts. He remained at the British Museum in one or other capacity for forty years, continually expanding and deepening his interests in eastern art and the Museum's oriental art collections: those interests, in fact, that his friendship with Ghose had first quickened in him. He wrote and gave lectures on non-western philosophies and world-views, and in the 1910s, in response to the work of the India Society, adapted a range of Asian classics and legends for the English stage, including *Sakuntala*. As well as serving as the keeper of Ghose's flame, Binyon also became a supportive mentor to many leading avant-garde artists and writers, though his own poetry is now best remembered for the four lines from his elegy 'For the Fallen' that are universally read at Remembrance Sunday services in England.[77] In his self-cast role of western interpreter of the east he played a crucial part in forging some of the intercultural alliances of early modernism, especially in so far as he introduced East Asian art forms to the poets who would soon come to call themselves Imagists (Ezra Pound, Richard Aldington, and H. D.).

Following this short overview of their biographies, it is appropriate to turn back to Ghose and Binyon's most significant joint achievement, *Primavera*. Initially, in reading the collection, the mutual involvements and muted cross-references that run between the young student-poets' lines give an impression of competitive posing. The four friends, but especially Binyon and Ghose, seem involved in trying to outdo one another in affecting *fin-de-siècle* attitudes of dreamy idealism and hopeless seeking. At the same time, however, each also moves thematically in unison with the other, in 'parallel attraction' (to use Binyon's phrase). Moved by that 'capacity to be intoxicated' by poetry that Binyon and Ghose had already found they shared, all the participating poets clearly had read and discussed their work with one another, developing their friendships through their poetic endeavours. Across the collection, a subtle and intriguing call-and-response pattern strings together and interconnects in particular the poems by the two friends, Ghose and Binyon. They are seen to hold certain concerns in common: a straining for 'Life', 'Love' and 'Youth', which is repeatedly overshadowed by a world-weary pessimism as to whether such visions of joy and promise might ever be realized, including the sense that it ultimately might be best to foster these as visions only.[78]

Of the *Primavera* poems, Binyon and Phillips supply four each, Cripps three, and Ghose five, the greatest number. As Binyon and Ghose's poems are longer, their work also covers more pages than does that of the other two. Thematic contrasts underpin these quantitative differences. All four *Primavera* poets are preoccupied with mutability and its inevitable outcome, mortality, transmuting these concerns into semi-allegorical forms and idealizations. In several poems, Youth, or analogues for Youth such as Beauty and Love are threatened by the world and death.[79] But whereas Cripps and Phillips seem particularly concerned with the antinomian pairing of Love and Death with which aesthetes were much involved, Binyon and Ghose share a poetic conversation about evanescence and the transitory quality of all life and desire. Their poems dwell on the inevitable movement from youth to age and the loss of aspiration and hope and onset of woe this brings. Throughout, there are felt echoes of 'Matthew-Arnoldian' solitude and pessimism (as most memorably expressed in his 'Dover Beach'), feelings that are only partially and fitfully allayed by the presence of love. Though their work is therefore superficially as preoccupied with abstractions as Phillips and Cripps, at the same time the poems are marked with more pronounced shifts and progressions, underpinned with a more visceral imagery, and so appear to spring directly from embodied experience. Binyon invokes a Ghose-type personage at least once in the poems, and Ghose more than once alludes to his position far from home (and to 'the pale long seas becoming golden' with the light of the east, that first emerged in his early poems, such as 'Towards the Morning', included in a letter to Binyon).[80] Taken together, the Ghose–Binyon poems therefore stand out as a particularly collaborative and even intimate interchange within the wider symposium of *Primavera*, a faithful and repeated taking account of the position of the friend.

Following directly after Stephen Phillips's opening poem in which the dreaming Muse of the 'later bards' is faced with the 'jarring Truth' of the present day, Binyon's keynote poem 'Youth' casts the personified Youth figure 'Thrilled with ethereal exultations/And a victorious expectancy', in the form of an Indian Bacchus facing the 'relentless Hours' of time and change (pp. 5–9). As captured in the epigraphic citation from the poem, above, apostrophized Youth, the 'bright new-comer' accompanied by tigers, striking out for the 'spacious earth', possessed by the 'longing for one perfect friend', bears more than a passing resemblance to Ghose. He, too, had set out as a conquering young poet, but, contemplating departure from Oxford at this time, faced disenchantment in the 'alien air' of 'others' commerce and economy'. In its final stanzas, with their constantly permutating *abcd* rhyme scheme, the poem modulates from elated apostrophe to fatalistic prayer—which, however, is still motivated by friendship and care, as the speaker entreats Nature to treat its 'child' well, despite the encroaching hostile conditions.

The untitled 'III', which follows, by Ghose, offers a partial response to 'Youth' (pp. 10–11). The poet-speaker, in his twentieth year, feels his youth stretching behind, and the world, 'Life, and thy visions of joy', 'Love' and the future, 'breaking' before him. Yet at the same time he casts himself as a poor dreamer, unaware of the ills that future holds in store. In this state, he is recalled to an image of his younger self, who, too, was possessed of a vision of brighter skies beyond the shores he then paced, and turned his face from the parting sorrows of loved ones. The poem, with its erratically half-rhyming alexandrines, ends on a jarringly visceral image of the family left behind 'on some tropic shore dying in fever and pain', a harsh reality that appears to confront not only the poet's former youthful self, but also the speaker in the present. As 'III' illustrates, those points of crisis and transition evoked in other of the *Primavera* poems are at times given autobiographical grounding in Ghose, as Binyon also appears to acknowledge with the evocation of his Indian Bacchus beset by hostile conditions. Binyon's sonnet 'Testamentum Amoris' addressed to a lover or dear friend, 'the lovely regent of my mind', follows 'III', and is itself followed by two poems about dead beloveds from Cripps and Phillips, which thus sustain the themes of love and loss through the first third of the collection.

In later poems, the reciprocated measures and symbolic resonances established in the opening lyrics, especially in those by Ghose and Binyon, are echoed and answered. In Ghose's 'Raymond and Ida' (VII), the nymph Ida, possessed by intimations of immortality, is comforted by her companion, Raymond (pp. 19–22). 'Psyche' by Binyon (VIII) evokes another interaction between two figures—the poet-speaker and Psyche, walking 'through enchanted lands of spring'—an interaction in which succour is again bestowed (pp. 20–2). In the second half of the poem, Psyche's healing presence returns to the poet in dreams despite the 'breaking in' of 'the world's strong strife'—'breaking' noticeably picks up a resonance from Ghose's line 'Breaking fresh at my feet . . . the world' in 'III' (pp. 20–2). Ghose's short and plangent 'A Lament' (IX) pictures the world as alive with leaping fishes and birds carrying music in their wings, yet the figure at the centre of this wheeling movement, separated from the speaker by heaven's 'wide spaces', lies apparently asleep, never to be seen again (p. 25). As in 'III', the accent on the forbidding lengths of the ocean separating the speaker and the loved one, and the western heavens arching above, introduces unmistakeable autobiographical reverberations.

'XII', again by Ghose, presents an exchange between a poet-speaker and a second poet he addresses as 'thou', and harks back to some of the top notes of 'Youth' (pp. 29–31; see also the third epigraph). The 'sad' poet, encased in some Keatsian grove (compare Ghose's 'unseen trees . . . softly real' and deep-shaded grove with 'I cannot see what flowers are at my feet' of 'Ode to a Nightingale'), does not feel equal to celebrating the beauties of Nature, much as they impel him to do so. Nature and the speaker together entreat him to resist the urge to slumber, at least until the always-oncoming autumn returns. As before, Nature, though changeable, represents a redemptive force that wards off dejection and sorrow. Though it is in vain, some hope lingers that the inevitable can be forestalled, at least for a while. Across the collection, the nature-worshipper Ghose is generally more even-tempered and hopeful than his friend Binyon (in spite of Binyon's 'XV', his six-line praise-song to life's sweetness).

Perhaps the clearest expression of Ghose's paganistic trust in nature comes in 'Mentem mortalia tangunt' ('this stuff of our mortality cuts us to the heart', from Virgil), the closing poem of the collection. Though Autumn has arrived and the speaker is again beset by the evanescence of all things, he gleans some spiritual sustenance from the very fact of the human yearning for the infinite, which the birds and flowers he admires do not share (pp. 38–41). That Nature has endowed human life with a sense of immortality brings hope: 'She will find out a way' (and the collection is named for the spring, after all). The images of trees, leaves, and birds as correlates for evanescence, and 'the lonely sea' as a symbol for loss, connect this closing poem back to the poems in the first half of the collection, particularly Ghose's own.

Overall, the cross-hatching of verbal echoes and shared emotions . . . draw the *Primavera* poems of Ghose and Binyon into what could very much, following Wilde, be called a 'bond of union'. The mood of wistful yearning that their poems together generate certainly captures something of the temper of the times: a sense of irrevocable change; of the world winding down like a clock. Indeed, the harmonies between the different poems suggest that the suture of the bond of union lay not just in Ghose's beguiling lyricism, but within the reciprocal movements of the poetic conversation itself. It lay in the resonance between Ghose's verses and those of his collaborator, his '[Friend] of one art'.[81]

IV 'SO IMPETUOUS AND SO SYMPATHETIC': SAROJINI NAIDU AS SELF-ORIENTALIST

In the pre-1914 period, the so-called 'Indian nightingale' Sarojini Naidu (1879–1949) succeeded perhaps more consistently even than the widely promoted seer-poet Rabindranath Tagore in representing herself as the definitive poet in English of the Orient.[82] It is telling that three of her poems, and not Tagore's verses, which were at that time better known, were chosen for the 1916 *Oxford Book of English Mystical Verse*, a collection to mark the time's rising new age of mysticism, according to the editors. Departing from Tagore's highly personalized, Vedantic sense of the divine, as well as her own sometimes trivializing whimsicality, Naidu's poems 'The Soul's Prayer', 'In Salutation to the Eternal Peace', and 'To a Buddha seated on a Lotus', capture the sharp contradictions and sense of awe through which the ineffable might be understood.[83] Of the three poems, the first is the closing poem to *The Golden Threshold*, and the second two appear among the closing poems to *The Bird of Time*. All three are imbued with the 'heavenward hungering of the soul' ('To a Buddha'), yet also, as is appropriate for closing poems, grant a sense of *Bhakha*-like spiritual transcendence that comes from contemplating 'the infinite essence of eternity' ('In Salutation').

Naidu styled herself in her work as in her person as an impassioned, spiritually enraptured 'woman of the East', to cite again from Symons, and manipulated with great deftness a mystical orientalist vocabulary. Despite, or perhaps even because of, her oeuvre's apparent complicity with received exotic and etherealized perceptions of Indians, it can be counted as among the most significant contributions made by an Indian visitor to London's metropolitan culture in the pre-First World War period. It is significant, first, because of how her poetry processed and subtly revised received ideas of the dominant west as set against its submissive, feminine, eastern fringe, India. To see how this operates, we must remember that Naidu always worked by design. She deliberately directed her poetry at a western audience, whom she never doubted would be susceptible to her careful orchestration of 'tropical and primitive' emotions (to quote from Gosse). Second, related to this, in so far as her poetry was effective in combining an established courtly Mughal style with voluptuous sensory effects, she was able to reconcile some of the countervailing imperial and decadent strains that marked the poetry of the time, both its stately themes and its lighter, more decorative preoccupations with beauty and style. Third, building on these first two factors, her work is significant for how it put in place a mixed interpretative framework of combined western and eastern, contrived and 'natural' elements through which modern Indian poetry, including that by Tagore, might be read and comprehended in Britain.

The critic Arvind Mehrotra finds fault with Naidu for taking no account in her work of contemporary modernist economies of style, yet in reading her we must allow for the fact that her most productive period precedes the advent of the lean *imagiste* poem with its predominantly visual effects by some fifteen years.[84] Her influences, as she was herself aware, came to her from W. B. Yeats in his dreamy 'Celtic Twilight' period and the languid, world-weary Symons. In other words, Naidu was a dynamic creation not so much of 'eastern magic' and 'western influences', as Symons put it, but rather of the process of cultural exchange and mutual translation between them, a process that helped to mould how 1890s culture was perceived, as this chapter contends throughout. Naidu's trend-setting interaction with avant-garde British culture therefore set a template which her near-contemporary Rabindranath Tagore would follow a decade-and-a-half later when, already hailed as a colossus in Indian letters, he acted as both foil to and interlocutor with the emergence of early Anglo-American modernism in London. As this implies, Naidu and Tagore, and Ghose to some extent, can be recognized as having built a subtradition of Indian writing in the heart of the west, styled to harmonize with European fashions and parsed using English rhythms, yet nonetheless moulded by Indian perceptions and beliefs. Or, as Naidu observed in one of her first political addresses, to students in Madras in 1903: to be a citizen of the world was predicated on being, first and foremost, a true Indian.[85] An attitude of open-minded worldly brotherliness did not preclude the assertion of an Indian identity.

Sarojini Naidu's name bulks large in the annals of India's twentieth-century history as one of the prominent leaders of the national independence struggle, as a campaigner for Indian women's rights gifted with remarkable oratorical skills, and as a lieutenant to M. K. Gandhi in the many campaigns he led against British rule (Civil Disobedience, Non-cooperation, Salt Satyagraha, and Quit India). Makarand Paranjape describes her as a 'minor poet in a major mode', the major mode being

Indian nationalist oratory.[86] Later in life, she was also the first Indian woman to serve as President of the Indian National Congress (1925), and the first woman governor of any state in independent India (Uttar Pradesh). Throughout, she was a strong advocate for the nationalist position that traditional Indian society had not universally degraded women or been restrictive of their self-expression, as the British authorities tended to believe. Women had been the upholders of Indian strength in the past, and could be so again.[87] Behind this story of towering political success, however, lies an earlier tale, of smaller scale yet just as glittering, of fame won in a very different quarter: the tale of a precocious poetic voice who gave up a promising career in Britain to dedicate her rhetorical gifts to the service of her nation (or, in her words, to carry 'the banner of song' into 'the throng and the tumult').[88] Viewed from the vantage point of 1900, therefore, or, even more so, 1905, the year of her first tour in her poetic persona to England, Naidu was the self-aware artist who, though there was much of the native informant to her self-presentation, at the same time consciously echoed and elaborated the symbolist and late Romantic tendencies that marked 1890s verse.

Naidu travelled to England first in 1895, and was back in 1905, 1912–13, 1914, 1919, and 1920–21, among many other visits, first as a student and a poet-in-the-making, as she introduced herself to Gosse, and then as a political activist campaigning for India's freedom and for representation for Indian women.[89] The two incarnations are linked, however, in her strong assertion throughout of a specifically *Indian* poetic identity that would nonetheless be legible to her western audiences—a mix that, as will be further discussed, played a part in the unfolding of 1890s Decadence. For Decadence, in so far as it encouraged artifice, also promoted role-play, exaggerated imitation, and self-transmogrification. These elements not only moulded the theatricality of Naidu's personal style, but also are constantly present in her poems. Their many scenes of dance and display might in fact be seen as themselves part-reflexive thematizations of performance.[90]

On one level, therefore, Naidu appears to have been willing to oblige her British mentors by living up to their image of her as an Indian poet-singer. Yet at another level, it is also important to recognize, she fostered this oriental style not merely as her signature, but, in the absence of precursors, as a literary tradition forged in the process of journeying, and hence as a mode of critical negotiation *between* the east and the west.[91] As we have already begun to observe, she in some respects knowingly cast herself as an oriental, yet was at the same time, as Chandani Lokugé writes, 'an astute dialogist'. (In a typical effusion, she wrote to Symons from Italy: 'One black night I stood in a garden with fireflies in my hair like darting restless stars caught in a mesh of darkness'.[92]) She was not so much assimilated to western trends and tastes as *self*-assimilated, which meant, importantly, that she exercised control in so projecting herself (there is a noteworthy similarity here to Sorabji). She challenged west–east hierarchies by performing and so reworking certain stereotypes of India, yet did so in a knowledgeable and modish way that, moreover, claimed historical and cultural depth for these eastern features. For example, though the focus in many of her poems on female self-sacrifice may at first come across as celebratory, at the same time that focus invites more complicated readings—in particular, as a subjective reappraisal of the power that is obtained through traditional forms of female submission.

Setting aside for a moment her years of apprenticeship in London, Naidu's most productive years as a poet span the period 1904–1917. In the early years of the new century, working from her base in Hyderabad, she prepared, with Arthur Symons's encouragement and guidance, her first collection of poems published in the west, *The Golden Threshold* (1905), which is still rightly regarded as her masterpiece. Yet, though the title's reference is to the Nizam's palace in Hyderabad, many of the poems in *The Golden Threshold*, like those in *The Bird of Time* which followed eight years later, stemmed from Naidu's extraordinarily productive period as a young student of poetry in 1890s London; the two collections follow a similar trajectory and invoke similar tones and colours. *The Bird of Time*, its title a reference to the bird in the Fitzgerald's *Rubáiyát of Omar Khayyám* that sings of both 'the joys and sorrows of life', set the seal on her reputation, yet also coincided with Tagore's glittering advent in London. Her third collection, *The Broken Wing: Songs of Love, Death and Destiny 1915–16*, more sombre, noticeably less innovative, and marked everywhere by her new political concerns (as in its opening dedication to the 'Hope of To-morrow', and its poems of homage to political leaders), came out in the penultimate year of the First World War, 1917, again from William Heinemann, but with little fanfare.[93] *The Feather of the Dawn* (1961), a posthumous collection, is once again repetitive of her 1900s trends and traits, down to its fondness for archaisms and balladic forms.[94]

From her publication dates it might appear that Naidu's most active poetic phase slips to the side of the 1890s period in which this reading would seek to place her. However, precocious student and hyper-adept networker that she was, it is also the case that all periods and phases in relation to her work must necessarily be taken as provisional. As even a cursory glance at one of her lyrics, whether early or late, will confirm, in her case continuities of style and theme overrode chronology. She began, as the orientalist yet also observant Symons and Gosse both noticed, 'mature' in bearing and exotic in aspect, and she persisted with more or less the same pitch and tone across her poetic career. This section's discussion therefore focuses without compunction on Naidu in her formative years as a young poet-apprentice in late nineteenth-century London, that time which proved the crucible of her most evocative work. In both 1905 and 1912, Naidu's years of greatest prominence as a poet, it was in her 1890s oriental guise that she was celebrated, and she in turn obliged those who praised her by maintaining throughout her characteristic accent on the ornamental, the ephemeral, the feudal, and the ritualistic (all features bearing orientalist overtones).

Born into a highly educated context, Naidu was herself the child of an east–west crossing. Her mother, Varada Sundari Devi, had spent time in a Brahmo Samaj institution for women founded by K. C. Sen, during the period that her father Aghorenath Chattopadhyay, a contact of Sen's, studied towards his doctorate in physics in Edinburgh. On his return to India, her father established what would become the Nizam's College in the princely state of Hyderabad, the Nizam or ruler at that time being the cultured and capricious Mir Mahboob Ali Khan (1866–1911). At twelve, Naidu took first-class honours in the Madras matriculation examination and rapidly made a name for herself at the Nizam's court with her intellectual and poetic precocity and knowledge of several languages, including Persian, Urdu, English, and her mother tongue, Bengali. She had by this stage also written several long poems, one of which, 'Mehir Muneer', a romance set in 'Persia's land long, long ago', was published in a local journal by her father. He also privately printed *Songs*, a collection of her juvenilia from the period 1892–96. 'Mehir Muneer', presented to the Nizam of Hyderabad, was instrumental in securing the scholarship, in his gift, that in due course sent Naidu to England on £300 a year, with her passage paid, to further her studies. This early close acquaintance with the feudal, paternalistic world over which the Nizam presided, clearly prepared the ground for those impressions of orientalist authenticity her work would later conjure. This is demonstrated in a number of her poems whose first drafts date from this period, not least 'Nightfall in the City of Hyderabad' and 'In praise of Gulmohur Blossoms', as well as 'Indian Dancers'—poems distinguished by their images of minarets, lattice windows, garlanded tresses, and other ornate *Arabian Nights* effects.[95] Inspired by the example of Toru Dutt, Naidu also attempted in this period to make contact with Edmund Gosse in England, although at this point unsuccessfully.

In 1893, at the age of fourteen, Sarojini Chattopadhyay fell in love with Govandarajulu Naidu, the non–Brahmin, whom her parents deemed unsuitable due to his caste and her age, but whom she would eventually marry. Concerned to keep her from her beloved, at least for the time being, her parents pressed Sarojini to take up the Nizam's scholarship. The emotional strain this caused brought on a nervous collapse, which gave the young poet's eventual departure for England, in the company of the theosophist Annie Besant, the appearance of a retreat and convalescence.[96] From this point on, separated from her lover, home, and family, Naidu's work became heavily infused with the heated desires and forbidden longings that would evolve into her trademark—emotions which the long period of separation in England only accentuated.

The original intention behind Naidu's scholarship was to send her to Girton College in Cambridge to further her studies, but because she was, at sixteen, too young to enrol, she began by boarding with a Miss Tagart in London and registering for classes at King's College Ladies' Department, at 13 Kensington Square. The King's College enrolment records and course catalogues show Sarojini Chattopadhyay, formerly of Hyderabad, now of Manor Lodge in Hampstead, registered in the 1895–96 session for courses of lectures in English Literature, for both terms, and in the 1897–98 session, for Michaelmas Term, in Shakespeare.[97] Interestingly, as has not to date been widely noted, 'Mr Gosse' was the English Literature tutor in Lent Term 1896: this correlates with biographer Padmini Sen Gupta's finding that Gosse and Chattopadhyay were introduced in January 1896 by a fellow student who 'entreated her to show her poems to the celebrated critic'.[98] Another tutor was 'Mr Plarr' or Victor Plarr, a Rhymers' Club poet. Sarojini's fellow students included Evelyn Underhill, later a well-known mystic, and the poet Alice Meynell. Even at this early stage, she was drawing close to the threshold of London's literary world and laying down the connections that would shape her poetic career. Indicatively, perhaps, Virginia Woolf, then Stephen, also attended King's College Ladies' Department classes, in her case between 1897 and 1901.

It is perhaps unlikely that the two future writers Naidu and Woolf, both moulded by the milieu of the 1890s, would have run into each other in the King's College corridors, especially as Woolf was a student of Greek, Latin, German, and (some) English History. However, assuming that Woolf was a reader of the King's College *Ladies' Department Magazine*, it still is interesting to speculate that she may have had some passing acquaintance with Naidu's poetry, which the magazine published on at least three occasions. She is perhaps unlikely to have seen the two nocturnal ballads 'Leili' and 'Poppy Land', already laden with Naidu's signature of floral imagery and other oriental—chiefly Persian—motifs, as these were published in the inaugural issue of 1896, when Virginia Stephen was not yet enrolled. Yet there is a chance that Woolf may have encountered the equally characteristic 'Past and Present' or 'The Song of Nurphan (from the Persian)', in which the speaker is a veiled woman. These appeared in the Michaelmas 1897 and Lent 1899 issues respectively, the latter after Sarojini's return to India.[99] 'The Song' later acquired the title 'The Song of Princess Zeb-Un-Nissa' and was juxtaposed with 'Indian Dancers' in *The Golden Threshold.* The appearance of these several poems suggests that Naidu must have been well known within the College, or at least to the editors of the magazine, as most of the other poems it published, alongside the usual club reports and translations from the classics, are spoofs, jingles, and 'effusions'. Moreover, the Lent 1900 issue broke with protocol in its announcement of the birth 'on September 26th, 1899' of Sarojini Chattopadhyay's first son, 'at Hyderabad, Deccan, India'.[100] The special emphasis gives an inkling of Naidu's cultural standing as a vibrant young Indian poet both in the College and the city at the time, something of which Virginia Stephen as herself a sensitive and sympathetic fellow student cannot have been entirely unaware.

Naidu formally began at Cambridge a year or so after her arrival in England, but her days there were short-lived. Academic study was isolating and uncongenial to her, whereas the 'new, large life of poetry' to which London had awoken her, as she wrote to Gosse, was busy and inspiring. However, frustrating and transitory as her time in Cambridge was, she did preside at an 1898 meeting of mainly 'English girls' to welcome the 'queenly' Lady Tata, the Bombay entrepreneur's wife, to the university.[101] The meeting once again demonstrates that way in which Indian presences in England and Scotland facilitated other and later Indian arrivals in a chain-reaction effect that was becoming almost conventional in this period. Other examples include the reception of Keshub Chunder Sen, and the hosting of both Naidu and Sorabji in London by Miss Elizabeth Adelaide Manning of the NIA. At Miss Manning's NIA lodgings, Naidu was bemused to observe, conversations tended to hark back several decades to the heyday of Keshub Chunder Sen and the Brahmo Samaj. Here she would also meet, amongst others, William Archer, the translator of Ibsen, and also William Heinemann, her future publisher, so gaining access to a cosmopolitan arts world which she now found far more stimulating and exciting than the rigours of academic study.

'Nilambuja: The Fantasy of a Poet's Mood', an atmospheric prose piece probably composed during Naidu's brief Cambridge period, gives an interesting autobiographical portrait of the young poet at this stage in her life (both Nilambuja and Sarojini signify the 'lotus born'). The eponymous Nilambuja is cast as separate both from her childhood companions and the 'purposeless' circumstances of their lives, as well as from the 'latticed chamber' of the 'temple of dreams' where she now finds herself.[102] She is evocatively represented in terms that Symons and Gosse were nurturing in Naidu's work at precisely this point, with the requisite encrusting of jewel-rich and dream-based images. Yearning to penetrate the mutable shows of her present life, Nilambuja is possessed by 'unattainable', 'insatiable', and 'unfulfilled' longings for something seemingly incommunicable, conveyed through the use of repetitive phrases and desperate exclamations, as in Naidu's poetry of this same period. As Nilambuja's strenuous reaching beyond her present circumstances anticipates, Naidu left Cambridge some time before the end of the academic year, and, back in London, effectively abandoned her studies in favour of poetry (though, as we saw, she did enroll for a course at King's College in the 1897 autumn term). She became a frequent visitor at her self-appointed mentor Edmund Gosse's 'friendly house', as she wrote in 1896 to her husband-to-be, where she found poets like Yeats, Symons, and William Watson were 'all gathered together'.[103]

As with Manmohan Ghose, Naidu's time in the capital conversing and networking operated as a kind of informal workshop for her verse, and her verse at the same time, reciprocally, contributed to a wider metropolitan conversation-in-progress about the proper concerns and preoccupations of late nineteenth-century poetry—not least 'primitive emotion' 'armed with... technical skill'. It was no doubt at this point that Gosse (whose quoted words these are) famously and also far-sightedly began to urge her to address eastern subjects in an eastern style—or at least a style recognized by Europe as eastern, as he recounted in the 1912 Introduction to her second volume, *The Bird of Time.* To succeed as an Indian-English poet in the metropolis, he famously advised, she should abandon the Romantic English mimicry she had been indulging in to date, and accentuate the Indian features of her work.

> The verses which Sarojini had entrusted to me were skilful in form, correct in grammar and blameless in sentiment, but they had the disadvantage of being totally without individuality. They were Western in feeling and in imagery; they were founded on reminiscences of Tennyson and Shelley... This was but the tone of the mocking-bird with a vengeance... I advised the consignment of all that she had written, in this falsely English vein, to the waste-paper basket. I implored her to consider that from a young Indian of extreme sensibility... what we wished to receive was, not a rechauffé of Anglo-Saxon sentiment in an Anglo-Saxon setting but some revelation of the heart of India, some sincere penetrating analysis of native passion, of the principles of antique religion, and of such mysterious intimations as stirred the soul of the East long before the West had begun to dream it had a soul.[104]

The language of Gosse's encouragement to Naidu to write as an impassioned and soulful Indian betrays some residual awareness of the culturally translated quality that 'true' or, in Gosse's terms, 'autochthonous' Indian identity, as viewed by Europe, bore: there is a strong, almost anxiously expressed concern that this hybrid creature lay claim to her indigenous birth-right (springing from 'the very soil of India'). At the same time, the confidence with which Gosse identifies what it is to be a true poet of the Indian Deccan points to the relative familiarity of Indian infusions into mainstream metropolitan culture.

For her part, when Naidu 'docilely' concurred with Gosse's advice, as he records, and set about orientalizing herself, she did not merely submit, in cynical fashion, to a cultural makeover in order to achieve poetic fame. Her turn to the 'dark places of the East' made possible an even more subtle mimicry than she had indulged in to date (a synthetic mixing of something that was already synthetic—easternness). She exercised, in effect, a reverse orientalism, and this afforded her verse a lightness and languor that chimed in with the characteristic chords of decadent verse. As is evident in many of *The Golden Threshold*'s lyrics, by manipulating so-called oriental tones and images she developed a voice with which to respond to the perfumed orientalist thematic of the day, yet one that also channelled her poetic interests in, for example, the song traditions of Islamic cultures, and Hindu Bhakti poetry (in which the poet addresses a personal god in the manner of a lover). Simply put, she utilized the literary resources she already had to hand in order to appeal to contemporary fashions, blending Persian and Islamic motifs drawn from her experience of the court and bazaars of Hyderabad with contemporary decadent motifs, of peacocks, lattices, and arabesque lines (a typical example is 'Ode to the Nizam of Hyderabad', which was presented at court during Ramadan). In this way, she was able to project a dual identity: a self that was at one level proudly and self-consciously Indian, yet at another transcultural and cosmopolitan; a poetic persona that allowed her to speak to at least two audiences at once, British and Indian.

Naidu's was a dreamy aesthetic not a world away from the verse written in imitation of the Romantics that Toru Dutt had produced, for related reasons and with similar effects, some decades before. It is suggestive, in this light, that in a prose work, 'Mah Rukh Begum: A Romance of Fate', written in London during these years, though not published in her lifetime, Naidu experimented with Indian materials—a 'Mohammedan love story' featuring peacocks under pomegranate trees—in order to tell a tale of a young woman poised between convention and modernity, but who, in rebelling against tradition, interestingly finds that the man of her choice is in fact the husband selected for her.[105] If we were to read into this stylized piece an object lesson for her own poetic practice of reverse orientalism, it is telling that the heroine's natural yet at first forbidden choice ultimately coincides with tradition. The Indian counterpart that initial prompting might have led her to forswear, is in fact her true and conventionally appointed partner: India turns from herself only to meet herself again.

In September 1898, Naidu returned to India without having taken a degree, thereby permanently closing a door on higher education. However, she left in place many deep-sea cables of literary connection that she would presently draw upon in order to establish herself as a published poet—initially in the pages of her College magazine, as was seen, and, from 1904, by planning her first collection, through correspondence with Symons and Gosse. In December 1898, in Madras, she at last married her long-term beloved, Govind Naidu, interestingly under the terms of the Brahmo marriages bill that had been proposed some decades back by Keshab Chandra Sen.[106] As Sarojini's husband worked in the Medical Services of the Nizam's Imperial Service troops, the marriage ensured that her close ties with the Hyderabad court were renewed and strengthened.

The sense of 'a new large life' of poetic endeavour that London had nurtured, strengthened by these royal connections, kept Naidu going through the years of childbirth and ill health that now followed. Giving birth to four children within the next five years she had little time for poetry, though she maintained a regular epistolary exchange with her London friends. The theatrical tone and heightened diction of these letters reflect an undisguised concern to keep her correspondents' attention focused on the easternized poetry and matching persona that she had so carefully fostered in their eyes. Repeatedly, in her correspondence, she reasserts her ambition to live, if not embody, the impassioned yet ethereal ethic of her work. Indeed, the heady vocabulary of her letters to Symons, for example, which he cites in his Introduction to *The Golden Threshold*, with their references to sumptuous colours and 'voluptuous scents', is hardly to be distinguished from the tonal palette of her poetry.

In her letters Naidu also expresses thoughtful, yet, once again, characteristic delight at having now experienced subjectively the *carpe diem* approach of living for the moment that was a signature of the 1890s ('I too have learnt the subtle philosophy of living from moment to moment').[107] Such hectic effects would continue into Naidu's correspondence dating from the period of her second career as a campaigning nationalist, to the extent that the later letters at times read as near-pastiches of her youthful lyrical effusions. Her transported, ecstatic voice had clearly become vital to her poetic self-image. To illustrate: in a 1919 letter from London, by which time Naidu had conclusively abandoned verse for politics, she painted the city as if with an Impressionist brush, washed in rain and mauve: 'I am walking the London streets in the early autumn dark that is veiled in lilac darkness and illuminated with shifting lamps rushing the darkness in an incessant stream.' And, writing to her daughter Padmaja on 2 August 1932 from prison, she described her high-walled garden as overflowing with those quintessential 1890s flowers, 'Lilies, lilies, lilies, foam-white, pearl-white as clouds and the breasts of swans, white as manna and milk and the miracle of silver filigree beaten out on fairy anvils into chalices of incense and nectar.'[108] The once evocative 'Indian' performance of 'tropical and primitive' emotions had become her default mode. Yet, though this is a factor sometimes cited to account for her relative lack of maturation as a poet, it can equally be submitted that her self-dramatization had been encouraged by her successes in persuading and inspiring audiences. She may have cast herself as a mere 'spectator from the watch-tower of dreams', yet she had nonetheless made of this a powerful position from which to urge all-India service to the motherland.[109]

At least half of *The Golden Threshold* comprises work held over from the previous decade, polished across the early Hyderabad years, as the inclusion of 'Indian Dancers' and poems published in the King's College magazine suggests. Contrary to Naidu's expectations when she contributed £14 to cover William Heinemann's printing costs, the collection was a critical success, garnering favourable, if inevitably orientalizing reviews from such journals and magazines as the *Review of Reviews, The Times,* the *Morning Post*, and the *Manchester Guardian*—all universally charmed at the 'fresh' 'Eastern colour' and 'delicate' touch of the work.[110] In 1906, a second edition appeared. In 1907, the collection's harmonies prompted the composer Liza Lehman to set fifteen of the poems to music, published under appropriately sunset-lit, impressionistic covers, and this, too, garnered praise, if for delicacy without depth.[111] A plan to make a cantata of the entire collection, however, did not bear fruit.

As the Edwardian public clearly entertained some lasting taste for the previous decade's exotic ornamentation, Naidu was now given the confidence she needed to work towards her second, 1912 collection, *The Bird of Time*, again published by William Heinemann. Introduced by the friend and mentor to whom the first collection had been dedicated, the book represented the fulfilment of Gosse's almost fifty-year mentoring of young Indian poets, and it, too, featured poems in Naidu's part-invented, part-adapted eastern song forms. Its *Manchester Guardian* reviewer, finding the poems at once 'sweet' and 'alien', drew from them a characteristic assurance of common humanity: 'over East and West one heaven stretches'.[112] The period leading from the book's publication to the outbreak of European hostilities in 1914, Naidu, often unwell, spent almost entirely in London, staying at the Lyceum when she was not in hospital, and engaged in political work. This interesting time also saw widespread suffragette protests in the capital, rising nationalist activity in India, and the foundation of the India Society, which would soon become influential (covered in Chapter 4). She gave readings and talks in her personae of both nationalist and nightingale, embracing in particular the cause of Indian women's education over that of their political liberation. Her appearances at such events as a Hotel Cecil dinner hosted by Yeats on 13 November 1913, a 5 March 1914 meeting of the Oriental Circle of the Lyceum Club, or a 1914 reading at the Harold Munro's Poetry Bookshop, were widely reported in the press, including in the *Daily News*, the *Pall Mall Gazette*, and the *Daily Telegraph*.[113] As for Naoroji in the 1880s and 1890s, or Sorabji in the 1890s and 1900s, these reports ensured that Indian presences continued to infiltrate London's sense of itself.

In the war collection *The Broken Wing*, with its unpropitious title, Naidu's balladic verse forms persisted, as was already noted, as did many of her dominant themes—in particular that of female submission in romance and marriage, and her preoccupation with the complicated enticements of passionate and self-sacrificing love. However, more loyal supporters like Gosse and G. K. Gokhale detected a sadder, more mature music in the collection's pages: certainly, the 'old lilting glad refrain' of Naidu's earlier work is significantly muted, as 'The Coming of the Spring' among other poems acknowledges (*BW*, pp. 49–50). To Tagore, Naidu wrote that these new poems contained 'less of my art and more of myself than hitherto'; Tagore, regardless, praised her oeuvre's 'lyric ease'.[114]

Across the first decade of the twentieth century, therefore, Naidu's growing political interests to a considerable extent intertwined with and underpinned her career as a poet. Both her political and her creative lives were preoccupied with questions of cultural authenticity, and, arguably, with unities of (national/poetic) form and purpose. By the second decade, however, Naidu's long-term reflections on what Indianness comprised and how it might be more fully expressed turned her ever more resolutely in a political direction—a tendency reinforced perhaps by the waning appeal among readers of the sensuous 'ease'ful 1890s themes and aural effects that had been her forte. The nationalist leader Gokhale, whom she first met in 1902, had for some time been introducing her to other senior nationalist politicians, who all recognized in her talent for oratory a potentially powerful instrument to move Congress, and, in the immediate term, a means through which to bridge the widening gulf between extremists and moderates that was threatening its political unity. As early as the 1904 Indian National Congress she was duly invited to recite the poem 'To India', a call to the nation to rise from the 'fettered darkness' of the colonial period—so instrumentalizing her creative work for the nationalist cause for the first time (*GT*, p. 94). She gave her first major political speech to the 1906 Congress meeting, and, in 1913, Gokhale, by now her close friend and mentor, asked her to pledge herself fully to the service of India.[115] In the same year, Rabindranath Tagore was awarded the Nobel Prize for Literature: the significance of this recognition for an Indian poet who had until very recently not been as well known as Naidu, at least in the west, and who now moved in the same literary circles, may have helped to seal her commitment to a political over a poetic life.

By the end of the First World War, when *The Broken Wing* was published, and undoubtedly by the time of Gandhian non-cooperation in the early 1920s, the call of the 'drum beat of [political] destiny' had grown so 'urgent' to Naidu's ears, as she writes in 'The Faery Isle of Janjira' (*BT*, pp. 79–80), that she steps outside of the literary purview of this discussion (though the Coda touches briefly on her war poem 'The Gift of India').[116] Even so, it is worth noting, her channels of political expression, like her literary networks, continued to be routed through London—and would remain so until Indian independence in 1947 (followed by her death two years later). Moreover, across her varied career, she continued to demonstrate what a *Manchester Guardian* reviewer called the 'inspired resolution' of the 'gulf-defying spider'.[117]

As the foregoing demonstrates, Naidu's 1890s poetic labours in London laid down indelible formal and thematic templates for her subsequent work, and these templates in turn established structures of reception for how her later oeuvre, and that of her compatriots, would be received (as eastern, feminine, spiritual, and so on). Self-invention and self-reproduction thus flowed into a smoothly repeating feedback loop. Hers was a poetry refracted through an aestheticized western framework of perception onto its eastern subject matter, but, conversely, her poems also infiltrate and inflect the western aesthetic forms in which they are ostensibly cast with Indian motifs, tones, and rhythms. As a young poet she presented herself as an avant-garde voice in eastern dress, reconciling the distant and the immediate, and the traditional and the new, in chiasmic ways.[118] It is in this sense that her oeuvre appears classically hybrid and postcolonial. She nativized her English mentors' Orient, framed it within tight metrical forms and alliterative lines (favouring sibilants and fricatives) drawn from the English tradition, introduced Persian and Hindu mythic features and figures (Radha, Savitri), combined these with poetic conceits from the Urdu ghazal, and laced the whole with a charged yet seemingly motiveless passion.[119]

In closing, Naidu's keynote is a plangent, on-flowing musicality. The insistently repeating motifs and rhythms of her best work, collected in *The Golden Threshold* and *The Bird of Time*, link across and weave between different poems. Tresses and silken skeins from one poem intertwine with garland and veil images in another, while poem after poem is studded with jewel-resembling colours ('onyx', 'peridote'). As in a song-cycle, different individual lyrics work together as refrain-like parts of a greater thematic, melodic, or painterly whole, reminiscent of how Ghose and Binyon's poems in *Primavera* come together in a dialogue of sorts. As in the 'Celtic Twilight' Yeats, generic and diaphanous images of moon, stars, and dreams gesture at an unseen world that is felt to be more psychologically or poetically true than everyday palpable reality.[120] Or, as the critic Ranjana Ash observes, Naidu's collected works form 'a continuity of poetic imagination', united by 'lilting cadences akin to song'—a musicality that was of course heard in the west as 'Oriental'.[121]

At the same time, Naidu's poetry unmistakeably tunes into the 1890s theme of evanescence that also marks Ghose's lyrics. If her poetic mode was ephemeral, as she told Symons early on, it was so in a peculiarly self-consistent way, in so far as the medium as well as the subject matter of her work repeatedly dealt in the transitory and the fleeting, down to the final twenty-four-poem sequence in *The Broken Wing*, recording a part-unrequited and diminishing love affair ('The Temple: A Pilgrimage of Love'). She spoke of the transitory nature of desire, love, and beauty using images of such inconstant entities as fire, flowers in bloom, and figures dancing, set in a persistent anapaestic or tripling metre that moves the reader on rapidly from one poem to the next. A number of the poems on mortality also carry a bi- or tri-partite structure that follows the diurnal or seasonal round or the phases of the human life cycle ('Indian Weavers' *GT*, p. 30, 'Bangle-sellers' *BT*, pp. 64–5, among many other examples). The suffering of the Indian widow denied the consummation of the funeral pyre is predictably a subject which recurs in the work, reflecting Naidu's abiding concern with Indian women's lives ('Suttee' *GT*, p. 46; 'Dirge' *BT*, pp. 13–14). Indeed, the confected and performative aspects of her work are perhaps most on show in her representation of women's suffering and endurance, in particular in purdah. In some ways like Cornelia Sorabji, the subject of Section V, from whom she differed strongly in other respects, the theme of women's seclusion facilitated the development of Naidu's literary voice. In the view of both writers, the *zenana*, for all its orientalized connotations, represented a space untouched by the modern world within which the veiled woman often demonstrated a remarkable resilience.

V CORNELIA SORABJI: 'GETTING ENGLAND INTO MY BONES'

Indian lawyer Cornelia Sorabji's memories of studying in Oxford between 1889 and 1892, and of her training as a solicitor at the London firm of Lee and Pemberton's until 1893, as described in her 1934 memoir *India Calling* (1934) and its part-sequel *India Recalled* (1936), hold up a finely bevelled, one might almost say recognizably Paterian lens to her time as a young Parsi woman in Britain.[122] Her first English period also embraced (at a stretch) her hidden years of 'exile' in London between 1901 and 1904, following an inappropriate love affair, while working as a trainee lawyer in India—as Richard Sorabji's 2010 biography *Opening Doors: The Untold Story of Cornelia Sorabji* lays bare for the first time.[123] During these early twentieth-century years in England she lived by her pen, producing atmospheric vignettes, stories, and sketches, largely set in India, which she gathered together in *Love and Life Behind the Purdah* (1901), and *Sun-babies: Studies in the Child Life of India* (1904), amongst other collections.[124]

Sorabji's evocations of her Oxford and London settings stand out for their polished and enamelled (even gemlike) aspect and their Impressionistic haziness: she retained a sharp recollection, for example, of 'the reds and russets and tawny greens of the Virginia creeper against the grey worn stone' of Oxford's college walls in autumn, and 'the exhilaration of London fogs: dream cities, the Towers of Westminster in a white mist'.[125] The beautiful gardens of her childhood, and the decorative and ceremonial features of her clients' homes and estates in India, met with the same exquisite, painterly treatment. To give only a sampling, she remembered in *India Calling* the particular beauty of the 'white-limbed', 'ivory-petalled' champak flowers in her garden at home, and how the beauty of 'the bell-shaped lilac flowers' under the moonlight 'squeezed her heart'. The lamp-lighting ceremony at the palace in Baroda, which she singled out in her depiction of her time spent in that royal household, produced to her eye the striking effect of fire-flies flitting through the darkness.[126] Even from these few details it is clear not only that Sorabji had a sophisticated feel for visual beauty, but also that her sensibility to a noticeable extent harmonized with lingering late nineteenth-century aestheticist preoccupations and therefore with some of the predominant moods of university life (consider, for example, the imagery of delicate flowers under moonlight).

For all that, Cornelia Sorabji was a self-proclaimed daughter of the empire, her writing about English cities, one small, one very large—both still, in pockets, under the binding spell of aestheticism—suggests that the relative conventionality of her imperialist views did not inoculate her against less-than-conventional late-century cultural influences such as might have appealed to one 'schooled' on two continents or 'home in two countries', as she was.[127] A delighted observer of Oxford's fritillaries and 'flaming' beeches, as she writes in her impassioned introduction to *India Calling*, she was also an admirer of its much celebrated medieval aspects. In her diaries and letters home, too, she comes across as a lively commentator on the daily life of Oxford and London, often singling out what might be called aestheticist effects, as the above examples illustrate. In later years, her descriptions of the confined conditions inhabited by the women in purdah she spent her career representing also carry embellished and fine-grained details that would not have been out of place in a sketch by Aubrey Beardsley.[128] Even when addressing a public that—by definition, in reading her—was largely interested in learning more about India, she appears to have lavished equal care on her British as well as her Indian backdrops. Through the medium of her articles in the *Nineteenth Century* and elsewhere, as well as via her books, her aestheticist evocations were transmitted to an even wider British audience than the young Naidu had had at her disposal five years or so before. In these ways her writing contributed subtle but important shades to the Indian patina through which, by the new century, 1890s aestheticist and Decadent effects were frequently viewed.[129] Not only was she receptive to these influences, but she to some degree also deepened and amplified their orientalist associations.

Antoinette Burton in *At the Heart of the Empire* has written what is still the most acute ethnographic portrait of Cornelia Sorabji (1866–1954) in late Victorian Oxford. Her study justly describes the young student of literature and then law from the large, Christianised Parsi family in Poona as a pioneering figure, an eventual barrister in the Indian High Court who was in many ways culturally hybrid, as she herself wrote (see, for example, the reference to 'getting England into my bones' in the subheading). Yet, in certain contexts, Sorabji was also viewed as typically Indian and exotic in her dress and manner.[130] Indeed, she positively liked to style herself as *the* Indian woman, especially in her beloved Oxford setting, despite its many Indian influences and presences. Moreover, in order to foreground her own uniqueness, she was sometimes standoffish towards other prominent Indians in Britain, especially women, such as Rukhmabai, or the Duleep Singh sisters, whose studies at Somerville interestingly overlapped with hers. In *India Calling*, she consistently presents herself as out-of-the-ordinary—one who could lay a unique claim to both English imperial and Indian Parsi identities, and whose academic and professional achievements were also exemplary for her time and background.

This relatively brief discussion, however, does not seek merely to go over the already well-covered biographical ground relating to Sorabji. Rather, the accent in these paragraphs is on her by and large occasional, yet nonetheless persistent interest in subscribing to the dominant exotic and orientalist literary codes of the day, whether in her depictions of Oxford and England, or of Indian life in purdah. Her descriptions in this respect are not noticeably remote from her nationalist countrywoman Naidu's wrought scene painting of London or Hyderabad.[131] As well as her concern to appeal to the eastern interests of the British public, the motivation behind Sorabji's aestheticist inclinations (though that is perhaps to overstate the matter) stemmed from her strong need for social approval, which was evident also in her elitist leanings, and an equally strong, related need to ward off disapprobation. As will be seen, these spurs are most dramatically on show in Sorabji's use of dress as both theatrical costume and as armoury, something that her memoir highlights on several occasions.

Oxford in Sorabji's time, as in Ghose's, was not only 'the heart of the heart of the Victorian empire' and Jowett's training ground for the Indian Civil Service, but also, a less examined aspect in respect of Sorabji, the aesthetes' city par excellence, at once its school and its laboratory, as she cannot have been unaware.[132] Its Gothic architecture of quad and cloister had been acclaimed in the art criticism of influential commentators like John Ruskin and William Morris, and also warmly promoted by Pater and Wilde. For Ruskin, and no doubt for Pater also, an Oxford education stood for the acquisition of 'noble human knowledge' in and for itself: it should not be end-directed, aimed at the training of imperial administrators, as was Jowett's plan.[133] So it followed that 'academical life', in Sorabji's phrase, bore utilitarian but also aestheticist features, as Manmohan Ghose and Laurence Binyon, too, had found—perhaps because that same academical life had informed the work of Pater and Wilde also.

Remarkably, as if by a stroke of aesthetic justice, during Cornelia's time at Somerville, Clara Pater, Walter's sister, was the College's Classics tutor, and 'presided' over the West Buildings where Cornelia lived. Cornelia regularly had dinners with Miss Pater in the latter's rooms in her capacity as Resident tutor, and it was here that Walter Pater often visited her, despite being known to fear 'petticoats'. Cornelia encountered him at Miss Pater's at least once. Though it is important not to over-read the epistemological significance of passing contacts, the association seems to suggest that the young Indian student would have had a sense of Pater's work and reputation, even if indirectly.[134] How much more she knew about the late-century critical veneration for medieval arts and crafts it is difficult to say. Yet there certainly is a distinctive aestheticist tone to

Sorabji's enchantment with Oxford life in her first letters home to Poona—even while her preoccupations are at the same time distinctly imperial. Pitched from the vantage point of the future, her sense in these letters is that the here-and-now, in 'this beautiful spot' Oxford, comes closer to an ideal of happiness than she will achieve at any other point in her life: 'I think one's ideal of a happy life is nearer being realised here than anywhere else: in the way of gentle and intellectual intercourse, with something of happiness for the future, as one looks back in after life on this beautiful spot in one's memory.'[135] As this appears to suggest, Oxford was already enshrined in her affections in a proleptic way, as a Paterian moment in time in which beauty, intellect, and emotion were concentrated.

It is clear from the lists of elite contacts Sorabji included in *India Calling* that she invested heavily in the class status and social respectability that Oxford afforded her as an Indian and a woman, building on this status in order to assert her citizenship of the empire in her legal and political work across her life. However, as her animated language in the relevant sections of the memoir suggests, there was something self-delighting as well as self-promoting in this investment: it pleased her to present herself in this way and reinforced her sense of uniqueness and inviolability. She made a particular friend of the Master of Balliol College, Benjamin Jowett, frequently presiding as his consort at the social evenings he held. She knew and was close to Max Müller and his family, as well as his rival Monier-Williams, and enjoyed excellent relations with Sir William Hunter, the then head of the Indian Institute, and the Reader in Indian law Sir William Markby. Across her early years in England she also met and impressed many other prominent and influential people, frequenting great country houses and salons, and enjoying many grand dinners, on which occasions she was often seated beside the host, as her letters recorded.[136]

To some extent, Sorabji's way into these networks had been prepared by her educationalist mother's charity work and contact-making English lecture tour in 1886. But Cornelia's networking also built on and extended the many India-in-Britain connections that had accumulated over the decades, as we have seen, for all that she styled herself as one of a kind. In *India Calling*, she conceded that though Indian women travellers still stood out in this period, 'Indian boys and men had long been coming [to Europe] in respectable numbers'. During her vacations she stayed with Miss Manning in London, whom she had first met in Bombay, and who also put up Rukmabai and, a little later, Naidu.[137] She was twice presented at Court, to Queen Victoria in 1892 and to Edward VII in 1903, wearing pink at the first reception (the Queen having granted her permission to depart from the conventional white), and sunset colours on the second, with French trimming.

On every one of the grand occasions Cornelia attended, not only at court, she paid special attention to the colour, texture, and decoration of her saris—which distinctively Indian garment she persisted in wearing in England, though in the Parsi way, usually over a puffy Victorian bodice or blouse. A great deal of her communication with her family in Poona was devoted to ordering and planning the design and colour of these saris and bodices. Inevitably, the rich details of dress with which both the letters and also her diary are filled, and the delight that is expressed in them, recall something of the brocaded opulence of Naidu's orientalist evocations. On Sorabji's second visit to the Warden of Merton, for example, she wrote that she wore 'a green velvet bodice and pale blue saree, and maiden's hair and white chrysanthemums' as a corsage. For a meeting with the Lord Chief Justice in early 1891, she chose 'white silk with a green velvet bodice accompanied with lilies of the valley'.[138]

However dimly, the young Sorabji was aware that the institutions in which she sought affirmation gave prominence to Indians who in some way embodied or played to western imaginings of India. She was also aware of how appropriate oriental effects might be relayed through dress and demeanour. At the same time, however, she sought to choreograph her style, both sartorially and kinetically, to project her own uniqueness and resilience, and was keen to collaborate with her English friends' interest in her as a remarkable 'Indian girl', to cite from the title of her first article for the *Nineteenth Century*, in October 1891.[139] Her colourful Indian 'draperies', in her terms, which her family in India had long eschewed, formed a core part of this self-presentation, a performance of otherness that would both attract and convince interested parties, yet hold interfering critics, and rivals, at bay. It is indicative that she rarely corrected 'proselytizing old ladies' who assumed she was a 'heathen' from her appearance, yet worried that the two daughters of the Maharajah Duleep Singh, her fellow students at Somerville, failed to dress in a way that befitted their status, by wearing 'uninteresting English garb'.[140] From the beginning, she identified with Oxford's and then the Bar's elitism in order to consolidate her own jealously guarded sense of specialness. Yet as that superiority in the case of Oxford was already overlaid with Wildean affectation, it could not but appear 1890s qua 'look'—as it did, if via different media, in the case of Manmohan Ghose (with whom she coincided in Oxford, but probably did not meet). Ultimately, therefore, Sorabji's 1890s traits, if such they may be called, rested on two main supports: first, on her claim of exceptionality, and second, on how this exceptionality was displayed sartorially. Both qualities bore obvious links to decadent preoccupations with the excessive, the extraordinary, the foreign, and the rare.

If Sorabji was frequently involved in the performance of her own extraordinariness, this was never more ostentatiously the case than on the occasion when she demonstrated sari wearing (or in fact sari disrobing) in front of customs officials at the Italian border.[141] It is an appropriately evocative scene with which to end-stop this chapter's final section. Travelling at the close of her second spring term with a friend of her mother's, Cornelia was challenged at Ventimiglia as to the contents of her luggage, the officials being incredulous that the folded silks in her luggage were in fact garments and not contraband goods. After some resistance, she met their display of disbelief ('movements of hands, shoulders, eyebrows') with a performance of her own, dropping her 'draperies' to her feet with a pull of the wrist. The officers standing round in a 'circle' were delighted, clamouring for an encore as if, as Sorabji herself noted, 'they were Alice in Wonderland or Peter Pan'—or at a performance of the same. She had given a display befitting the veiled dance of Salomé in Oscar Wilde's eponymous play, or the Indian dancers in Naidu's poem of that name, one that both invited, yet ultimately withstood European scrutiny. The 'allure or suggestion . . . of foreignness', as Cornelia herself wrote, at once depended upon yet exceeded sartorial display, but at the same time the display was sufficiently important for her to agree to a striptease of a kind, rather than risk relinquishing her eastern apparel.

The three *fin-de-siècle* Indian writers in English profiled in this chapter in different ways responded to their time's interest in the sensuous and the exotic and, in responding, added to this interest Indian hues and flavours. Participating in the mannered and perfumed tendencies that characterized 1890s art and literature through their close friendships with some of the key cultural commentators of the day—most prominently, Edmund Gosse, Arthur Symons, and Laurence Binyon—they found that within the aesthetic traditions from which they wrote which deepened those tendencies. Both Naidu and Ghose were interested in the transient and the ephemeral; Sorabji and Naidu delighted in colourful adornment. While Naidu was perhaps the most prominent painter of eastern effects in her work, all three, whether through their use of imagery and allusion or their mode of address, bestowed an Indian inflection upon the orientalist associations of Decadence. However, as this inflection was something they contributed from their position as cosmopolitan Anglophone Indians—or, as Salman Rushdie might say, as translated men and women—the connotations that they added were not mere orientalist confections, but nuanced and multivoiced, homed in two continents, to quote Sorabji once again, or pitched from more than one cultural vantage point.

It is due in no small part to their contribution, added to that of other Indian travellers discussed in this book, that Naipaul's reclusive landlord in *The Enigma of Arrival*, a century on from the 1890s, makes strong associations between Indian tradition and the culture of Decadence. Specifically, he links the *Yellow Book* art of Aubrey Beardsley with both 'the poems of Krishna and Shiva' and associations of 'imperial glory' beyond its prime, declining to satiety:

> Ruskinianism, a turning away from the coarseness of industrialism, upper-class or cultivated sensibilities, sensibilities almost drugged by money, the Yellow Book, philosophy melting away into sensuousness, sensation—my landlord's Indian romance partook of all of those impulses and was rooted in England, wealth, empire, the idea of glory, material satiety, a very great security.[142]

The looping-back of Naipaul's enumerations underlines the recursive patterning that was involved in the process of recreating India for imperial readerships already fatted with images of the east in Indian guises. Yet, even so, poets like Ghose and Naidu who hybridized Romantic symbols with nostalgic yearnings for Indian horizons, or English meters with Persian ghazal forms, contributed to laying down some of the circuitous yet also circular pathways of arrival in the heart of empire that Naipaul would tread a century on: pathways whereby the 'typically Indian' would be that which was manufactured on British shores, for the benefit of western eyes.

As the chapter's emphasis on literary composition and hence agency suggests, the 1890s Indian writers' participation in a displaced or distributed orientalism was not the response of a mimic or parrot, as might appear on the surface, or as a superficial reading of Gosse's introduction to Naidu's work might imply. They did not merely cast back at their audience the image of the east that they expected to see.[143] On the contrary, as is clearest in the case of Ghose, they exercised a complex agency and ingenuity in forging these images, working together with a small, largely well-disposed readership in a collaborative and even assertive way. Aware that the west would not admire what it did not in part contain, they pointed to the ways in which England was interpenetrated by objects and cultural influences from outside, including from India, and so interrogated, even if obliquely, the artificiality of the oriental India construct (not to say of the Orient *tout court*). But they were also concerned to endow the figure of 'India' with inner cultural strengths (consider the resilience of Naidu's self-sacrificing female personae, for example), while, at the same time, giving that figure and its stereotypical oriental associations (of sensuality, excess, and the like) the more positive inflection that the Aesthetic and Decadent movements in the arts afforded.

In forging these more positive associations, they effected a powerful doubling manoeuvre whereby they found resonances for their seemingly 'Indian' preoccupations in British culture, just as Britain, through the medium of their work, was finding resonances for its *fin-de-siècle* weariness in the east. Through 'a Western language and under partly Western influences', as Symons recognized, they channelled an 'Eastern magic'.[144] They stage-managed the east–west divide in order to demonstrate their proficiency in traditions on both sides of it, but they also overrode the divide when they wished to present themselves as the cosmopolitan artists, urban agents, and imperial citizens they in fact also were, confidently tracing their different social and cultural pathways through the British towns and cities they inhabited.

NOTES

1. Sarojini Naidu, 'An Anthem of Love', in *The Bird of Time: Songs of Life, Death & the Spring*, intr. Edmund Gosse (London: William Heinemann, 1912), p. 89. The references to the collections cited in the epigraphs appear below.
2. See Holbrook Jackson, *The Eighteen Nineties* (1913: London: Jonathan Cape, 1931), p. 48. The poem appears in Sarojini Naidu, *The Golden Threshold* (London: William Heinemann, 1905), pp. 71–2; and in Makarand Paranjape, ed., *Sarojini Naidu: Selected Poetry and Prose* (New Delhi: Rupa Press, 2010), pp. 118–19.
3. Paranjape, 'Introduction', in *Sarojini Naidu: Selected Poetry and Prose*, pp. 22–3.
4. Edmund Gosse, 'Introduction', in *The Bird of Time: Songs of Life, Death & the Spring*, pp. 4–5.
5. Arthur Symons, 'Introduction' to *The Golden Threshold*, by Sarojini Naidu (London: William Heinemann, 1905), pp. 16, 19; Talia Schaffer and Kathy Alexis Psomiades, eds., *Women and British Aestheticism* (Charlottesville, VA: University Press of Virginia, 1999), p. 144.
6. See Elleke Boehmer, 'East is East: Where Postcolonialism is Neo-orientalist: The Cases of Sarojini Naidu and Arundhati Roy', in *Stories of Women: Gender and Narrative in the Postcolonial Nation* (Manchester: Manchester University Press, 2005), pp. 158–71; Marina Warner, *Stranger Magic* (London: Chatto & Windus, 2011), p. 24. On the cultural 'counter-invasion' of the west by the east, which came with colonial penetration, see J. Jeffrey Franklin, *The Lotus and the Lion: Buddhism and the British Empire* (Ithaca, NY, and London: Cornell University Press, 2008), especially p. 7.

7. As we will see in Chapter 4, Yeats, Pound, and others to some extent played up their 'wise imperialist' reception of Tagore in order to promote the emergent modernist effects in their own work.
8. Maud Gonne, *A Servant of the Queen* (London: Victor Gollancz, 1938), p. 331; Ronald Schuchard, *The Last Minstrels: Yeats and the Revival of the Bardic Arts* (Oxford: Oxford University Press, 2008), pp. 130–1.
9. Symons, 'Introduction' to *The Golden Threshold*, pp. 15–16.
10. Anna Snaith writes illuminatingly of the ways in which Naidu's remarkable career-long cross-border mobility shaped her transnational poetics. See Anna Snaith, 'Sarojini Naidu: Feminist Nationalism and Cross-cultural Poetics', in her *Modernist Voyages: Colonial Women Writers in London, 1890–1945* (Cambridge: Cambridge University Press, 2014), pp. 67–89.
11. Naidu's father financed the publication of her juvenilia, under the title *Songs* and the name Sarojini Chattopadhyaya, in Hyderabad in 1896. However, as this collection was for private circulation only, in what follows *The Golden Threshold* will be referred to for convenience as Naidu's first, or first British, collection, *The Bird of Time* as her second, and *The Broken Wing* as her third.
12. An excellent study of M. M. Dutt is offered in Alexander Riddiford, *Madly After the Muses: Bengali Poet Michael Madhusudan Dutt and his Reception of the Graeco-Roman Classics* (Oxford: Oxford University Press, 2013). See also Rosinka Chaudhuri, *Gentlemen Poets in Colonial Bengal: Emergent Nationalism and the Orientalist Project* (Calcutta: Seagull, 2002), pp. 87–126. Nursing a lifelong ambition to reach 'Albion's distant shore', M. M. Dutt in the period 1862–7 finally made it to Britain and then, for a longer period, France, where he trained as a barrister. M. M. Dutt's Bengali, as well as his English poetry, is interestingly infused with the extensive knowledge of the Indian classics that he developed alongside his reading in the western classics.
13. Chaudhuri, *Gentlemen Poets*, pp. 170–86. See also Edward Fitzgerald, *Rubáiyát of Omar Khayyám* (1859; London: Collins, 1954).
14. Manmohan Ghose, Letter of 12 December 1887, in *Collected Poems*, ed. Lotika Ghose (1924; Calcutta: University of Calcutta, 1970), p. 153.
15. Edward Said, *Orientalism: Western Conceptions of the Orient* (London: Penguin, 1978; rev. edn 1995).
16. Ruvani Ranasinha with Rehana Ahmed, Sumita Mukherjee, and Florian Stadtler, eds., *South Asian Writers in Twentieth-century Britain* (Oxford: Oxford University Press, 2007), pp. 5–6.
17. See 'Extract 1: Textual and Cultural Reception', in Ruvani Ranasinha, with Rehana Ahmed, Sumita Mukherjee, and Florian Stadtler, eds., *South Asians and the Shaping of Britain 1870–1950: A Sourcebook* (Manchester: Manchester University Press, 2012), pp. 175–8.
18. And who herself, in the medium of prose, cultivated aestheticist images of Oxford—and of India.
19. For a still effective, if inevitably dated characterization of the time, see Elaine Showalter, *Sexual Anarchy: Gender and Culture at the Fin-de-siècle* (London: Bloomsbury, 1991), in particular pp. 1–18.

20. Like Sorabji, Naidu deftly used dress to project herself as a poet of the east, and 'adored beautiful jewels and clothes', yet at the same time was always aware of the western contexts and audiences to whom she primarily targeted this mode of dress. In a 4 September 1905 letter to Edmund Gosse from Hyderabad, she went so far as to develop what can best be called an inter-cultural synaesthesia by finding analogies for the fabrics she proposed to wear in the attributes of English poets:

    > There is a great excitement about the coming royal visit and at this moment my soul runs not on lyrics but on clothes—as gorgeous as the verse of Milton, brocaded with gold and silver on philox red and iris purple silk, and delicate and diaphanous as the lyrics of Shelley, all floating gauzes edged with silver fringe and pearls, coloured like the petals of rose and and [*sic*] the heart of a Konark champa. Can you imagine anything more eastern or more sumptuous—as to the sound of it and the 'verbal vision'.

    See Tara Ali Baig, *Sarojini Naidu* (New Delhi: Ministry of Information and Broadcasting, Government of India, 1974), p. 29; Makarand Paranjape, ed., *Sarojini Naidu: Selected Letters, 1890s–1940s* (New Delhi: Kali for Women, 1996), p. 48.
21. Ranasinha et al., eds., *A Sourcebook*, p. 175.
22. Arthur Symons, 'The Decadent Movement in Literature', *Harper's New Monthly Magazine* (November 1893); collected in his *Dramatis Personae* (London: Faber and Gwyer, 1923), pp. 96–117, especially pp. 96–7.
23. As Symons wrote of the 'delicate, subtle, aspiring, unsatisfied' artistic personality in his essay 'Walter Pater' in *Studies in Prose and Verse* (London: J. M. Dent, 1904), pp. 62–76, especially p. 67, it is one 'withdrawn from action . . . solitary with its ideals, in the circle of its "exquisite moments" in the Palace of Art, where it is never quite at rest'. He was, of course, directly referencing Pater himself on the immortalization of 'vivid moments' in art.
24. See, for example, Oscar Wilde, *The Picture of Dorian Gray* (1890/91; Oxford: Oxford World's Classics, 2008), pp. 18–19, 21, 22, 111, 182.
25. On the mannered imitation of the 1890s, see David Weir, *Decadence and the Making of Modernism* (Amherst, MA: University of Massachusetts Press, 1995), especially p. 23.
26. Quoted in Showalter, *Sexual Anarchy*, p. 1.
27. Jackson, *The Eighteen Nineties*, in particular, pp. 12–13, 21, 63, 84.
28. As Weir, *Decadence and the Making of Modernism*, xi–xii aptly puts it, in a commentary on Charles Baudelaire's poem 'Une Charogne' [A Corpse]: 'civilization is itself the corpse upon which the decadent sensibility feeds, nourished by the prospect of its own annihilation'.
29. Wilde, *The Picture of Dorian Gray*, pp. 5, 27, 106, 154.
30. Warner, *Stranger Magic*, especially pp. 25–30; Ros Ballaster, *Fabulous Orients: Fictions of the East in England 1662–1785* (Oxford: Oxford University Press, 2005).
31. See Ronald Inden, *Imagining India*, 2nd edn (1990; Bloomington, IN: Indiana University Press, 2000).

32. Wilde, *The Picture of Dorian Gray*, p. 118.
33. Showalter, *Sexual Anarchy*, pp. 144–68. See also H. Rider Haggard, *She*, ed. Daniel Karlin (1897; Oxford: Oxford World's Classics, 1991).
34. Jackson, *The Eighteen Nineties*, p. 231.
35. Franklin, *The Lotus and the Lion*; David Scott, 'Kipling's Encounters with Buddhism and the Buddhist Orient: "The Twain Shall Meet"?' *Cultural History* 1 (April 2012): 36–60, available at: <http://www.euppublishing.com/doi/abs/10.3366/cult.2012.0005> (accessed 14 February 2015). See also Rudyard Kipling, *Kim*, ed. Edward W. Said (1901; London: Penguin, 1987).
36. Mary Ellis Gibson, *Anglophone Poetry in Colonial India* (Athens, OH: Ohio University Press, 2011); Makarand Paranjape, *Making India: Colonialism, National Culture and the Afterlife of Indian English Authority* (Dordrecht, NL: Springer, 2013), pp. 171–3.
37. See also Robert H. MacDonald, *The Language of Empire: Myths and Metaphors of Popular Imperialism: 1880–1918* (Manchester: Manchester University Press, 1994), pp. 49–50, 55, 211.
38. Arthur Conan Doyle, *A Study in Scarlet* (1887; London: Penguin, 2008), pp. 1–5; Wilde, *The Picture of Dorian Gray*, p. 43.
39. See Patrick Brantlinger, 'Imperial Gothic: Atavism and the Occult in the British Adventure Novel', *English Literature in Transition 1880–1920* 28.3 (1985): 243–52; Wilde, *The Picture of Dorian Gray*, p. 109.
40. Wilde, *Dorian Gray*, p. 41; Leela Gandhi, *Affective Communities: Anticolonial Thought and the Politics of Friendship* (Durham, NC: Duke University Press, 2006), pp.141–76, especially pp. 144, 61. Later twentieth-century writers like Evelyn Waugh, or Nancy Mitford in the *The Pursuit of Love* (London: H. Hamilton, 1945), flippantly amplified the stereotype of the gilded Rajah whose wealth whitened and enhanced his status within the upper-class marriage market.
41. Schuchard, *The Last Minstrels*, pp. 28–31, 258. This was Hulme's characterization. See also Pound, 'The Later Yeats', *Poetry* 4 (May 1914): 65.
42. Antoinette Burton, '"Stray Thoughts of an Indian Girl" by Cornelia Sorabji', *Indian Journal of Gender Studies* 3.2 (1996): 249–56.
43. Alex Owen, *The Place of Enchantment: British Occultism and the Science of the Modern* (Chicago, IL: Chicago University Press, 2004), pp. 29–30.
44. When MP Mr Burnie asked Naoroji to make an approach to the India Office on the Indian oculists' behalf, Naoroji responded he could do nothing, presumably because the destitute Indians were not in his constituency. See IOR: L/PJ/6/373, f.828 ('Indian Oculists in a Destitute Condition in Swansea (1894)'). India Society, *Proceedings of the London India Society 1910* (London: India Society, 1911): in particular, in this file, the letter from James Fox, Proprietor of *The Cambria Daily Leader*, 1 May 1894, to Mr Burnie, MP in Swansea, concerning the plight of these 'natives of the Punjab (named Bukhsh)', who had been practicing in Cumbria and 'latterly in Neath'. Comment is also made on their being 'high caste' Muslims for whom it would be scandalous to be sent to the workhouse, especially in a

Christian (that is, God-fearing) country. See also Sumita Mukherjee, 'A Warning Against Quack Doctors': The Old Bailey Trial of Indian Oculists, 1893', *Historical Research* 86.231 (February 2013): 76–91.

45. In his discussion *Poetry of the Period* (1870), for example, the (later) Poet Laureate Alfred Austin lamented the bifurcation within contemporary British poetry between 'great poetry' and 'beautiful poetry', in which the former was addressed to the world of action, conflict, and public statement, the latter to the world of dreams. See Alfred Austin, 'Summary in *The Poetry of the Period*', in *The Victorian Poet*, ed. Joseph Bristow (Beckenham: Croom Helm, 1987), pp. 123–4.
46. Ronald Schuchard, *The Last Minstrels: Yeats and the Revival of the Bardic Arts* (Oxford: Oxford University Press, 2008), pp. xxi, 5.
47. The quotations are from the letters of 1890s poet Ernest Dowson and are cited in John Hatcher, *Laurence Binyon: Poet, Scholar of East and West* (Oxford: Clarendon Press, 1995), p. 34. The poet Manmohan Ghose should not be confused with the Indian National Congress campaigner who also plied between India and Britain, though somewhat earlier than Ghose, from the 1860s.
48. Laurence Binyon, 'Introductory Memoir', in *Songs of Love and Death* (Oxford: Basil Blackwell, 1926), pp. 7–23. See also the same essay, 'Manmohan Ghose', in *Collected Poems*, p. vii. For her critical theoretical yet also biographical account of the lifelong Ghose–Binyon friendship, see Gandhi, *Affective Communities* pp. 162–71.
49. See Elleke Boehmer, *Empire, the National, and the Postcolonial: Resistance in Interaction* (Oxford: Oxford University Press, 2002) for two chapters of extended discussion of Aurobindo Ghose.
50. Binyon, 'Introductory Memoir', pp. 7–23.
51. Hatcher, *Laurence Binyon*, pp. 31–5.
52. Binyon, 'Introductory Memoir', p. 10.
53. Ghose, Letter of 2 September 1888, in *Collected Poems*, pp. 190–2.
54. Binyon, 'Introductory Memoir', pp. 9–10, 13–14.
55. Ghose, Letters April 15 and 20 1887, July 1887 and [Summer] 1887, in *Collected Poems*, pp. 111–14, 123–4, 131–3.
56. See Laurence Binyon Collection, British Library, vol. 5. The letters that appear in *Collected Poems*, edited by Lotika Ghose, cover the period 1887–90, the last two being 22 December 1890 from Earls Court and 7 January 1916 about Ghose's wife's illness. This gives the misleading impression that the friends did not correspond between 1890 and 1916, whereas in fact, between 1894 and 1904, they exchanged on average about five or six letters a year. On the 'zig-zag' matching of late nineteenth-century heterodoxies, see Gandhi, *Affective Communities*, pp. 122–6.
57. Kwame Anthony Appiah, *Cosmopolitanism: Ethics in a World of Strangers* (London: Allen Lane, 2006).
58. Appiah, *Cosmopolitanism*, in particular pp. xv, 85. Pheng Cheah and Bruce Robbins, eds., *Cosmopolitics: Thinking and Feeling Beyond the Nation*

(Minneapolis, MN: University of Minnesota Press, 1998) likewise insists that the once free-floating view of cosmopolitanism rather be anchored in the particularities of place and history (much as the other is seen as 'out beyond' rather than, as here, within).

59. 'Four authors' [Laurence Binyon, Arthur C. Cripps, Manmohan Ghose, Stephen Phillips], *Primavera* (Oxford: B. H. Blackwell, 1890). Phillips, who became a respected actor, is mentioned in Jackson, *The Eighteen Nineties*, p. 40.
60. Gandhi, *Affective Communities*, pp. 142–3; Hatcher, *Laurence Binyon*, p. 30.
61. Walter Pater, *Studies in the History of the Renaissance* (1873; Oxford: Oxford University Press, 1986), p. 40.
62. Ghose, *Collected Poems*, p. 196.
63. Hatcher, *Laurence Binyon*, pp. 9–10. See also A. B. Purani, *Sri Aurobindo in England* (Pondicherry: Sri Aurobindo Ashram, 1956), p. 21.
64. 'Introductory Memoir', pp. 7–23. The quotations are from pp. 7–9.
65. Hatcher, *Laurence Binyon*, p. 156.
66. Hatcher, *Laurence Binyon*, pp. 45–7; Ghose, *Collected Poems*, pp. 125–6.
67. Ghose, *Collected Poems*, pp. 159ff., 179. As a further expression of his loneliness, in a 12 December 1887 letter, Ghose appears to question Binyon about a poem that hinted at a homoerotic affair.
68. See the charged political letter of 1887 in Ghose, *Collected Poems*, pp. 135–43.
69. Hatcher, *Laurence Binyon*, p. 11; Gandhi, *Affective Communities*, pp. 162–71.
70. Ghose, *Collected Poems*, p. 222; Ranasinha et al., eds., *A Sourcebook*, p. 178. It was fair of Wilde to single him out in this way. As the Acknowledgements show, four of the *Primavera* poems had been published before, but none by Ghose.
71. Gandhi, *Affective Communities*, pp. 168–70.
72. Ghose, Letters of 4 and 28 August 1890 in particular, *Collected Poems*, pp. 232–6, 237–9; also p. 242.
73. See Yeats, 'The Trembling of the Veil', in *Autobiographies*; Gandhi, *Affective Communities*, pp. 231–2.
74. Gandhi, *Affective Communities*, pp. 169–71.
75. Ghose, Letters of 3 February 1890 and November 1890, *Collected Poems*, pp. 239–41, 247–9.
76. Book 42040 (Lionel Johnson copy of *Primavera*), Rare Books Department, Huntingdon Library, San Marino, California. See also Gandhi, *Affective Communities*, p. 169; Hatcher, *Laurence Binyon*, pp. 26–9, 31–2.
77. Binyon would supervise the subsequent publication of Ghose's work in England. As the later letters record, he oversaw the 1898 publication of his *Love Songs and Elegies*, as Garland no. 9 in Elkin Matthews's Shilling Series, and the 1926 posthumous appearance of *Songs of Love and Death*.
78. See, in particular, Binyon et al., *Primavera*, pp. 5–9 ('Youth' by Binyon; III by Ghose). Further page references to *Primavera* will be included in the text.

79. Considering the influence of both Wilde and Pater upon the collection, the reader might recall the Lord Henry's fateful invocation in Wilde's *The Picture of Dorian Gray*, p. 23: 'Youth! Youth! There is absolutely nothing in the world but youth!'
80. Ghose, *Collected Poems*, pp. 120–1.
81. Ranasinha et al., eds., *A Sourcebook*, pp. 175–8; Book 42040 (Lionel Johnson's copy of *Primavera*). See also Gandhi, *Affective Communities*, pp. 142–3; Hatcher, *Binyon*, p. 30. Curiously, the Italian monarch Victor Emmanuel II in the 1860s praised a poem of M. M. Dutt's on Dante Alighieri in terms very similar to those of Wilde. He wrote that the poem would be like a ring 'which will connect the Orient with the Occident'.
82. J. J. Wilhelm, *Ezra Pound in London and Paris 1908–1925* (London: Pennsylvania State University Press, 1990), p. 129. For the subheading quotation, see again Gosse, 'Introduction', *The Bird of Time*, p. 3.
83. C. H. S. Nicholson and A. H. E. Lee, eds., *The Oxford Book of English Mystical Verse* (Oxford: Clarendon Press, 1916), pp. 610–12. In the 'Introduction', pp. v–ix, they allow that 'any poetry written in English, from whatever country' is acceptable. The three poems appear in *The Bird of Time*, pp. 81 and 97; and *The Golden Threshold*, p. 97. Page references for quotations from Naidu's poems will henceforth be included in the text, with the abbreviations *BT* and *GT*.
84. See Arvind Krishna Mehrotra, ed., *The Oxford Anthology of Twelve Modern Indian Poets* (New Delhi: Oxford University Press, 1992), pp. 1–2.
85. Baig, *Sarojini Naidu*, p. 31.
86. Paranjape, 'Introduction', *Sarojini Naidu: Selected Poetry and Prose*, p. 14.
87. See BL: Mss Eur F341/152. Ruth F. Woodsmall, 'Notes on Sarojini Naidu: Interview' (New Delhi, 20 March 1931): 'There is no thought in the East of women being pitted against men. The Indian movement has come much more naturally than the Western feminism and must be kept true to its genius.' See also Baig, *Sarojini Naidu*, p. 46.
88. Naidu, 'The Fairy Isle of Janjira', in *The Bird of Time*, pp. 79–80.
89. Index 15: Manuscript Poems and Letters of Sarojini Naidu, National Archives of India. On Gosse, see also Chapter 1, Section VI.
90. See Lisa Rodensky, ed. and intro., *Decadent Poetry from Wilde to Naidu* (London: Penguin, 2006), pp. xxiii–xlviii, especially, pp. xlii–xliii.
91. See R/E/O 821.91 N 143a and R/E/O 821.91, vols. 1–3. Sarojini Naidu papers, Special Collections, National Library, Calcutta.
92. Chandani Lokugé, 'Dialoging with Empire: The Literary and Political Rhetoric of Sarojini Naidu', in *India in Britain*, ed. Susheila Nasta (London: Palgrave, 2012), pp. 115–33 (the quotation is from p. 115); Symons, 'Introduction', in *The Golden Threshold*, p. 21.
93. Sarojini Naidu, *The Broken Wing: Songs of Love, Death and Destiny 1915–16* (London: William Heinemann, 1917). As the collection's opening poem (also called 'The Broken Wing', pp. 3–4) confirms, the title was again significant, both a pessimistic retrospective reference to Omar Khayyam's

singing bird, and to a question Gokhale posed in 1914, apparently referring to Naidu's always uncertain health and changing priorities, which was here used as an epigraph: 'Song-bird, why dost thou bear a broken wing?' The answer given in the poem about the attempt to fly ever higher is defiant but indirect.

94. Sarojini Naidu, *The Feather of the Dawn*, ed. Padmaja Naidu (Bombay: Asia Publishing House, 1961).
95. Baig, *Sarojini Naidu*, pp. 18–19, 22; Hasi Banerjee, *Sarojini Naidu: The Traditional Feminist* (Calcutta: K. P. Bagdhi and Co., 1998), pp. 4–5.
96. Baig, *Sarojini Naidu*, pp. 18–19. Naidu would once again travel at Besant's side in 1915–17 during the latter's period as President of the Indian National Congress.
97. KW/SYL 5a and SYL 6, KWA RAD 2, KWA RAD 3. King's College London Archives: the syllabus of lectures 1895–96 and 1897–98, the address book and course 1895–96 and 1897–98, respectively. I am grateful to Anna Snaith and the staff of the King's College London Archives, for introducing me to the archive and pointing these records out to me. On Naidu's 'colonial modernism', see also Snaith's chapter on Naidu in *Modernist Voyages*, pp. 67–89.
98. Padmini Sen Gupta, *Sarojini Naidu* (New Delhi: Sahitya Akademi, 1974), p. 13.
99. K/SER1/170. *King's College Magazine, Ladies' Department*, numbers I, IV, VII, Michaelmas 1896, Michaelmas 1897, Lent 1899, Lent 1900, pp. 11, 8, 43, and 30, respectively. See also Christine Kenyon Jones and Anna Snaith, 'Tilting at Universities: Virginia Woolf at King's College London', *Woolf Studies Annual* 16 (2010): 1–44.
100. *King's College Magazine, Ladies' Department,* Number X, Lent 1899, p. 30.
101. Cited in Mss Eur F341/118: 'Memorial Meetings and Resolutions, Town Hall, Bombay, 29 June 1931', from Sarojini Naidu, *Lady Tata: A Book of Remembrance* (Bombay: Commercial Printing Press, 1932), pp. 55–6.
102. Paranjape, ed., *Sarojini Naidu: Selected Poetry and Prose*, pp. 202–5. 'Nilambuja' was first published in *The Indian Ladies' Magazine* (December 1902).
103. Paranjape, ed., *Sarojini Naidu: Selected Letters,* p. 3.
104. Gosse, 'Introduction', *The Bird of Time*, pp. 4–5. Curiously perhaps, Gosse had invoked a similar premature consignment to the waste-paper basket in his account of first encountering Dutt's collection, thirty years before.
105. Paranjape, ed., *Sarojini Naidu: Selected Poetry and Prose*, pp. 197–201.
106. Baig, *Sarojini Naidu*, p. 20; Sen Gupta, *Sarojini Naidu*, p. 9.
107. Symons, 'Introduction', in *The Golden Threshold*, pp. 17–19.
108. Paranjape, ed., *Sarojini Naidu: Collected Letters,* for example, pp. xxxviii.
109. Baig, *Sarojini Naidu*, pp. 54–5.
110. Paranjape, ed., *Collected Letters,* p. 47. See also Anonymous, 'Recent Verse', *Manchester Guardian* (20 December 1905), p. 5.
111. Sarojini Naidu and Liza Lehman, *The Golden Threshold: An Indian Song-garland* (poems by Sarojini Naidu; music by Liza Lehmann) (London:

Boosey and Co., 1907). See also Anonymous, 'Music in London', *Manchester Guardian* (30 April 1907).

112. See Anonymous, 'An Indian Poetess', *Manchester Guardian* (27 January 1913), p. 7. For a representative sampling of Naidu's reviews, see also A. A. S. [Miss A. A. Smith], 'How Far That Little Candle Throws its Beams', *Indian Magazine and Review* 519 (March 1914), p. 72; J. D. W., 'Review of *The Bird of Time*', *The Indian Magazine and Review* 508 (April 1913), p. 89; Anonymous, 'Poet-President of Indian National Congress', *Manchester Guardian* (28 December 1925), p. 2, which expressed a punning respect for Naidu's 'soul-force'.
113. Hasi Banerjee, *Sarojini Naidu: The Traditional Feminist* (Calcutta: K. P. Bagdhi and Co., 1998), pp. 23–9; W. B. Yeats, *Memoirs: Autobiography—First Draft; Journal*, ed. Denis Donoghue (London: Macmillan, 1972), p. 175.
114. Baig, *Sarojini Naidu*, p. 59; Sen Gupta, *Sarojini Naidu*, p. 34.
115. Interestingly, it was on the same east–west routes which she had begun to map from the time of her first Suez journey, traced in Chapter 1, that Naidu found another congenial fellow traveller in Gokhale himself. She was a faithful member of the Lyceum Club, where she usually stayed while in London; he was a frequenter of the London Liberal Club, a venue in which he enjoyed playing bridge. The Liberal Club, it will be recalled, was also a sometime residence of the Ghose brothers. Naidu was to be seen on occasion driving to the Kensington Gardens address together with her mentor.
116. Naidu, *The Bird of Time*, p. 79–80; *The Broken Wing*, pp. 5–6. In the discussion of Naidu's poetry that follows, page references to individual poems will be included in the text together with the abbreviations *GT*, *BT*, and *BW*.
117. Baig, *Sarojini Naidu*, p. 34; Sen Gupta, *Sarojini Naidu*, pp. 37–9.
118. See Haun Saussy, 'Chiasmus', *Comparative Literature* 57.3 (2005): 234–8.
119. Ranjana Ash, 'Two Early Twentieth-century Indian Women Writers: Cornelia Sorabji and Sarojini Naidu', in *A History of Indian Literature in English*, ed. Arvind Mehrotra (London: Hurst and Company, 2003), pp. 126–34.
120. In symbolist poetry, wrote Symons, 'the visible world is no longer a reality, and the unseen world is no longer a dream'. See Arthur Symons, *The Symbolist Movement in Literature* (London: Heinemann, 1899), p. 4.
121. Ash, 'Two Early Twentieth-century Indian Women Writers', p. 131.
122. Cornelia Sorabji, *India Calling*, ed. Elleke Boehmer and Naella Grew (1934; Nottingham: Trent Editions, 2004), pp. 21–2. This is an extraordinary metaphor for an Indian writing at this time; one that suggests a certain porosity or sponginess, indeed, an accessibility, to settled, racially defined ideas of Englishness, and so of Britishness more broadly. In a fascinatingly contradictory and yet far-sighted way, Sorabji allows for an eclectic make-up of British identity, even while in the same paragraph asserting the power of 'Breed' over 'Feed' (nature over nurture).

123. Richard Sorabji, *Opening Doors: The Untold Story of Cornelia Sorabji* (London: IB Tauris, 2010).
124. Cornelia Sorabji, *Love and Life Behind the Purdah* (London: Freemantle and Co., 1901), which presents portraits of the *purdahnashin* or women in purdah she represented in India in the 1890s, and *Sun-babies: Studies in the Child Life of India* (London: John Murray, 1904), based on observations of the lives of her domestic servants. *Between the Twilights* (London: Harper, 1908), a retelling of Hindu myths featuring women, again drew on Sorabji's Indian experiences.
125. Sorabji, *India Calling*, pp. 5–6 and 20. See also the final epigraph at the start of this chapter.
126. Sorabji, *India Calling*, pp. 14 and 52. See also p. 135 for the description of another beautiful, though more retiring, lamp-lighting ceremony.
127. Sorabji, *India Calling*, p. 5.
128. Back in India after Oxford, Sorabji worked in a self-styled position as legal adviser to the Indian Courts of Wards.
129. Sorabji published articles and essays in the *Nineteenth Century*, and the *Nineteenth Century and After*, in 1891, 1893, 1896, 1899, 1900, 1901, and 1903, most of which she later collected, edited, and published in book form, such as in *Love and Life* and *India Calling*. She also published on babuisms and F. Max Müller, amongst other topics, in the *Temple Bar* magazine.
130. Burton, *At the Heart of the Empire*, pp. 110–51, especially pp. 111 and 145. See also Ash, 'Two Early Twentieth-century Indian Women Writers', pp. 126–34.
131. As is not surprising in respect of two such prominent and outspoken Indian women, Cornelia Sorabji's path intersected at several points with Sarojini Naidu's following their first meeting in Hyderabad in 1904. They saw each other relatively often in London in 1914. The two women were appreciative of one another's interests and faculties, while also registering strong political differences. R. Sorabji, *Opening Doors*, pp. 336–8.
132. 'Heart of the heart' is Burton's locution. See Burton, *At the Heart of the Empire*, pp. 114, 127–30.
133. See again Richard Symonds, *Oxford and Empire: The Last Lost Cause?* (New York, NY: St Martin's Press, 1986).
134. C. Sorabji, *India Calling*, p. 26; R. Sorabji, *Opening Doors*, p. 23.
135. Burton, *At the Heart of the Empire*, pp. 129, 132–3, which quotes MS EUR F 165/1 (letter of 10 November 1889).
136. R. Sorabji, *Opening Doors*, pp. 59, 105–6, 117.
137. R. Sorabji, *Opening Doors*, pp. 30–2.
138. R. Sorabji, *Opening Doors*, pp. 38, 40.
139. Burton, *At the Heart of the Empire*, pp. 60–1, 145. The article was entitled 'Stray Thoughts of an Indian Girl'.
140. C. Sorabji, *India Calling*, pp. 36–7.
141. The remarkable scene is described in *India Calling*, p. 36 (pp. 50–1 in the first edition). See also R. Sorabji, *Opening Doors*, p. 45.

142. Naipaul, *The Enigma of Arrival*, pp. 192–3.
143. For a different reading, see Lotika Basu, *Indian Writers of English Verse* (Calcutta: University of Calcutta Press, 1933), pp. 94–5, in which Naidu is criticized for being a creator of 'the picture of India painted by Anglo-Indian and English writers'.
144. Symons, 'Introduction', in *The Golden Threshold*, p. 10.

4

Edwardian Extremes and Extremists, 1901–13

. . . her heart gave a quick beat of recognition. Several pieces of furniture had been set out of the van upon the pavement. There was a beautiful table of elaborately wrought teakwood, and some chairs, and a screen covered with rich Oriental embroidery. The sight of them gave her a weird, homesick feeling. She had seen things so like them in India.

Frances Hodgson Burnett, *A Little Princess* (1905)[1]

the unwritten text of Anarchism: the right of the oppressed to overthrow the oppressor; the divinity of violence; the sacredness of sacrifice and martyrdom in the cause of enlightenment.

Edgar Wallace, *The Four Just Men* (1905)[2]

Where the mind is without fear and the head is held high;
Where knowledge is free;
Where the world has not been broken up into fragments by narrow
domestic walls;
Where words come out from the depth of truth;
Where tireless striving stretches its arms towards perfection;
Where the clear stream of reason has not lost its way into the dreary
desert sand of dead habit;
Where the mind is led forward by thee into ever-widening thought
and action—
Into that heaven of freedom, my Father, let my country awake.

Rabindranath Tagore, 'XXXIII', *Gitanjali: Song Offerings* (1912)[3]

I DIFFERENCE WITHIN

By the beginning of the new twentieth century—the century that would be eventually distinguished as an era of transcontinental migration par excellence—small clusters of Indian scholars, academics, activists, politicians, entrepreneurs, seers, and seamen had become established in British cities, towns, and universities, even if mostly in niches and pockets. These Indian residents of places like London, Cambridge, and Bristol contributed not only to how India was perceived internationally, when seen from the vantage point of the west, but also to an understanding of Britain, London in particular, as an intercultural cosmopolitan hub, in which Indians abroad could potentially play politically and culturally significant roles.

By the beginning of the first decade of the new century, therefore, South Asians in Britain had developed for themselves a terrain described by Avtah Brah as 'diaspora space': a concept which places emphasis not merely on the inputs of the migrant community to their new country, but also keeps in play both the receiving and the arriving groups' investments in the experience of contact and exchange.[4] As many of the case studies highlighted in this book bear out, 'diaspora space' is an appropriate and productive term because, instead of focusing solely on communities on the move, as 'diaspora' alone might, it captures the intertwining experiences of both those who have migrated and those who have stayed put. As Brah explains: 'diaspora space as a conceptual category is "inhabited", not only by those who have migrated and their descendants, but equally by those who are constructed and represented as indigenous'.[5] In a word, citizens' *in situ* understanding of their space, especially of how their spaces are bounded by other spaces, including those of their families, neighbourhood, and country of origin, comprise multiple and diverse connotations, held in tension with the understandings of other communities.[6] So it followed that, at the turn of the nineteenth century, as diasporic communities grew, Indian migrants' lives and doings became increasingly more intercalated with those of other migrants, as well as with those of the resident British population.

As Manmohan Ghose and Sarojini Naidu's shaping involvement in late-century Decadence encapsulates, this multivalent, intercultural 'inhabitation' related also to imaginative experience.[7] In poetry, literary sketches, stories, letters, and public statements, Indian inhabitants' conceptualization of their space both in the here-and-now (Britain), and in relation to faraway (South Asia), became increasingly more braided with a sense of other cultural presences. This involvement is vividly reflected, for example, in Frances Hodgson Burnett children's classic, *A Little Princess*, in which Sara Crewe, a native of India and a homesick resident of London, gains to her amazement a sense of the capital as imbued with Indian influences (captured in the epigraph above). But Madan Lal Dhingra's justification of his own urban terrorism in London only a few years after the publication of Burnett's book, in dialogue with the anarchist discourse of London's many East European revolutionaries and radicals (corroborated in the above quotation from Wallace), demonstrated a related sense of imaginative embedding also; of feeling sufficiently in place in Britain to mount such a critique. Even in these relatively early days for migration from South Asia, the Indian migrants' sense of their movement through, and belonging in, Britain, their route-ing and their rooting, was therefore complex and intersectional, and this pertained even where stays and obstructions to such inhabitation began to arise in the form of a rising nationalist extremism, as well as of countervailing expressions of racism.[8]

As the twentieth century began to unfold, diasporic and progressive spaces in Britain, including those relating to Indians, came under growing pressure from several different corners. This new polarization in perceptions of Indians in Britain marked what is conventionally known as the Edwardian period—here, the long Edwardian decade—and laid down patterns in race relations that would be influential for years to come. It is this gradual polarization, as mapped and analysed through a range of novels, memoirs, portraits, photographs, and a collection of poetry (Tagore's *Gitanjali*, which furnishes the third epigraph), that forms the core subject of this chapter. The culmination of this period is not so much Virginia Woolf's watershed moment of December 1910, 'on or about' which, she claimed, 'human character changed' (or at least the representation thereof), but one of the pre-war highpoints of Indian–British interaction, 7 July 1912, the meeting of the poet Rabindranath Tagore and the portraitist and art critic William Rothenstein, along with other friends and well-wishers, not least W. B. Yeats, in the portraitist's London home.[9] The presence of Indians at different cultural interfaces during these crucial years was brought to an intriguing climax at this point, as will be seen, in the form of the simultaneous understanding yet misunderstanding that the meeting created. This neatly dramatizes Brah's notion of mutual contact, though here between migrant rather than strictly diasporic individuals, while it also usefully complicates once again Appiah's account of cosmopolitanism. At this point, the understanding of the modern as something pertaining exclusively to the west changed fundamentally, for those in positions to see it.

The focus on 1912, however, should not cast other possible watershed moments or contiguous years as of lesser importance. The year 1910, chosen by Woolf as a landmark year in the light of how the first Post-Impressionist Exhibition had revised representational conventions in art (it opened on 8 November 1910), was also a key year for the reception of Indian arts in Britain. It was in January that the India Society was formed by Rothenstein and others, with the date engraved into its badge or logo. It was in this year, too, that Rothenstein travelled to India, where he met Tagore for the first time, and Forster, already feeling drawn to India, published *Howards End*, his last English novel before *A Passage to India*, in which the brown metropolis of London inexorably encroaches on the English pastoral scene. Also in 1910, Sarojini Naidu, who had reported some years before to R. C. Dutt that her muse was at last working again, was writing at high intensity, in order to produce a volume of poetry in time for the Delhi Durbar of 1911 to mark the visit of George V to India.[10] And in November 1910, too, K. K. Aziz launched a project to build a mosque in London, though the project application was refused by the Secretary of State, Morley. In the same year, however, he did form the British Red Crescent Society as the Muslim world's counterpart to the British Red Cross.[11] Yet 1913, too, was a significant year, and not just because it was the last year of the peace.[12] In 1913, G. H. Hardy first encountered the remarkable mathematical work of Ramanujan, who then embarked for England at Hardy's invitation. In 1913, too, Tagore was awarded the Nobel Prize, as we will see, the first writer from outside Europe to be so honoured; and Leonard Woolf, already married to Virginia, published his fascinating study in Sinhalese otherness, *The Village in the Jungle*, based on his experiences as a colonial officer. The year 1912 therefore forms a prominent point of intercultural concentration, around which related Indian–British developments in neighbouring years may be seen to cluster.

Across the 1890s and into the new century, Britain's declining economic power on the world stage, at least in relative terms, had heightened imperial rivalries in relation to both Germany and the USA. In 1900, both countries, as well as Japan, succeeded in outstripping Britain's levels of industrial production. The Anglo-Boer hostilities of 1899–1902 then further isolated Britain among the great powers and exposed the empire's serious military and political weaknesses. On the home front, such imperial and international stresses exacerbated existing social, political, cultural, and what would now be called ethnic tensions—tensions that were sensed and expressed both within mainstream culture, and inside migrant enclaves such as that of (loosely conceived) India-in-Britain. Even as anxieties about national and imperial degeneration became more widely prevalent in the wider public sphere, anarchist, socialist, suffragette, and other radical groupings grew more organized, as well as increasingly vociferous and insistent in their demands. In their turn, these developments inevitably aggravated an already rising jingoism and accelerated the decline of the political middle ground—that ground which Gladstonian Liberalism once had furnished.[13] The 'vast fatigue' that Max Nordau had diagnosed as besetting Europe lost many of the attractive aspects it had presented in the etiolated 1890s and was now increasingly viewed as the symptom of a grave and rapidly oncoming civilizational crisis.[14] As the new century dawned, therefore, with Hong Kong secured and the Boer

Republics defeated, the empire's vast expansion across the final decade of Queen Victoria's reign paradoxically produced in the new Edwardian decade both an entrenchment of imperialist attitudes and a deepening of colonial divisions. A general defensiveness about propagating the empire abroad dampened the congenial spirit that to date had accompanied, at home, ecumenical ideas of imperial citizenship shared by all peoples under the crown.

The layered social experiences or 'intersectionality' that distinguishes diasporic space may to some degree have contributed to these rising tensions—though Indians for a considerable time remained relatively free from the racially coded suspicion meted out to other migrant groups, in particular Jews. Almost everywhere, the potential fallout of the new and more frequent contact between different migrant communities, as well as between hosts and migrants, was, once again, a rise in political radicalism as anti-imperial views and values were compared and exchanged across the multiplying contact zones of the ever-more-networked empire. The repressive and divisive measures taken against already existing nationalist formations, such as in Ireland, Egypt, and Bengal, also heightened these exchanges.[15]

In Bengal, for example, the politically motivated partition of 1905 introduced an aggressive new extremism to nationalist politics, the repercussions of which were felt as far afield as Europe and the West Coast of the United States.[16] In the same year that Sister Nivedita (Margaret Noble), a collaborator of Manmohan's younger brother Aurobindo Ghose, unfurled an extremist banner at a meeting of the Indian National Congress in Calcutta, the Parsi revolutionary Madame Cama flew an Indian freedom flag at the 1907 International Socialist conference in Stuttgart, and repeated the symbolic gesture in the radical cell of India House in London, in order to mark the 50th anniversary of the Indian Rebellion. In short, as Rabindranath Tagore for one was well aware, the tensions generated by imperial anxieties and rising nationalist feeling aggravated already existing social and cultural fault-lines—and these fault-lines themselves deepened as extremist politics intensified across the polarized decade. As Arthur Symons symptomatically observed in a commentary on Joseph Conrad's novel about inner-city anarchism, *The Secret Agent*—a novel to which this chapter shall again have occasion to refer—that bloodletting which the novelist in his early work had observed as rife in the Malayan Peninsula seemed to be threatening and even infiltrating the heart of empire. To Symons, this new violence and vengefulness was concentrated in *The Secret Agent* in the point of Winnie Verloc's carving knife.[17]

Inevitably, even as Indian residents' activities in Britain came little by little to be perceived as woven in with strands of British social, political, and cultural life, these migrant entanglements and interactions became noticeably more cordoned off than before, or more prone, in the corners and cliques they inhabited, to contention and division. Instead of underpinning those experiences of commonality, amity, and living side by side that previous decades had started to put in place, even if in partial ways, as was seen, these pressures, taken together, rather heightened that sense of alienness in Britain that Indians still experienced. As destitute Indians became steadily more numerous in port cities, which newspapers reported, and as rumours of Indian students' radicalization emanated from the India Office in London, the image of the Indian-in-Britain shifted from that of exotic but generally benign itinerant traveller, and took on connotations of danger, threat, and encroachment.[18] Certainly, after the extremist Madan Lal Dhingra's assassination of the Secretary of State for India, Sir William Curzon Wyllie, in London in early July 1909, the India Office began to consider most Indian students at English universities as radicals in the making.[19] Angered to the extreme by the treatment of Indians at the hands of the British in India, Dhingra had shot the high-ranking Indian civil servant at a no less intercultural and symbolic event than a National Indian Association concert and reception in the Imperial Institute, South Kensington. From this point on, it appeared, an Indian could just as likely be an unsavoury extremist as a handholding friend.

In the years leading up to the First World War, therefore, Indians studying, travelling, or settling in Britain were perceived much more sharply than before in bifurcated ways: still in many circles as welcome arrivants and aspirant citizens, but also as potentially dangerous aliens. In this they were not unduly singled out; far from it. Across society cosmopolitan attitudes were on the wane, and Indians were not the first to bear the brunt of the shift. Both Joseph Conrad and Edgar Foster Wallace in their novels of urban terrorism, *The Secret Agent* (1907) and *The Four Just Men* (1905), published within a couple of years of one another, registered a growing anarchist and revolutionary presence in London, and the increasing wariness of the establishment in response to this perceived foment. The middle years of the long Edwardian decade saw extensive debate both within and outside Parliament—with which Wallace and Conrad engaged—concerning the Aliens Act of 1905, the first legislation since the time of Napoleon to restrict immigration to England. Though it was aimed at migrants from Eastern Europe and not the empire, the law nonetheless threatened to undermine, or at least circumscribe the haven for refugees and visitors from elsewhere that England had offered across the nineteenth century. The rise of an increasingly more vociferous Indian nationalism in the 1900s, and the sharpened regional, racial, and political identifications that accompanied this development contributed to this new vigilance and aggravated the sense that resident Indians may have harboured of their otherness or 'unhomeliness' in Britain.[20] Even as some Indians continued to sculpt from their expatriate vantage point a sense of themselves as being at once future citizens of an independent Indian nation, yet also at home in the imperial metropolis, as in Gandhi's model, at the same time their interpretation of the idea of independence and its cognates, such as freedom and self-determination, cut across their experience of integration. It intruded upon their experience of living amicably together with other communities.[21]

So far, this study has explored the different ways in which Indian students, seers, activists, maharajahs, and other travellers moving through Britain in the turn-of-the-century period laid emotional and imaginative claim to its intercultural meeting-places and pathways, especially within London, an experience to which they encountered relatively few hindrances. Indeed, as late as the 1920s, as Richard Sorabji observes, Cornelia Sorabji and her siblings encountered no difficulties in relocating semi-permanently from India to England.[22] In India they simply secured their passports; then set out. Even by the end of the century's first decade, though the Indian nationalist attachment to their distant homeland had made its presence uncompromisingly felt in metropolitan life, such anti-imperial sentiments were still perceived as containable—managed and controlled as they were by the diligent attentions of the India Office. Across the broad social spectrum Indian extremism was perceived to occupy a limited range, especially when compared to the other lively and heterogeneous expressions of India abroad to which Britain was pleased to play host.

Yet, even as Indians developed a sense of belonging to, and even entitlement within, British public spaces, as previous chapters in this volume show, there had remained certain resistances and barriers to their arrival and to their passing, in the sense of their being socially accepted. Such resistances paradoxically only seemed to intensify as the empire widened and the decade turned. The 1910 foundation of the India Society and the subsequent feting of the Bengali poet Rabindranath Tagore threw into relief some of these distinctions. As the final sections of this chapter trace, the India Society had been established to promote Indian arts, yet some of its work confirmed widely held primitivist readings of Asian cultural production as alien and pre-modern, rather than as advanced, complicated, and hence proximate to Europe, as had been the original aim. Indeed, by the time Tagore arrived in 1912 as a guest of the Society to present his work to London audiences, he was celebrated not so much as a modern contemporary, but as a tradition-bound troubadour poet, a foil to the iconoclastic nay-saying modernist artist.

The embedded presences of Indians in Britain, including in its rural areas, yet their continuing sense of mixed familiarity and foreignness, are delicately captured in Julian Barnes's historical novel *Arthur & George* (2005), a portrait of the encounter between the Indian-British lawyer George Edalji and Sir Arthur Conan Doyle. Barnes's subtly postcolonial narrative is woven around a series of actual incidents that took place in the village community of Great Wyrley in Staffordshire in early 1903, which brought the creator of Sherlock Holmes together with the relatively obscure, yet remarkable figure of Edalji, whose Parsi father was a Church of England-educated vicar. Both the historical incidents involving Edalji and their dramatization in the novel pick out the countervailing keynotes of this chapter—that the more established diasporic presence of Indians in British society, far from bringing about a new flush of hospitality in this period of relative stability and prosperity before the First World War, came in certain quarters to be as much rejected as accepted, as much held at arm's length as embraced. In other words, the relatively positive interactions between individual Indians and Britons in previous decades offered no guarantees as to the fostering of amity between migrants and hosts in the new century. As Wilkie Collins had presciently observed of the 'foreign'-looking colonial Ezra Jennings in *The Moonstone*, the dark-skinned outsider might be respected within his community, yet he was also treated with circumspection.

Beginning in February 1903, the rural village community of Great Wyrley in Staffordshire was beset by the repeated mutilation of horses kept in the fields surrounding the town. Up until this point, Great Wyrley had carried the modest distinction of being among the first, if not the first, English village to house in its midst an Indian-born Church of England vicar, Sharpurji Edalji, who, though trained in Canterbury and Evangelical Oxford, was a Bombay Parsi. The relatively unusual occurrences might not, however, have attracted the county—and later nationwide—attention they did, had it not been for an organized campaign of malicious letters that were posted to the family and appeared in the local press within only a day or so of the first maiming incident. The letters implicated Sharpurji's mixed-parentage son George—a trained solicitor and author of a book on railway law—and were racially inflected. George Edalji, who saw himself as 'a freeborn Englishman', in the letters was referred to as 'the black' and as oriental-looking, in language loaded with insinuation and resentment.[23] As this showed, when it came to rural areas relatively unfamiliar with strangers from other cultures, racial feeling ran not far below the surface. Jawaharlal Nehru, a student at Harrow School in London at the time, rightly observed that these troubles had been laid at Edalji's feet 'because he was an Indian'.[24] Nehru also acknowledged thereby the extent to which the incident had captured public attention. Although Indians were accepted in some, mostly elite, social circles, it seemed that in society at large they were generally tolerated only when they did not stand out in any way, where they either kept to themselves or stuck to the company of other foreigners.

Sir Arthur Conan Doyle's January 1907 articles in the *Daily Telegraph*, written in an attempt to clear Edalji's name by creating 'as big a stir as . . . with Dreyfus', first apprised Nehru of the Great Wyrley Outrages.[25] However, by the time the articles appeared, Edalji had already been convicted and imprisoned for his alleged crime, and, in October 1906, released after serving only three years. His family had waged an eventually successful campaign against the Home Office about the case, which was how it first came to Conan Doyle's attention. It then became the writer's aim to have the wrongful conviction overturned, on the convincing grounds of Edalji's ocular impairment, in order to allow him to practice again as a lawyer. The alliance that thus unfolded between the two men told a remarkable story, which Julian Barnes distils in *Arthur & George*: of the great detective writer, upholder of the status quo, putting his own legendary skills of detection to use in order to clear the name of an obscure second-generation Indian; of rationality shown up as powerless in the face of misperception and misunderstanding; and yet of the power of collaboration to overcome that misunderstanding.

In *Arthur & George*, the unlikely interaction between the Scottish Sir Arthur and the Parsi-British younger Edalji that trumps their differences of character and ethical approach is built at least in part on shared principles of common decency—a decency which Edalji even more than Sir Arthur terms 'English'.[26] In chapters entitled 'George', 'Arthur', or 'Arthur & George' (where joint action is concerned), Barnes neatly extracts from the fictionalized alliance some of the salient features of one-on-one Indian–British friendships that have threaded through the case studies in this book: in particular, that such relationships often emerge out of unlikelihood and inadvertency, yet that their hybridizing and entangling effects precisely give them their strength.[27] Edalji, for example, asserts a more convinced law-abiding Britishness than Sir Arthur; Sir Arthur, burdened by marital grief, becomes more of a spiritualist than the putatively 'spiritual' Indian. Indeed, Shapurji Edalji believes that the new century will bring a more harmonious 'commingling of the races', though in the event the commingling is mainly one-on-one, piecemeal, and unpredictable. It is also dependent, as we saw before, on similarities of class outweighing differences of race.[28] Even so, the novel's retelling of the Sir Arthur Conan Doyle and George Edalji story provides an effective illustration of that core tenet of imperial cosmopolitanism developed in this book; namely, that amity expressed between similarly positioned individuals, and asserted in the face of misunderstanding, can work to some degree, one-on-one, to counteract the negative effects of racial prejudice in society at large.

As a terrifying, if not terroristic eruption of seeming difference in the English countryside, the Edalji case, regardless of the perspective from which it is viewed, marks an interesting tipping point in perceptions of Britons in respect of India, and of India-in-Britain. Fittingly, for those who would wish to read significance into watershed periods, it was also, as it turned out, a development that fell in the very first years of the twentieth century, not long after Queen Victoria's death and the formal close of the era designated by her name. Up to this point, Indians in Britain had 'passed' as at once hyper-visible yet to some extent invisible foreigners, exotic yet relatively unthreatening. However, the charges and counter-charges, accusations, and slurs that emerged from the Great Wyrley case, as Barnes perceives, anticipated the ways in which Indians would, before too long, come to be viewed as dangerous and dissident presences, and ostracized as irredeemably foreign and irretrievably other. Despite Conan Doyle's advocacy, this happened not just in Britain but in Europe more widely—even, as the Coda shows, on the Western Front.

II INDIA HOUSED AND UNHOUSED

Edgar Wallace's thriller *The Four Just Men* and Joseph Conrad's dark satirical comedy *The Secret Agent* chart the sharpening political tensions and increasing fear of the stranger that in the opening years of the new century accompanied the rising presence of foreigners in London.[29] Symptomatically, however, neither work gives the least attention to places east of Suez as sources of the new urban threat. Rather, it is continental Europe—especially its eastern fringes, not least Russia—that forms the hotbed from which dangerous new ideas and ideologues are perceived to arise—dangers which then encroach upon and exploit the freedoms of liberal England, and the complacent working of its 'social mechanism'.[30] In both novels, complicated though largely ineffectual games of surveillance and manoeuvre play out between the London police, the British secret service, and foreign agitators at work in London. However, it is a London that is almost exclusively white—as even a cursory comparison with Wilkie Collins's *The Moonstone* would show.[31] Even so, the two novels do attend to that growing polarization of the city's cosmopolitan underworld in which politicized Indian students and activists were soon to become more involved. Both works are keenly aware of the potential for disruption of the 'queer foreign fish that can be seen of an evening... flitting around the dark corners', as Conrad's Assistant Commissioner observes.[32] The works' various boundaries, divides, and hidden niches outline by implication those subversive subterranean spaces where Indians, too, would begin to foment dissent, even though most published works, in this case the novel, might not yet have been able to register them.

The Four Just Men directly addresses the question of the good that inheres in giving hospitality to aliens (the contemporary resonances hardly need spelling out). Taking a double-thriller form, comprising versions of the locked-room mystery in both part I, 'The Secretary of State for Foreign Affairs', and part II, 'The Council of Justice', the novel's relentless build-up of suspense encourages a subtle identification with the elite terrorists as well as their victims, and in this differs markedly from Conrad's deeply pessimistic view of anarchist politics. As such, Wallace's novel can be seen to work as a symbolic methodology, in Cara Murray's terms, through which London's intermixing of the alien and the familiar is critically investigated. Motivated by an ideal of pure justice, the eponymous group of international vigilantes who mastermind the novel's action seek to deal summarily with those they deem over-powerful wrong-doers, such as government officials and international capitalists, against whom ordinary citizens are no match (*FJM*, p. 5). Very differently from Conrad's dissolute anarchists or embittered nihilists, the just men are sophisticated cosmopolitan intellectuals as well as self-appointed crusaders: Manfred is an artist, Gonsalez an urban anthropologist, Poiccart a chemist. Only Thery, their new fourth, is represented as an unreflective thug; in part II he is replaced by a utopian aristocrat.

In part I, which constituted Wallace's original pot-boiler, the Just Men's plan is to prevent the British Foreign Secretary from pushing an 'Aliens Political Offences Bill' through Parliament and so shut down the safe haven that Britain, with its rule of law, has become for freedom fighters and political agitators: those 'who are patriots and who are destined to be the saviours of their countries'—words which Madan Lal Dhingra might well have applied to himself (*FJM*, pp. 17–18, 163–4). The Bill aims to restrict their right to asylum or political sanctuary and deliver them back into the hands of their oppressive home governments. With *The Four Just Men*, Wallace therefore entered an ongoing debate concerning the threat of subversion from foreign elements brought in by immigration, and the robustness of the law in dealing with political dissidence—a debate that the build-up to the *actual* Aliens Bill restricting immigration from Russian and East European Jews, of January 1906, had ignited.[33] By implication, he also interrogated the political weakness of terrorism, in so far as terrorists are 'self-appointed', as was Dhingra, and lack the mandate of mass support (though the Just Men, due to their charisma, excellent command of communications, and general effectiveness, do claim this).[34]

Part II is an espionage narrative, which Wallace added in 1908, interestingly in the wake of *The Secret Agent*'s appearance. In this second section, the Just Men turn their attention to the complacency, parochialism, and internal conflict bedevilling Britain's anarchists and so seek to fight 'terror with terror', as well as brio (*FJM*, p. 170). They demonstrate through their own daring and discipline (for example, springing one of their number from gaol), how 'the unwritten text of Anarchism' might best be followed: the text, that is, as in the epigraph, dictating 'the right of the oppressed to overthrow the oppressor; the divinity of violence; the sacredness of sacrifice and martyrdom in the cause of enlightenment' (*FJM*, pp. 30, 115). Interestingly, in both parts, but especially the first, the Just Men, in order to mount their terroristic resistance, exploit precisely those heterogeneous and diverse features of London life they are fighting to preserve. They also realert the public to an anxiety—'the hidden terror in the metropolis itself'—of which it would have been intermittently aware since the 'Fenian outrages' of the mid-1880s: namely, that the proximities involved in city life entailed rubbing along unconsciously with terrorists (*FJM*, p. 21). Once again, however, the fear of foreign agitators and their methods expressed in the novel does not deploy a language of race targeting darker-skinned people.

Like *The Four Just Men*, Conrad's *The Secret Agent* is preoccupied with the perceived need on the part of the European powers forcibly to dissuade the British establishment from giving undesirable continentals political asylum. The novel is also intensely aware of the 'close-woven stuff of relations between the conspirator and the police' that makes up everyday life in London's 'inhospitable accumulation of bricks, slabs and stones' (*SA*, pp. 42, 63). The twist the plot offers, however, is that it is not London's underground anarchists but rather a foreign Embassy that provokes the terrorist 'outrage' intended to encourage more stringent immigration policies. The indolent *agent provocateur* Verloc is goaded into demonstrating his usefulness to the Embassy, not by 'setting' his ineffectual anarchist friends 'to work', but by hoodwinking his 'idiot' brother-in-law into committing the 'propaganda by deed' of bombing Greenwich Observatory (*SA*, p. 22). As with other isolated and therefore accident-prone acts of terrorism, or what the Assistant Commissioner calls 'unauthorized scoundrelism', not least perhaps Madan Lal Dhingra's, the attempt goes horribly awry (*SA*, p. 103). There is a sudden localized erruption of the violence, the 'ferocity from the age of caverns', that in the novel's view subtends but also maintains social convention, as much in the 'monstrous' city as out in the darkest reaches of the empire (*SA*, pp. 219–20). The scenes leading up to and following the explosion describe a gap in the narrative chronology that is the moment of the 'outrage' itself, the sudden 'hole in space and time' from which anarchy bursts, as Inspector Heat is well aware (*SA*, p. 63). In its chronological as well as its metaphorical structure, *The Secret Agent* offers a complex reflection on how terror is bound up in the 'relations of force and discourse' it seeks to destroy, yet through which it is also mediated, in Alex Houen's terms.[35] Flowing more or less indiscriminately through the urban 'stream of life', terror is also an impulse, as Conrad observes, that is blind as to the social or racial identity either of its propagators or of its victims.

Taking Wallace and Conrad's novels as evidence, in the early years of the new century Indians in Britain continued to occupy a charmed, or at least separate sphere when it came to metropolitan perceptions of dangerous aliens. They blended into the modern city's 'dark corners' and monotonous streets, the 'holes in space and time' that defied even the most vigilant of policemen (*SA*, pp. 108, 220). If we are able to read significance into the silences of both works, therefore, Indian visitors to the metropolis were by and large still taken as politically invisible, even if they were at the same time, at other levels, extravagantly visible; at once out-of-the-ordinary, yet unthreatening. Such perceptions harmonized with the temper of the times. In a reaction to the high moral seriousness that had distinguished the long Victorian period, a strongly contrasting new sense of fun, abandon, sexiness, and exuberance distinguished at least middle- and upper-class social life in the first decade of the new century—of which A. S. Byatt's *The Children's Book* (2009), for example, gives a keen-eyed account.[36] The presence of exotic-looking Indians on London's streets embellished and heightened this interest in newness and difference—and would again with the advent of the sage-seeming, bearded and robed Tagore in 1912. As before, the Indians' by-and-large elite or respectable social status continued at this stage, too, to mediate any incipient problems of race.

Frances Hodgson Burnett's *A Little Princess* gives an interestingly detailed texture to this now seemingly widespread acceptance of India in well-off urban Britain. In contrast with the two novels just described, Burnett's children's classic subtly but convincingly evokes Indians' metropolitan presence, but not through the medium of terror. Though the novel's representation of Indians and Indian objects as part and parcel of British life might by this stage be seen as predictable, a feature reminiscent of Wilkie Collins's 1860s descriptions, at the same time there is something unusually reassuring and familiar, as well as hyperbolic, about how India relentlessly crops up in heroine Sara Crewe's life, as if it were interpellating yet also incorporating her foreignness. Though her parentage is Anglo-French, Sara, the eponymous 'little princess', is both Indian-born and described in Indian terms. It is whispered that with her dark hair and 'queerly' coloured eyes, 'she must be at least some foreign princess—perhaps the little daughter of an Indian rajah', as if the place of her birth and upbringing had nativized her.[37] Wherever Sarah goes in the metropolis, though her routes are understandably controlled, India appears to seek her out. Indian presences materialize not only in the street, but on the rooftops, and wherever they appear they bring brightness, colour, excitement, and a sense of familiarity, epitomized in the seemingly miraculous yet ultimately comforting appearance of a 'lascar'-looking face at her sky-light.

At the start of the novel, Sara Crewe is sent home from India to attend school in London, and is dubbed 'Little Princess' on account of her rich clothes and other fine possessions (*LP*, p. 18 ff). However, she is stripped of everything on the sudden death of her father, caused by shock following the bankruptcy of his Indian diamond-mining ventures. Despite this setback, her sense of self remains resiliently grounded in her sense of her own otherness and the fantastical powers of her imagination, and this supplies her with the means to survive by telling stories, draping the drab surfaces of her London attic with eastern dreams: she '[paints] pictures . . . of labyrinthine passages in the bowels of the earth, where sparkling stones studded the walls and roofs and ceilings, and strange dark men dug them out with heavy picks' (*LP*, p. 55; also pp. 32, 53–4, 103, 128). In due course, material help comes to her in the form of the Anglo-Indian Mr Carrisford (whom Sara calls 'the Indian gentleman'), a new neighbour of the school, who is accompanied by his 'lascar' servant and go-between, Ram Dass. On the gentleman's moving day, Sara observes with a deep sense of recognition and homesickness his possessions standing out on the street, including a Buddha in a shrine. The association of fine fabrics, wrought goods, religious objects, and jewels—of India within the imperial metropolis—is a clear continuation from the 1880s and 1890s representations featured in previous chapters. Sara's intense feelings of homesickness are also reminiscent of Kipling's first responses to London as a Bombay-born arrivant (*LP*, pp. 119–21).[38] London both conjures, yet cannot fully replicate, a sense of India to the Anglo-Indian, the foreigner who is also native. Yet at the same time, Sara (and Kipling) seems to find India everywhere embedded in London, not in spite of but due to its foreignness reflecting and matching her own.

It is first Ram Dass's monkey and then Ram Dass himself who forge a bond of friendship with Sara across the rooftops. This represents an important link in the plot as it at long last communicates her invisible presence upstairs to 'the Indian gentleman'. At their first meeting, Sara straightaway feels a strong affinity with Dass, in that they are able to speak Hindustani together and share a similar sense of marvel, carrying obvious *Arabian Nights* overtones. Just as Sarah decodes the presence of Indian objects on the London street with relative ease, so, too, brought up in India, does she find Ram Dass legible, as the description of their encounter powerfully suggests:

> ... it was the picturesque white-swathed form and dark-faced, gleaming-eyed, white-turbaned head of a native Indian man-servant—'a lascar', Sara said to herself, quickly—and the sound she had heard came from a small monkey he held in his arms as if he were fond of it, and which was snuggling and chattering against his breast ... She turned to the lascar, feeling glad that she remembered still some of the Hindustani she had learned when she lived with her father. She could make the man understand. She spoke to him in a language she knew.

Though it is clear that the servant has emerged on the roof to claim his monkey, she also empathetically speculates that he first came up to 'look at the sun, because he had seen it so seldom in England' (*LP*, pp. 124–7). At once Indian and Anglo-French, Sara has traversed a wide continuum of cultural difference in her short life, and so, it is implied, is able as comfortably to receive Ram Dass's salaams as to interact with Becky, the school's 'maid of work'. As with Becky, the understanding with Ram Dass is mutual: he tells his 'Sahib', the 'child is the little friend of all things' and 'not as other children', much as if Kipling's Kim, the Friend of all the World, had been brought to London. Perceiving the state she is in—'I see her when she does not see me. I slip across the slates and look at her many nights to see that she is safe. I watch her from my window when she does not know I am near ... she is treated as a pariah'—Ram Dass revisits her room in secret, as a benign visitant or voyeur. He lays out hot food and adorns the place with expensive, unmistakeably eastern things: a 'curious wadded silk robe', 'quilted slippers', a 'rosy lamp', 'odd materials of rich colours', and 'brilliant fans', all of which he appears to have easily to hand (*LP*, pp. 152, 156). The mutual understanding, therefore, extends further than mere sympathy. Eavesdropping on Sara's tales told to her friends, Ram Dass is inspired by a common cultural store of 'oriental' reference-points. He furnishes Sara's room as in her make-believe, 'like a story from the "Arabian Nights"': 'Without the help of an agile, soft-footed Oriental like Ram Dass, however, it could not have been done' (*LP*, pp. 156, 202).

In a plot twist worthy of the same fantastical 'Arabian Nights' tales Sara likes to tell, it transpires that the Indian gentleman is her father's former business partner and fellow speculator who, his 'possessions [having] been restored to him', has been conducting a Europe-wide search for her (*LP*, p. 133). She is duly taken under his wing and her status is again transformed. However, the somewhat incredible overlaps and coincidences that resolve Sara's Cinderella tale, though they may on one level be explained as a function of the story's romantic machinery, on another level highlight the presence of a widely ramifying cultural network within Britain that is perceived to link the metropolis to the subcontinent, the 'foreign fish' at home and abroad. Operating at levels both high and low, on the rooftops and in the street, this network supplies a logic and a sequence to encounters that might otherwise seem entirely random. Indeed, in *A Little Princess*, the focus on elevated, 'overground' connections provides an interesting (if unintentional) mirroring of the secret, underground connections that were fomenting at the very same time within the heart of London.

The generous embrace of India by London in Burnett's work could in part be explained with reference to *A Little Princess*'s status as a book appealing to the power of the child's imagination to comfort and inspire. India is delightful and reassuring to Sara Crewe not only because it was her first home, but also because it is associated in her mind with the *Arabian Nights*, the source she taps to tell her stories. Yet the influence of ancient eastern legend is not on its own enough to account for this prevalence of India in the story; equally important is Burnett's palpable awareness of the history of India-in-Britain. In support, we might consider a mainstream Raj novel like F. E. Penny's *The Inevitable Law* (1907), published in the same year as *A Little Princess*, which concedes, as it does, to the spaces of cultural assimilation that Britain afforded for Indians and their British hosts. Though Penny's Anglo-Indian fiction was preoccupied in predictable ways with India's allegedly unbridgeable racial and caste divides, and drew sharply contrasting portraits of social integration in England as against that in India, she, too, allows for some degree of mixing between 'educated', relatively assimilated Indians in Britain ('witnesses of western education') and their British hosts.[39] It is an important and revealing concession in a writer habituated to the hierarchies of the Raj.

The Inevitable Law opens with a suggestive scene in which Dolores Avondean, a blind Englishwoman, the daughter of an ICS examinations tutor based in Bristol, is taken out on the river at Maidenhead by Rama Rajah, the (already married) son of an Indian estate owner who has lived with her family for ten years. Much of the rest of the novel, which is set in India, concerns the restrictiveness of caste barriers ('the inevitable law') as these apply even to returning western-educated Indians like

Rama—details of which do not concern us here. In terms of this reading, it is rather the quintessentially English bucolic scene on the Thames, in which an English girl is rowed by a charming Indian man of whom she is fond, that stands out as a high-water mark of Indian–British interaction, at least for the Anglo-Indian novel within this period. Though the blind Dolores is pardoned her racially unsuitable infatuation by her ocular impairment, and is soon put on the right social track by the ICS officer Newent, who becomes her love interest, *The Inevitable Law*, albeit in only one chapter, though a significantly placed one, concedes that the potential for Indian–British romance exists in Britain, given sufficient assimilation and education.

A telling contrast to Penny's passing tableau of Indian–British companionship is presented in Alice Perrin's slightly later *The Anglo-Indians* (1912), which follows the fortunes of an Anglo-Indian family from their days of personal and professional fulfilment in India to their shabby retirement in England, lacking both income and capital.[40] Given their sentimental connection to India, the family's move 'Home' represents as much arrival as return, as it might to the middle- or upper-class Indian travellers featured in previous chapters. Fay, the youngest daughter of the family, who is beloved both of a colonially educated Indian, Rajah Rotan, and an English colonial officer, channels the paradoxical conflict of loyalties that shapes the condition of the arrivant or 'Britain-Returned'.[41] She feels more alive and at home in 'foreign' India than her ancestral homeland, though, in the event, the return to England consolidates her love for the Englishman, Somerton. As in Penny, the attraction between Englishwoman and the highborn, highly educated Indian is briefly portrayed as titillating (and a catalyst for Somerton's feelings), even though the bond is rapidly undone and hence recuperated by his unsuitability (which his precocious sexuality highlights). Later, when Rajah Rotan visits England with his desperately homesick wife Rani, he is represented as socially remote from Fay. The Indian couple keeps to a hotel that '[specializes] in accommodation for Eastern visitors of wealth and rank', where the best society magazines such as *The Queen* (which once recounted Sorabji's social successes), are available to guests.[42]

Not unlike anglicized and self-assimilated Indian travellers, the Anglo-Indians in Perrin's novel outline those complex lineaments of diasporic displacement that often dictated a stronger connection to the adopted country than to the cultural motherland. At the same time, the Anglo-Indian novel as represented here by both Penny and Perrin (and in a specialist sense by Burnett) recognized that in Britain, despite a certain degree of social exclusion, elite Indians still moved relatively easily through the public sphere, without police hindrance. They were well received in both private and semi-private spaces: the boat on the river; the attic bedroom; the bespoke London hotel that, as Perrin is so careful to observe, is receptive to Indians. Significantly, the remarkable Indian-English novel of the same period, *The Prince of Destiny: The New Krishna* (1909), by migrant author and one-time Gresham College student Sarath Kumar Ghosh, to a large extent corroborates these perceptions, adding to the viable spaces where Indians might mix with Britons, the railway carriage, the mentor's cottage, and the Oxbridge Union.[43] The outbreak of revolutionary politics, when it occurs in Ghosh's novel, is set far away in India. Pressing this home, Ghosh's central character, Barath, while in England feels himself to be a participant in English social life, 'not an external observer'.

It is not to the novel therefore but to the on-the-ground, testimonial form of memoir that we must turn to gain a sense of the rather different migrant spaces that emerged at this time, subtending and cross-cutting the niches of relative assimilation. For it was now, as it were under cover of South Asians' flamboyant display on British city streets, and under the very noses of the police, that certain Indians abroad, often radicalized by their experiences of racial exclusion at home, and by anti-colonial and anarchist ideas in circulation in the capital, began even at the height of empire and in the imperial heartland to organize themselves into radical nationalist groups and cells, by far the most influential of which was that attached to India House in Highgate. In these relatively out-of-the-way spaces, ignited also by the mid-decade divisive situation in Bengal, the at once externally and internally defined 'boundaries of exclusion' that mark out migrant or arrivant spaces, according to Brah, were deepened and reinforced. Given government surveillance, however, these migrant activists left few traces of their activity. As 'excluded' individuals on the run, they rarely turned even to the transitory and intermittent form of notes or letters. Rather, it was left to Indian students slightly further afield, like Jawaharlal Nehru, or other interested parties and observers, such as in the special case represented by David Garnett's close, if passing acquaintance with Vinayak Savarkar, to provide some record of Indians' migrant dissidence. It was a dissidence that was at one and the same time pitched in opposition to all that Britain represented as an imperial power, and yet, being 'home'-grown, was defined in partnership with ideas of anti-colonial resistance often propagated by Britons (such as Edward Carpenter or H. M. Hyndman).

The tipping point in perceptions of Indians abroad came with the shocking 1909 murder of Sir Curzon Wyllie by the sometime associate of India House, Madan Lal Dhingra. In the view of many at the time, the five shots Dhingra fired at point blank range into Sir Curzon Wyllie, missing his main target the colonial civil servant Sir William Lee-Warner, but killing also a Parsi physician standing nearby, Dr Cawas Lalcaca, brought the mutinous energies and *thuggee* long associated with a violent and insurrectionary India, even from before the time of the 1857 Rebellion, into the heart of imperial London.[44] For radicals like Dhingra himself, however, such outbreaks represented a justified recursion of colonial violence to its source, given that 'Englishmen only understand force'. Wherever the root cause lay, it was now made very clear that Indians had joined forces with extremists from other more obviously threatening nations like Russia, and this at a time when invasion fears were rife, as Bram Stoker's *Dracula* had anticipated as early as 1897.[45] The influential *Times* journalist Valentine Chirol, for one, saw July 1909 as an eye-opener for Britain, a development that would alert the public to the nature of the 'revolutionary propaganda' being carried on not merely 'outside India' but in the imperial capital, aided and abetted by anti-British activists in India.[46] It is a similar shock effect that Mr Vladimir, the First Secretary of the foreign Embassy in *The Secret Agent*, hopes Verloc's trumped-up explosion will have.

Establishment figure though he was, Valentine Chirol was right in his implied charge that, up until this moment, neither Indian political intelligence nor the Special Branch in Britain had properly considered young Indians in Britain, and in particular the India House group, to pose as grave a threat as they now appeared to do. He was also right in suspecting, first, that the sedition that had now surfaced in the metropolis was part of the warp and weft of the colonial encounter, not separate from it, as had previously been thought, and, second, that this internalized violence would fundamentally redefine the relationship between India and Britain. Already, in 1907, the top-secret Lee-Warner committee (which included Curzon Wyllie, Lee-Warner's companion on the fateful night) had been set up to investigate the radicalization of Indian students in Britain. However, its findings—that westernized Indians with a radical tendency were growing more rather than less dissatisfied with colonial rule during their time in Britain and therefore needed to be more effectively assimilated within domestic systems of control—were deemed so incendiary that the report was not published until 1922. The committee's reliance on interviews with students meant, however, that its existence even so inevitably became known.[47] In the case of Dhingra, as well as his forming part of the radical India House community, the racist abuse he suffered while working as a stoker on a P & O liner first turned him to extremism, which his reading of reports on the consequences of imperialism in India in the British press further reinforced.[48] In an extempore speech at his trial, he spoke of the illegal occupation of his homeland by Britain and made it clear he understood himself to be waging a permanent war of national self-defence. Taken together, therefore, the counter-terroristic initiatives of 1907, followed by the actual terroristic event of July 1909, painted from the state's perspective a disturbing picture of an Indian student community in Britain that had grown isolated and untrustworthy, and therefore required state-sponsored regulation. Interestingly, the eradication or extradition of the community was not considered, and this in spite of Lee-Warner's disturbing evocation of railway stations and cheap lodging houses infiltrated by radicals, and the newspaper stories that were widespread at the time about destitute and other troublesome Indians at large in Britain (including the oculist-mendicants encountered in Chapter 3).[49] It would only be with the outbreak of war and the introduction of the new legislation to convict suspected terrorists, most notably the 1914 Defence of the Realm Act, that the relative freedom that Indians in Britain had enjoyed up to this point became formally circumscribed.

The large house at 65 Cromwell Avenue, Highgate, dubbed Bharat Bhavan or India House, had been bought in 1905 by Shyamaji Krishnavarma, in many ways a typical product of India-in-Britain, born in the year of Indian Rebellion, whom readers first encountered in his early role as Professor Monier-Williams's research student at the Oxford Indian Institute. Krishnavarma returned to India after Oxford to practice as a lawyer, and in the 1890s held a series of posts in various princely states, growing wealthy through his investments in cotton mills. His observation of imperial rule on the ground, in particular during the famines that gripped India in this period, deeply disillusioned him, and from 1897, following his return to Britain and the Inner Temple, he began to espouse Herbert Spencer's ideas of liberal evolutionism. As well as establishing India House, he inaugurated the Herbert Spencer lectureship at Oxford and travelling scholarships for Indian students. He also set up the *Indian Sociologist* as a journal of his Indian Home Rule Society and a mouthpiece of Spencer's *laissez faire* Social Darwinist teaching, thus demonstrating once again, as Alex Tickell, too, observes, the 'eclecticism of expatriate Indian nationalist thought', yet an eclecticism predicated on an understanding of the active interpenetration of Britain by India.[50] Injustice in the empire, Krishnavarma believed, restricted justice at home; therefore boycott in India, to protest at the 1905 partition of Bengal, demanded the propagation of a politics of non-cooperation in Britain. Under intense police surveillance, Krishavarma left England for Paris in June 1907, handing the directorship of India House over to the charismatic Vinayak or Veer Savarkar, a Hindu nationalist ideologue, law student, and the holder of a Krishnavarma scholarship. The changeover took place against a background of increasing radicalism in the Indian National Congress at home and abroad, and within the expatriate Indian student body in Britain.

Though Krishnavarma first established India House merely as an alternative to the government-sponsored residences for Indian students that existed in the NW1 area of London around University College, the house turned rapidly into a hot-housing seminar for radical nationalist thought. Modelled on Oxford's Ruskin College for adult education, and opened on 1 July 1905 by H. M. Hyndman, the leader of the Social Democratic Federation, India House sought to replicate the cosmopolitan situation of Krishnavarma's own university education, while at the same time offering an institutional structure to act as a counterpoint to the liberal-colonial network that to date had shaped the involvements of the migrant student elite. Across its five years of existence, India House would provide a roof for a significant group of both extremist and more moderate figures, including some leading theorists of active resistance as a decolonizing strategy: the later House leader Savarkar; Virendranath Chattopadhyaya, Sarojini Naidu's radical younger brother; and the revolutionary nationalist Lala har Dyal, the founder of the expatriate Ghadr party in San Franscisco. Both Lenin and Gandhi would be visitors. In the House's final year of existence, Asaf Ali, studying for the Bar at Lincoln's Inn (1909–12), was also a frequent visitor, later writing that the atmosphere 'surcharged with politics, got on my nerves'.[51]

Veer Savarkar was, like Krishnavarma, an adherent of a theory of aggressive Hindu nationalism, based on a radical reading of the *Bhagavadgita* as a text that sanctioned anti-colonial violence as a mode of self-making. Similar to Gandhi's self-transformation through his reading of the *Gita* in London, therefore, the expatriate Savarkar became a more self-conscious Hindu through his encounter in Britain with this translated and transplanted Indian text. His idea of an essential and united India also matched European nationalist templates in the characteristic derivative ways described by Partha Chatterjee.[52] Again, like Krishnavarma, Savarkar was also keenly aware of the advantages of organizing his campaign for the freedom of India as a cross-border, transnational project, especially given that the legal status of political dissidents such as himself was markedly different in Britain than under the repressive colonial situation in India (Vladimir's view in *The Secret Agent* again).[53] To this end of national freedom, Savarkar in London formed links with Irish and Egyptian nationalists, wrote a revisionist history of 1857, entitled *The Indian War of Independence* (1909), translated the Italian nationalist Mazzini's autobiography into Marathi, and, more practically, smuggled arms and bomb-making manuals back to India. He also befriended the young English student David Garnett and enlisted him for a time as a largely unwitting helpmeet in his political cause.

Subsequent to Curzon Wyllie's assassination, Savarkar's attempt to escape the British police was foiled, despite the assistance of his friends. He was then deported to India and charged with sedition. Contemporary official reports on his activity such as Chirol's, however, rarely designate revolutionaries like him by name, rather speaking of an undifferentiated extremism. Treading carefully, the young Jawaharlal Nehru in his *An Autobiography* also desists from naming individuals, though he was a student in England at the time of the Imperial Institute assassination and would have been aware through his political contacts of the existence of India House. Writing about his time at Harrow School (1906–7), Cambridge (1907–10), and then at the Inns of Court, Nehru in his autobiography does, however, show an insightful, if oblique awareness of the political potential for nationalist Indians that lay in cross-border collaboration and solidarity, especially in relation to Sinn Fein. He perceives that Indians might learn from the example of Irish nationalists and anti-colonialists, and not merely at a remove, through hearsay and newspaper reports, but through on-the-spot observation, especially considering that they are active within the precincts of the same cosmopolitan city, London. In chapter 4 of *An Autobiography*, entitled 'Harrow and Cambridge', he also traces the gradual 'agitation' he felt at school at following the news 'from India', 'meagre' as the accounts in the English papers were.[54] The Cambridge Majlis, however, did not provide him with an outlet for this growing political awareness. In contrast with the effectiveness of political movements in London, its political discussions appeared 'unreal' and ineffectual: 'Ireland and the suffrage movement interested me especially. I remember how, during a visit to Ireland in the summer of 1910, the early beginnings of Sinn Fein had attracted me.'[55]

For an individualized, more calibrated account of Veer Savarkar, and the India House community more broadly, we must turn from Nehru to an unexpected, un-Indian source: Garnett's retrospective youth memoir, *The Golden Echo*, published many years after the events it describes took place, in 1953. David Garnett had connections through his prominent literary family with a wide network of socialists, Fabians, and European revolutionary exiles (his mother was Constance Garnett, the acclaimed translator of Tolstoy and other Russian authors). In several ways, therefore, he may have been more confident about encountering the unconventional Indian students he met at the tutorial college or 'cramshop' he attended in Red Lion Square in order to prepare for the London matriculation than other English eighteen-year-olds in his position might have been. In a sustained piece of what might be called domestic adventure writing, around the mid-point of the first volume of *The Golden Echo*, he recounts his experience of falling into a fascinated if politically naive friendship with some of India House's major radicals.[56] At his revision class, Garnett writes, his first encounter is with 'a brown young man with a head of luxuriant black ringlets' called Dutt, whose appearance rouses in him a hodge-podge of exotic associations from his childhood and his adult reading. He wonders if Dutt is 'a Madagascan', as he knew 'Robert Drury's account of his experiences as a slave in Madagascar in the early eighteenth century', and then, when he hears of his 'Bengali' background, thinks (ironically perhaps) of 'what I had picked up from Colonel Meadows Taylor's *The Confessions of a Thug*', as well as of a childhood rhyme connecting 'Bengal tigers in the zoo' to 'Little Black Sambo'. At the India House meeting to which Dutt then takes him, where he meets the 'magnetic' Savarkar for the first time, and at tea at Dutt's 140 Sinclair Road lodgings thereafter, the combined orientalist and erotic sensory impressions are for him seemingly inescapable: the 'hot air'; the 'cheap', 'sweet', 'sweaty', and spicy smells; the Indian music that reminds him of 'pomegranates... jewelled seed, pale nipples of garnets breaking through the brown rind', and, as if in an illustrated article on India in the *Strand Magazine*, 'king cobras, their coils rising above the cross-legged circle of musicians'.

Importantly, however, this stock imagery is in almost every case counterbalanced by assertions of youthful fellow feeling. Garnett's seemingly natural openness to strangers in almost every case overrides the stereotyping language, which itself is used in part for effect, to quicken the reader's surprise at the alien and out-of-the ordinary, yet ultimately legible, presences that London incorporates. So, after the visit to Dutt's lodgings, Garnett and Dutt enjoy a lunch of 'poached eggs on toast' at the A. B. C. in Southampton Row. And at the India House meeting, Garnett reports, there are jokes at Krishnavarma's expense, implicitly among the younger activists (about his seriousness). Even after the Curzon Wyllie assassination, when Savarkar and Dutt come to live over a small Indian restaurant in Red Lion Passage, close to where Dutt and Garnett first met, Garnett notes that he often eats lunch at the restaurant and so continues to see a good deal of Savarkar.

Garnett gave up the London Tutorial College soon after his first meetings with the India House residents, in order to attend drama school, yet he continued to meet with his new friends and, significantly, invited three of them to his family house at Caerne for a weekend stay when his parents were away. To some extent he remained aware of a 'gulf between me and these brown men'. The Indian classics they recommended he read, including *Sakuntala*, the *Bhagavad-gita*, the *Mahabharata*, and the *Ramayana*, he found to be miserable, unimaginative, and 'nag-ridden by religion'. Overall, however, his contact with 'these Hindus' was as much a fascinating as a disconcerting experience, as is corroborated in Garnett's willingness to assist with Savarkar's attempt to escape from Brixton prison, following his arrest on suspicion of involvement in the Curzon Wyllie shooting, also described in *The Golden Echo*.[57] True, Garnett cannot have been oblivious of the tenor of Savarkar's extremist politics, and was aware, too, of the operation of anti-colonial networks in London, as is reflected in his recourse to Sinn Fein support for the gaol-break, which in Paris triggers a warning message from Yeats's nationalist muse Maud Gonne. Nonetheless, for Garnett the value that lay in the contact with Savarkar's 'fight' for a period of time weighed against the danger that the radical link represented. Race and politics did not at first break the bond of youthful friendship. Indeed, Garnett travelled as far as Paris to make sure of an (eventually insecure) escape route for Savarkar, and wrote a short exculpatory letter about him for the *Daily News*. Even after Dhingra's act of violence aroused in Britain more circumspect, suspicious perceptions of Indians, Garnett was prepared to seek publication for Dhingra's manifesto (though in vain), and to wonder in print whether the 'Byronic' nationalist had wished for events to go quite as far as they did.

Garnett's remarkable ethnographic account in *The Golden Echo* of the deepening radicalism of Indian students in London is not much longer than a standard essay in length. However, it provides a surprisingly fine barometer of the flickering changes in British attitudes to Indians that the long Edwardian decade brought about, as comfortable impressions of friends at the gate transmogrified into frightening images of strangers within. Throughout, domestic points of contact—the family home, the tea-shop—are stitched together with unfamiliar, and indeed alien referents in a way that disturbs the signification of both the native and the strange within Britain. Yet perhaps the most outstanding feature of the memoir, above even this, is the relative unawareness of its youthful author and protagonist as to the political radicalism into which he inadvertently stumbles. Indeed, it is indicative of the relatively advanced incorporation of India in British social and cultural life not only that his account is as hybridizing as it is (in a postcolonial sense), but also that the protagonist is so unfazed about the extremism into which he briefly lands.

III INDIAN BLOOMSBURY

As the topography of Garnett's inner London meetings with Indians demonstrates, the mix of India-and-Britain was especially interwoven in central London, including the area of Bloomsbury that gave the India-involved

'Bloomsbury group' its name. It was this cosmopolitan context that both facilitated and moulded the Indian–British exchanges that subtly yet indelibly marked Bloomsbury arts and letters, not least the important 1912 meeting of Bengali poet Rabindranath Tagore with his promoters in the west, which provides the focus of the final section. Tagore's reception would prove symptomatic of how India was perceived in London before the First World War; therefore the outline of 'Indian Bloomsbury' that follows not only sets the scene for the meeting, but also provides an index of Indian–British urban interaction at this time—of both its extent, and its general hues and patterns.

As we have seen, the mesh of India with London was always most concentrated in its inner city spaces, in the East End in particular, but also in west central areas like Bloomsbury and South Kensington, as the location of David Garnett's London crammer suggests. By the turn of the century, the streets around University College and the British Museum, including Tottenham Court Road, featured numerous curry houses and Indian boarding houses. Bayswater was referred to as 'India minor', as Rozina Visram records.[58] On his first visit to England as a student in 1879, Tagore had stayed with a host family, the Scotts, at 10 Tavistock Square.[59] Across the board, it was a time of new intellectual and cultural foment involving little magazines, poetry clubs, arts societies, and their splinter groups, such as Hulme's Secessionist group.[60] In the wider London area, including Hampstead, many of the organizations that had brought Indians and Britons together since the 1880s continued to meet, at once forging new links and maintaining already existing acquaintance. Organizations such as the Theosophical Society, the London Vegetarian Society, the Oriental Circle of the Lyceum Club and the National Indian Association remained conduits for Indian traffic into and around the metropolis. In 1911, Annie Besant brought Krishnamurti, the young man theosophists believed to be the new 'World Teacher', together with his brother Nitya, over from the theosophical headquarters in Adjar, India, to meet London members and to be introduced to the Society's global networks outside India.[61] New India-related societies sprang up with the aim of promoting specific Indian arts and, once again, bolster 'east–west' understanding or, in the more politically polarized landscape, of providing an alternative to those groups whose established status was seen as too close to the authorities. These new groupings included the India Society, as will be seen; the Indian Art and Dramatic Society, founded by the activist Kedar Nath Das Gupta in 1912; and the London Indian Association Jinnah founded in 1913 while visiting London on Congress business. Central London also continued to be the meeting- and party-ground for the 'upper ends' of Indian and British high society, not excluding members of the British aristocracy and the court of the extravagant Edward VII.

Personal narratives of the time give depth and detail to this picture of lively, if largely elite, intercultural connectivity. The young Muslim student Atiya Fyzee, in her Urdu travel diary *Zamana-i-tahsil* (*A Time of Education*, 1921), records her time in teacher training at Maria Grey College in London in 1906–7. She describes racially mixed 'At Homes' and lectures at the Imperial Institute in Kensington, as well as meetings with dozens of prominent Britons and Muslim intellectuals, in a way reminiscent of her mentor Cornelia Sorabji's *India Calling*, as Siobhan Lambert-Hurley writes.[62] Fyzee's writing testifies to the presence of a thriving Muslim community in London, which by the start of the Edwardian period numbered in the higher thousands. She also met many interesting young Indian women on her journeys through and around London, including the prominent, if retiring suffragette Sophia Duleep Singh, the daughter of the Maharaja, and Janaka Bonnerjee, W. C. Bonnerjee's daughter. As Fyzee piquantly wrote, 'Whichever educational institution I go to, I always find some or other Indian girl.'

Nehru's *An Autobiography* bears witness to the fact that Indian students in Cambridge and Oxford continued to maintain close ties with social, political, and cultural developments relating to India in London. When Sarojini Naidu lived in London in the years 1912–14, convalescing from illness as well as engaging in political work for India, she met frequently with Indian student nationalists, as well as with many of the English or British literary friends of her youth. In his memoirs, Asaf Ali records organizing a dinner in her honour, to which Robert Bridges, Alice Meynell, Henry Newbolt, Walter de la Mare, and Edmund Gosse were invited, and which Yeats chaired.[63] In the years immediately before the First World War, London theatres such as the Royal Court staged Indian dramas, tableaux vivants, and spectacles, including the 1911 *Birth of the War-God*, based on Kalidasa, at the Royal Court, and *Buddha*, derived from Edwin Arnold's work. Several of these productions were led by Das Gupta of the Indian Art and Dramatic Society.[64] Like the political work of Sophia Duleep Singh, or Naidu's well-attended readings, dramatic spectacles such as these gave further prominence to Indian voices and letters within the capital's public sphere. Another maverick mid-Edwardian figure was the Anglo-Indian or Eurasian performer Olive Christian Malvery, who established herself on the London scene under several guises, in 'Indian' costume for her recitals of 'picture poems' based on Indian legends, and under her married name, Mrs Archibald Mackirdy, when reporting as a journalist for *Pearson's Magazine* on the plight of London's working women.[65]

The Indian presence in central London almost inevitably impinged on the cultural formation called Bloomsbury, as was most vividly exemplified after the First World War in the contact that the up-and-coming novelist Mulk Raj Anand was able to forge with authors like E. M. Forster and Virginia Woolf, and the profile the Woolfs' Hogarth Press gave to Indian writing in the 1940s (though this history must be held over for another book).[66] At the same time, however, the Bloomsbury circle to an interesting degree also advanced and heightened these exchanges with India. A mere sampling of the biographies of some of the key Bloomsbury figures reflects close family involvements with the Raj, while at the level of aesthetic and cultural engagement, the formal and conceptual experiments that interested members of Bloomsbury, not least Virginia Woolf, acknowledged and responded to the interpenetration of the capital by multiple cultural influences flowing in from the empire, here in particular India.

Named for a Viceroy, the biographer Lytton Strachey came from a leading Anglo-Indian family and wrote in vindication of Warren Hastings's 'love of India'.[67] E. M. Forster's 1906 relationship with his tutee Syed Ross Masood (grandson of the Indian educationalist Syed Ahmed Khan), made him, he later wrote, 'half an oriental' even before he himself had had a chance to travel to India. Though he may not have been part of Bloomsbury's inner circle, his feelings of affiliation to India related to those of his Bloomsbury peers.[68] In the case of Virginia Woolf, her mother Julia Stephen was born in Calcutta and her paternal uncle James Fitzjames Stephen was the legal member of the Colonial Council in India. Anglo-Indian society was 'embedded in the fabric' of Woolf's maternal ancestry, as her biographer Hermione Lee writes, 'just as the history of colonial government [in India] ran as the main thread though the Stephen family tree'.[69] It seems likely, therefore, that Virginia found a certain genealogical comfort in her marriage in 1912 to the imperial civil servant, Leonard Woolf, recently returned from Ceylon, and she herself wrote always with a strong awareness of the stamp of the Indian Empire on London, as is most clear, perhaps, in *Mrs Dalloway* (1925). Though it is impossible to determine whether Bloomsbury's relative openness to cultural influences from without was directly affected by personal exposure, or whether an already existing ethical openness was enhanced by Indian contact, it certainly is the case that in the long Edwardian decade cultural and artistic formations like Bloomsbury provide a persuasive illustration of the mutual intercultural inhabitation that takes place in city spaces receptive to migrants, that is, in 'diaspora space'.

The core Bloomsbury group grew out of a circle of student friends at Cambridge, in particular Trinity College, who consolidated their friendships through the secret Apostles Society: they included Clive Bell, Lytton Strachey, Thoby Stephen, and the slightly younger Leonard Woolf. The Apostles also counted among their number E. M. Forster and the art critic Roger Fry, and would only a few years later induct the mathematician G. H. Hardy, who became in 1913 a host and mentor to the Indian mathematical genius Srinivas Ramanujan. The philosophical openness of many of these men to structures of value outside the utilitarian norm hinged on the work they took as their ethical handbook, their tutor G. E. Moore's *Principia Ethica* (1903). For Moore, 'the good' pertained not to the phenomena of the empirically verifiable world, but rather to the pleasures of discourse between friends, and the contemplation of beautiful objects.[70] It was this pre-eminent importance he ascribed to conversation, hospitality, and friendship that ignited many of the cross-cultural, outward-looking interests that distinguished Bloomsbury, despite its cliquey make-up—interests that went into the making of what Woolf took to be 'the common mind' that interconnected all readers regardless of nationality and '[bound] the whole world together'.[71] The premium on an openness to others intercalated also with Bloomsbury's predilection for unconventional, 'inverted', often homosexual or homoerotic partnerships—those forms of relationship which, in previous decades, had often stimulated and heightened anti-colonial critique, as we saw in the case of Edward Carpenter. 'Tolerate the spasmodic, the obscure, the fragmentary, the failure', Woolf enjoined modern writers in the conclusion to her previously cited essay 'Character in Fiction'.[72] The injunction can be read to apply not only aesthetically to her experiments in the novel, but, more broadly, to the revivifying forms of interrelationship and contiguity she fostered within her own creative practice, as well as in her wider social circle.[73]

The regenerative energies of cultural influences from without were recognized as part of two major developments involving Bloomsbury and its satellites in 1910, the year Woolf marked as a watershed. The first was the formation of the Indian Society at the beginning of that year, which was followed, towards its end, by the so-called First Post-Impressionist Exhibition, formally entitled *Manet and the Post-Impressionists*, which gave prominence to African motifs and forms. On several levels, both organizational and interpersonal, the establishment of the India Society in February 1910 evoked within London a new awareness of Indian art and artistic networks, and so prepared the stage for the reception only two years later of Rabindranath Tagore by Rothenstein, W. B. Yeats, Ezra Pound, and their associates. From henceforth, as Richard Davis and Sarah V. Turner recognize, Indian 'idols' would be reappraised as works of art, and Indian ethnography renamed 'fine art'.[74]

The catalyst for the India Society's formation arose from an incident at the 13 January 1910 meeting of the Royal Society of Arts in London. E. B. Havell, the influential former principal of the Calcutta School of Art and a friend of the Tagores, gave a paper on British imperial arts education, to which Sir George Birdwood, then exhibitions organizer for the India Office, slightingly responded that Indian religious objects could not be regarded as fine art, regardless of the religious emotions they might inspire. A. K. Coomaraswamy, the influential Ceylonese-British art critic, at once hit back with an attack on the poor conditions that existed in Britain for the exhibition and appreciation of Indian art—art which, he further asserted, showed no division between so-called fine and decorative concerns (thereby discounting Birdwood's critique as an ignorant misreading or a category mistake).[75] A 'disgusted' William Rothenstein 'then and there' followed up, as he wrote, by proposing the creation of a new society to widen public understanding of Indian painting, sculpture, and music. Only a month later, in February 1910, the new India Society was formed.

The list of the founder members of the India Society gives a fascinating snapshot of elite India-and-Britain *c.*1910. Abanindranath Tagore, Rabindranath's nephew, the then President of the Indian Society of Oriental Art, Calcutta; the eminent industrial magnate and philanthropist Sir Ratan Tata; the sculptors Eric Gill and Jacob Epstein and the novelist H. G. Wells; the powerful Gaekwar of Baroda; the Arts and Crafts designer Walter Crane; Jawaharlal Nehru; the theosophist Annie Besant; and the two originators Coomaraswamy and Rothenstein: prominent Indian arrivants stand cheek-by-jowl with leading British Indianists and friends of India.[76] Though the Society was designed to be non-political, it nonetheless opened within London a significant arena for intercultural Indian–British contact, where new, boundary-shifting discussions about Indian visual representation might be held, on more equal terms than had existed before. Through its publications to members, the Society also provided new access to Indian art works (including, in the case of Tagore, poetry), and, in so doing, helped to encourage actual journeys of artistic exploration to India. As Sarah Turner observes, the Society's extensive reproduction and sharing of images and objects thus became a 'crucible' of interconnection between the Indophile and Indian scholars and friends whom the metropolis had brought into conjunction.[77]

Soon after the India Society's formation, one of its chief supporters, Lady Christiana Herringham, set out for India on what was for her a second trip to copy the 'great wall paintings' or Buddhist frescoes in the Ajanta rock temples, and successfully 'pressed' William Rothenstein into accompanying her. Prompted by Havell and Coomaraswamy, who was also in India at the time, Rothenstein went on from Ajanta to draw at 'wonderful' Chitor, the 'dream city' Udaipur, 'beautiful' Delhi, and 'enchanting' and revelatory Benares, everywhere exploring the 'cosmic energy' and mobility of temple art. 'Richer' for his contact with what he took to be 'a classical land' whose beauty was at once 'antique' yet lived (and uncorrupted by commercialism), Rothenstein finally visited Calcutta, as the guest of Abanindranath, and to meet Tagore's other artist nephew Gaganendranath. It was in this way that he first crossed paths with the poet Rabindranath Tagore and made his now famous set of portrait drawings of him, straightaway intuiting something of the future significance to his life of the poet's personality: 'I discerned an inner charm as well as great physical beauty, which I tried to set down with my pencil.'[78]

In November 1910, nine months after the formation of the India Society, Roger Fry forged another new channel for creative energy to flow into London from abroad when he organized at the Grafton Gallery the two-month First Post-Impressionist Exhibition (followed in 1912 by the Second Post-Impressionist Exhibition, in which he tried to amplify the First's 'awful excitement'). In his 1910 manifesto for the first exhibition, Fry claimed that the work which was featured, by radical French colourists like Matisse and Picasso, sought not to imitate life but to create 'significant form'—form which found 'an equivalent for life' yet also embodied raw vitality.[79] Importantly, his preparation for the job of curator had included reviewing Helen Tongue's study of 'Bushmen' paintings.[80] As Woolf observes in her biography of Fry, at the time he had also grown excited about Manchester manufactures destined for Africa, in particular their bold, colourful prints 'to suit the taste of negresses', and big sun-hats 'to delight [their] untutored taste', which were displayed at the Grafton Gallery as part of the exhibition.[81] These hues and patterns coincided, in his view, with the vibrant decoration and extravagant coloration that also distinguished the art on the walls. Widely perceived as an '[outrage]', threatening to the sexual, national, and racial status quo, the First Post-Impressionist Exhibition and its sequel represented that chiasmic break with Victorian realism to which Woolf referred in her 'Character in Fiction' essay. She correctly identified that the pulse of transformative energy that was perceived to emanate from this art had as its source the 'primitive' African motifs and fetish objects that Picasso and his cohort had admired—objects first encountered in museum and photographic collections in Paris. Therefore, differently from his sympathizer Rothenstein (who by November was travelling in India), Fry at this point leaned to African over Indian cultural artefacts as touchstones for the aesthetic revival he sought. Indian antiquity he may have perceived as too smoothly continuous with European civilizational history to constitute a significant enough break in western representation.

Yet if in the domain of the visual arts, art criticism, and architecture, Africa at this point was perceived by some as more 'primitive' and hence more productive of new meanings, India was not overlooked as a source of new vitalism (as Rothenstein's descriptive terms above indeed suggest). Indian images and ideas were certainly in circulation alongside other influences from abroad, not least within Bloomsbury. In such areas as body figuration and architectural design, as Rupert Arrowsmith observes, artists like Jacob Epstein and Eric Gill in these years tapped the Indian points of cultural reference which lay to hand in museum collections, in innovative if sometimes predictable ways.[82] More so than in the 1890s, Indian cultural forms like dance and music were gradually loosened from the all-embracing categories of the exotic and the esoteric, as the art criticism of Ananda Coomaraswamy dynamically demonstrates. At the same time, however, the more knowledgeable and sophisticated narratives through which Indian art could now be understood did not stand entirely free of the homogenizing interpretations of the past. As will be apparent also in the reception of Tagore, Indian arts and letters continued to be seen in contradistinction to Europe, as more mystical and idealist than anything the west had to offer.

The geologist turned art historian Ananda Kentish Coomaraswamy was Britain's foremost expert on Indian culture in the pre-1914 period and a leading spokesperson for what in his respect can very justly be termed India-in-Britain. His influential readings in books including *Medieval Sinhalese Art* (1908) and *Indian Drawings* (1912) brought Indian aesthetic energies and forms to the attention of English artists such as Eric Gill while at the same time, much like Gill, he drew on the inspiration of the English Arts and Crafts Movement.[83] A collaborator of Herringham and Rothenstein's, and a correspondent of Havell's, Coomaraswamy contributed in substantial ways to the busy cultural networks connecting India with Britain at this time. His work on the continuities between the useful and abstract arts in India was published in such leading journals as the *Nineteenth Century and After* and the *New Age*, and found a responsive audience among Indian and British critics and artists alike. He shared his organicist commitments with the Arts and Crafts practitioner C. R. Ashbee, as with the Omega Workshop started by Fry, Vanessa Bell, and others. Ceylon-born and UCL-educated, the son of a Tamil aristocrat and an English mother, Coomaraswamy self-consciously carried in his own person the contact zone between India and England, and his scholarship furnished perhaps the most important conduit into England of new perceptions of Indian art. As he himself wrote, in art, 'Europe and

Asia are united'.[84] He particularly encouraged an approach to Indian art that saw universal humanity as encapsulated in local folk traditions, and the periphery as inextricably connected to wider global or metropolitan cultures, and so was an important precursor to Tagore, who was also his interlocutor and friend.

Yet if Coomaraswamy cherished an idealized image of a 'true' India unadulterated by contact with Europe, at the same time he conceded in interesting ways that there were perspectives discernible within seemingly alienated and fragmented modern art that resonated with eastern art forms. As in his discussion of the 'idea-world' of eighth-century Indian art in *The Dance of Shiva*, he read characteristic modernist techniques into Indian antiquity and also projected past traditions into present-day forms. The dancing figure of Shiva with his raised arms as depicted in Elura stone sculpture, he suggested, could be seen as an anticipation of the 'synthetic and symphonic art representing a continuity of thought, or action' of the present day.[85] Yet he was also a strenuous advocate for the conservation of traditional crafts like temple decoration and weaving, which he saw as essential to resisting the encroachment in South Asia of mass-produced commercial design, an approach that was once again inspired by William Morris's ideas concerning the organic integration of the arts into the social fabric. Coomaraswamy's uncompromising critique of British imperialism was motivated by these same principles, and in this his thinking bears comparison with that of Gandhi, Edward Carpenter, or indeed Vinayak Savarkar. As these details variously suggest, Coomaraswamy's work provides a vivid illustration of how Indian ideas, broadly conceived, helped to shape British cosmopolitan society and networks of affiliation in the period, not least that culture designated by the term 'Bloomsbury'. It also counteracts the impression given in colonial literature, even including E. M. Forster's *A Passage to India*, that the influence was mainly projected in the other direction, from Britain on to India.

IV ON OR ABOUT 1912

The legendary advent of the Bengali poet Rabindranath Tagore in the west on 16 June 1912 (as opposed to that of the student Tagore in the 1870s), which forms the focus of this final section of the chapter, is probably the most exhaustively discussed episode in Indian–British cultural relations pre-1947, and certainly the highpoint of this narrative of Indian arrival in Britain. The 1912–13 visit to England and America had as its aim the publication in English and promotion of Tagore's collection *Gitanjali: Song Offerings*, which he famously (and controversially) produced in collaboration with W. B. Yeats and others, so pursuing, yet also extending that complicated path of Indian–British poetic affiliation and mentorship which Naidu had first begun to forge in her relations with Gosse. Perhaps the most influential, yet also the most patronized Indian traveller in the west in this long turn-of-the-century period, Tagore himself descended from a privileged lineage of peripatetic Bengali social reformers, and had acquired as part of his upbringing a cultural stance vis-à-vis Britain that was self-assured and transnational.[86] This allowed him to deal at least at first in effective ways with his western friends' misinterpretations of his poetic vision—a vision that, unlike that of many of his late nineteenth-century precursors, was rural, retiring, and quietist.[87] Rapturously received by both mainstream and avant-garde poetic circles, Tagore was from the first day of his arrival in London widely hailed as the quintessential 'troubadour' poet, to quote Yeats in his 'Introduction' to *Gitanjali*. The image captured how, in the eyes of his British admirers, it was as if a travelling medieval singer equipped with a holistic sense of speaking for 'the whole people' had emerged fully formed within the broken heart of the modern world.[88]

Rabindranath Tagore's name became for a time therefore ubiquitous in the imperial metropolis as *the* sign of India—an India that was at once 'true' and yet translated, grounded, and yet at large, medieval but modern (and hence, as previous chapters have suggested, that could be regarded as typical of the India to which Europeans were now exposed). Even some of his closest supporters in the west tended to laud him in overweening and ultimately objectifying ways, as a mystic figure or wise man from the east, in the mould of Swami Vivekananda or K. C. Sen, an image that his bearded and robed appearance obviously did much to enhance. When Tagore visited Oxford in 1913, and was garlanded by Indian students (including later Indian ambassador Shahid Suhrawaddy) at the railway station before being taken for lunch at the home of Poet Laureate Robert Bridges, the students unsurprisingly hailed him as an embodiment of eastern grace, especially in contradistinction to the 'unexotic' Bridges.[89] Rupert Brooke, on his way home from Tahiti to England in April 1914 after time spent there with his lover Tatamata, remarked in a letter to a friend in defensive self-justification how Tagore had instructed him in the merits of Indian women compared to white: the anecdote again holding Tagore up as a source of eastern wisdom.[90] And the Chinese modernist poet Xu Zhimo carried a Sanskrit inscription of a poem by Tagore on the friendship hand-scroll he brought to Cambridge on a 1922 visit (in which, by contrast, Tagore's name signified both modernity and the east).[91] Yet, alongside these two-dimensional representations, Tagore's metropolitan hosts were able—even as they stereotyped him—to acknowledge the cultural validity of his work, especially in so far as it represented a more expansive and inclusive India than countenanced by either imperialists or nationalists, and a viable spiritual alternative to the godless west.

As a keynote event in Indian–British interaction, Tagore's 1912 coming was thrown into relief by two contrasting factors: first, the almost instant interest he roused and the acclaim he received in literary London, which culminated just over a year later in his achievement of the Nobel Prize on the strength of the work he had presented to Rothenstein, Yeats, and others; and, second, the outbreak of the First World War only a year after that, which brought a very different kind of Indian incursion to the west (as this book's Coda shows). Set against the bloody horrors of war, Tagore's seemingly sentimental mystical verse soon appeared impossibly ethereal, an effect heightened by the complicated process of translation to which it was subjected. Within the decade had fallen into critical neglect. However, in the light of the several prominent studies published to mark the 2013 centenary of Tagore's Nobel Prize, in particular by William Radice and Michael Collins, this section does not propose to add to the bibliographic and cultural history of Tagore's (mis)reception.[92] Rather it sets out to observe, necessarily in overview, aspects of Tagore's 1910s involvement in 'the complex web of influence and acknowledgement' rising out of more than two decades of east–west exchange, with which all Indian-English poetry at the time had necessarily to deal, as Mary Ellis Gibson writes.[93] It will consider also how his arrival was mediated by his interaction with his chief promoters, in particular the choreographer of July 1912, William Rothenstein. Although Tagore was recognized as a modernizing poetic force in his native Bengal, his leading London-based advocates, W. B. Yeats and Ezra Pound, acted on what they themselves termed a 'wise imperialism' (that is, patronizing yet promotional) when they elevated Tagore as the exemplar of tradition against which to pit their own modernist experiments, and then proceeded to distance themselves from him for the reason that he too perfectly embodied that tradition.[94] In contrast, Tagore's collaboration with William Rothenstein, the art critic, portraitist, and anglicized Jew, operated on a more reciprocal and horizontal footing, and so provides a more sensitive measure of the genuine, if circumscribed, sympathy with which India was received in these pre-war years.

When William Rothenstein welcomed Tagore to his Hampstead home in early July 1912, probably on the 7th, as the honoured guest in a large gathering of friends and acquaintances, the occasion was marked by several photographs taken by John Trevor in Rothenstein's drawing room.[95] At subsequent meetings, Rothenstein would draw portraits of a reposeful Tagore, as he had in India, one of which features as a frontispiece to the

1912 *Gitanjali*. A valuable visual record therefore exists of a number of the meetings that took place between the two friends across that summer. On or about that same July day, according to Rothenstein, Tagore 'begged' him to accept his translations of what would become *Gitanjali* (in fact, extracts from three different Bengali collections), though Tagore later admitted to considerable hesitation in making the request, which suggests that the pressure, if such there was, may have operated more forcefully in the other direction.[96] Yeats had probably already had sight of Tagore's poems, having invited him to one of his Monday evenings, and from around this time began to work on correcting and improving the translations. He read out loud from the poems to the 7 July gathering, which included many influential or soon-to-be-influential literary and cultural figures, including Robert Bridges, John Galsworthy, Alice Meynell, Ezra Pound, Bernard Shaw, H. G. Wells, Ernest Rhys, Thomas Sturge Moore, and also C. F. Andrews, the Christian missionary who was also an intimate of Gandhi's. 'It was pleasant to see homage paid so readily to an Indian; for nothing of the kind had happened before', Rothenstein observed, though in retrospect he regretted that the 'mystical element in [Tagore's] poetry' had attracted so many western 'sentimentalists'. In the beginning, however, it was 'easy to protect him', given that in London he was able to direct and manage Tagore's affairs at first hand. As for the younger poets Rothenstein described as '[sitting] at Tagore's feet[,] Ezra Pound the most assiduously', the presence of the Indian poet seems to have galvanized them into shaping their voice as modern poets, though some listeners, including Yeats's friend Thomas Sturge Moore, found Tagore's poetry too gentle in its effects.[97]

Of the 7 July 1912 photographs, perhaps the most evocative and salient in the context of this study, is that of Rothenstein and Tagore seated side by side on a sofa (Figure 3)—an image so modern and fresh it gives the impression it might have been taken in a large English drawing room just yesterday, not over a hundred years ago. There is certainly nothing shadowy, fussy, or 'Victorian' about the interior. The sofa on which the two sitters are posed is light in colour. The floor-to-ceiling shelving behind, painted white, displays a tasteful arrangement of small sculptures and other *objets d'art*, some with a Buddha-like aspect. On the wall are large drawings of bold statuesque figures—pictures that we can surmise from their outlines to be those done by Rothenstein himself, some in India.[98] The two sitters are likewise very much in their place, though interestingly one, Tagore the visitor, looks the more comfortably settled against the back of the sofa than the other. From other photographs taken on the same occasion, we know that William Rothenstein changed places with his children, while Tagore, the honoured guest and primary subject,

Figure 3. Photograph of William Rothenstein and Rabindranath Tagore, 7 July 1912, by John Trevor

was allowed to keep to the same position and aspect. As if he had hurriedly slipped into place, the host William Rothenstein sits at a slight angle to the camera, though he faces forwards, his left arm solicitously resting on the back of the sofa, almost touching the shoulder of his guest. The pose suggests a respectful welcome and acceptance, though Rothenstein's face, in particular the wide open eyes, could be read as surprised, the picture having been taken perhaps moments after slipping into place. In contrast, the unsmiling Tagore looks almost self-assured, the famous Bengali poet surveying the promise of a career in the west from an already eminent vantage point.

At the time the photograph was taken, as we now know, Tagore was about to embark on one of the most successful and concentrated publicity campaigns in modern literary history, piloted by the man on his right, but it would be difficult to read this off from either man's aspect, so unperturbed are they and, clearly, so comfortable in one another's company. Indeed, the ways in which the different elements of the photograph come together, and inform the history that subsequently unfolded from the July meeting, cast it as emblematic not only of the elite Indian–British encounters described in this book, taken as a whole (various as they were), but also of the enduring presence of a certain spiritual India-in-Britain across the long twentieth century to come. Especially when held against the background of the quiet, intensely private portraits of Tagore that Rothenstein drew that summer, the two faces gaze out, as Leela Gandhi might put it, through a felicitous 'breach... in the fabric of imperial inhospitality'.[99] That breach would give a determining outline to the encounter between modernist endeavours in London and Calcutta that unfolded in the months ahead, and this, in turn, shaped the integrative ways in which India and Indians would be viewed in avant-garde British society in the years leading up to the war. Tagore would write in 1914 of the portraits Rothenstein drew that he took his friend's love evident from the sketches as 'a lasting memorial of our friendship'. He also repeatedly spoke of Rothenstein's friendship as a 'divine' gift, and Rothenstein in his turn referred many times to feeling blessed by his encounter with a mind 'so wonderfully in sympathy' with his own.[100]

The depth of intimacy between the two men testifies to the fact that 7 July 1912 did not represent their first meeting. It was rather a consolidation in interpersonal terms of that already established bond of sympathy with India that Rothenstein had laid down first in the foundation of the India Society, and then on his remarkable 1910–11 journey to the subcontinent, when he had found out, as 'no English artist' had before, 'how much good Eastern and Western art have in common'.[101] Visiting the Tagore family house in the Jorasanko district of Calcutta, as we began to see, Rothenstein had felt 'an immediate attraction' to the poet Tagore, and this set off what Radice calls the 'cultural chain reaction' that would connect the Bengali poet to Rothenstein's extensive networks in London and so launch him in the west.[102] An important ingredient in this chain reaction therefore was that Rothenstein had been drawn into the circle around Tagore as a brother artist and a fellow cosmopolitan interested in visiting an alternative centre of modernist activity. Moreover, it was a centre that was, despite its stylish old 'ways', self-consciously modern, networked, and 'worlded'. Though Rothenstein did not at this stage yet understand how 'remarkable' Tagore was already considered to be in his own country, he was able to observe that Rabindranath was viewed by Indians not merely as a representative of tradition, as Yeats might have wished to see him, but as himself a seeker of new forms of perception that went beyond narrowly local and nationalist concerns. Rothenstein's west–east journey, therefore, would have clarified the extent to which Tagore's travels were in some sense always in the west, where the west is understood as the networked empire, yet at the same time drew on bonds of sympathy and inspiration from outside the west. This is a crucial factor in assessing

Rothenstein's genuine and lasting openness to Tagore. Indeed, throughout, his account of his aesthetic pilgrimage in India testifies to a remarkable sensitivity to the grace and style of Indian life and art.[103]

The next important link in the 'cultural chain reaction' that brought Tagore to the attention of London was the widely acclaimed 10 July 1912 India Society dinner in the Trocadero restaurant on the Soho outskirts of Bloomsbury, attended by seventy artists, authors, and critics, that embedded the work of welcome which the first meetings had set in train. It also drew Yeats to the forefront of the campaign to promote Tagore in Britain and America, a development that for a time eclipsed Rothenstein's role. Introducing Tagore's work, Yeats spoke in terms that he would hone in his autumn 'Introduction' to *Gitanjali*. He said that he found represented in Tagore's poetry a unity of culture that he hoped to retrieve for Ireland also, and that he believed this unity to be expressed in aural traditions in particular, or what Yeats chose to regard as Tagore's minstrelsy, an art form that spoke to an entire people.[104] Different from the 'instrumentalised' relationship built on a wilfully simplified reading of Tagore's work that Michael Collins finds existed between Yeats and the Bengali poet, this emphasis on a live bardic tradition suggests that the disillusioned cultural nationalist Yeats was quite genuinely attempting to find sources of Irish revival through his depiction of a distant, non-Christian, yet mythically related culture in India.[105] Not unlike Tagore, Yeats was in the midst of mounting his own offensive against narrow-minded nationalism and utilitarianism in his homeland. Therefore, far from cynically using the Bengali poet, he believed, for a time at least, to have found in him an interlocutor on shared questions of cultural retrieval and spiritual renewal, which for Yeats was never merely a Eurocentric project, as it also was not, though in a more marked way, for Rothenstein. Far from seeing Tagore as a mere emissary of an idealized and intuitive east, Yeats in 1912–13 felt that Tagore's work brought him closer to the underlying affinities that connected all cultures. Even as far back as the 1880s, as Chapter 3 showed, Yeats had begun sifting through the symbolic systems of other cultures, not least Indian legends, to stock his personal myth-system, in a spirit of sincere involvement. Later, however, in the 1930s, he did become jaded with Tagore's work, which he felt had declined in visionary and poetic quality.[106]

The extent of Yeats's participation in the making of the English *Gitanjali* will probably never be fully known. The only source that might provide verification one way or another, the typed copy to which Yeats made his changes, has been lost. The manuscript of Tagore's own translations from the Bengali, preserved among the William Rothenstein papers at Harvard, contains only 83 poems, not the 103 of 1912, arranged in a different order from the first English edition, as *Gitanjali*'s 2011 translator and editor William Radice writes.[107] Published in November 1912 in a limited edition by the India Society, and then reprinted in March 1913 by Macmillan, the English *Gitanjali* overlaps with the Bengali *Gitanjali* by just over half. As Radice speculates, Yeats probably had more of a hand in the creation of the 1912 *Gitanjali* than to date he has been allowed, '[playing] a highly active role in the preparation of the book for the press' in ways that changed the text from 'the thematically and structurally coherent, song-based collection Tagore had brought with him to Europe'.[108] Yet there is also evidence to suggest that Tagore made adjustments to and even resisted Yeats's emendations, which he remembered as 'sparing', though, as he later conceded, memory could delude, especially when it came to matters of literary fame.[109] Certainly, the lack of clarity in respect of the creation of the English *Gitanjali* provided fertile ground in ensuing years for the making of myths as to Tagore's contribution. The ground was especially fertile in so far as pre-existing ideas about Indian art already in circulation, as we saw, represented Indian cultures as primitive, 'raw', and in need of western polish. It is perhaps unsurprising, therefore, that William Rothenstein, loyal friend to Tagore and to Indian art, expressed no doubt as to provenance of *Gitanjali*:

> I knew that it was said in India that the success of *Gitanjali* was largely owing to Yeats' re-writing of Tagore's English. That this is false can easily be proved. The original MS of *Gitanjali* in English and in Bengali is in my possession. Yeats did here and there suggest changes but the main text was printed as it came from Tagore's hands.[110]

Having travelled in India, met Tagore in his own domestic context, and witnessed the onslaught of western consumer goods brought by colonialism, Rothenstein was in a better position than any of Tagore's western friends to see that, more than being merely the *Gitanjali* poet, he was an inventive and visionary cross-cultural traveller. Though Rothenstein's views were broadly liberal and far from anti-imperial, he may also have understood something of what motivated Tagore when he undertook his journey to the west in 1912. For, though Tagore was known to describe the venture as an accident and an experiment, in time he came to view it as providential, an emotional and spiritual quest impelled by a transformational disillusionment with both imperialism and nationalism, and by a guiding belief that greater harmony between societies and nations could only come through intercultural commingling.[111] Having spent the 1890s in bucolic isolation, managing Shelidah, his family estate in eastern Bengal, Tagore had become in the politicized new century dejected at what seemed to him to be the destructive extremism that had flared up in response to the 1905 partition of Bengal. On his western pilgrimage he hoped to discover whether and how new bridges of understanding might be built between Britain and India outside the realm of nationalist politics. India, he believed, was a capacious category that in principle could comprise 'all humanity'.[112]

Tagore's keynote 1917 essay 'Nationalism', presented as a series of lectures in Japan during the First World War, crystallizes many of these core ideas. Throughout, he expresses the wish to distance himself from Europe's 'cannibalistic' civilization which 'overrunning the whole world like some prolific weed, is based upon exclusiveness'.[113] Yet at the same time he feels that western civilization contains immortal 'living seeds', which India might assimilate through forging bonds of friendship and reconciliation. The close tie of friendship, he further insists, 'is the only natural tie that can exist between nations' in order that spiritual beauty might be developed and nationalist selfishness combated. (In this regard, it is interesting that even during periods of disagreement he and Rothenstein addressed one another as 'My dear friend'.) Moreover, he continues, as empire had created a political and philosophical submissiveness in Indians, it was important that India's spirit now be strengthened through greater international openness and inclusiveness. The poetry for which in 1912 he aimed to find a western audience, would, he believed, provide one means of forging such ties. Therefore, though he sometimes spoke in letters of the translation into English of his *Gitanjali* and other poems as merely an exercise undertaken to calm his mind while travelling on 'the high seas', it is clear from other writings at the time that his journey was motivated by a clear vision of the need for rapprochement between east and west. Indeed, since at least 1908 he had been encouraged by friends, including A. K. Coomaraswamy, to find avenues outside the Bengali language for his work: it was only through the contact with other cultural worlds that translation facilitated, that the 'bridges' of art 'uniting one country with another' could be built. The key point to make here therefore is that Tagore did not come to England in 1912 as either a proselytizer for India or a supplicant before the west, in pursuit of its approbation. Rather it was as a sophisticated advocate of what he himself in 1907 called *visva-sahitya* or 'world literature', and as himself a practitioner of world letters promoting international understanding, that he made his journey and overcame the many resistances to his vision that he would encounter en route.[114]

This outline of the different threads of political, emotional, and aesthetic investment in July 1912 and subsequently will have given some impression of the still complicated process of coming together that joined Britons and Indians in the heart of 1910s London. Marked by many of the intercultural impulses to find familiarity in the strange that have been traced across this study, this process had consequences that were unprecedented for all the parties concerned. At their various meetings, as Rothenstein, Yeats, and others presented Tagore and his work first to their wider literary circle and then to the reading public, what took place was not simply an east–west encounter in which the two sides objectified each other in by now predictable ways. The cosmopolitan embedding of India in Britain by this stage was too deep for that to be the case.

Instead, as Yeats was to acknowledge in his 'Introduction' to *Gitanjali*, if in backhanded fashion, the different parties to the encounter detected in each other's work, even if intermittently, flashes of their own most heartfelt concerns. The now obtuse, now heartfelt interchange between Tagore's plangent lyrical verse, which was collected in the English, Nobel-winning *Gitanjali*, and the modernist experiments of Yeats, Pound, and others, was to have a profound effect on the work of all involved. It was an encounter that contributed to the formation of the spare, stripped-down style with which modernists like Woolf and T. S. Eliot, as well as Yeats and Pound were to become associated. In this respect, Tagore was a key contributor to the symbiotic formation of early Indian Bloomsbury—a process that after the First World War was taken forward in the work of other 'foreign' writers, here most notably Mulk Raj Anand. Though during the war years the acclaim that Tagore had received hardened in the public mind into a fixed image of an Indian seer or mystic (which the sentimental collections he produced across the 1910s did nothing to challenge), a countervailing perception remained that Tagore's verses were not out of place in the heart of the metropolis. They may have been lyrical and Romantic, but their emotion was also perceived as poignant, hard-hitting, and modern. In the poems, wrote the Irish poet James Cousins, could be felt a new revelation of spiritual beauty, one in which several writers, as well as the sympathetic Rothenstein, found aspects of themselves.[115]

The identification that sprang up between Rothenstein and Tagore in 1912 persisted despite the predictable corrosions of war, nationalist politics, geographical distance, and ongoing questions as to Yeats's contribution to the founding of Tagore's reputation. In 1917, Rothenstein importantly declared himself 'in sympathy' with Tagore's *Nationalism*, which he had sent him.[116] After the war, both still longed to be in one another's company. Even following a cooling of the friendship in the early 1920s, Rothenstein continued to write empathetically of the 'subtle admixture of gravity and sensuousness' in Tagore's writing, as well as in Indian art. In 1931, Rothenstein spoke of theirs as a 'perfect friendship': 'something in my nature responded, from the beginning, to your own, and has since always responded'. This was followed by a vehement letter from Tagore in November 1932 in which he roundly accused his western friends, Rothenstein first and foremost, of having parachuted him into the alien world of English letters, an unwished-for fate, which had distorted his true majesty. Yet Tagore also wrote more appreciatively in a different letter that Rothenstein's friendship had given him 'two births', one among his own people, another in the 'freedom of humanity'. Even through the 'disengagement' of old age, to use Mary Lago's term, the two men continued to write kindly, if more intermittently to one another, raising ongoing interests in common, in particular as to the derivativeness of modern Indian art.

The depth of feeling they shared and would continue to share, however, was already succinctly demonstrated at the very beginning of their long epistolary friendship in the exchange of a poem. Rothenstein, whose mother died in July 1912, not long after the Hampstead gathering, was deeply moved when Tagore sent him, by way of condolence, verses he had written in 1902 upon the death of his wife, which became poem LXXXVII in the English *Gitanjali*: 'My house is small, and what once is lost from there can never be regained'. 'Your "songs on death"', Rothenstein replied, felt so poignant and real that they gave him comfort.[117]

*

As can be distilled from this chapter's readings, across the early years of the twentieth century, up to the outbreak of the First World War, the Indian presence in Britain, or, in a phrase, diasporic India-in-Britain, was perceived under two predominant aspects. These might broadly be described as India emergent, a nationalist development, and esoteric or 'authentic' India, an ongoing but deepening tendency, especially in the arts. Yet, though these aspects might on one level be perceived as distinct, on another they shared certain key features, rising from aesthetic and political interests and passions held in common. In particular, as in the Edalji affair, in Anglo-Indian fiction, or in the reception of Tagore, these common features unfurl from the orientalist tendencies that Chapter 3 already discerned in 1890s letters and arts, yet which were now cast further into relief first by the build-up of nationalist sentiment in India, and then the onset of Indian political extremism on British ground.

As this suggests, self-assertion by recourse to ancient tradition and primitive vitalism to some extent distinguished the practice of both modernists and nationalists. Poets, lawyers, artists, activists, and priests, Indian and British alike, contrapuntally developed in diaspora space ideas of a transnational modernity in which both the west and the east could take part and in which colonial migrants played a key role, as self-conscious moderns *and* as themselves a foil against which modernity might be asserted. In this sense, both India House and the India Society were crucibles of a modern self-consciousness stirred by 'primitivist' findings from ethnography. And Tagore's literal translations of his own poems in Bengali into cadenced and epigraphic English blank verse participated in the creation of the modernist prose poem.[118] Tagore the 'sermonizing spiritual guru', the orientalized confection of the modernist 'men of 1914', as Amartya Sen recognizes, was at the same time an interpreter of the modern world with a commitment to the 'clear stream of reason' as a means of transcending social, cultural, and national barriers.[119] For this reason, not only Rothenstein but also his friend T. W. Rolleston, not only Leonard Woolf but also, within only a few years, Forster, would find their sensual and emotional worlds expanding through their contact with South Asian cultures, broadly speaking. And in return, South Asians felt their 'life' '[enlarging]' through their exchanges with British moderns, to cite from another letter from Tagore to Rothenstein.[120] In some areas, therefore, India might be deemed to have arrived in Britain; in other areas, however, it remained nativized and objectified, still not quite arriving, yet always about to arrive, poised invitingly on the threshold.

NOTES

1. Frances Hodgson Burnett, *A Little Princess* (London: Warne, 1905; Penguin 1970), pp. 118–19.
2. Edgar Wallace, *The Four Just Men*, intr. David Glover (1905; Oxford: Oxford University Press, 1995), pp. 30, 115.
3. Rabindranath Tagore, *Gitanjali*, intr. W. B. Yeats (London: India Society, 1912), p. 27.
4. See Avtah Brah, *Cartographies of Diaspora* (London and New York: Routledge, 1996). See also Ghassan Hage, *White Nation: Fantasies of White Supremacy in a Multicultural Society* (New York and London: Routledge, 2000); Nira Yuval-Davis, *The Politics of Belonging: Intersectional Contestations* (London: Sage, 2011).
5. Brah, *Cartographies of Diaspora*, p. 209.
6. Yuval-Davis, *The Politics of Belonging*, 2011; Hage, *White Nation*, 2000; Linda McDowell, 'Thinking Through Work: Complex Inequalities, Constructions of Difference and Trans-national Migrants', *Progress in Human Geography* 32:4 (1998): 491–507.
7. In combination with Avtah Brah, see Peter D. McDonald, 'Thinking Interculturally: Amartya Sen's Lovers Revisited', *Interventions* 13.3 (2011): 367–85. McDonald helpfully defines intercultural interaction as 'risky' and 'illimitable', 'in which each source culture, or aspects of each, could potentially transform the other, for better or worse, without the kaleidoscopic play of "different pieces" ever settling down into a final pattern and without the future survival of either culture ever being guaranteed' (pp. 380, 384).

8. See Paul Gilroy, *The Black Atlantic: Modernity and Double Consciousness* (London: Verso, 1993); James Clifford, *Routes: Travel and Translation in the Late Twentieth Century* (Cambridge, MA: Harvard University Press, 1997).
9. Virginia Woolf, 'Character in Fiction', *Selected Essays*, ed. David Bradshaw (Oxford: Oxford World's Classics, 2008), p. 38. The essay was first read as a paper to the Heretics Society in 1924.
10. Makarand Paranjape, ed., *Sarojini Naidu: Selected Poetry and Prose* (New Delhi: Rupa Press, 2010), p. 55.
11. See K. K. Aziz, *Ameer Ali: His Life and Work* (Lahore: Publishers United, 1968), which is indebted to Syed Razi Wasti, ed., *Memoirs and Other Writings of Syed Ameer Ali* (Lahore: Peoples' Publishing House, 1968). Ali regularly spent time in England across his career, from the time he studied for the Bar during 1869–73, to when he settled permanently in England in 1904. He also founded, in 1908, the non-separatist London Muslim League, and wrote for such journals and newspapers as the *Nineteenth Century and After* and *The Times*.
12. See Margaret Macmillan, *The War that Ended the Peace: How Europe Abandoned Peace for the First World War* (London: Profile Books, 2013). See also Charles Emmerson, *1913: The World Before the Great War* (London: Bodley Head, 2013); Florian Illies, *1913: The Year Before the Storm* (London: Clerkenwell, 2013).
13. On George Dangerfield's 1935 *The Strange Death of Liberal England*, see Stuart Hall, *The Hard Road to Renewal: Thatcherism and the Crisis of the Left* (London: Verso, 1988).
14. See Elleke Boehmer, 'Introduction', in *Scouting for Boys*, Robert Baden-Powell, (Oxford: Oxford University Press, 2004), p. xix; Max Nordau, *Degeneration,* 2nd edn (1893: London: William Heinemann, 1895); Eric Hobsbawn, *The Age of Empire, 1875–1914* (London: Weidenfeld and Nicholson, 1987); James Lawrence, *The Rise and Fall of the British Empire* (London: Little, Brown, 1994).
15. Alex Tickell, *Terrorism, Insurgency, and Indian-English Literature* (London and New York: Routledge, 2011), p. 2. See also Elleke Boehmer, *Empire, the National, and the Postcolonial: Resistance in Interaction* (Oxford: Oxford University Press, 2002).
16. On the Bengal resistance and its extremist repercussions, see Boehmer, *Empire, the National, and the Postcolonial*, chs. 1 and 2.
17. Arthur Symons, *Dramatis Personae* (London: Faber and Gwyer, 1923), p. 22.
18. Between 1904 and 1909, fifty-two cases involving sixty-one people of all professions were brought before the India Office, but only eight people were repatriated. As the number of Indians in Britain falling destitute was increasing, the India Office commissioned a report into 'Distressed Colonial and Indian Subjects'. The 1910 report recognized that Indian seamen were protected by the Imperial Merchant Shipping Act but that the India Office did not have any guidelines for other classes of destitute Indian. See BL: L/PJ/6/925, file 830. 'Committee on Distressed Colonial Seamen' (1909, 1910).

19. For a thoughtful study of terrorism and sedition in India, which includes substantial treatment of the Dhingra case, see Tickell, *Terrorism, Insurgency, and Indian-English Literature*. See also Rozina Visram, *Asians in Britain: 400 Years of History* (London: Pluto Press, 2002), especially pp. 56–62.
20. Homi Bhabha, *The Location of Culture* (London: Routledge, 1994), p. 9.
21. In his travelogue *From Adam's Peak to Elephanta: Sketches in Ceylon and India* (London: Swan Sonnenschein and Co., 1892), p. 51, Edward Carpenter presciently observed à propos of his friend Arunachalam and the retreat from westernization that his nationalism represented: 'My friend . . . became thoroughly Anglicised while studying in England, and like many of the Hindus who come to London or Cambridge or Oxford, did for a time quite outwesternise us in the tendency towards materialism and the belief in Science, "comforts", representative institutions, and "progress" generally. Now however he seems to be undergoing a reaction in favour of caste and the religious traditions of this own people, and I am inclined to think that other westernizing Hindus will experience the same reaction.'
22. Richard Sorabji, *Opening Doors: The Untold Story of Cornelia Sorabji* (London: IB Tauris, 2010), p. 278.
23. Roger Oldfield, *Outrage: The Edalji Five and the Shadow of Sherlock Holmes* (Cambridge: Vanguard Press, 2010), p. 101; Julian Barnes, *Arthur & George* (London: Vintage, 2005), pp. 126, 148, 154, 157, 300, 303–4, 327.
24. Sarvepalli Gopal ed., *Selected Works of Jawaharlal Nehru* (New Delhi: Orient Longman, 1972), p. 16.
25. Barnes, *Arthur & George*, pp. 339, 423; Oldfield, *Outrage*, p. 323.
26. Barnes, *Arthur & George*, pp 303–4, 377.
27. In the novel, the Parsi Edalji family are—very fittingly in the context of this study—aware of forming part of a tradition of Parsi migration to Britain. In a poignant speech, Edalji senior asks his son to remember that Naoroji was for many years a Professor of Gujerati at University College London, and was elected an MP in 1892. He also notes the fact that the Prime Minister Lord Salisbury was in 1888 rebuked by Queen Victoria herself when he said that a black man 'should not and would not be elected to Parliament' (also observed in Chapter 2 of this volume). Barnes, *Arthur & George*, pp. 58–9.
28. Barnes, *Arthur & George*, p. 298.
29. Page references to the 1995 OUP edition of *The Four Just Men* will be cited in the text, together with the abbreviation *FJM*. Glover's 'Introduction', pp. ix–xxv, provides an excellent contextual analysis of the suspicion towards strangers that motivates most of the characters.
30. Joseph Conrad, *The Secret Agent*, intro. John Lyon (Oxford: Oxford World's Classics, 2004), pp. 11, 22.
31. That said, the Assistant Commissioner's colonial background in *The Secret Agent* comes through in his reference to Alfred Russel Wallace's works on the Malay and his comparison of the office desks with the jungle. I am grateful to Charne Lavery for this reminder.
32. Conrad, *The Secret Agent*, p. 108. Page references henceforth will be cited in the text together with the abbreviation *SA*.

33. David Glover, 'Introduction', in *The Four Just Men*, p. xviii.
34. See Robert Young, 'Terror Effects', in *Terror and the Postcolonial*, ed. Elleke Boehmer and Stephen Morton (Oxford: Blackwell, 2010), pp. 307–28, in particular p. 318.
35. Alex Houen, *Terrorism and Modern Literature* (Oxford: Oxford University Press, 2002), p. 18. On 'propaganda by deed', see pp. 34–5.
36. A. S. Byatt, *The Children's Book* (London: Chatto & Windus, 2009), p. 300.
37. Hodgson Burnett, *A Little Princess*, pp. 12, 14, 19, 92, 107, 193, 194. Further page references will be cited in the text together with the abbreviation *LP*.
38. Alexander Bubb, 'Tracing the Legacy of an Experimental Connection', in *India in Britain: South Asian Networks and Connections, 1858–1950*, ed. Susheila Nasta (Basingstoke: Palgrave Macmillan, 2013), pp. 46–63.
39. F. E. Penny, *The Inevitable Law* (London: Chatto & Windus, 1907), in particular p. 31.
40. Alice Perrin, *The Anglo-Indians* (London: Methuen, 1912).
41. On Anglo-Indian feelings of unexpected alienation in their long-missed 'Home'land, see Georgina Gowans, 'Imperial Geographies of Home: Memsahibs and Miss-Sahibs in Indian and Britain, 1915–1947', *Cultural Geographies* 10.4 (2003): 424–41.
42. Perrin, *The Anglo-Indians*, p. 230.
43. Sarath Kumar Ghosh, *The Prince of Destiny: The New Krishna* (London: Rebman, 1909). I am indebted to Alex Tickell's reading of this novel, in *Terrorism, Insurgency, and Indian-English Literature*, pp. 169–83.
44. For a detailed, analytical account of India House and its main resident thinkers, see Tickell, *Terrorism, Insurgency, and Indian-English literature*, pp. 138–54.
45. See Elleke Boehmer, 'Empire and Modern Writing', in *The Cambridge History of Twentieth-Century English Literature*, ed. Laura Marcus and Peter Nichols (Cambridge: Cambridge University Press), pp. 50–60.
46. Valentine Chirol, *Indian Unrest* (London: Macmillan, 1910).
47. 'Report of the Committee Appointed by the Secretary of State for India in 1907 to Inquire into the Position of Indian Students in the United Kingdom', Appendix IV to India Office, Report of the Committee on Indian Students, 1921–22 (London, 1922). The Committee had investigated sixty-five Europeans and thirty-five Indians connected with Oxbridge, London, and Edinburgh, and reported *inter alia* that of the 700 Indian students then in Britain, nearly half enrolled in the Inns of Court were 'of second-rate ability'. See James D. Hunt, *Gandhi in London*, rev. edn (1978; New Delhi: Promilla and Co., 1993), pp. 15–16; Tickell, *Terrorism, Insurgency, and Indian-English Literature*, pp. 154–9; Visram, *Asians in Britain*, pp. 156–60.
48. These reports are likely to have commented on the drain of wealth from India to Britain, and the loss of 80 million Indian lives due to the famine and war occasioned by empire. If the former were the case, the reports may well have been written up by disciples of Naoroji and R. C. Dutt.

49. From the later decades of the nineteenth century, the India Office in London was from time to time approached by destitute Indians (including also abandoned ayahs and unsuccessful litigants), who had made their way to Britain for various different reasons, mainly to do with employment, and then could not afford to return to India. As the responsibility of the India Office and the Secretary of State for India, these destitute Indians sought the Office's financial assistance for their passage home. The press coverage and subsequent public discussion about the Indian 'student problem', as well as the interest generated by the Lee Warner report and the 1909 murder, proved fruitful for British novelists with Indian interests, not least Edmund Candler in *Siri Ram—Revolutionist* (1912) and Edward Thompson in *Farewell to India* (1931), though in both novels the revolutionary Indian characters are based in India, not Britain (as they also are in Sarath Kumar Ghosh). In his reflections on India, *The Other Side of the Medal* (London: Hogarth Press, 1925), Thompson spoke of the 'madness' generated within Indian students by their radicalization—a madness which he significantly saw as internal to Britain, '[shadowing] Indians studying in our midst today' (p. 122).
50. Tickell, *Terrorism, Insurgency, and Indian-English Literature*, p. 146.
51. See G. Ragahavan, *M. Asaf Ali's Memoirs: The Emergence of Modern India* (Delhi: Ajanta, 1994). After his time in India House, Ali moved in with a Scottish family, the Wills, in Finsbury Park. He knew Dhingra and was dismayed by the Curzon Wyllie murder. The shock-waves of the event were understandably felt across the community of Indian students in England, as is registered also in Jagmenderlal Jaini, *Fragments from an Indian Student's Notebook*, ed. M. Amy Thornett (London: Arthur H. Stockwell, 1934), covering the years 1904–09.
52. Partha Chatterjee, *Nationalist Thought and the Colonial World: A Derivative Discourse?* (London: Zed Books, 1986). See also Mrinalini Sinha, *Specters of Mother India: The Global Restructuring of an Empire* (Durham, NC: Duke University Press, 2006).
53. Kevin Grant, Philippa Levine, and Frank Trentham, *Empire and Transnationalism 1880–1950* (Basingstoke: Palgrave, 2007), pp. 1–7, reminds us: 'Empires . . . were critical sites where transnational social and cultural movements took place.'
54. Jawaharlal Nehru, *An Autobiography* (London: Bodley Head, 1936), pp. 18–25.
55. In his English chapters, Nehru is largely intent on portraying himself as a political dilettante lacking in purpose. For a period of time, he writes, especially at Cambridge, he continued to indulge himself in a hedonistic Wildean 'cyrenaicism', 'partly natural to youth, partly the influence of Oscar Wilde and Walter Pater'—not the first Indian to feel the attraction of this brand of homegrown exoticism. Even so, there is some residual perception in these pages, even at this early stage, as there is in Gandhi's autobiographical writing, of the Indian nation as a concept that might be conceived far from home and that, vitally, might be shaped in dialogue with other nationalist

thinkers and activists that the great colonial cities had also thrown into concatenation. Empire in this sense facilitated, though it could also impede, cross-national—and diasporic—solidarity. See Nehru, *An Autobiography*, pp. 18–25. It is worth setting alongside Nehru's example that of another influential figure in the making of modern India, Subhas Chandra Bose. A student in Cambridge after the war, Bose in his *An Indian Pilgrim: An Unfinished Autobiography*, ed. Sisir K Bose and Sugata Bose (Delhi: Oxford India, 1997), p. 115, observes how the news from India, and the discussion amongst the students, stimulated nationalist thought: 'Even one who has never thought of his own country cannot help doing so after coming here', and 'we have got to make a nation, and a nation can only be made by... uncompromising idealism'.

56. David Garnett, *The Golden Echo*, vol. 1 (London: Chatto & Windus, 1953), the quotations following being from pp. 137–9, 140, 143.
57. See, in particular, Garnett, *The Golden Echo*, pp. 143, 146, 149.
58. Rozina Visram, *Ayahs, Lascars and Princes: Indians in Britain, 1700–1947* (London: Pluto Press, 1986), p. 92.
59. Krisha Dutta and Andrew Robinson, *Rabindranath Tagore: The Myriad-minded Man* (London: Bloomsbury, 2000), p. 75.
60. Ron Schuchard, *The Last Minstrels: Yeats and the Revival of the Bardic Arts* (Oxford: Oxford University Press, 2008), p. 259. See Tara Ali Baig, *Sarojini Naidu* (New Delhi: Government of India Publications Division, 1974), p. 41.
61. Mary Lutyens, *Krishnamurti: The Years of Awakening* (New York, NY: Farrar, Straus, Giroux, 1975), pp. 50–2.
62. See Siobhan Lambert-Hurley and Sunil Sharma, *Atiya's Journeys: A Muslim Woman from Colonial Bombay to Edwardian Britain* (Delhi: Oxford University Press, 2010); Siobhan Lambert-Hurley, 'Atiya Fyzee in Edwardian London', in *India in Britain*, ed. Susheila Nasta (London: Palgrave, 2012), pp. 64–79, in particular pp. 70 and 71.
63. Ragahavan, *M. Asaf Ali's Memoirs*.
64. Colin Chambers, '"A Flute of Praise"–Indian Theatre in Britain in the Early Twentieth Century', *India in Britain*, ed. Nasta, pp. 149–63.
65. See Shompa Lahiri, *Indians in Britain: Anglo-Indian Encounters, Race and Identity* (London: Frank Cass, 2000), pp. 5, 9–32, 142; Judith Walkowitz, 'The Indian Woman, the Flower Girl, and the Jew: Photojournalism in Edwardian London', *Victorian Studies* 42 (Autumn 1998): 3–46.
66. See, for example, Jessica Berman, 'Comparative Colonialisms: Joyce, Anand and the Question of Engagement', in *Modernism/Modernity* 13.3 (2006): 465–86; Kristin Bluemel, *George Orwell and the Radical Eccentrics: Intermodernism in Literary London* (Basingstoke: Palgrave Macmillan, 2004), pp. 69–92; Sumita Mukherjee, 'Thomas Sturge Moore and his Indian friendships in London', *English Literature in Transition 1880–1920*, 56.1 (2013): 64–82; Susheila Nasta, 'Between Bloomsbury and Gandhi? The

Background to the Publication and Reception of Mulk Raj Anand's *Untouchable*', in *Books Without Borders: Perspectives from South Asia*, vol. 2, ed. Robert Fraser and Mary Hammond (Basingstoke: Palgrave, 2008), pp. 151–69. The reference to Indian interests at the Hogarth Press in the 1940s points in particular to the publication of R. Palme Dutt's work and Ahmed Ali's 1940 *Twilight in Delhi*, as well as Leonard Woolf's correspondence relating to these. See MS 2750 (files 2, 74, 75). Hogarth Press Archive, University of Reading Special Collections. Susheila Nasta is preparing a study entitled 'Asian Bloomsbury'.

67. S. P. Rosenbaum, *Edwardian Bloomsbury: The Early Literary History of the Bloomsbury Group*, vol. 2 (Basingstoke: Macmillan, 1994), pp. 117–39.
68. Antony Copley, *A Spiritual Bloomsbury: Hinduism and Homosexuality* (Lanham, MD, and Oxford: Lexington Books, 2006), p. 129.
69. Hermione Lee, *Virginia Woolf* (London: Chatto & Windus, 1996), pp. 87–8.
70. Lee, *Virginia Woolf*, pp. 253, 302.
71. Rosenbaum, *Edwardian Bloomsbury*, p. 143; Virginia Woolf, *A Passionate Apprentice: The Early Journals, 1897–1909*, ed. Mitchell A. Leaska (London: Hogarth, 1990), pp. 178–9.
72. Woolf, 'Character in Fiction', in *Selected Essays*, ed. David Bradshaw (Oxford: Oxford World's Classics, 2008), p. 54.
73. Amit Ray reminds us that high modernist experimentation at the time used 'primitivist and Orientalist appropriations' in order to break down representational norms and 'defamiliarise . . . European audience[s]'. See Amit Ray, *Negotiating the Modern: Orientalism and Indianness in the Anglophone World* (London and New York: Routledge, 2007), p. 107.
74. Richard Davis, *The Lives of Indian Images* (Princeton, NJ: Princeton University Press, 1999), p. 177; Partha Mitter, *Much Maligned Monsters: A History of European Reaction to Indian Art* (Oxford: Clarendon Press, 1977); Sarah V. Turner, 'Crafting Connections: The India Society and the Formation of an Imperial Artistic Network in Early Twentieth-Century Britain, in *India in Britain*, ed. Nasta, pp. 96–114.
75. William Rothenstein, *Men and Memories: Recollections of William Rothenstein, 1900–1922*, vol. 2 (London: Faber and Faber Ltd, 1932), pp. 231–2; Turner, 'Crafting Connections', pp. 104–7.
76. India Society, *Proceedings of the London India Society, 1910* (London: India Society, 1911), p. 8.
77. Turner, 'Crafting Connections', p. 104.
78. Rothenstein, *Men and Memories*, pp. 236, 237, 239, 245, 247, 249; William Rothenstein, *Examples of Indian Sculpture at the British Museum* (London: Indian Society, 1923), pp. 7–12.
79. Lee, *Virginia Woolf*, p. 324.
80. Frances Spalding, *Roger Fry: Art and Life* (Berkeley, CA: University of California Press, 1980), pp. 122–3, 157.

81. Virginia Woolf, *Roger Fry: A Biography* (London: Hogarth Press, 1940), p. 152. In fact, Woolf and her sister Vanessa attended the Post-Impressionist Ball in November 1920 swathed in this Manchester cloth.
82. As exemplified in how Epstein's 1908–9 carvings for British Medical Association building drew on the iconography of Indian temple culture. See Rupert Arrowsmith, *Modernism and the Museum: Asian, African and Pacific Art and the London Avant-Garde* (Oxford: Oxford University Press, 2011).
83. An evocative expression of Gill and Coomaraswamy's appreciation for one another's work is captured in a woodcut bearing distinct 'Asian' marks (exotic leopard-print motifs on the trees, the Japanese-like lack of background), that Gill produced as an illustration for a sheaf of three erotic poems Coomaraswamy published in 1920. See A. K. Coomaraswamy, *'New England Woods': Three Poems* (Ditchling, Sussex: St Dominic's Press, 1920). See also Rupert Richard Arrowsmith, 'Transcultural Literature and Art', *Wasafiri* 26.3 (2011): 38–49.
84. Turner, 'Crafting Connections', p. 110.
85. A. K. Coomaraswamy, *The Dance of Shiva: Fourteen Indian Essays* (Bombay: Asia Publishing House, 1948), p. 70.
86. His father, Debendranath Tagore, was a founder of the Brahmo Samaj, and friend to Max Müller, as we saw before; his grandfather Dwarkendranath, a wealthy landowner, had been an early Indian traveller to London in the 1840s and had dined with Queen Victoria.
87. As he wrote to William Rothenstein on 27 October 1912 from New York, every time he was confronted with a modern city he was reminded that his ancestors had been forest dwellers. He saw the city in recognizable modernist terms as a 'giant engine' propelling 'streams of people' in various directions, and 'the thick solitude of the crowd' as 'oppressive'. It is indicative that even from the time of his first letters from England written as a student in 1879, Tagore's impressions were not of the natural world, as they might have been in India, but of the British interior, upholstered, enclosing, static, respectable. Even so, for all that Tagore positions himself at a remove from the materialist western world, he reads its information, including its less familiar data, with relative ease, occasional humour, and without deference. See Mary Lago, *Imperfect Encounter: Letters of William Rothenstein and Rabindranath Tagore, 1911–1941* (Cambridge, MA: Harvard University Press, 1972, p. 97; Krishna Dutta and Andrew Robinson, eds., *Selected Letters of Rabindranath Tagore* (Cambridge: Cambridge University Press, 1997), pp. 8–10.
88. See W. B. Yeats, *Autobiographies* (London: Macmillan, 1956), p. 190.
89. Shahid Suhrawardy, 'Tagore at Oxford', *Calcutta Municipal Quarterly: Tagore Memorial Special Supplement* (13 Sept 1941), n. p. Robert Bridges later wrote that Tagore's presence 'gave reality to the honest but vain profession of the university to be a home for all creeds and nations'.
90. Rupert Brooke, Letter to Cathleen Nesbit, in *The Letters of Rupert Brooke*, ed. Geoffrey Keynes (London: Faber and Faber, 1968), pp. 570–2.

91. Patricia Lawrence, *Lily Briscoe's Chinese Eyes: Bloomsbury, Modernism and China* (Columbia, SC: University of South Carolina Press, 2003), pp. 7, 10, 32, 33.
92. See Michael Collins, *Empire, Nationalism and the Postcolonial World: Rabindranath Tagore's Writings on History, Politics and Society* (London and New York: Routledge, 2011); William Radice, 'Introduction' to *Gitanjali*, by Rabindranath Tagore, trans. William Radice (New Delhi: Penguin, 2011), pp. xv–lxxxiv. Boehmer, *Empire, the National, and the Postcolonial*, ch. 4, to which Collins several times refers, explores the ways in which the two poets Tagore and Yeats shaped their divergent modernist responses through their encounter and interaction with one another's work. See also Sirchendu Majumdar, *Yeats and Tagore: A Comparative Study of Cross-Cultural Poetry, Nationalist Politics, Hyphenated Margins and the Ascendancy of the Mind* (Palo Alto: Academica Press, 2013).
93. Mary Ellis Gibson, *Anglophone Poetry in Colonial India 1780–1913: A Critical Anthology* (Athens, OH: Ohio University Press, 2011), pp. 3, 310–14.
94. The term 'wise imperialism' comes from a November 1912 letter from W. B. Yeats to Edmund Gosse concerning Tagore's proposed election to the India Society, in which Yeats observed that: 'from the English point of view it would be a fine thing to do, a piece of wise imperialism, for he is worshipped as no poet of Europe is . . . I believe that if we pay him honour, it will be understood that we honour India also for he is its most famous man today.' The term neatly encapsulates Yeats, Pound, and others' self-serving patronage of Indian and other colonial poetic voices in Europe in order to bring out and develop mainstream modernist effects. The condescension involved does not need further spelling out; however, as this chapter shows, Yeats fully intended the contradictory coupling of wisdom with imperialism in this phrase to provoke and to promote in equal measure. See W. B. Yeats to Edmund Gosse, 25 November 1912: W. B. Yeats Correspondence Files. Rabindranath Tagore Papers, Rabindra Bhavana, Santiniketan, West Bengal. The letter also appears in Allan Wade, ed., *The Letters of W. B. Yeats* (London: Rupert Hart-Davis, 1954), pp. 572–3. As Christopher Balme, *Pacific Performances* (Basingstoke: Palgrave Macmillan, 2007), p. 7, perceptively observes: 'one essential condition of modernity is that it creates its own antithesis through an interest in traditional societies'.
95. Kalyan Kundu, Sakti Bhattacharya, and Kalyan Sircar, *Imagining Tagore: Rabindranath and the British Press, 1912–1941* (Calcutta: Shishu Sahitya Samsad, 2000), give the date as 7 July 1912; Hugh Tinker, *The Ordeal of Love: C. F. Andrews and India* (Oxford: Oxford University Press, 1979), p. 56, as 30 June. Rathindranath Tagore, *On the Edges of Time* (Calcutta: Orient Longmans, 1958), pp. 101–3, corroborates the former date. Lago, *Imperfect Encounter*, frontispiece, and pp. 45 and 60, shows the John Trevor photographs.
96. See Rothenstein, *Men and Memories*, part 2, pp. 262–6; Schuchard, *The Last Minstrels*, pp. 270–83. Tagore's considerable diffidence as to his poems'

reception comes through in Tagore's letter to Rothenstein of 26 November 1932, in Lago, *Imperfect Encounter,* pp. 344–7. See also Mary Lago, 'The Parting of the Ways: A Comparative Study of Yeats and Tagore', *Indian Literature* 6.2 (1963): 4. James Cousins and Margaret E. Cousins, *We Two Together* (Madras: Ganesh and Company Ltd, 1950), p. 161, describes Yeats taking the poems, possibly typed up, along with him on holiday to Normandy.

97. An early proselytizer alongside Yeats for the modern significance of Tagore's work, yet one more quickly disillusioned by 'King Rabindra''s seemingly grandiloquent and conceited posturing, Ezra Pound wrote on Tagore for *Poetry* (December 1912) and the *Fortnightly Review* (March 1913), saying that his poetry contained both the 'properties of action' and the 'stillness of nature'. Listening to Tagore's singing in September 1912 (while Rothenstein drew him), Pound tried to find parallels between the Provençal troubadour traditions and song-based traditions in Bengal. Tagore's singing confirmed for him that English metrics followed 'the sequence of the musical phrase', not 'the sequence of a metronome', as he wrote in *Poetry* (March 1913)—something that he had first learned from Yeats and his psaltery-playing friend Florence Farr. As in the case of Naidu in relation to Symons, Pound and Yeats enlisted Tagore to define by contradistinction the robust modernist interventions of their ensuing years, or, in the case of Yeats, to seek distance from a disillusioned cultural nationalism. See Schuchard, *The Last Minstrels*, p. 278.
98. William Rothenstein's Indian drawings are now held in the Tate Britain archive. I am grateful to Sarah V. Turner for showing them to me in May 2008. In 1912, Rothenstein also made nine portrait drawings of Tagore, which are held at Tate Britain and at the British Museum.
99. Leela Gandhi, *Affective Communities: Anti-colonial Thought and the Politics of Friendship* (Durham, NC: Duke University Press, 2006), p. 189.
100. Letter from Rabindranath Tagore to William Rothenstein, 29 April 1914, MS ENG 1148/1457/46. William Rothenstein Papers, Houghton Library, Harvard University: quoted in Turner, 'Crafting Connections', p. 109; Lago, *Imperfect Encounter*, pp. 65, 121.
101. Rothenstein, *Men and Memories*, pp. 249–55.
102. Radice, 'Introduction', *Gitanjali*, p. xxii.
103. His preference for drawing over painting, he felt, lent itself to an admiration for the vibrant, mobile forms of Indian temple art. Rothenstein, *Men and Memories*, p. 232.
104. Schuchard, *The Last Minstrels*, p. 281; James Cousins, 'Introduction', to Abinash Chandra Bose, *Three Mystic Poets: A Study of W. B. Yeats, A. E. and Rabindranath Tagore* (Kolhapur: School and College Bookstall, 1946), pp. v–vi.
105. Collins, *Empire, Nationalism and the Postcolonial World*, pp. 112–21; Joseph Lennon, *Irish Orientalism: A Literary and Intellectual History* (New York, NY: Syracuse University Press, 2004), pp. 265–81; W. B. Yeats, *Autobiographies* (London: Macmillan, 1926), p. 164.

106. Michael Collins points out that the seven Tagore poems Yeats included in his 1936 *Oxford Book of Modern Verse* were selected from just the two books Tagore had published in their shared idealist heyday of 1913 (p. 119).
107. Radice, 'Introduction', *Gitanjali*, pp. xvi–xix.
108. Radice, 'Introduction', *Gitanjali*, p. xviii.
109. Letter to William Rothenstein (4 April 1915), in Dutta and Robinson, eds., *Selected Letters*, pp. 161–2; Lago, *Imperfect Encounter*, pp. 194–6; Rothenstein, *Men and Memories*, pp. 300–1.
110. Rothenstein, *Men and Memories*, vol. 2, p. 301. On p. 267 he includes a reproduction of a page from this *Gitanjali* MS, by way of proof. See also MS 429(i), Facsimile of the Harvard MS of *Gitanjali*, Rabindranath Tagore Papers, Rabindra Bhavana, Shantiniketan, West Bengal.
111. Rabindranath Tagore to Indira Devi (6 May 1913), in Krishna Kripalani, *Tagore: A Life* (Delhi: National Book Trust, 1986), p. 123. An alternative translation can be found in Krishna Dutta and Andrew Robinson, eds., *Selected Letters of Rabindranath Tagore* (Cambridge: Cambridge University Press, 1997), p. 117.
112. Rabindranath Tagore, 'The Future of India', *The Modern Review* 9.3 (1911): 240–1.
113. Rabindranath Tagore, *Nationalism* (Harmondsworth: Penguin, 2010), pp. 7–10, 69; and also 'The Future of India' (1911): 240–2; Literatus, 'Rabindranath Tagore in America', *Modern Review* 21.6 (1917): 666. For related references, see Collins, *Empire, Nationalism and the Postcolonial World*, pp. 44–7; Dutta and Robinson, eds., *Selected Letters*, pp. 89, 90, 97–8, 117; Kripalani, *Tagore: A Life*, pp. 122–3. In the years leading up to the publication of *Nationalism*, Tagore developed his critique both of western imperialism and of narrow-minded nationalism in a number of essays published in the Calcutta-based *Modern Review*.
114. Supriya Chaudhuri, 'The Idea of a World Literature', in *Towards Tagore*, ed. Sanjukta Dasgupta, Ramkumar Mukhopadhyay, and Swati Ganguly (Kolkata: Visva-Bharati, 2014), pp. 273–83. Tagore's essay 'Vishva Sahitya' is collected as 'World Literature' in Rabindranath Tagore, *Selected Writings on Literature and Language*, ed. Sukanta Chaudhuri, Sisir Kumar Das, and Sankha Ghosh, trans. Swapan Chakravorty (Delhi: Oxford University Press, 2001).
115. Radice, 'Introduction', in *Gitanjali*, pp. xxiv–xxv.
116. References for the quotations from the Tagore–Rothenstein letters in order are: Rothenstein to Tagore (19 September 1917); Rothenstein to Tagore (15 March 1927); Rothenstein to Tagore (15 July 1931); Tagore to Rothenstein (26 November 1932); Tagore to Rothenstein (26 June 1931), in Lago, *Imperfect Encounter*, pp. 240–2, 319–20, 337–8, 344–7, 336–7. The final letters between Yeats and Tagore that can be found in the archives profess continuing loyalty, yet also a sense of distance. As with Tagore and Rothenstein, an enduring sense of connection is refracted through memories of their first heady period of contact. See W. B. Yeats

to Tagore (7 September 1931); Tagore to Yeats (4 October); Tagore to W. B. Yeats (16 July 1935). See W. B. Yeats Correspondence Files. Rabindranath Tagore Papers, Rabindra Bhavana, Shantiniketan, West Bengal.

117. Tagore to Rothenstein (16 July 1912); Rothenstein to Tagore (18 July 1912), in Lago, *Imperfect Encounter*, pp. 49–50, 50–1.
118. Gibson, *Anglophone Poetry*, p. 314.
119. Amartya Sen, 'Tagore and his India', *The Argumentative Indian* (London: Penguin, 2005), pp. 89–120. To illustrate, see Collins, *Empire, Nationalism and the Postcolonial World*, p. 119, and note 106 above.
120. Tagore to Rothenstein (19 November 1912), in Lago, *Imperfect Encounter*, pp. 64–5.

5

Coda—Indian Salients

Recognition of sameness [is] at work, not only curiosity about difference.

Marina Warner, *Stranger Magic* (2011).[1]

This man in his own country prayed we know not to what Powers.
We pray Them to reward him for his bravery in ours.

Rudyard Kipling, 'Hindu Sepoy in France', from
'Epitaphs of the War 1914–18'.[2]

I cannot do more than assure you that the unfailing kindness with which I have been greeted in England has moved me far more than I can tell. I have learned that though our tongues are different and our habits dissimilar, at the bottom our hearts are one. The monsoon clouds, generated on the banks of the Nile, fertilise the far distant shores of the Ganges: ideas may have to cross from East to Western shores to find a welcome in men's hearts and fulfill their promise.

Rabindranath Tagore, words of thanks in response to
W. B. Yeats's introductory address, Trocadero Restaurant,
10 July 1912.[3]

In early spring 1914, the self-taught Indian mathematician Srinivas Ramanujan travelled from Madras, where he had worked as a clerk in the Port Trust Office, to Trinity College, Cambridge, at the invitation of the English mathematician and Apostle G. H. Hardy. As David Leavitt describes in his fictionalization of their friendship, *The Indian Clerk* (2007), the two mathematicians spent the next five years in close collaboration—across the entire period of the First World War—developing new theorems and testing proofs, and working through different hypergeometric series, which led to one of the most efficient formulas for the calculation of pi.[4] For Hardy, though he was by no stretch a part of Bloomsbury, this mathematical conversation with Ramanujan became a living expression of his belief, in part derived from his Apostle 'father' G. E. Moore's thought, that one-to-one friendship between like-minded men, regardless of race, was pivotal to intellectual life. 'All my best work', he later wrote in his memoir, *A Mathematician's Apology*, 'has been bound up with [Ramanujan's]': this association, and that with the mathematician Littlewood, was the 'decisive event of [his] life'.[5] For Ramanujan, a religious man whose approach to his subject was always more instinctual and impulsive, the patterns of ideas that made up mathematics rather came from the ministrations of the goddess Namalgiri, who did not however, or not at first, neglect him in England. Though it may seem trivializing to read mathematical concepts metaphorically, nonetheless it is noteworthy that whereas Hardy was particularly concerned with the Riemann hypothesis and prime numbers, Ramanujan arrived in Cambridge reflecting in particular on what he called highly composite numbers or 'anti-primes', like 24, whose salience lies in their divisibility rather their singularity, their openness to accommodating divisors, rather than refusing such accommodation, as do primes.[6]

Though Ramanujan's early months in England coincided with the legendary glorious summer of 1914, loneliness, near-starvation, and illness overshadowed most of his time in a Cambridge emptied of students due to the war. War shortages also meant that good vegetarian food was hard to come by for a reclusive mathematician who did not have access to the contacts that Gandhi had found in London some decades previously. Not long after his return to India in 1919 Ramanujan died of either tuberculosis or liver infection. Before he left England, however, he was elected, in 1918, Fellow of the Royal Society and Fellow of Trinity College, respectively the second and the first Indian to be thus honoured.

In the town of Ypres or Ieper in Flanders, Belgium, the imposing Menin Gate, designed by Reginald Blomfield, stands as a memorial to the 54,332 missing of the Salient who have no known grave. The long lists of the war dead carved into the stone plaques that line the inner walls of the monument, especially those on the city side of the Gate, show the names of *subedars*, *havaldars*, and *naiks* from the Indian Army who in 1914–15 died in action in the vicinity, especially in the long defensive action around Ypres, or, as Sarojini Naidu wrote in her obliquely patriotic poem 'The Gift of India', were 'strewn like blossoms mown down by chance/On the blood-brown meadows of Flanders and France'.[7] At Neuve-Chapelle, some twenty-seven miles away across the border, the Indian Memorial, designed by Herbert Baker, lists the 5,015 names of those of the Indian Army who were killed in France in 1914–15, but whose bodies were never found or could not be identified, having been either blown to pieces by mines or buried by collapsing trenches. As these memorials suggest, the Indian troops' stay in Europe was far from long, diverting, or in any sense celebrated, or not until recently.[8] However, their unequivocal presence in the form of these carved names, and of a small memorial or *chatri* to Indian soldiers that stands on the Ypres ramparts, testifies to the decisive role they played on the Western Front during the dark early months of the First World War, first holding the critical Ypres salient, a 16-mile perimeter line around the Belgian town, and then taking part in some of the heaviest action at nearby Neuve-Chapelle and Loos. The year of 1915, which marks their departure, has therefore been chosen as the end-date of this study.

The Indian Corps, the world's largest standing army, first came to the assistance of the beleaguered British Expeditionary Force in October 1914. At the outbreak of war, troops from the white Dominions were not yet properly trained, therefore the one source of regular manpower that Britain could turn to in its time of grave crisis was the Indian Army, in spite of official apprehension at the deployment of non-white troops. Until they were withdrawn in 1915, in large measure in response to such racially motivated concerns, these Indian arrivals in Europe effectively held the Western Front for the Allies or, as Corrigan writes, they 'arrived in Belgium just in time and in just sufficient strength to block the gaps in a very stretched British line and prevent the Germans from breaking through to the Channel ports'—and mounting a direct threat to the British mainland.[9] Though overextended and underequipped, lacking proper reinforcement, and unused to the terrain, the cold, and defensive entrenchment, these soldiers protected the west of the Western Front in a series of major battles extending across nearly twelve months. Overall, the Indian Army supplied the war in Europe in this first year with 140,000 men, both combatants and non-combatants, of which over a third were wounded, and 8,000 killed. In material terms, the Indian units were also supported by a vast outlay of funding from the Indian princes. Ranjitsinhji, the cricketer, an honorary major with the Inniskillin Dragoon Guards, channelled recruits and funds from his princely state of Nawanagar.[10]

Though at the time it went largely unrecognized, the Sepoys' crucial presence at this point in the war represents perhaps the most historically important instance of Indian arrival covered in this book, and the first time that non-elite Indians in significant numbers shaped the military and political history, not only of Britain, but also of Continental Europe. In total, India contributed around 1.4 million men to the First World War effort, who, after the removal from France in 1915, served in Mesopotamia, Persia, Gallipoli, and the Far East. As the majority of these men were illiterate, and their dictated letters home heavily censored, we have little direct sense of how they experienced the war.[11] Their truncated messages, combined with the reports of their British officers, and some oral testimony, do, however, give an impression of the remarkable courage and the strong sense of honour, or *izzat*, with which they approached the remote

King Emperor's war, though also of their fear and bewilderment at fighting so far from home, in a cold and unfamiliar climate, with obsolete rifles, among people who tended to treat their presence with considerable circumspection.[12] In official circles, too, the deployment of the 'coloured races' in Europe raised official dismay and disapproval on both sides in the war, in Germany and in parts of the British Empire.

This circumspection extended even to the Indian wounded, who in 1914–15 were treated in six Indian military hospitals set up in southern England, including at Bournemouth and in the converted Brighton Pavilion. Though the India Office and the War Office took pains to respect the religious and cultural sensibilities of these troops, and the Indian Soldiers Fund (operating out of Lord Curzon's London residence) arranged for entertainments like London tours, their hospital compounds were strongly guarded, especially at night, in order to avoid any possibility of consort between the soldiers and local women. In the hospitals, too, male rather than female nurses were used. In spite of his capacity as a soldier fighting in defence of the imperial motherland, the non-elite Indian was not at this time permitted to 'arrive' or move about freely in England, although the residents of Brighton do seem to have appreciated the 'picturesqueness' of the South Asians in their midst, as local newspaper reports suggest.[13] In general, papers like the *Illustrated London News* and the *Daily Mail* represented the Indian presence on the Western Front in exotic and primitivist terms but reported nothing of their actual heroism, including in reports on Neuve-Chapelle.[14]

Among the first Indian troops to land at Marseilles, and the first to be involved in action, the 3rd Lahore Division occupied trenches near Wijtschate and Mesen in Flanders on 22 October 1914, and staged an attack to the south of Hollebeke four days later, as part of the protracted First Battle of Ypres (19 October–22 November 1914). For racial reasons, the division was not yet permitted to operate as one distinct unit, but rather was divided and utilized as reinforcements or stopgaps in the line. However, their worth was amply demonstrated during their first battle, at the La Bassée Canal in late October, when their arrival in support of the retreating British forces stabilized the line in the face of powerful German attacks. The 47th Sikhs and two British sapper companies also contributed substantially to a British attack on Neuve-Chapelle on 28 October, repulsing a German push down the Menin road, though their capture of the town by hand-to-hand fighting was almost immediately cancelled by a German counterattack. The Sikhs lost 289 men. Severely depleted, this 2nd Corps was incorporated into the Indian Corps, which was thus at last involved in action as a distinct unit and, after 10 November, completely took over the line previously occupied by the 2nd Corps.

In March 1915, Indian troops were again involved in an attack on Neuve-Chapelle, which broke through the German line, though the British forces could not then advance further due to a lack of ammunition. The Lahore Division participated also in Second Ypres, from 26 April–1 May 1915, once again stopping the German advance into the Salient. Indians also helped to mount a diversionary attack on the first day of the Battle of Loos, on 30 August 1915, in which the battalions were composed of men from many different regiments. After Loos, the Indian front stretched for six-and-a-half miles, from the north of Neuve-Chapelle to the La Bassée canal, which meant that the Indian Corps had maintained their hold on more or less the same sector of the Front since arriving in France. From this point on, however, the Indian Corps battalions began to be withdrawn from France, bound for the Middle East and Egypt, where Turkey was proving stronger than expected. With reinforcements arriving from Canada, the maintenance of a significant non-white force in the west came now to be regarded as less viable than before. By the end of 1915, most Indian Sepoys had departed from Europe, bringing to an end the largest and most significant Indian 'arrival', at least in military terms, which the continent had yet seen.

Wilfred Owen, the soldier-poet whose work so powerfully evoked the experience of the British armed forces during the First World War, found his own particular salience in Indian lines—in his case, lines of poetry by Rabindranath Tagore. As echoes between his and Naidu's sibilant sound patterns suggest (following Santanu Das's reading), Owen may have shared with both contemporary Indian writers a delight in the sinuous sonic effects of turn-of-the-century and Edwardian poetry.[15] Certainly, Owen copied into the pocket-book that he took with him to war, poem XCVI, from the final ten poems of Tagore's *Gitanjali*, which begins: 'When I go from hence let this be my parting word, that what I have seen is unsurpassable.'[16] Owen had first encountered Tagore's work in the 1915 *Times* War Poems supplement, which included the Indian poet's 'The Trumpet', and also heard his poetry read at the Harold Monro's Poetry Book shop in the same year. But it was *Gitanjali* that drew him, touched perhaps by its mystical sense of human divinity, of God in man, as Tagore might have put it, or by the awareness that Tagore's work had brought to so many of his first British readers in 1912–13: that western poetry, to be renewed, should open to other traditions. In pre-war London, such openness and exchange had been felt not only to be possible but intellectually desirable, as we saw in Chapter 4.

Owen scrawled the lines from *Gitanjali* on the back of a January 1917 message from the Acting Adjutant of his battalion, and then also quoted them to his mother Susan on the last day of his leave before his final embarkation. He was killed on 4 November 1918 north of Ors in France. Nearly two years later, in August 1920, Susan Owen wrote Tagore a letter about the inscription in her 'dearest eldest' son's pocket-book, telling him how he quoted it when they stood with 'breaking hearts' looking across the 'sun-glorified' sea to France. She went on to ask where she might find the whole poem.[17] The heart-sore letter with its sometimes sprawling and erratically slanting handwriting is a poignant document of contact requested but not reciprocated. There is no record of Tagore ever replying, perhaps because he was travelling at the time, though the facsimile of the letter is preserved in his papers at Shantiniketan. Yet for a book interested in harmonies and counterpoint, such as this, and one that began with a reading of Toru Dutt's poem 'Near Hastings', it is still fitting that Owen and his mother were close to Hastings looking out over the Channel to France when he spoke Tagore's lines recounted in the letter. As for Ramanujan and Hardy, who explored through the universal language of mathematics a means of communicating that transcended cultural divides, Owen appears to have found in Tagore a deep and convincing sense of human oneness, of something innately understood between a speaker and a listener bound together by kindness, regardless of the cultural boundaries that might divide them.

Indian Arrivals has explored in depth Indian involvements in British metropolitan life, especially as expressed in literary writing, in the high imperial decades 1870–1915. As these three First World War tableaux suggest by way of closing, visitors from India in the long turn of the century contributed in a number of significant ways to the make-up of cosmopolitan British society, culture, and letters. Their arrivals—their conversations and interactions, their labour, and their writing—flowed into the ongoing story of layering and mixing which has defined lives and selves on these islands from as far back as 'Britain began'.[18] Whether we consider the Suez crossings of Chapter 1, or the encounters staged in Dutt's and Ghose's poetry, or whether we trace, as in Chapter 4, the complicated creative genealogy of Rabindranath Tagore's *Gitanjali*, lines of which were recalled by Wilfred Owen at Hastings in 1918, the different case studies evoke the extent to which Indian intellectuals, writers, and travellers in Britain helped to mould some of the leading literary-cultural movements, ideas, styles, and identities of the day. These included the colonial travelogue, perceptions of the imperial city, the orientalist inflection of late-century Decadence, the sinuous shape and sound of Edwardian poetry, and, throughout, concepts of the modern and mobile western self—movements, ideas, styles, and identities which across most of the twentieth century were rarely seen as shaped by Indian hands.

In the decades following the First World War, the material and psychic devastation that had been wreaked on Europe, and the political polarization and 'race conflict' that then developed, as Tagore predicted, to a considerable extent erased the memory of that contribution.[19] As a war between emergent, mature, and collapsing empires, 1914–18 precipitated a mass imperial decline which exacerbated that erasure, in part because intercultural contact had been so intricately associated with expressions of both imperial confidence and anxiety. To contend with these historical oversights, this book has required strategic manoeuvres of retrieval and re-reading, inspired throughout by the object lessons that the different migrant encounters might be seen to have offered. Contrary to the experiences of racially motivated ostracism and exclusion which post-1945 Indian migrants faced, early India-in-Britain, as we have seen, placed an exemplary emphasis on the mutual exchange of philosophical, literary, and cultural perceptions. As in the poetry of Manmohan Ghose or Sarojini Naidu that crossed English Romantic symbols with a nostalgic yearning for Indian horizons, or the letters and travel writing of R. C. Dutt, M. K. Gandhi, or even Rabindranath Tagore, Indian pathways of arrival in the heart of empire tended often to be recursive as well as circuitous, and the 'typically Indian' would be that which was made on British shores, for the benefit of western eyes. Aware from their outsider (and usually elite) perspectives that the west could not admire what it did not in part contain, Indian arrivants and travellers by their presence enacted how England was interpenetrated by material and cultural influences from abroad.[20]

Through their various acts of arrival, Indian visitors to Britain forged modern selves that were made up out of contingent experiences and chance encounters, of different intersecting '[processes] of movement and mediation'.[21] They not only contributed by their presence to creating the new social fluidities and speeded-up interactions that defined the high imperial metropolis, but also analysed the complexity and heterogeneity of that intercultural world by virtue of participating in it and writing about it. As does the protagonist of a *Bildungsroman*, according to Franco Moretti, Indian poet travellers and other literary migrants sought through the medium of their writing for an accommodation between self-expression on the one hand and the necessity to fit in with their changing social context on the other.[22] They wrote their way from a position in the wider west, deeper into the west—from an outlying city into the *ur*-city—reflecting critically on their new cross-border involvements even as they engaged in them.

The dialogues, relationships, and conversations that *Indian Arrivals* has drawn together, illuminate intersecting lines and links in a multilayered network that began to connect India more closely with Britain from the mid-to-late nineteenth century onwards. Throughout, these connections have pointed to the ways in which the conventional centre of the late nineteenth-century imperial world was criss-crossed by its margins, much as the margins of that world were by the centre. Whereas, in India, the British had tried to make the Indian in their image, though an imperfect one, the Indian in Britain in this period, a citizen of empire among equals, experienced such assimilation as a self-directed and even mutual process, seeing Britain from a cosmopolitan perspective first developed in India, and turning the experience of arrival into something of a process of re-entry. As this suggests, rather than standing in a polar relationship to the wider empire, the metropolis existed in dynamic relationship with it: the networks of the one were folded back upon and crosshatched with those of the other. It is a mingling that provided suggestive models for the India-in-Britain of the future, of which these early travellers at the time could barely have conceived—a Britain in which curry, popadoms, bindis, and salwar kameez would be seen, legitimately, as a quintessential part of the culture of these islands.

NOTES

1. Marina Warner, *Stranger Magic* (London: Chatto & Windus, 2011), p. 24.
2. Rudyard Kipling, *Complete Verse: Definitive Edition* (London: Hodder and Stoughton, 1989), p. 387.
3. Carbon copy following Letter 23, W. B. Yeats Correspondence Files. Rabindranath Tagore Papers, Rabindra Bhavana, Shantiniketan, West Bengal.
4. David Leavitt, *The Indian Clerk* (London: Bloomsbury, 2007). See also Simon McBurney, *A Disappearing Number* (London: Oberon, 2008), the script of the award-winning 2007 Théatre de Complicité play about the Hardy–Ramanujan friendship, staged at the Theatre Royal, Plymouth, and at the Barbican. I am grateful to Marcus du Sautoy for clarification concerning the nature of the two mathematicians' collaborative work.
5. G. H. Hardy, *A Mathematician's Apology*, foreword by C. P. Snow (1936; Cambridge: Cambridge University Press, 1967), p. 48.
6. Leavitt, *The Indian Clerk*, pp. 140–1.
7. Sarojini Naidu, 'The Gift of India', in *The Broken Wing: Songs of Love, Death and Destiny 1915–1916* (London: William Heinemann, 1917), pp. 5–6. Written in praise of India's sons who had given their lives in Flanders, Gallipoli, and Mesopotamia, the poem reflects Naidu's belief in the right of Indian men to bear arms as a birthright and a guarantee of their manhood. She first read 'The Gift of India' at the Hyderabad Ladies' War Relief Association in December 1915, and referred to it in her 1916 address to Congress, hoping,

along with many other Indians, that Britain would reward the sacrifice of the hundreds of thousands of Indian soldiers who had died and were wounded in helping to defeat the Axis Powers with a move towards greater political autonomy. See Tara Ali Baig, *Sarojini Naidu* (New Delhi: Ministry of Information and Broadcasting. Government of India, 1974), p. 57; Padmini Sen Gupta, *Sarojini Naidu* (New Delhi: Sahitya Akademi, 1974), p. 39. See also Santanu Das's important work recovering the Indian First World War experience, summarized in 'India, Empire and First World War Writing', *The Indian Postcolonial: A Critical Reader*, ed. Elleke Boehmer and Rosinka Chaudhuri (London: Routledge, 2011), pp. 297–315, which offers a reading of Naidu's 'slyly subversive' poem; and also his 'Introduction' and chapter, 'Indians at Home, Mesopotamia and France, 1914–1918: Towards an Intimate History', in his edited *Race, Empire and the First World War* (Cambridge: Cambridge University Press, 2011), pp. 1–32, 70–89.

8. As well as the work cited immediately above, see also Dominiek Dendooven, 'Troops of British India in Flanders', in *World War I: Five Continents in Flanders*, ed. Dominiek Dendooven and Piet Chielens (Tielt, Belgium: Lannoo, 2008), pp. 117–29; David Omissi, *The Sepoy and the Raj* (Basingstoke: Macmillan, 1994); and Florian Stadtler, 'Britain's Forgotten Volunteers: South Asian Contributions to the Two World Wars', in *South Asians and the Shaping of Britain, 1870–1950: A Sourcebook*, ed. Ruvani Ranasinha et al. (Manchester: Manchester University Press, 2012), pp. 80–135.
9. Gordon Corrigan, *Mud, Blood and Poppycock* (London: Orion, 2003), p. 64, and the more detailed account in his *Sepoys in the Trenches: The Indian Corps on the Western Front 1914–15* (Stroud: Spellmount, 2006), pp. 50, 51, 77 in particular. Corrigan, *Sepoys in the Trenches*, p. 73 relatedly comments: 'While it was perhaps hyperbole to say that they had "Saved the Empire", it was certainly true that they had saved the [British Expeditionary Force]', so preventing a German breakthrough to the coast.
10. David Cannadine, *Ornamentalism: How the British Saw Their Empire* (London: Allen Lane, 2001), p. 54; Satadru Sen, *Migrant Races: Empire, Identity and K. S. Ranjitsinjhi* (Manchester: Manchester University Press, 2005), p. 139.
11. However, new publications emerging to coincide with the 2014–18 centenary of the Great War are helping to fill in these gaps. As well as the work cited in notes 6 and 7 above, see Santanu Das, ed., *The Cambridge Companion to the Poetry of the First World War* (Cambridge: Cambridge University Press, 2013).
12. Corrigan, *Sepoys in the Trenches*, pp. 11, 16–17, 21, 33–4, 72. So, for example, a naik of the 47th Sikhs, invalided in England, wrote to a relative in Amritsar: 'our brothers who are in the trenches have endured sufferings beyond the powers of words to describe. When God grants me to see you again I will tell you the whole story. I think you will not believe what I tell you of the fighting, of our ships and of our fights with the bayonet. I have seen such sights my wits are still amazed' (p. 72).

13. Rozina Visram, *Asians in Britain: 400 Years of History* (London: Pluto Press, 2002), p. 191.
14. In contrast, Lieutenant General Sir James Willcocks, the Commander of Indian troops, wrote to the Viceroy of India after the 1915 battle of Neuve-Chapelle: 'The fighting was very severe and the losses heavy, but nothing daunted them, their tenacity, courage and endurance were admirable, and worthy of the best traditions of the soldiers of India.' See Corrigan, *Sepoys in the Trenches*, p. 169.
15. Das, 'India, Empire and First World War Writing', pp. 297–315.
16. See Jon Stallworthy, *Wilfred Owen*, 2nd edn (1974; London: Pimlico, 2013), p. 267, but also pp. 124, 125, 129, 159. It was the same line that the Reverend Stopford Brooke, a Unitarian minister and a friend of William Rothenstein, picked out of the 1912 *Gitanjali* for encapsulating his delight in 'nature's sumptuousness'. See William Rothenstein, *Men and Memories: Recollections of William Rothenstein, 1900–1922*, vol. 2 (London: Faber and Faber Ltd, 1932), p. 263. Sebastian Faulks also quotes the line as epigraph to his Great War novel *Birdsong* (1996). By contrast, the reviewer 'HWN' writing in the suffragette journal *Votes for Women* in 1913 chose the *Gitanjali* poem LII (beginning 'I thought I should ask of thee') as an anthem for British women's campaign for the vote and for political representation in the modern world.
17. Letter 279, Rabindranath Tagore Papers, Rabindra Bhavana, Shantiniketan, West Bengal.
18. Barry Cunliffe, *Britain Begins* (Oxford: Oxford University Press, 2013).
19. Rabindranath Tagore, *The Crescent Moon* (London: Macmillan, 1913), quoted in Michael Collins, *Empire, Nationalism and the Postcolonial World: Rabindranath Tagore's Writings on History, Politics and Society* (London and New York: Routledge, 2011), pp. 58–9.
20. As Ferdinand de Saussure pointed out in his *Course in General Linguistics*, trans. Wade Baskin (1966), the value of a thing arises from 'the concurrence of everything that exists outside it'. Quoted in Patricia Lawrence, *Lily Briscoe's Chinese Eyes: Bloomsbury, Modernism and China* (Columbia, SC: University of South Carolina Press, 2003), pp. 114–15.
21. See Paul Gilroy, *The Black Atlantic* (London: Verso, 1993), ch. 1. As Said also reminds us in *Reflections on Exile*, 'the traveller *crosses over*, traverses territory, and abandons fixed positions all the time', '[suspending] the claim of customary routine in order to live in new rhythms and rituals'. It is a definitively modern set of involvements and undertakings. See Edward W. Said, 'Identity, Authority and Freedom', *Reflections on Exile and Other Essays* (London: Granta, 2000), p. 404.
22. Franco Moretti, *The Way of the World: The Bildungsroman in European Culture* (London: Verso, 1987), p. 16.

Works Cited

1. MANUSCRIPT SOURCES

BL: L/PJ/6/925, file 830. 'Committee on Distressed Colonial Seamen' (1909, 1910)

BL: Mss Eur F341/152. Ruth F. Woodsmall, 'Notes on Sarojini Naidu: Interview' (New Delhi: 20 March 1931)

Book 42040 (Lionel Johnson copy of *Primavera*). Rare Books Department, Huntingdon Library, San Marino, California

IOR: L/PJ/6/209, f.1299. 'Pauper Natives of India and Other Countries Relieved by Certain Workhouses' (6 August 1887)

IOR: L/PJ/6/373, f.828 ('Indian Oculists in a Destitute Condition in Swansea (1894)'). India Society, *Proceedings of the London India Society, 1910* (London: India Society, 1911)

K/SER1/170. *King's College Magazine, Ladies' Department*, numbers I, IV, VII, Michaelmas 1896, Michaelmas 1897, Lent 1899, Lent 1900

KW/SYL 5a and SYL 6, KWA RAD 2, KWA RAD 3. King's College London Archives

Lockwood Kipling letter. Bateman's Archive, Box 1, Item 7, Wimpole Papers, SxMs38/1/7

Manuscript Poems and Letters of Sarojini Naidu, Index 15. National Archives of India, New Delhi

MS 2750 (files 2, 74, 75). Hogarth Press Archive, University of Reading Special Collections

MS Eng. 1148.1457/46. William Rothenstein Papers, Houghton Library, Harvard University

MS. Eng. d. 2352. F. Max Müller Correspondence book. Bodleian Library, Oxford

Rabindranath Tagore Papers. Rabindra Bhavana, Santiniketan, West Bengal. Including MS 429(i). Facsimile of the Harvard MS of *Gitanjali*

R/E/O 821.91 N 143a and R/E/O 821.91, vols. 1–3. Sarojini Naidu papers, Special Collections, National Library, Calcutta

Report of the Committee on Indian Students, 1921–22. 'Report of the Committee Appointed by the Secretary of State for India in 1907 to Inquire into the Position of Indian Students in the United Kingdom'. Appendix IV to India Office, Report of the Committee on Indian Students, 1921–22 (1922)

W. B. Yeats Correspondence Files. Rabindranath Tagore Papers, Rabindra Bhavana, Santiniketan, West Bengal

2. PRIMARY PRINTED TEXTS

'Four authors' [Laurence Binyon, Arthur C. Cripps, Manmohan Ghose, Stephen Phillips], *Primavera* (Oxford: B. H. Blackwell, 1890)

Bose, Subhas Chandra, *An Indian Pilgrim: An Unfinished Autobiography*, ed. Sisir K. Bose and Sugata Bose (Delhi: Oxford India, 1997)

Brathwaite, E. K., *Arrivants: A New World Trilogy* (comprising *Rights of Passage*, 1967; *Masks*, 1968; *Islands*, 1969) (Oxford: Oxford University Press, 1973)

Burnett, Frances Hodgson, *A Little Princess* (1905; London: Penguin, 1970)

Collins, Wilkie, *The Moonstone*, ed. and intr. Sarah Kemp (1868/1871; Oxford: Oxford World's Classics, 2008)

Conrad, Joseph, *The Secret Agent*, intr. John Lyon (2007; Oxford: Oxford World's Classics, 2004)

Dickens, Charles, *The Mystery of Edwin Drood*, ed. Margaret Cardwell (1870; Oxford: Oxford World's Classics, 1992)

Dutt, Romesh Chunder, *Three Years in Europe 1868–71*, 4th edn (1872; Calcutta: S. K. Lahiri, 1896)

Dutt, Toru, *Ancient Ballads and Legends of Hindustan*, intr. Amaranatha Jha (Allahabad: Kitabistan, 1941)

Dutt, Toru, *Collected Poetry and Prose*, ed. Chandani Lokugé (New Delhi: Oxford University Press, 2006)

Malabari, B. M., *The Indian Muse in English Garb* (Bombay: Reporters' Press, 1879)

Malabari, B. M., *The Indian Eye on English Life; or, Rambles of an Indian Reformer* (London: Archibald Constable, 1893); 2nd edn (Bombay: Apollo Printing Works 1895)

Meredith, George, *One of Our Conquerors* (London: Chapman and Hall, 1892)

Mukharji, T. N., *A Visit to Europe* (Calcutta: W. Newman and Co./London: Edward Stainford, 1889)

Naidu, Sarojini, *The Golden Threshold* (London: William Heinemann, 1905)

Naidu, Sarojini, *The Bird of Time: Songs of Life, Death & the Spring*, intr. Edmund Gosse (London: William Heinemann, 1912)

Naidu, Sarojini, *The Broken Wing: Songs of Love, Death and Destiny 1915–16* (London: William Heinemann, 1917)

Naidu, Sarojini, *Lady Tata: A Book of Remembrance* (Bombay: Commercial Printing Press, 1932), pp. 53–6

Naidu, Sarojini, *The Feather of the Dawn*, ed. Padmaja Naidu (Bombay: Asia Publishing House, 1961)

Nehru, Jawaharlal, *An Autobiography; with Musings on Recent Events in India* (London: Bodley Head, 1936)

Ondaatje, Michael, *The Cat's Table* (London: Jonathan Cape, 2011)

Pandian, Rev. T. B., *England to an Indian Eye* or *English Pictures from an Indian Camera* (London: Elliot Stock, 1897)

Paranjape, Makarand, ed., *Sarojini Naidu: Selected Poetry and Prose* (New Delhi: Rupa Press, 2010)

Sorabji, Cornelia, *Love and Life Behind the Purdah* (London: Freemantle and Co, 1901)

Sorabji, Cornelia, *Sun-babies: Studies in the Child Life of India* (London: John Murray, 1904)

Sorabji, Cornelia. *Between the Twilights* (London: Harper, 1908)
Sorabji, Cornelia, *India Revisited* (London: Nisbet, 1936)
Sorabji, Cornelia, *India Calling*, ed. Elleke Boehmer and Naella Grew (1934; Nottingham: Trent Editions, 2004)
Sorabji, Cornelia, *An Indian Portia: Selected Writings of Cornelia Sorabji, 1866–1954*, ed. Kusoom Vadgama (New Delhi: Blacker, 2011)
Tagore, Rabindranath, 'The Future of India', *The Modern Review* 9.3 (1911): 240–1
Tagore, Rathindranath, *Gitanjali*, intr. W. B. Yeats (London: Indian Society, 1912)
Tagore, Rathindranath, *On the Edges of Time* (Calcutta: Orient Longmans, 1958)
Tagore, Rabindranath. *An Anthology*, ed. Krishna Dutta and Andrew Robinson (London: Picador, 1997)
Tagore, Rathindranath, *Selected Letters*, ed. Krishna Datta and Andrew Robinson (Cambridge: Cambridge University Press, 1997)
Trollope, Anthony, *The Eustace Diamonds* (1873; Oxford: Oxford World's Classics, 1982)
Woolf, Leonard, *Growing: An Autobiography of the Years 1904–1911* (London: The Hogarth Press, 1964)
Woolf, Leonard, *The Journey Not the Arrival Matters: An Autobiography of the Years 1939–1969* (London: Hogarth Press, 1969)
Woolf, Leonard, *An Autobiography 1: 1880–1911* (Oxford: Oxford University Press, 1980)
Woolf, Leonard, *Letters*, ed. Frederic Spotts (London: Bloomsbury, 1990)
Woolf, Leonard, 'Pearls and Swine', *Empire Writing*, ed. Elleke Boehmer (Oxford: Oxford University Press, 1998), pp. 415–30

3. SECONDARY PRINTED TEXTS

Ali, Ahmed, *Twilight in Delhi* (London: Hogarth Press, 1940)
Alexander, Meena, *The Shock of Arrival* (Boston, MA: South End Press, 1996)
Alexander, Michael and Sushila Anand, *Queen Victoria's Maharajah: Duleep Singh 1838–93* (London: Phoenix Press, 1980); 2nd edn (London: Phoenix Press, 2001)
Anand, Mulk Raj, *Conversations in Bloomsbury* (London: Wildwood House, 1981)
Anderson, Benedict, *Imagined Communities*, rev. edn (1983; London: Verso, 1991)
Anderson, Benedict, *The Spectre of Comparisons: Nationalism, South-East Asia and the World* (London: Verso, 1998)
Anonymous [Ceylonese participant in 1886 Exhibition], 'A Stranger Within Our Gates', *Daily News* (8 and 9 October 1886)
Anonymous, 'India in London', *Pall Mall Gazette* (6 February 1888)
Anonymous, 'A Lady's Day at the Glasgow Exhibition', *The Indian Magazine* 214 (October 1888): 540–6

Anonymous, 'Annie Besant and Theosophy', *Lucifer* iv.24 (15 August 1889): 486–99

Anonymous, 'Theosophical Activities', *Lucifer* xiii.73 (15 September 1893): 7

Anonymous, 'Recent Verse', *Manchester Guardian* (20 December 1905)

Anonymous, 'Music in London', *Manchester Guardian* (30 April 1907)

Anonymous, 'An Indian Poetess', *Manchester Guardian* (27 January 1913)

Anonymous, 'Poet-President of Indian National Congress', *Manchester Guardian* (28 December 1925)

A. A. S. [Miss A. A. Smith], 'How Far That Little Candle Throws Its Beams', *Indian Magazine and Review* 519 (March 1914): 70–2

Appiah, Kwame Anthony, *Cosmopolitanism: Ethics in a World of Strangers* (London: Allen Lane, 2006)

Araeen, Rasheed, 'A Very Special British Issue: Modernity, Art History and the Crisis of Art Today', *Third Text* 22.2 (March 2008): 125–44

Arnold, Edwin, *India Revisited* (London: Trübner and Co., 1886)

Arnold, Edwin, *The Light of Asia* (1879; London: Senate, 1998)

Arrowsmith, Rupert, *Modernism and the Museum: Asian, African and Pacific Art and the London Avant-Garde* (Oxford: Oxford University Press, 2011)

Arrowsmith, Rupert, 'Transcultural Literature and Art', *Wasafiri* 26.3 (2011): 38–49

Ash, Ranjana, 'Two Early Twentieth-century Indian Women Writers: Cornelia Sorabji and Sarojini Naidu', in *A History of Indian Literature in English*, ed. Arvind Mehrotra (London: Hurst and Co., 2003), pp. 126–34

Aziz, K. K., *Ameer Ali: His Life and Work* (Lahore: Publishers United, 1968)

Baig, Tara Ali, *Sarojini Naidu* (New Delhi: Government of India, 1974)

Baijnath, Lala, *England and India: Being Impressions of Persons and Things, English and Indian, and Brief Notes of Visits to France, Switzerland, Italy and Ceylon* (Bombay: Jehangir B. Karani and Co., 1893)

Ballaster, Ros, *Fabulous Orients: Fictions of the East in England 1662–1785* (Oxford: Oxford University Press, 2005)

Balme, Christopher, *Pacific Performances* (Basingstoke: Palgrave Macmillan, 2007)

Banerjee, Hasi, *Sarojini Naidu: The Traditional Feminist* (Calcutta: K. P. Bagdhi and Co., 1998)

Banerjee, Sukanya, *Becoming Imperial Citizens: Indians in the Late-Victorian Empire* (Durham, NC, and London: Duke University Press, 2010)

Barnes, John, Bill Bell, Rimi B. Chatterjee, Wallace Kirsop, and Michael Winship, 'A Place in the World', *The Cambridge History of the Book in Britain*, vol. 6: 1830–1914 (Cambridge: Cambridge University Press, 2009), pp. 595–634

Barnes, Julian, *Arthur & George* (London: Vintage, 2005)

Bartlett, E. Ashmead, M. P., *The Conference and Mr Gladstone's Proposals* (London: The Patriotic Association, 1885)

Basu, Lotika, *Indian Writers of English Verse* (Calcutta: University of Calcutta Press, 1933)

Bell, Duncan, *The Idea of Greater Britain: Empire and the Future of World Order* (Princeton, NJ, and Oxford: Princeton University Press, 2007)
Berman, Jessica, 'Comparative Colonialisms: Joyce, Anand and the Question of Engagement', *Modernism/Modernity*, 13.3 (2006): 465–85
Berman, Jessica, *Modernist Commitments: Ethics, Politics, and Transnational Modernism* (New York, NY: Columbia University Press, 2011)
Besant, Annie, *Why I Became a Theosophist* (New York, NY: Aryan Press, 1890)
Bhabha, Homi, *The Location of Culture* (London and New York: Routledge, 1994)
Binyon, Laurence, 'Introductory Memoir', in *Songs of Love and Death* (Oxford: Basil Blackwell, 1926), pp. 7–23
Blanchot, Maurice, *Friendship*, trans. Elizabeth Rottenberg (Stanford: Stanford University Press, 1997)
Blavatsky, H. P., *The Secret Doctrine: The Synthesis of Science, Religion and Philosophy*, 2 vols., 2nd edn (London: Theosophical Publishing House, 1888)
Bluemel, Kristin, *George Orwell and the Radical Eccentrics: Intermodernism in Literary London* (Basingstoke: Palgrave Macmillan, 2004)
Boehmer, Elleke, ed., *Empire Writing: An Anthology of Colonial Literature 1870–1920* (Oxford: Oxford University Press, 1998)
Boehmer, Elleke, *Empire, the National, and the Postcolonial: Resistance in Interaction* (Oxford: Oxford University Press, 2002)
Boehmer, Elleke, 'Empire and Modern Writing', in *The Cambridge History of Twentieth-Century English Literature*, ed. Laura Marcus and Peter Nichols (Cambridge: Cambridge University Press, 2004), pp. 50–60
Boehmer, Elleke, 'Introduction', in *Scouting for Boys*, Robert Baden-Powell (Oxford: Oxford University Press, 2004), pp. xi–xxxix
Boehmer, Elleke, *Colonial and Postcolonial Literature: Migrant Metaphors*, 2nd edn (Oxford: Oxford University Press, 2005)
Boehmer, Elleke, *Stories of Women: Gender and Narrative in the Postcolonial Nation* (Manchester: Manchester University Press, 2005)
Boehmer, Elleke and Stephen Morton, eds., *Terror and the Postcolonial* (Oxford: Blackwell, 2010)
Boehmer, Elleke, 'Circulating Forms: The Jingo Poem at the Height of Empire', *English Language Notes* 49.1 (Spring/Summer 2011): 11–28
Boehmer, Elleke and Anshuman Mondal, 'Networks and Traces: Interview with Amitav Ghosh', *Wasafiri* 27.2 (June 2012): 30–5
Boehmer, Elleke, 'The Zigzag Lines of Tentative Connection: Indian–British Contacts in the Late Nineteenth Century', in *India in Britain 1858–1950*, ed. Susheila Nasta (London: Palgrave Macmillan, 2013), pp. 12–27
Borthwick, Meredith, *Keshub Chunder Sen: A Search for Cultural Synthesis* (Calcutta: Minerva Associates, 1977)
Bose, Sugata, *A Hundred Horizons: The Indian Ocean in the Age of Global Empire* (Cambridge, MA: Harvard University Press, 2006)
Brah, Avtah, *Cartographies of Diaspora* (London and New York: Routledge, 1996)

Brantlinger, Patrick, 'Imperial Gothic: Atavism and the Occult in the British Adventure Novel', *English Literature in Transition 1880–1920* 28.3 (1985): 243–52
Brantlinger, Patrick, *Rule of Darkness: British Literature and Imperialism, 1830–1914* (Ithaca, NY, and London: Cornell University Press, 1988)
Brennan, Timothy, *At Home in the World: Cosmopolitanism Now* (Cambridge, MA: Harvard University Press, 1997)
Bristow, Joseph, ed., *The Victorian Poet* (Beckenham: Croom Helm, 1987)
Brooke, Rupert, *The Letters of Rupert Brooke*, ed. Geoffrey Keynes (London: Faber and Faber, 1968)
Brown, J. M., *Windows into the Past: Life Histories and the Historian of South Asia* (Notre Dame, IN: Notre Dame Press, 2009)
Brown, Judith, *Gandhi: Prisoner of Hope* (New Haven, CT, and London: Yale University Press, 1989)
Bubb, Alexander, 'Tracing the Legacy of an Experimental Connection', in *India in Britain: South Asian Networks and Connections, 1858–1950*, ed. Susheila Nasta (Basingstoke: Palgrave Macmillan, 2013), pp. 46–63
Buck-Morss, Susan, *The Dialectics of Seeing: Walter Benjamin and the Arcades Project* (Cambridge, MA, MIT Press, 1997)
Buettner, Elizabeth, *Empire Families: Britons and Late Imperial India* (Oxford University Press, 2004)
Bulfin, Ailise, 'The Fiction of Gothic Egypt and British Imperial Paranoia: The Curse of the Suez Canal', *English Literature in Transition* 54.4 (2011): 411–43
Burton, Antoinette, 'Making a Spectacle of Empire: Indian Travellers in Fin-de-siècle London', *History Workshop Journal* 42 (1996): 126–46
Burton, Antoinette, '"Stray Thoughts of an Indian Girl", by Cornelia Sorabji', *Indian Journal of Gender Studies* 3.2 (1996): 251–5
Burton, Antoinette, *At the Heart of the Empire: Indians and the Colonial Encounter in Late Victorian Britain* (Berkeley, CA: University of California Press, 1998)
Burton, Antoinette, *Empire in Question: Reading, Writing and Teaching British Imperialism* (Durham, NC, and London: Duke University Press, 2011)
Burton, Antoinette and Isabel Hofmeyr, eds., *Ten Books that Shaped the British Empire: Creating an Imperial Commons* (Durham, NC: Duke University Press, 2014)
Byatt, A. S., *The Children's Book* (London: Chatto and Windus, 2009)
Candler, Edmund, *Siri Ram—Revolutionist: A Transcript from Life* (London: Constable & Co., 1914)
Cannadine, David, *Ornamentalism: How the British Saw Their Empire* (London: Allen Lane, 2001)
Carey, Daniel and Lynn Festa, eds., *Postcolonial Enlightenment* (Oxford: Oxford University Press, 2009)
Carpenter, Edward, *From Adam's Peak to Elephanta: Sketches in Ceylon and India* (London: Swan Sonnenschein and Co., 1892)
Carpenter, Edward, *My Days and Dreams* (London: Allen and Unwin, 1916)
Carter, Marina and Khal Torabully, *Coolitude: An Anthology of Indian Labour Diaspora* (London: Anthem, 2002)

Carter, Paul, *The Road to Botany Bay* (London: Faber, 1987)

Cavafy, C. P., *Collected Poems*, trans. Edmund Keeley and Philip Sherrard (Princeton, NJ: Princeton University Press, 1992)

Cave, Terence, *Recognitions: A Study in Poetics* (Oxford: Clarendon Press, 1988)

Cave, Terence, 'Cognitive Affinities', *Times Literary Supplement*, 5739 (29 March 2013): 22–3

Cave, Terence, *Thinking with Literature* (Oxford: Oxford University Press, 2015)

Chakrabarty, Dipesh, *Provincializing Europe: Postcolonial Thought and Historical Difference* (Princeton, NJ: Princeton University Press, 2000)

Chambers, Colin, '"A Flute of Praise"–Indian Theatre in Britain in the Early Twentieth Century', in *India in Britain*, ed. Susheila Nasta (London: Palgrave, 2012), pp. 149–63

Chatterjee, Partha, *Nationalist Thought and the Colonial World: A Derivative Discourse?* (London: Zed Books, 1986)

Chatterjee, Partha, 'Nationalism, Colonialism and Colonized Women', *The American Ethnologist* 16.4 (1989): 622–33

Chatterjee, Rimi, 'Macmillan in India: A Short Account of the Company's Trade with the Sub-continent', in *Macmillan: A Publishing Tradition from 1943*, ed. Elizabeth James (Houndmills: Palgrave, 2001), pp. 153–69

Chaudhuri, Rosinka, *Gentlemen Poets in Colonial Bengal: Emergent Nationalism and the Orientalist Project* (Calcutta: Seagull, 2002)

Chaudhuri, Supriya, 'The Idea of a World Literature', in *Towards Tagore*, ed. Sanjukta Dasgupta, Ramkumar Mukhopadhyay, and Swati Ganguly (Kolkata: Visva-Bharati, 2014), pp. 273–86

Cheah, Pheng and Bruce Robbins, eds., *Cosmopolitics: Thinking and Feeling Beyond the Nation* (Minneapolis, MN: University of Minnesota Press, 1998)

Chirol, Valentine, *Indian Unrest* (London: Macmillan, 1910)

Chopra, Preeti, *A Joint Enterprise: Indian Elites and the Making of British Bombay* (Minneapolis, MN: University of Minnesota Press, 2011)

Choudhury, Deep Kanta Lahiri, *Telegraphic Imperialism: Crisis and Panic in the Indian Empire, c. 1830–1920* (New York, NY: Palgrave Macmillan, 2010)

Clarke, Norma, 'Excellent Larders', *Times Literary Supplement* 5705 (3 August 2012): 3–4

Clifford, James, *Routes: Travel and Translation in the Late Twentieth Century*, (Cambridge, MA: Harvard University Press, 1997)

Coetzee, J. M., *White Writing* (Cambridge, MA: Harvard University Press, 1988)

Collins, Michael, *Empire, Nationalism and the Postcolonial World: Rabindranath Tagore's Writings on History, Politics and Society* (London and New York: Routledge, 2011)

Coomaraswamy, A. K., *Medieval Sinhalese Art* (Broad Campden: Essex House Press, 1908)

Coomaraswamy, A. K., *Indian Drawings: Second Series* (London: The India Society, 1912)

Coomaraswamy, A. K., *'New England Woods': Three Poems* (Ditchling, Sussex: St Dominic's Press, 1920)

Coomaraswamy, A. K. *The Dance of Shiva: Fourteen Indian Essays* (Bombay: Asia Publishing House, 1948)
Cooper, Frederick, *Colonialism in Question: Theory, Knowledge, History* (Berkeley, CA: University of California Press, 2005)
Cooper, Frederick and A. Laura Stoler, eds., *Tensions of Empire: Colonial Cultures in a Bourgeois World* (Berkeley, CA: University of California Press, 1997)
Copley, Antony, *A Spiritual Bloomsbury: Hinduism and Homosexuality in the Lives and Writings of Edward Carpenter, E. M. Forster and Christopher Isherwood* (Lanham, MD, and Oxford: Lexington Books, 2006)
Corrigan, Gordon, *Mud, Blood and Poppycock* (London: Orion, 2003)
Corrigan, Gordon, *Sepoys in the Trenches: The Indian Corps on the Western Front 1914–15* (Stroud: Spellmount, 2006)
Cousins, James, '"Introduction" to Abinash Chandra Bose', in *Three Mystic Poets: A Study of W. B. Yeats, A. E. and Rabindranath Tagore* (Kolhapur: School and College Bookstall, 1946), pp. v–vi
Cousins, James and Margaret E. Cousins, *We Two Together* (Madras: Ganesh and Company Ltd, 1950)
Cunliffe, Barry, *Britain Begins* (Oxford: Oxford University Press, 2013)
Das, Santanu, 'India, Empire and First World War Writing', in *The Indian Postcolonial: A Critical Reader*, ed. Elleke Boehmer and Rosinka Chaudhuri (London and New York: Routledge, 2011), pp. 297–315
Das, Santanu, ed., *Race, Empire and the First World War* (Cambridge: Cambridge University Press, 2011)
Das, Santanu, *The Cambridge Companion to the Poetry of the First World War* (Cambridge: Cambridge University Press, 2013)
David, Deirdre, *Rule Britannia: Women, Empire and Victorian Writing* (Ithaca, NY, and London: Cornell University Press, 1995)
Davis, Richard, *The Lives of Indian Images* (Princeton, NJ: Princeton University Press, 1999)
de Certeau, Michel. *The Practice of Everyday Life* (Berkeley, CA: University of California Press, 1984)
Dendooven, Dominiek and Piet Chielens, eds., *World War I: Five Continents in Flanders* (Tielt, Belgium: Lannoo, 2008)
Doss, N. L., *Reminiscences: English and Australasian* (Calcutta: M. C. Bhowmick, 1893)
Doyle, Arthur Conan, *A Study in Scarlet* (1887; London: Penguin, 2008)
Driver, Felix and David Gilbert, eds., *Imperial Cities: Landscape, Display and Identity* (Manchester: Manchester University Press, 1999)
Dutt, R. C., *Three Years in Europe: Being Extracts from Letters Sent from Europe*, 2nd edn (1872; Calcutta: Thacker, Spink and Co., 1873)
Dutt, R. C., *Three Years in Europe: Being Extracts from Letters Sent from Europe*, 4th edn (1872; Calcutta: S. K. Lahiri, 1896)
Dutta, Krisha and Andrew Robinson, eds., *Selected Letters of Rabindranath Tagore* (Cambridge: Cambridge University Press, 1997)
Dutta, Krisha and Andrew Robinson, *Rabindranath Tagore: The Myriad-minded Man* (London: Bloomsbury, 2000)

Eliot, T. S., *Four Quartets* (London: Faber and Faber, 1944)
Ellman, Richard, *Yeats: The Man and the Masks* (London: Macmillan, 1949)
Emery, Mary Lou, *Modernism, the Visual, and Caribbean Literature* (Cambridge: Cambridge University Press, 2007)
Emmerson, Charles, *1913: The World Before the Great War* (London: Bodley Head, 2013)
Faulks, Sebastian, *Birdsong* (London: Vintage, 1993)
Fergusson, Niall, *Empire: How Britain Made the Modern World* (London: Allen Lane, 2003)
Fisher, Michael H., *Counterflows to Colonialism: Indian Travellers and Settlers in Britain, 1600–1857* (Delhi: Permanent Black, 2004)
Fitzgerald, Edward, *Rubáiyát of Omar Khayyám* (1859; London: Collins, 1954)
Forster, E. M., *Howards End* (London: Edward Arnold, 1910)
Forster, E. M., *A Passage to India* (1924; London: Penguin, 1967)
Foster, R. F., *Modern Ireland, 1600–1972* (London: Allen Lane, 1988)
Foster, R. F., *W. B. Yeats: A Life*, 2 vols. (Oxford: Oxford University Press, 1997–2003)
Franklin, J. Jeffrey, *The Lotus and the Lion: Buddhism and the British Empire* (Ithaca, NY, and London: Cornell University Press, 2008)
Fyzee, Atiya, *Zamani-i-tahsil* (*A Time of Education*) (Agra: Matba' Mafid-i-'Am, 1921)
Gandhi, Leela, *Affective Communities: Anti-colonial Thought and the Politics of Friendship* (Durham, NC: Duke University Press, 2006)
Gandhi, M. K., *An Autobiography; or the Story of my Experiments with Truth* (1927; Ahmedabad: Navajivan Publishing House, 1958)
Garnett, David, *The Golden Echo*, vol. 1 (London: Chatto & Windus, 1953)
Ghose, Manmohan, *Collected Poems*, ed. Lotika Ghose (1924: Calcutta: University of Calcutta Press, 1970)
Ghosh, Amitav, *The Circle of Reason* (London: Hamish Hamilton, 1986)
Ghosh, Amitav, *In an Antique Land* (Delhi: Seagull, 1992)
Ghosh, Amitav, *Sea of Poppies* (London: John Murray, 2008)
Ghosh, Amitav, *River of Smoke* (London: John Murray, 2011)
Ghosh, Sarath Kumar, *The Prince of Destiny: The New Krishna* (London: Rebman, 1909)
Gibson, Mary Ellis, *Anglophone Poetry in Colonial India 1780–1913: A Critical Anthology* (Athens, OH: Ohio University Press, 2011)
Gifford, Zerbanoo, *The Golden Thread: Asian Experiences of Post-Raj Britain* (London: Pandora, 1990)
Gilroy, Paul, *The Black Atlantic: Modernity and Double Consciousness* (London: Verso, 1993)
Gilroy, Paul, *Between Camps: Nations, Cultures and the Allure of Race* (London and New York: Routledge, 2004)
Glendinning, Victoria, *Leonard Woolf* (London: Simon and Schuster, 2006)
Gonne, Maud, *A Servant of the Queen* (London: Victor Gollancz, 1938)
Gopal, Sarvepalli, ed., *Selected Works of Jawaharlal Nehru* (New Delhi: Orient Longman, 1972)

Gosse, Edmund, 'Toru Dutt: Introductory Memoir', in Toru Dutt, *Ancient Ballads and Legends of Hindustan* (London: Kegan, Paul, Trench and Co., 1882), pp. vii–xxvii

Gosse, Edmund, *Father and Son*, ed. and intr. Michael Newton (1907; Oxford: Oxford University Press, 2004)

Gowans, Georgina, 'Imperial Geographies of Home: Memsahibs and Miss-Sahibs in Indian and Britain, 1915–1947', *Cultural Geographies* 10.4 (2003): 424–41

Grant, Kevin, Philippa Levine, and Frank Trentham, *Empire and Transnationalism 1880–1950* (Basingstoke: Palgrave, 2007)

Green, Nile, 'Among the Dissenters: Reciprocal Ethnography in Nineteenth-century Inglistan', *Journal of Global History* 4 (2009): 293–395

Greenhalgh, Paul, *Ephemeral Visits: The Expositions Universelles, Great Exhibitions and World's Fairs, 1851–1939* (Manchester: Manchester University Press, 1988)

Guha, Ramachandra, *Gandhi Before India* (London: Allen Lane, 2013)

Gui, Weihsin, 'Post-heritage Narratives: Migrancy and Travelling Theory in V. S. Naipaul's *The Enigma of Arrival* and Andrea Levy's *Fruit of the Lemon*', *Journal of Commonwealth Literature* 47.1 (2012): 73–90

Gupta, Pamila, Isabel Hofmeyr, and Michael Pearson, eds., *Eyes Across the Water: Navigating the Indian Ocean* (Pretoria: UNISA Press, 2010)

Haddad, Emily, 'Digging to India: Modernity, Imperialism and the Suez Canal', *Victorian Studies* 47.5 (2005): 363–96

Hage, Ghassan, *White Nation: Fantasies of White Supremacy in a Multicultural Society* (London and New York: Routledge, 2000)

Haggard, H. Rider, *She*, ed. Daniel Karlin (1897; Oxford: Oxford World's Classics, 1991)

Halbfass, Wilhelm, *India and Europe: An Essay in Understanding* (New York, NY: SUNY Press, 1988)

Hall, Catherine, *Civilising Subjects: Metropole and Colony in the English Imagination 1830–1867* (Cambridge: Polity Press, 2002)

Hall, Stuart, *The Hard Road to Renewal: Thatcherism and the Crisis of the Left* (London: Verso, 1988)

Hardy, G. H., *A Mathematician's Apology*, foreword C. P. Snow (1936; Cambridge: Cambridge University Press, 1967)

Harlow, Barbara and Mia Carter, eds., *Imperialism and Orientalism: A Documentary Sourcebook* (Oxford: Blackwell, 1999)

Harris, Jose, *Private Lives, Public Spirit: A Social History of Britain 1870–1914* (Oxford: Oxford University Press, 1993)

Harvey, David. *The Condition of Postmodernity: An Enquiry into the Origins of Cultural Change* (Oxford: Blackwell, 1990)

Hatcher, John, *Laurence Binyon: Poet, Scholar of East and West* (Oxford: Clarendon Press, 1995)

Hensher, Philip, Review of *The Cat's Table*, *The Telegraph* (5 September 2011). See <http://www.telegraph.co.uk/culture/books/bookreviews/8735345/The-Cats-Table-by-Michael-Ondaatje-review.html> (accessed 8 January 2015)

Hillcoat, Charles H., *A Mystery of the Suez Canal* (Glasgow: David Bryce and Son, 1896)

Hobsbawn, Eric, *The Age of Empire, 1875–1914* (London: Weidenfeld and Nicholson, 1987)

Hoffenberg, Peter H., *An Empire on Display* (Berkeley, CA: University of California Press, 2001)

Hofmeyr, Isabel, 'The Complicating Sea: The Indian Ocean as Method', *Comparative Studies of South Asia, Africa and the Middle East*, 32.3 (2012): 584–90

Höhner, Terrance D. and Carolyn B. Kenny, *Chronology of Swami Vivekananda in the West* (Portland, OR: Prana Press, 2000)

Houen, Alex, *Terrorism and Modern Literature* (Oxford: Oxford University Press, 2002)

Hunt, Bruce J., *Pursuing Power and Light: Technology and Physics from James Watt to Albert Einstein* (Baltimore, MD: The Johns Hopkins University Press, 2010)

Hunt, James D., *Gandhi in London*, rev. edn (1978; New Delhi: Promilla and Co., 1993)

Illies, Florian, *1913: The Year Before the Storm* (London: Clerkenwell, 2013)

Inden, Ronald, *Imagining India* (Bloomington, IN: Indiana University Press, 1990; 2nd impression, 2000)

Iyer, Pico, 'Kip and Kim: How Michael Ondaatje is Subtly Remaking the English Novel', *Times Literary Supplement* 5660 (23 September 2011): 14–15

J. D. W., 'Review of *The Bird of Time*', *The Indian Magazine and Review* 508 (April 1913): 89

Jackson, Holbrook. *The Eighteen Nineties* (1913; London: Jonathan Cape, 1931)

Jaini, Jagmenderlal, *Fragments from an Indian Student's Note-book*, ed. M. Amy Thornett (London: Arthur H. Stockwell, 1934)

Jameson, Fredric, 'Modernism and Imperialism', in *Nationalism, Colonialism and Literature* (Minneapolis, MN: University of Minnesota Press, 1990), pp. 60–4

Jones Kenyon, Christine and Anna Snaith, 'Tilting at Universities: Virginia Woolf at King's College London', *Woolf Studies Annual* 16 (2010): 1–44

Joshi, Priya, *In Another Country: Colonialism, Culture and the English Novel in India* (New York, NY: Columbia University Press, 2002)

Karabell, Zachary, *Parting the Desert: The Creation of the Suez Canal* (London: John Murray, 2003)

Khalidi, Omar, ed., *An Indian Passage to Europe: The Travels of Fath Nawaz Jung* (Karachi: Oxford University Press, 2006)

Kinross, Lord, *Between Two Seas: The Creation of the Suez Canal* (London: John Murray, 1968)

Kipling, Rudyard, *Kim*, ed. Edward W. Said (1901; London: Penguin, 1987)

Kipling, Rudyard, *Complete Verse: Definitive Edition* (London: Hodder and Stoughton, 1989)

Kripalani, Krishna, *Tagore: A Life* (Delhi: National Book Trust, 1986)

Kundu, Kalyan, Sakti Bhattacharya, and Kalyan Sircar, *Imagining Tagore: Rabindranath and the British Press, 1912–1941* (Calcutta: Shishu Sahitya Samsad, 2000)

Lago, Mary, 'The Parting of the Ways: A Comparative Study of Yeats and Tagore', *Indian Literature* 6.2 (1963): 1–34

Lago, Mary, *Imperfect Encounter: Letters of William Rothenstein and Rabindranath Tagore, 1911–1941* (Cambridge, MA: Harvard University Press, 1972)

Lahiri, Shompa, *Indians in Britain: Anglo-Indian Encounters, Race and Identity, 1880–1930* (London: Frank Cass, 2000)

Lal, Victor, 'Encounter and Response: The British Unitarians and Brahmo Samajees at Manchester College, Oxford, 1896–1948', *Faith and Freedom: Journal of Progressive Religion*, 2 parts, 68.1 (Spring/Summer 2015) and (Autumn/Winter 2015) (forthcoming)

Lambert, David and Alan Lester, eds., *Colonial Lives Across the British Empire: Imperial Careering in the Long Nineteenth Century* (Cambridge: Cambridge University Press, 2006)

Lambert-Hurley, Siobhan and Sunil Sharma, *Atiya's Journeys: A Muslim Woman from Colonial Bombay to Edwardian Britain* (Delhi: Oxford University Press, 2010)

Lambert-Hurley, Siobhan, 'Atiya Fyzee in Edwardian London', in *India in Britain*, ed. Susheila Nasta (London: Palgrave, 2012), pp. 64–79

Lavery, Charne, 'Writing the Indian Ocean in Selected Novels by Joseph Conrad, Amitav Ghosh, Abdulrazak Gurnah and Lindsey Collen', D.Phil. thesis, University of Oxford (2013)

Lawrence, James, *The Rise and Fall of the British Empire* (London: Little, Brown, 1994)

Lawrence, Patricia, *Lily Briscoe's Chinese Eyes: Bloomsbury, Modernism and China* (Columbia, SC: University of South Carolina Press, 2003)

Leask, Nigel, *British Romantic Writers and the East: Anxieties of Empire* (Cambridge: Cambridge University Press, 1992)

Leavitt, David, *The Indian Clerk* (London: Bloomsbury, 2007)

Lee, Hermione, *Virginia Woolf* (London: Chatto & Windus, 1996)

Lennon, Joseph, *Irish Orientalism: A Literary and Intellectual History* (New York, NY: Syracuse University Press, 2004)

Levi-Strauss, Claude, *Tristes Tropiques*, trans. John and Doreen Weightman (New York, NY: Atheneum, 1973)

'Literatus', 'Rabindranath Tagore in America', *Modern Review* 21.6 (1917): 659–66

Lokugé, Chandani, ed. *Toru Dutt: Collected Poetry and Prose* (New Delhi: Oxford University Press, 2006)

Lokugé, Chandani, 'Dialoging with Empire: The Literary and Political Rhetoric of Sarojini Naidu', in *India in Britain*, ed. Susheila Nasta (London: Palgrave, 2012), pp. 115–33

Lootens, Tricia, 'Bengal, Britain, France: The Locations and Translations of Toru Dutt', *Victorian Literature and Culture* 34.2 (2006): 573–90

Lootens, Tricia, 'Alien Homelands: Rudyard Kipling, Toru Dutt and the Poetry of Empire', in *The Fin-de-siècle Poem: English Literary Culture and the 1890s*, ed. Joseph Bristow (Athens, OH: Ohio University Press, 2007), pp. 284–310

Lutyens, Mary, *Krishnamurti: The Years of Awakening* (London: J. Murray, 1975)
Lynch, T. K., *A Visit to the Suez Canal* (London: Day and Son Ltd, 1866)
Macaulay, Thomas Babington, *Critical and Historical Essays* (1840; London: Dent, 1907)
Macaulay, Thomas Babington, *Prose and Poetry*, ed. G. M. Young (Cambridge, MA: Harvard University Press, 1952)
MacDonald, Robert H., *The Language of Empire: Myths and Metaphors of Popular Imperialism, 1880–1918* (Manchester: Manchester University Press, 1994)
MacKenzie, John, *Imperialism and Popular Culture* (Manchester: Manchester University Press, 1986)
Macmillan, Margaret, *The War that Ended the Peace: How Europe Abandoned Peace for the First World War* (London: Profile Books, 2013)
Majumdar, Sirchendu, *Yeats and Tagore: A Comparative Study of Cross-Cultural Poetry, Nationalist Politics, Hyphenated Margins and the Ascendancy of the Mind* (Palo Alto: Academica Press, 2013)
Mars-Jones, Adam, 'Confusing Rites of Passage Tale', review of *The Cat's Table, Observer New Review* (25 September 2011), p. 38
Marsh, Richard, *The Beetle* (London: Skeffington, 1897)
Marshall, Peter, *Bengal: The British Bridgehead: Eastern India, 1740–1828* (Cambridge: Cambridge University Press, 1987)
Max Müller, Friedrich, *Biographical Essays* (London: Longmans, Green and Co., 1884)
Max Müller, Friedrich, *Biographies of Words and the Home of the Aryas* (London: Longmans, Green and Co., 1898)
Max Müller, Friedrich, *Ramakrishna: His Life and Sayings* (London: Longmans, Green and Co., 1898)
McBurney, Simon, *A Disappearing Number* (London: Oberon, 2008)
McClintock, Anne, *Imperial Leather: Race, Gender and Sexuality in the Colonial Contest* (London and New York: Routledge, 1995)
McDonagh, Josephine, 'Rethinking Provincialism in Mid-nineteenth-century Fiction: *Our Village* to *Villette*', *Victorian Studies* 55.3 (Spring 2013): 399–424
McDonald, Peter D., 'Thinking Interculturally: Amartya Sen's Lovers Revisited', *Interventions* 13.3 (2011): 367–85
McDowell, Linda, 'Thinking Through Work: Complex Inequalities, Constructions of Difference and Trans-national Migrants', *Progress in Human Geography*, 32:4 (1998): 491–507
McGlamery, Gayla S., '"The Malady Afflicting England": *One of Our Conquerors* as Cautionary Tale', *Nineteenth-century Literature* 46.3 (December 1991): 327–50
McLaughlin, Joseph, *Writing the Urban Jungle: Reading Empire in London From Doyle to Eliot* (Charlottesville, VA, and London: University Press of Virginia, 2000)
Mehrotra, Arvind Krishna, ed., *The Oxford Anthology of Twelve Modern Indian Poets* (New Delhi: Oxford University Press, 1992)
Melville, Herman, *Redburn: His First Voyage* (New York, NY: Harper and Brothers, 1850)

Metcalf, Thomas R., *Imperial Connections: India in the Indian Ocean Arena, 1860–1920* (Berkeley, CA: University of California Press, 2007)
Mitford, Nancy, *The Pursuit of Love* (London: H. Hamilton, 1945)
Mitter, Partha, *Much Maligned Monsters: A History of European Reaction to Indian Art* (Oxford: Clarendon Press, 1977)
Mitter, Partha, *The Triumph of Modernism* (London: Reaktion, 2009)
Mohanram, Radhika, *Imperial White: Race, Diaspora and the British Empire* (Minneapolis, MN, and London: University of Minnesota Press, 2007)
Monteith, Ken, *Yeats and Theosophy* (London and New York: Routledge, 2008)
Moore, G. E., *Principia Ethica* (Cambridge: Cambridge University Press, 1903)
Moretti, Franco, *The Way of the World: The Bildungsroman in European Culture* (London: Verso, 1987)
Morgan, P. D., 'Encounters Between British and "Indigenous" Peoples, *c.* 1500–*c.* 1800', in M. J. Daunton and R. Halpern, eds., *Empire and Others: British Encounters with Indigenous Peoples, 1600–1800* (London: UCL Press, 1999), pp. 42–78
Mukharji, T. N., *A Visit to Europe* (Calcutta: W. Newman, 1889)
Mukherjee, Meenakshi, *An Indian for all Seasons: The Many Lives of R. C. Dutt* (New Delhi: Penguin, 2009)
Mukherjee, Pablo, *Crime and Empire: The Colony in Nineteenth-century Fictions of Crime* (Oxford: Oxford University Press, 2003)
Mukherjee, Sumita, *Nationalism, Education and Migrant Identities: The England-Returned* (London and New York: Routledge, 2010)
Mukherjee, Sumita, '"A Warning Against Quack Doctors": The Old Bailey Trial of Indian Oculists, 1893', *Historical Research* 86.231 (February 2013): 76–91
Mukherjee, Sumita, 'Thomas Sturge Moore and his Indian Friendships in London', *English Literature in Transition 1880–1920*, 56.1 (2013): 64–82
Murray, Cara, *Victorian Narrative Technologies in the Middle East* (London and New York: Routledge, 2008)
Nagarajan, K., 'Lawyer at Large', unpublished autobiography, Centre for South Asian Studies, Cambridge, n.d.
Naidu, Sarojini and Liza Lehman, *The Golden Threshold: An Indian Song-garland* (poems by Sarojini Naidu; music by Liza Lehmann) (London: Boosey and Co., 1907)
Naipaul, V. S., *The Enigma of Arrival: A Novel* (London: Penguin, 1987)
Naipaul, V. S., *Half a Life* (London: Picador, 2001)
Naoroji, Dadabhai, *The Poverty of India* (London: Vincent Brooks, Day and Son, 1878)
Naoroji, Dadabhai, *Poverty and Un-British Rule in India* (London: Swan Sonnenschein and Co., 1901)
Nasta, Susheila, 'Between Bloomsbury and Gandhi? The Background to the Publication and Reception of Mulk Raj Anand's *Untouchable*', in *Books Without Borders: Perspectives from South Asia*, vol. 2, ed. Robert Fraser and Mary Hammond (Basingstoke: Palgrave, 2008), pp. 151–69
Nasta, Susheila, *India in Britain* (London: Palgrave, 2012)

Nehru, Jawaharlal, *The Discovery of India* (London: Meridian Books, 1946)
Nehru, Jawaharlal, *Jawaharlal Nehru: An Autobiography: With Musings on Recent Events in India* (London: Bodley Head, 1936)
Nelson, Dana D., *National Manhood: Capitalist Citizenship and the Imagined Fraternity of White Men* (Durham, NC: Duke University Press, 1998)
Nicholson, C. H. S. and A. H. E. Lee, eds., *The Oxford Book of English Mystical Verse* (Oxford: Clarendon Press, 1916)
Nord, Deborah Epstein, *Walking the Victorian Streets* (Ithaca, NY, and London: Cornell University Press, 1995)
Nordau, Max, *Degeneration*, 2nd edn (1893; London: William Heinemann, 1895)
Oldfield, Roger, *Outrage: The Edalji Five and the Shadow of Sherlock Holmes* (Cambridge: Vanguard Press, 2010)
Omissi, David, *The Sepoy and the Raj* (Basingstoke: Macmillan, 1994)
Ondaatje, Michael, *The English Patient* (London: Bloomsbury, 1992)
Owen, Alex, *The Darkened Room: Women, Power and Spiritualism in Late Victorian England* (London: Virago, 1989)
Owen, Alex, *The Place of Enchantment: British Occultism and the Science of the Modern* (Chicago, IL: Chicago University Press, 2004)
Palumbo-Liu, David, Bruce Robbins, and Nirvana Tanoukhi, eds., *Immanuel Wallerstein* (Durham, NC: Duke University Press, 2011)
Paranjape, Makarand, ed., *Sarojini Naidu, Collected Letters, 1890s to 1940s* (New Delhi: Kali for Women, 1996)
Paranjape, Makarand, *Making India: Colonialism, National Culture and the Afterlife of Indian English Authority* (Dordrecht, NL: Springer, 2013)
Pater, Walter, *Studies in the History of the Renaissance* (1873; Oxford: Oxford University Press, 1986)
Pearsall, Cornelia, *Imperial Tennyson: Victorian Poetry and the Expansion of England* (forthcoming)
Penny, F. E., *The Inevitable Law* (London: Chatto & Windus, 1907)
Perrin, Alice, *East of Suez* (London: Anthony Treherne and Co., 1901)
Perrin, Alice, *The Anglo-Indians* (London: Methuen, 1912)
Pietsch, Tamson, *Empire of Scholars: Universities, Networks and the British Academic World* (Manchester: Manchester University Press, 2013)
Plotz, Joseph, *Portable Property: Victorian Culture on the Move* (Princeton, NJ, and Oxford: Princeton University Press, 2008)
Pound, Ezra, 'The Later Yeats', *Poetry* 4 (May 1914): 65
Pratt, Lloyd, *Archives of American Time: Literature and Modernity in the Nineteenth Century* (Philadelphia, PA: University of Pennsylvania Press, 2010)
Pratt, Mary Louise, *Imperial Eyes: Travel Writing and Transculturation* (London and New York: Routledge, 1992)
Proulx, Annie, Review of *The Cat's Table*: 'Journey from Childhood', *The Guardian Review* (3 September 2011)
Purani, A. B., *Sri Aurobindo in England* (Pondicherry: Sri Aurobindo Ashram, 1956)

Radice, William, 'Introduction' to *Gitanjali*, by Rabindranath Tagore, trans. William Radice (New Delhi: Penguin, 2011), pp. xv–lxxxiv

Ragahavan, G. M., *Asaf Ali's Memoirs: The Emergence of Modern India* (Delhi: Ajanta, 1994)

Raghu, A., 'Yeats's "Mohini Chatterjee"', *Explicator* 51:3 (Spring 1993): 170–2

Rahman, A., 'The Burden of Imagination: Mapping the Centre Through the Colonised Gaze', *SACS* 3.1 (October 2011): 1–16, available at: <http://blogs.edgehill.ac.uk/sacs/files/2012/05/Document2-A.-Rahman-The-burden-of-imagination-FINAL.pdf>

Ramanujan, A. K. 'Annayya's Anthropology', trans. Narayan Hegde, in Ramachandra Sharma ed., *From Cauvery to Godavari: Modern Kannada Short Stories,* (New Delhi: Penguin,1992), p. 44

Ramazani, Jahan, *The Hybrid Muse: Postcolonial Poetry in English* (Chicago, IL: University of Chicago Press, 2001)

Ramazani, Jahan, *A Transnational Poetics* (Chicago, IL: University of Chicago Press, 2009)

Ramazani, Jahan, *Poetry and Its Others: News, Prayer, Song, and the Dialogue of Genres* (Chicago, IL: University of Chicago Press, 2013)

Ranasinha, Ruvani, *South Asian Writers in Twentieth-century Britain* (Oxford: Oxford University Press, 2007)

Ranasinha, Ruvani, with Rehana Ahmed, Sumita Mukherjee, and Florian Stadtler, eds., *South Asians and the Shaping of Britain 1870–1950: A Sourcebook* (Manchester: Manchester University Press, 2012)

Ray, Amit, *Negotiating the Modern: Orientalism and Indianness in the Anglophone World* (London and New York: Routledge, 2007)

Raychaudhuri, Tapan, *Europe Reconsidered: Perceptions of the West in Nineteenth-century Bengal*, 2nd edn (New Delhi: Oxford University Press, 2002)

Reddy, J. P., *Down Memory Lane: The Revolutions I have Lived Through* (Hyderabad: Booklinks, 2000)

Riddiford, Alexander, *Madly After the Muses: Bengali Poet Michael Madhusudan Dutt and his Reception of the Graeco-Roman Classics* (Oxford: Oxford University Press, 2013)

Rodensky, Lisa, ed., *Decadent Poetry from Wilde to Naidu* (London: Penguin, 2006)

Rosenbaum, S. P., *Edwardian Bloomsbury: The Early Literary History of the Bloomsbury Group*, vol. 2 (Basingstoke: Macmillan, 1994)

Rothenstein, William, *Examples of Indian Sculpture at the British Museum* (London: Indian Society, 1923)

Rothenstein, William, *Men and Memories: Recollections of William Rothenstein, 1900–1922*, vol. 2 (London: Faber and Faber, 1932)

Rothkopf, Carol Zeman, *The Opening of the Suez Canal* (New York, NY: Franklin Watts, 1973)

Rowbotham, Sheila, *Edward Carpenter: A Life of Liberty and Love* (London and New York: Verso, 2008)

Rylance, Ralph, *The Epicure's Almanac: Eating and Drinking in Regency London—The Original 1815 Guidebook*, ed. Janet Ing Freeman (1815; London: British Library, 2012)
Said, Edward W., *Culture and Imperialism* (London: Cape, 1993)
Said, Edward W., *Orientalism: Western Conceptions of the Orient*, rev. edn (1978; London: Penguin, 1995)
Said, Edward W., 'Identity, Authority and Freedom', *Reflections on Exile and Other Essays* (London: Granta, 2000)
Joshi, V. C., ed., *Rammohun Roy and the Process of Modernization in India* (New Delhi: Vikas, 1975)
Saussy, Haun, 'Chiasmus', *Comparative Literature* 57.3 (2005): 234–8
Savarkar, Vinayak, *The Indian War of Independence (National Rising of 1857)* (Bombay: Sethani Kompani, 1909)
Schaffer, Talia and Kathy Alexis Psomiades, eds., *Women and British Aestheticism* (Charlottesville, VA: University of Virginia Press, 1999)
Schneer, Jonathan, *London 1900* (Yale: Yale University Press, 1999)
Schuchard, Ron, *The Last Minstrels: Yeats and the Revival of the Bardic Arts* (Oxford: Oxford University Press, 2008)
Schwarz, Bill, *The White Man's World*, vol.1: *Memories of Empire* (Oxford: Oxford University Press, 2012)
Scott, David, 'Kipling's Encounters with Buddhism and the Buddhist Orient: "The Twain Shall Meet"?' *Cultural History* 1.1 (April 2012): 36–60, available at: <http://www.euppublishing.com/doi/abs/10.3366/cult.2012.0005>
Searight, Sarah, *Steaming East: The Forging of Steamship and Rail Links Between Europe and Asia* (London: The Bodley Head, 1991)
Selig de Kusel, Baron Samuel, *An Englishman's Recollections of Egypt 1863–1887* (London: John Lane, 1915)
Sen, Amartya, *The Argumentative Indian: Writings on Indian History, Culture and Identity* (London: Penguin, 2005)
Sen, K. C., *Keshub Chunder Sen in England: Diary, Sermons, Addresses & Epistles* (Calcutta: Navavidhan Publication Committee, 1938)
Sen, Satadru, *Migrant Races: Empire, Identity and K. S. Ranjitsinjhi* (Manchester: Manchester University Press, 2005)
Sen Gupta, Padmini, *Sarojini Naidu* (New Delhi: Sahitya Akademi, 1974)
Showalter, Elaine, *Sexual Anarchy: Gender and Culture at the Fin-de-siècle* (London: Bloomsbury, 1991)
Singh, Raja-i-Rajgan Jagatjit of Kapurthala, *My Travels in Europe and America 1893* (London: George Routledge and Sons, 1895)
Sinha, Mrinalini, *Colonial Masculinity: The 'Manly Englishman' and the 'Effeminate Bengali' in the Late Nineteenth Century* (Manchester: Manchester University Press, 1995)
Sinha, Mrinalini, *Specters of Mother India: The Global Restructuring of an Empire* (Durham, NC: Duke University Press, 2006)
Snaith, Anna, *Modernist Voyages: Colonial Women Writers in London, 1890–1945* (Cambridge: Cambridge University Press, 2014)

Sorabji, Cornelia, *India Calling*, ed. Elleke Boehmer and Naella Grew (1934; Nottingham: Trent Editions, 2004)
Sorabji, Richard, *Opening Doors: The Untold Story of Cornelia Sorabji* (London: IB Tauris, 2010)
Spalding, Frances, *Roger Fry: Art and Life* (Berkeley, CA: University of California Press, 1980)
Stadtler, Florian, 'Britain's Forgotten Volunteers: South Asian Contributions to the Two World Wars', in *South Asians and the Shaping of Britain, 1870–1950: A Sourcebook*, ed. Ruvani Ranasinha et al. (Manchester: Manchester University Press, 2012), pp. 80–135
Stallworthy, Jon, *Wilfred Owen*, 2nd edn (1974; London: Pimlico, 2013)
Steiner, Rudolf, *Spiritualism, Madame Blavatsky and Theosophy: Lectures*, ed. Christopher Bamforth (Great Barringon, MA: Anthroposophic Press, 2001)
Stoker, Bram, *Dracula*, ed. Maud Ellman (1897; Oxford: Oxford World's Classics, 1996)
Suhrawardy, Shahid, 'Tagore at Oxford', *Calcutta Municipal Quarterly: Tagore Memorial Special Supplement* (13 September 1941): n. p.
Symonds, Richard, *Oxford and Empire: The Last Lost Cause?* (New York, NY: St Martin's Press, 1986)
Symons, Arthur, *The Symbolist Movement in Literature* (London: Heinemann, 1899)
Symons, Arthur, *Studies in Prose and Verse* (London: J. M. Dent, 1904)
Symons, Arthur, 'Introduction' to *The Golden Threshold*, by Sarojini Naidu (London: William Heinemann, 1905), pp. 9–23
Symons, Arthur, *Dramatis Personae* (London: Faber and Gwyer, 1923)
Tagore, Rabindranath, *Selected Writings on Literature and Language*, ed. Sukanta Chaudhuri, Sisir Kumar Das, and Sankha Ghosh, trans. Swapan Chakravorty (Delhi: Oxford University Press, 2001)
Tagore, Rabindranath, *Nationalism* (1917; Harmondsworth: Penguin, 2010)
Tennyson, Lord Alfred, *The Poems of Tennyson*, vol. iii, 2nd edn, ed. Christopher Ricks (Berkeley, CA: University of California Press, 1987)
Thomas, Nicholas, *Colonialism's Culture: Anthropology, Travel and Government* (Cambridge: Polity Press, 1994)
Thompson, Edward, *The Other Side of the Medal* (London: Hogarth Press, 1925)
Thompson, Edward, *A Farewell to India* (London: E. Benn, 1931)
Thwaite, Ann, *Edmund Gosse: A Literary Landscape, 1849–1928* (Oxford: Oxford University Press, 1985)
Tickell, Alex, *Terrorism, Insurgency, and Indian-English Literature, 1830–1947* (London and New York: Routledge, 2012)
Tinker, Hugh, *The Ordeal of Love: C. F. Andrews and India* (Oxford: Oxford University Press, 1979)
Torabully, Khal, *Cale d'étoiles-Coolitude* (Réunion: Editions Azalées, 1992)
Trouillot, Michel-Rolphe, *Global Transformations: Anthropology and the Modern World* (Basingstoke: Palgrave Macmillan, 2003)
Turner, Sarah V., 'Crafting Connections; The India Society and the Formation of an Imperial Artistic Network in Early Twentieth-century Britain', in *India in Britain*, ed. Susheila Nasta (London: Palgrave, 2012), pp. 96–114

Vadgama, Kusoom, *India in Britain: The Indian Contribution to the British Way of Life* (London: Royce, 1984)

Visram, Rozina, *Ayahs, Lascars and Princes: Indians in Britain, 1700–1947* (London: Pluto Press, 1986)

Visram, Rozina, *Asians in Britain: 400 Years of History* (London: Pluto Press, 2002)

Viswanathan, Gauri, *Masks of Conquest: Literary Study and British Rule in India* (New York, NY: Columbia University Press, 1989)

Viswanathan, Gauri, 'The Ordinary Business of Occultism', *Critical Inquiry* 27:1 (2000): 1–20

Viswanathan, Gauri, 'Ireland, India and the Poetics of Internationalism', *The Journal of World History* 15.1 (2004): 7–30

Viswanathan, Gauri, 'Spectrality's Secret Sharers', in Walter Goebel and Saskia Schabio, eds., *Beyond the Black Atlantic* (London and New York: Routledge, 2006), pp. 135–45

Viswanathan, Gauri, 'The Great Game: The Geopolitics of Secret Knowledge', in *Locating Transnational Ideals*, ed. Walter Goebel and Saskia Schabio (London and New York: Routledge, 2009), pp. 191–204

Vivekananda, Swami, *The Complete Works of Swami Vivekananda*, 8 vols. (Calcutta: Advaita Ashrama, 1991–92)

Wade, Allan, ed., *The Letters of W. B. Yeats* (London: Rupert Hart-Davis, 1954)

Wainwright, Martin, *'The Better Class of Indians': Social Rank, Imperial Identity, and South Asians in Britain, 1858–1914* (Manchester: Manchester University Press, 2008)

Wainwright, Martin, 'Royal Relationships as a Form of Resistance: The Cases of Duleep Singh and Abdul Karim', in *South Asian Resistances in Britain, 1858–1947*, ed. Rehana Ahmed and Sumita Mukherjee (London: Continuum, 2012), pp. 91–105

Walkowitz, Judith, 'The Indian Woman, the Flower Girl, and the Jew: Photojournalism in Edwardian London', *Victorian Studies* 42 (Autumn 1998/1999): 3–46

Wallace, Edgar, *The Four Just Men*, intr. David Glover (1905; Oxford: Oxford University Press, 1995)

Wallerstein, Immanuel, *Historical Capitalism with Capitalist Civilization* (London: Verso, 1996)

Wallerstein, Immanuel, *World Systems Analysis: An Introduction* (Durham, NC: Duke University Press, 2004)

Walvin, James, *Passage to Britain: Immigration in British History and Politics* (London: Penguin, 1984)

Warner, Marina, *Stranger Magic* (London: Chatto & Windus, 2011)

Wasti, Syed Razi, ed., *Memoirs and Other Writings of Syed Ameer Ali* (Lahore: Peoples' Publishing House, 1968)

Weedon, Alexis, *Victorian Publishing: The Economics of Book Production for a Mass Market 1836–1916* (Aldershot: Ashgate, 2003)

Weir, David, *Decadence and the Making of Modernism* (Amherst, MA: University of Massachusetts Press, 1995)

White, Daniel E., *From Little London to Little Bengal: Religion, Print, and Modernity in Early British India, 1793–1835* (Baltimore, MD: Johns Hopkins University Press, 2013)
White, Hayden, *Tropics of Discourse: Essays in Cultural Criticism* (London: Johns Hopkins University Press, 1978)
Whitman, Walt, *Leaves of Grass*, ed. Michael Moon (New York and London: W. W. Norton Co., 2002)
Wilde, Oscar, *The Picture of Dorian Gray* (1890/91; Oxford: Oxford World's Classics, 2008)
Wilhelm, J. J., *Ezra Pound in London and Paris 1908–1925* (London: Pennsylvania State University Press, 1990)
Woodward, E. L., *Age of Reform 1815–1879* (Oxford: Clarendon Press, 1938)
Woolf, Leonard, *The Village in the Jungle* (London: Edward Arnold, 1913)
Woolf, Virginia, *Mrs Dalloway* (London: Hogarth Press, 1925)
Woolf, Virginia, *Roger Fry: A Biography* (London: Hogarth Press, 1940)
Woolf, Virginia, *A Passionate Apprentice: The Early Journals, 1897–1909*, ed. Mitchell A. Leaska (London: Hogarth, 1990)
Woolf, Virginia, *Selected Essays*, ed. David Bradshaw (Oxford: Oxford World's Classics, 2008)
Yeats, W. B., *Memoirs: Autobiography—First Draft; Journal*, ed. Denis Donoghue (London: Macmillan, 1972)
Yeats, W. B., *Autobiographies* (1955; London: Macmillan, 1979)
Yeats, W. B., *The Poems*, ed. and intr. Daniel Albright (London: Everyman, 1992)
Young, Robert J. C., *Colonial Desire: Hybridity in Theory, Culture, and Race* (New York and London: Routledge, 1995)
Young, Robert J. C., *The Idea of English Ethnicity* (Oxford: Blackwell, 2008)
Yule, Henry, *Hobson-Jobson*, ed. Kate Teltsher (Oxford: Oxford University Press, 2013)
Yuval-Davis, Nira, *The Politics of Belonging: Intersectional Contestations* (London: Sage, 2011)

Index